Leading *with* Character

BARBARA W. FARMER

EDGAR I. FARMER

JAMES L. BURROW

THOMSON

SOUTH-WESTERN

Australia · Brazil · Canada · Mexico · Singapore · Spain · United Kingdom · United States

THOMSON

SOUTH-WESTERN

Leading with Character

Dr. Barbara W. Farmer, Dr. Edgar I. Farmer, Dr. James L. Burrow

VP/Editorial Director:
Jack W. Calhoun

VP/Editor-in-Chief:
Karen Schmohe

Executive Editor:
Eve Lewis

Senior Developmental Editor:
Dr. Inell Bolls

Senior Marketing Manager:
Nancy Long

Content Project Manager:
Colleen A. Farmer

Marketing Coordinator:
Angela Glassmeyer

Technology Project Editor:
Scott Hamilton

Manufacturing Coordinator:
Kevin Kluck

Production House:
ICC Macmillan Inc.

Printer:
Courier, Kendalville

Art Director:
Tippy McIntosh

Internal Designer:
Design Matters, Diane and Nick Gliebe

Cover Designer:
Design Matters, Diane and Nick Gliebe

Cover Images:
© Getty Images

For more information about our products, contact us at:

Thomson Higher Education
5191 Natorp Boulevard
Mason, Ohio 45040
USA

Cathy Bishop
Teacher, Marketing Education
Bartlett High School
Bartlett, Tennessee

Brian Ferrell, CMP
Communications Manager
Future Business Leaders
*   of America—Phi Beta Lambda*
Reston, Virginia

Britt James
JAG Specialist
Springdale High School
Springdale, Arkansas

Karen Joslin
Teacher, Career Technology Department
Hobbs High School
Hobbs, New Mexico

Christina L. Hain
FACS and Workforce Education Teacher
Bismarck Public Schools
Bismarck, Arkansas

Maurice Henderson
State Director
Business Professionals
*   of America—Michigan*
Ypsilanti, Michigan

Kristine Labbus
Teacher, Business and
*   Information Technology*
Neenah High School
Neenah, Wisconsin

Sissy Long
Marketing Specialist
DECA Inc.
Birmingham, Alabama

Judith A. Moore
Director of Career Development
Columbia City High School
Columbia City, Indiana

Christopher Oechsner
Business and Information
*   Technology Teacher*
Hartford Union High School
Hartford, Wisconsin

Randy Poland
Marketing Teacher/Coordinator
Park View High School
Sterling, Virginia

Mark Steedly
Sports Marketing Instructor
Great Oaks/Winton Woods
*   High School*
Cincinnati, Ohio

Don Shumacher
Marketing Teacher and DECA Advisor
Spring Valley High School
Las Vegas, Nevada

Barbara W. Farmer, Ed.D., is a principal in the State College (Pennsylvania) Area School District. She hosts the "What Matters" program on WPSU Television and Radio at the Pennsylvania State University. A former business education teacher in the Hampton City (Virginia) Schools and the Wake County (North Carolina) Public Schools, Dr. Farmer received her Bachelor of Science degree from Hampton University. She received a master's degree from North Carolina A & T State University, and a Doctor of Education in Educational Leadership degree from the University of North Carolina, Chapel Hill. Dr. Farmer is a co-editor of *Diversity in America: Visions of the Future.*

Edgar I. Farmer, Ed.D., is Professor of Education and Director of Postsecondary Technical and Community College Leadership in the Workforce Education and Development program at the Pennsylvania State University, University Park. He is also the Site Director for the National Research and Dissemination Centers for Career and Technical Education. Dr. Farmer works extensively with school districts, government agencies, and other universities as a consultant in career and technical education programs. He holds degrees from Norfolk State University, Hampton University, and the Pennsylvania State University.

James L. Burrow, Ph.D., has a background in marketing and human resource development. Dr. Burrow works regularly with the business community and other organizations as a consultant on marketing and performance improvement strategies. Recently retired from North Carolina State University, he served as professor and Coordinator of the Graduate Training and Development program. Dr. Burrow received degrees from the University of Northern Iowa and the University of Nebraska-Lincoln in marketing and marketing education.

Learning to Lead

What makes a good leader? Explore the types of character and virtue needed to be a respected leader. **Leading with Character** prepares students for leadership roles in school, extra-curricular, and community activities, and for future academic, career, and citizenship responsibilities. Multiple projects and activities encourage students to work cooperatively in groups and to do independent reflection.

- *WinningEdge* exposes students to opportunities for involvement in a variety of student organizations
- *Accepting the Challenge* is an ongoing project that assesses personal growth
- Internet activities at thomsonedu.com/school/leading encourage research and reinforce key concepts

Flexible Package Packed with Power

Student Text/CD (0-538-44486-X) Explore the leadership potential in each of us using this full-color, 12-chapter, activity-laden text and CD package.

Adobe eBook (0-538-44491-6) Enjoy the entire text in a pdf format on your computer.

ExamView® (0-538-44489-4) Make assessment quick and easy using this electronic test bank and grade book.

Instructor's Resource CD (0-538-44488-6) Access PowerPoint presentations and lesson plans with ease at your computer.

Annotated Instructor's Edition (0-538-44487-8) Teaching material is included in the margin, right at point of use.

Website (thomsonedu.com/school/leading) Find more activities on the free website.

"I believe this text is excellent!"
Britt James, Reviewer

Leadership: Experienced

Take a look for yourself at how this dynamic text brings leadership principles to life for your students day after day with proven learning features and unmatched teaching support. It's everything you need for today's classroom and the understanding that extends well beyond.

Throughout 12 chapters, the strong link between character and leadership is explored using activities, quotes, features, and research:

1. There Is a Leader in You
2. Understanding the Characteristics of Leadership
3. Character Matters
4. Becoming a Leader: Developing Your Personal Plan
5. Developing and Demonstrating Character
6. Teams and Teamwork
7. Effective Groups and Organizations
8. Understanding and Supporting Diversity
9. Personal Characteristics Build Character
10. Relationships with Others Build Character
11. Modeling and Mentoring: Helping Others to Lead
12. Leading into the Future

Chapters are broken into several class-length Lessons. The Lesson Numbers and Titles provide an overview of the chapter content.

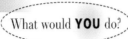

Heighten student interest at the beginning of every chapter with **What Would You Do?**, a student-focused scenario related to the upcoming chapter content.

What would **YOU** do?

BECKY'S JUDGMENT OF OTHERS

It's that time of year again when homeroom classes must select class officers. Since Becky is a new student at her high school, she does not think she has a chance of winning an office. Members of the football team and cheering squad are in her homeroom, and she believes the elections will be just a popularity contest. Even though she is a member of the theater group, Becky believes she cannot win over the "popular, athletic, and pretty" people.

Before passing judgment on some of the students in this group, Becky began paying closer attention to their behaviors in class, in the halls, and in the cafeteria. She noticed that they had positive, friendly attitudes when dealing with others. They greeted others with pleasant and enthusiastic words or actions and parted with messages about meeting or talking later.

As she began to take risks in responding to their acts of friendliness, Becky began to realize that if she acted friendly to them, they responded positively to her. She also realized that the way she saw herself—her attitude toward others, personality style, and work ethic—affected the way they saw her. She saw that the way she treated them had a lot to do with the way they treated her. She realized that what she gave was usually what she got in return. This new awareness helped Becky become a responsible and responsive member of the school community.

By working to build relationships, Becky gained a sense of trust and risk taking that motivated her to run for a classroom office. She won the office she was running for and became a leader in her classroom and in her school. Today, as a college student, Becky knows that an awareness of others and herself can help her connect with and fit in with the people in her new setting.

THINK CRITICALLY

1. What did Becky learn about others by withholding judgment of them?

2. What did she learn about herself?

3. Why is it important to take risks and trust others in order to reach your goals?

CHARACTER *Builder*

In the workplace, social skills are highly valued. The ability to get along well with other people, coupled with self-confidence, is not as easy to teach as other skills.

Character Builders present real-world examples of how character is a significant aspect of being a true leader.

Prepare students to **READ** each lesson effectively by previewing the goals and key terms.

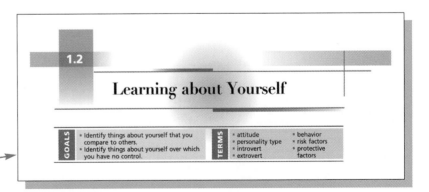

1.2 Learning about Yourself

GOALS	TERMS
▪ Identify things about yourself that you compare to others. ▪ Identify things about yourself over which you have no control.	▪ attitude ▪ behavior ▪ personality type ▪ risk factors ▪ introvert ▪ protective ▪ extrovert factors

"Great 'Leadership Tips' in this chapter. Very well connected to the topic and the content."
Maurice Henderson, Reviewer

Student-Focused Features

A **TEAM** *Effort*

People tend to be one of two personality types—introvert or extrovert. Work as a team to develop a questionnaire or checklist that can be used by others to help determine if they are an introvert or extrovert. It may be helpful to use the Internet to research introvert and extrovert characteristics.

THINK *CRITICALLY*

Do you think people can have behaviors that represent both personality types and not have one dominant style? Could this be revealed in your questionnaire or checklist? Explain how.

A TEAM Effort offers in-class collaborative activities. Students work in small groups while developing leadership skills and knowledge.

Show students how to become leaders in their local communities with these ideas on participating and volunteering.

Building **COMMUNITIES**

In your history class, you have been studying the value and power of voting. A local election will take place in your community. You have decided to become involved by leading a group that will develop campaign flyers and posters that communicate the importance of voting.

THINK *CRITICALLY*

1. What type of information would you include on the flyers to explain the benefits of voting in a local election?
2. How would you organize the planning process for constructing, placing, and removing posters?

What About **ME** ?

Reflect back over your life. Think about the experiences you have had with leaders. Perhaps someone in your family or one of your friends took on a leadership role to carry out a plan. Now, think of at least two occasions when you were chosen as a leader—no matter how insignificant they may have seemed at the time.

THINK *CRITICALLY*

1. Did you see yourself as a leader at the time? Why or why not?
2. Did anyone else identify you as being a leader?
3. Describe both of these experiences in detail. Were they positive or negative experiences?
4. If you were asked to be a leader, did it boost your self-confidence? Did you like being a leader? Why or why not?

What About ME? asks students to reflect on their personal leadership traits and decision-making abilities.

COMMUNICATE

Goal setting and planning help people make decisions about the direction to take in their lives. If you are new to goal setting, you may want to get started by using a to-do list and checking off your accomplishments as you complete each one. As you gain confidence in completing the list, you will want to commit to completing even bigger goals. Keep in mind that you will need a more detailed plan to support your efforts in reaching bigger goals. Success in your personal goal setting can set the stage for goal setting as a leader in your group.

THINK *CRITICALLY*

Explain how setting goals can help you in school. How can setting goals help you be a better leader?

COMMUNICATE allows students to actively learn about the strong link between leadership, attitude, and communication.

LEADERSHIP *Tip*

Knowing what you are passionate about can help you direct your energy toward work that is rewarding and satisfying. Your enthusiasm then begins to rub off on others around you.

Students will be interested in these insightful, practical tips on how leaders act and make decisions.

> Whenever you're in conflict with someone, there is one factor that can make the difference between damaging your relationship and deepening it. That factor is attitude.
>
> — Timothy Bentley

Helpful quotes are included to offer practical perspectives and advice on leadership.

CHECKPOINTS throughout the chapter provide opportunities for informal evaluation of learning.

 CHECKPOINT

Describe the two most common personality types.

_____

_____

"I am able to relate the scenarios to actual situations that I have observed, and I believe that students will associate the scenarios with situations they face by using the 'Think Critically' questions for class discussion."

Christina Hain, Reviewer

Integrated Assessment

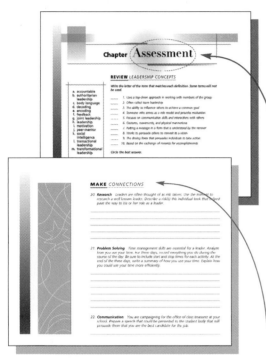

Lesson Assessment at the end of every lesson allows you to evaluate student comprehension and progress frequently.

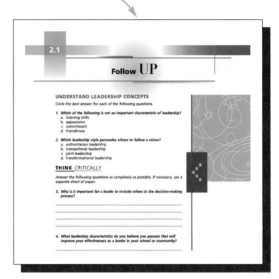

Chapter Assessment covers basic understanding through critical-thinking applications. **Make Connections** cross-curricular assessment activities connect leadership and character to the related communication, writing, reading, technology, research, and other academic subjects.

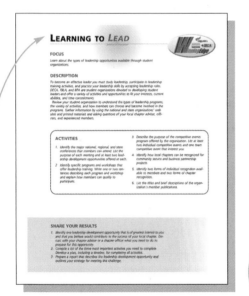

Students have the option of using the forms and calendars on the CD to complete **Accepting the Challenge** projects on the computer.

Complete the **Learning to Lead** activities and give students the *WinningEdge* in co-curricular student organizations.

Accepting the Challenge presents case studies and goal-setting activities that encourage students to internalize the leadership concepts and skills presented in each chapter. Students read about a relevant scenario, and then apply personal development goals as a follow-up.

Contents

CHAPTER 1
THERE IS A LEADER IN YOU 2

LESSON 1.1	Inventory of Past Experiences and Opportunities	4
LESSON 1.2	Learning about Yourself	11
LESSON 1.3	Seize the Moment	18

CHAPTER ASSESSMENT | LEARNING TO LEAD | ACCEPTING THE CHALLENGE

CHAPTER 2
UNDERSTANDING THE CHARACTERISTICS OF LEADERSHIP 30

LESSON 2.1	Leadership Characteristics	32
LESSON 2.2	Leadership Skills	38
LESSON 2.3	Social Intelligence and Communication	44

CHAPTER ASSESSMENT | LEARNING TO LEAD | ACCEPTING THE CHALLENGE

CHAPTER 3
CHARACTER MATTERS 56

LESSON 3.1	What Is Character?	58
LESSON 3.2	When Character Is Missing	64
LESSON 3.3	Acting Ethically	70

CHAPTER ASSESSMENT | LEARNING TO LEAD | ACCEPTING THE CHALLENGE

CHAPTER 4
BECOMING A LEADER: DEVELOPING YOUR
PERSONAL PLAN 82

Lesson 4.1 Being a Leader in Your School and Community... 84
Lesson 4.2 Creating a Sense of Community within
Your School 91
Lesson 4.3 Planning for Servant Leadership............................ 98
Chapter Assessment | Learning to Lead | Accepting the Challenge

CHAPTER 5
DEVELOPING AND DEMONSTRATING
CHARACTER 110

Lesson 5.1 Your Path to Character.. 112
Lesson 5.2 How You Demonstrate Character 120
Lesson 5.3 A Path to Personal Improvement........................... 125
Chapter Assessment | Learning to Lead | Accepting the Challenge

CHAPTER 6
TEAMS AND TEAMWORK.................................. 138

Lesson 6.1 The Need for Teams and Teamwork 140
Lesson 6.2 Character of Teams and Team Members 146
Lesson 6.3 Making Teams Work 151
Chapter Assessment | Learning to Lead | Accepting the Challenge

CHAPTER 7
EFFECTIVE GROUPS AND ORGANIZATIONS.. 164

Lesson 7.1   Understanding Groups.................................... 166
Lesson 7.2   Followership in Support of Leadership............. 172
Lesson 7.3   The Changing Work Ethic................................. 177

Chapter Assessment | Learning to Lead | Accepting the Challenge

CHAPTER 8
UNDERSTANDING AND SUPPORTING DIVERSITY 188

Lesson 8.1   Recognizing, Respecting, and Valuing Diversity .. 190
Lesson 8.2   Working Effectively in Diverse Groups............... 196
Lesson 8.3   Fitting in Without Fading Out........................... 201

Chapter Assessment | Learning to Lead | Accepting the Challenge

CHAPTER 9
PERSONAL CHARACTERISTICS BUILD CHARACTER 212

Lesson 9.1   Being Honest and Truthful............................... 214
Lesson 9.2   Being Reliable and Responsible........................ 221
Lesson 9.3   Exhibiting Self-Discipline................................. 228

Chapter Assessment | Learning to Lead | Accepting the Challenge

CHAPTER 10

RELATIONSHIPS WITH OTHERS BUILD CHARACTER **240**

Lesson 10.1 Relationships and Character 242
Lesson 10.2 Respect and Fairness.................................... 250
Lesson 10.3 Trust, Loyalty, and Caring........................... 257
Lesson 10.4 Organizational and Community Citizenship 263

Chapter Assessment | Learning to Lead | Accepting the Challenge

CHAPTER 11

MODELING AND MENTORING: HELPING OTHERS TO LEAD **274**

Lesson 11.1 Role Models... 276
Lesson 11.2 Finding Role Models 281
Lesson 11.3 Mentors and Mentoring 286

Chapter Assessment | Learning to Lead | Accepting the Challenge

CHAPTER 12

LEADING INTO THE FUTURE **300**

Lesson 12.1 Future Leadership Roles 302
Lesson 12.2 What Employers Expect 307
Lesson 12.3 Visionary Leadership 313

Chapter Assessment | Learning to Lead | Accepting the Challenge

Glossary **324**
Index **328**

 Pages 128, 169, 217, 303

 Pages 14, 39, 65, 85, 118, 152, 175, 191, 222, 245, 282, 308

 Pages 5, 59, 148, 277

 Pages 33, 99, 202, 265

ACCEPTING THE *CHALLENGE* Pages 28, 54, 80, 108, 136, 162, 186, 210, 238, 272, 298, 322

 Pages 19, 46, 72, 92, 121, 141, 179, 198, 232, 251, 292, 314

 Pages 27, 53, 79, 107, 135, 161, 185, 209, 237, 271, 297, 321

Chapter 1

There Is a Leader in You

© Digital Vision/Getty Images

1.1 *Inventory of Past Experiences and Opportunities*

1.2 *Learning about Yourself*

1.3 *Seize the Moment*

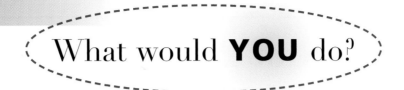

BECKY'S JUDGMENT OF OTHERS

It's that time of year again when homeroom classes must select class officers. Since Becky is a new student at her high school, she does not think she has a chance of winning an office. Members of the football team and cheering squad are in her homeroom, and she believes the elections will be just a popularity contest. Even though she is a member of the theater group, Becky believes she cannot win over the "popular, athletic, and pretty" people.

Before passing judgment on some of the students in this group, Becky began paying closer attention to their behaviors in class, in the halls, and in the cafeteria. She noticed that they had positive, friendly attitudes when dealing with others. They greeted others with pleasant and enthusiastic words or actions and parted with messages about meeting or talking later.

As she began to take risks in responding to their acts of friendliness, Becky began to realize that if she acted friendly to them, they responded positively to her. She also realized that the way she saw herself—her attitude toward others, personality style, and work ethic—affected the way they saw her. She saw that the way she treated them had a lot to do with the way they treated her. She realized that what she gave was usually what she got in return. This new awareness helped Becky become a responsible and responsive member of the school community.

By working to build relationships, Becky gained a sense of trust and risk taking that motivated her to run for a classroom office. She won the office she was running for and became a leader in her classroom and in her school. Today, as a college student, Becky knows that an awareness of others and herself can help her connect with and fit in with the people in her new setting.

THINK *CRITICALLY*

1. What did Becky learn about others by withholding judgment of them?

2. What did she learn about herself?

3. Why is it important to take risks and trust others in order to reach your goals?

Think Critically Answers
1. Becky learned that if she acted friendly to others, they responded positively to her.
2. Becky learned that the way she viewed herself affected the way others viewed her.
3. Answers will vary. You cannot reach your goals if you hold back and do not extend yourself to others in a positive way.

TEACHING RESOURCES
Instructor's Resource CD
Lesson Plans, Ch. 1
PowerPoint Slides, Ch. 1

Student Activity CD, Ch. 1

thomsonedu.com/school/leading
Crossword Puzzle, Ch. 1
Flash Cards, Ch. 1

Exam*View*® CD, Ch. 1

CHAPTER OVERVIEW
Chapter 1 helps students evaluate their experiences, identify their skills and personality traits, and set a new vision for becoming a leader.

Lesson 1.1
Identifies beliefs that people have about being a leader and describes personal qualities that result in leadership opportunities.

Lesson 1.2
Describes personality traits and discusses the importance of behavior in dealing with others.

Lesson 1.3
Explains how to create a new vision for your life.

WHAT WOULD YOU DO?
Ask students why they think someone might hesitate to approach the "popular, athletic, and pretty" people in school. Do they know people who have used Becky's approach to build new relationships? What were the results?

Inventory of Past Experiences and Opportunities

GOALS
- Identify your beliefs about being a leader.
- Describe personal qualities that result in leadership opportunities.

TERMS
- leader
- skill
- skill level
- affirmation
- conflict resolution

SCHEDULE
Block 45 minutes
Regular 1 class period

FOCUS
Ask students what personal qualities they think make a person a good leader. Write their answers on the board.

TEACH
Have students name people whom they would identify as leaders. Ask students what traits these individuals have in common. How are they different?

BELIEFS ABOUT BEING A LEADER

When you hear the word *leader*, you may assume that you need to have the courage to speak in front of large groups of your peers or belong to a certain group or clique. You may think you need to wear specific types of clothing, come from a certain type of home life, or have a particular physical appearance. The thought of these things can be frightening if you view yourself as a shy, quiet person who does not belong to the "right" group, wear "cool" clothes, come from a certain neighborhood or income bracket, or have the "right" look. It also can feel frightening if you believe that others think you lack the courage or ability to do the things required of a leader.

The word *leader* can be applied to someone who displays courage, brings forth ideas, and exhibits speaking skills. On a smaller scale, the word *leader* might simply apply to someone who motivates his or her peers to do their part of a class project. A leader possesses certain traits and characteristics such as honesty, integrity, encouragement, dependability, responsibility, fairness, truthfulness, sympathy, and empathy.

A **leader** is someone with the ability to guide others toward accomplishing a goal. Regardless of how the word *leader* might be used, at some point in your life, you have most likely led or guided others.

© PhotoLink/Photodisc/Getty Images

Reflect back over your life. Think about the experiences you have had with leaders. Perhaps someone in your family or one of your friends took on a leadership role to carry out a plan. Now, think of at least two occasions when you were chosen as a leader—no matter how insignificant they may have seemed at the time.

THINK *CRITICALLY*

1. *Did you see yourself as a leader at the time? Why or why not?*

2. *Did anyone else identify you as being a leader?*

3. *Describe both of these experiences in detail. Were they positive or negative experiences?*

4. *If you were asked to be a leader, did it boost your self-confidence? Did you like being a leader? Why or why not?*

▍Past Experiences

The journey on the path to becoming a leader began with the small steps that you took at an early age. Maybe you were the line leader in elementary school who guided your classmates to the library. Maybe you sounded like a leader when you encouraged members of your little league team to play hard and do their best. You could have shown traits of a leader when you did not go along with the crowd in teasing the new kid at school. You may even act like a leader at home by displaying personal traits that show you are responsible about your behavior and assigned tasks. You show responsibility when you do your homework without being told. You show that you are considerate when you start dinner before your parents arrive home from work or when you volunteer to clean the kitchen after dinner.

Think about the times when you have volunteered to do something extra or different. Think, too, about some of the times when your friends or teammates have recommended you for a leadership role. All of these opportunities or experiences show the leader in you. But because these have been everyday, ordinary things, you may not have thought you were being a leader. You may have thought that you were just doing what you were asked to do or what you knew was the right thing to do. Whether or not you realize it, you demonstrate your leadership ability through many of your daily actions. As you go about your day, try to recognize those times that you exhibit leadership skills.

CHECKPOINT

What are two beliefs that people sometimes have about leaders?

They may believe that leaders must have the courage to speak in front of large groups or must wear certain clothes, come from certain homes, or have a specific appearance.

TEACH
Discuss the definition of a leader. Have students review the list they made at the beginning of the chapter. Do the personal qualities of a leader that they identified agree with the definition?

TEACH
Explain that leadership may be demonstrated through daily actions. Ask students to think of ways they have demonstrated leadership at home, at school, on a job, or in their community. Ask several people to give examples.

WHAT ABOUT ME?
Too often, students think of leadership in terms of major events. Point out that leadership can involve small, daily activities that may even feel "ordinary."

Think Critically Answers
1. Answers will vary.
2. Answers will vary.
3. Answers will vary.
4. Answers will vary.

ONGOING ASSESSMENT
Use the Checkpoint as an opportunity to conduct ongoing assessment of student comprehension of the lesson material.

OPPORTUNITIES TO LEAD

Opportunities to be a leader come in different ways, at different times, and for different reasons. An opportunity to lead may relate to a particular situation that matches the qualities you possess. The personal qualities you possess that may result in a leadership role include the following:

- physical size
- physical attractiveness
- skill level
- academic ability
- emotional stability
- honesty and truthfulness
- treatment of others

Any one, or combination, of these traits will cause others to see you as a leader. The situation will dictate which of these traits is used, whether in a positive or negative way, to enable you to take on the role of leader.

Physical Size

A person's height, weight, and strength are viewed by many as positive traits that can be used to give a group a winning edge. But tall students are not automatically basketball players, and all muscular students are not wrestlers or weightlifters. Students of any height and build can be good athletes under the right circumstances. How many times have you seen people selected or rejected to lead because of their physical size? Individuals should not be penalized for something over which they have no control. Physical size does not take into account the character of a person.

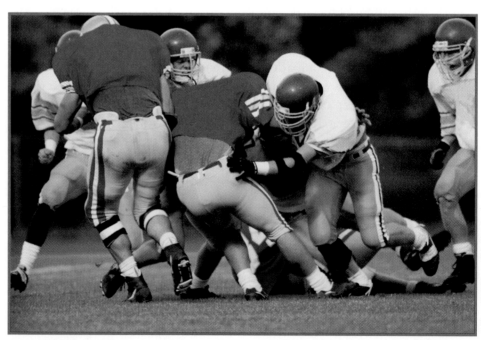

© PhotoLink/Photodisc/Getty Images

Physical Attractiveness

Unfortunately, in some cultures, there is a standard of beauty, or a "certain look," that allows a physically attractive person to get special treatment. You might assume that people you view as being more attractive are smarter, more important, more popular, happier, and more satisfied with their lives. Based on this perception, individuals who are physically attractive may be chosen to be leaders even if they are less qualified or less skillful. For this reason, it is important that you look beyond physical appearances. Begin appreciating the positive inner qualities that you possess. Focus on your attitude and personality. A person's inner qualities far outweigh physical appearance when it comes to being a good leader.

TEACH
Ask students if they have ever known a physically attractive person who got special treatment because of his or her looks. Do they think it was fair? How did it make them feel?

TEACH
Ask students to think of the special skills they possess. Why do they think that skill level is one of the best indicators of a good leader?

Skill Level

A **skill** is a learned ability or strength that allows an individual to do something well. A **skill level** is a measure of a person's ability, talent, or expertise in performing a task. There are times when skill level is not easily identified because it is observable only if the person chooses to demonstrate that skill in the presence of others. As you interact with your peers on a daily basis, you are able to recognize the things that they do really well. It is important that you give them recognition for those things. Your compliments can encourage them to share their skills for the good of the group.

© F64/Photodisc/Getty Images

Skill level is one of the best indicators of a good leader. There are a variety of skills that are important to a leader, including social skills, communication skills, decision-making skills, self-control skills, and technical or mechanical skills.

Social Skills

Individuals with social skills display friendly, outgoing, and confident behaviors toward others. These skills usually are exhibited when you have social confidence. Social confidence allows you to move freely and favorably in and out of social situations. You appear to be comfortable with yourself and are able to offer understanding, sympathy, and empathy to others. You are comfortable "in your own skin."

Communication Skills

Being a good communicator is one of the most important skills you can have as a leader. Communication skills are displayed by speaking, writing, or using body language to send information or messages to others. The information can be delivered to another individual through everyday interactions or to a large group through speeches and

TEACH
Some students may have better developed social skills than others. Ask students how they think individuals can develop better social skills.

TEACH
Ask students how they think they communicate through body language. Discuss things like posture and stance, facial expressions, and gestures.

presentations. You can easily identify this skill in yourself and others because it is used to build relationships with others.

Decision-Making Skills

As you have developed through the years, you have been given opportunities to make both large and small decisions. The small decisions, such as what snack to eat, what color shoe laces to buy, and what costume to wear for a special holiday, helped give you the confidence to make increasingly more difficult decisions. Your decision-making skills will continue to grow stronger throughout the years. You still will make a bad decision occasionally. Bad decisions should be viewed as part of the learning process because you can learn from your mistakes.

When you make good decisions, you often receive affirmation from others. **Affirmation** involves agreeing with, validating, or confirming the actions or behaviors of another person. Affirmation makes you feel secure and satisfied, leading you to take increased risks when making decisions. This is why individuals with good decision-making skills are sometimes considered risk takers.

As you grow and take on more responsibilities, you will begin to realize that the decisions you make can affect the lives of others. It is important to think through the consequences of your decisions. Be aware of how you make decisions. Do you think things through? Do you plan ahead and look at all the options? Good leaders will make careful decisions and do what is best for the group.

Self-Control Skills

Being able to control your emotions and behaviors requires self-control skills. Individuals with good self-control are usually good at conflict resolution. **Conflict resolution** is the ability to find acceptable solutions to problems and experiences to benefit both you and the others involved.

Technical/Mechanical Skills

Some individuals can fix anything. They can take apart things, such as a stereo or computer, and put them back together again. They seem to understand how and why things work the way they do. When it comes to complex tasks, individuals with technical or mechanical skills are often chosen to lead.

© Jeff Maloney/Photodisc/Getty Images

Academic Ability

The grades that you get on your report cards and on class projects indicate your academic ability. You may receive recognition, praise, financial reward, and other things for performing well academically. Academic ability is one of the most frequently rewarded skills. If you get good grades, teachers may call on you in class to showcase your academic abilities. You may be labeled by others as "smart." Most of the individuals who carry this label are hard-working students who put a lot of time and effort into their work. Most people can improve their academic standing by changing their work and study habits. Individuals who have the drive to work hard often are selected as leaders.

Emotional Stability

How you accept, treat, and view yourself and others shows your emotional stability. The developmental, emotional, and social changes you experience as you grow and mature will increase your emotional stability. Individuals who seem to display a sense of maturity, calmness, and acceptance of themselves and others are the ones people look to as leaders. A person who has low or no acceptance and tolerance for others may be passed over and not seen as someone to represent the good of the group. Individuals who are able to remain calm and level-headed are sought out by their peers for emotional support and friendship. They often take on leadership roles.

Honesty and Truthfulness

Honesty and truthfulness usually go hand in hand. These character traits are at the core of a person in whom others are willing to place their trust and confidence. From the time you have understood the difference between right and wrong, you have been held responsible for doing and saying the right things. You can see these traits in individuals who are sincere in their dealings with others. You also should be able to identify these traits in yourself. Your family and friends need to know that if they confide in you, you will honor their privacy. They need to know that you will follow through with your promises. Honesty and truthfulness are necessary qualities for all leaders.

Treatment of Others

It is important to treat people the way you would want to be treated. During your early childhood years, you were taught to be nice to your siblings and your parents. You were taught to share and to respect others' feelings. At this point in your life, you now realize that others deserve to have rights and privileges just as you have. Based on this realization, you will begin to show increased respect and personal regard for others as human beings worthy of acceptance, love, fairness, and respect.

 CHECKPOINT

List and describe two personal qualities that result in leadership opportunities.

Qualities that may result in leadership opportunities include physical size, attractiveness, skill level, academic ability, emotional stability, honesty, and treatment of others.

TEACH
Ask students if they have ever been around someone who had low acceptance and tolerance for others. How did they feel being around that person? Would they view that person as a good leader? Why or why not?

TEACH
Ask students if they have ever had a friend tell them something and follow it by saying, "Please don't tell anyone. I promised I wouldn't tell." How did that make them feel about that friend? Would they feel comfortable confiding in that person?

TEACH
Ask students if they are familiar with the Golden Rule: Treat others the way you want to be treated. Have several students give examples of ways that they can demonstrate the Golden Rule in their daily interactions with others.

TEACHING STRATEGIES
LEP Students
Many different cultures have some version of the Golden Rule. Ask students to share the "rules" they have learned in their own culture relating to the proper treatment of others.

ONGOING ASSESSMENT
Use the Checkpoint as an opportunity to conduct ongoing assessment of student comprehension of the lesson material.

Follow UP

UNDERSTAND LEADERSHIP CONCEPTS

Circle the best answer for each of the following questions.

1. Which of the following beliefs about a leader is true?
   a. A leader must always be able to speak in front of large groups.
   b. Only physically attractive people can be leaders.
   c. Most individuals have past experience in leading others.
   d. A leader must have technical and mechanical skills.

2. Which of the following qualities may result in an opportunity to lead?
   a. physical size
   b. skill level
   c. emotional stability
   d. all of the above

THINK *CRITICALLY*

Answer the following questions as completely as possible. If necessary, use a separate sheet of paper.

3. Why is it helpful to think about past experiences of being a leader?

Recognizing past experiences of being a leader helps you realize that you have

leadership abilities that you may not have realized. You demonstrate leadership

ability through many daily activities.

4. Describe the qualities that you have that would help you be a good leader.

Answers will vary but may include various skills, academic ability, emotional stability,

honesty and truthfulness, and proper treatment of others.

5. Why are honesty and truthfulness necessary qualities for a leader?

Leaders must be honest and truthful so that people will be willing to trust them, place

their confidence in them, and know that they will follow through with their promises.

ASSESS
Reteach
Have students work with a partner to discuss the past experiences and personal qualities that they have identified as a foundation for leadership.

Enrich
Have students interview a leader in their school or community. Questions might include, "What past experiences do you think prepared you to become a leader?" and "What personal qualities do you think helped you become a good leader?" Have students prepare a brief oral report summarizing their interview.

Close
Have students review the opportunities to lead discussed in this lesson. Ask them to identify what they think are their strongest personal qualities.

10   Chapter 1   There Is a Leader in You

Learning about Yourself

GOALS
- Identify things about yourself that you compare to others.
- Identify things about yourself over which you have no control.

TERMS
- attitude
- personality type
- introvert
- extrovert
- behavior
- risk factors
- protective factors

COMPARING YOURSELF TO OTHERS

As a human being, you sometimes compare yourself to others. This comparison usually begins at home as you become aware of the differences between you and others in your family. At other times, you may be aware of differences in the way you are treated compared to the way others in the same situation are treated. Keep in mind that at an early age, you did not have much control over certain elements of your life, such as where you lived, what you wore, or what you looked like. However, you have now reached a stage in your life where you can have an impact upon how you live, what you wear, and what you look like, so making comparisons is common.

You still probably have very little or no control over where your home is located. But you do have some control over how you manage your space within your home. For example, you can decide how neat you want to keep your room. As your family members observe the way you take care of your possessions, they often want to give you more responsibility or reward you with more things to manage. If they see that you are irresponsible in taking care of your things, they assume that you will not be responsible in taking care of theirs. They may take away privileges and deny some of your requests.

The way you come to see and accept yourself is shaped by your early childhood experiences with your family members and friends. These people help establish the direction you take and your successes or failures in the future. Negative feedback and lack of encouragement from family and friends may delay your growth physically, emotionally, academically, and socially. If this occurs, you may experience dysfunctional or inappropriate behaviors in your life. If family and friends provide positive feedback, support, and praise for

SCHEDULE
Block 45 minutes
Regular 1 class period

FOCUS
Ask students how they feel when they are around people who have a positive attitude and who behave appropriately. How do they feel around people who have a negative attitude or who behave badly?

TEACH
Ask students if they see a direct relationship between the decisions they make and the amount of responsibility they are given.

© Barbara Penoyar/Photodisc/Getty Images

TEACH

Ask students to explain the difference between self-awareness and self-image. Have several students give examples of positive and negative self-image.

TEACH

Ask students if they know someone who has a poor self-image. How does that person's poor self-image affect his or her attitude and personality?

TEACH

Ask students to explain what it means to say either "the glass is half full" or "the glass is half empty." Point out that in each case the person is viewing the same glass. The difference is in the individual's attitude.

Discuss the margin quote. Ask students to explain how attitude can damage or strengthen a relationship.

> " Whenever you're in conflict with someone, there is one factor that can make the difference between damaging your relationship and deepening it. That factor is attitude.
>
> — Timothy Bentley

things you do well, you will grow confident and strong in the important areas of your life.

You Are Who You Are

Self-awareness helps you understand who you are. You can become more self-aware by taking an inventory or doing a self-assessment of your traits and characteristics. Before making judgments about yourself, however, keep several important things in mind:

- Remember that you did not create yourself. You inherited your body frame, hair texture, height, weight potential, structure, and features from your biological parents. In addition, your parents and others who may have helped raise you have greatly influenced your personality and attitude.
- Recognize and accept the things you cannot change about yourself. For example, if your mother and father both wear eyeglasses, chances are that you also will need to wear eyeglasses.
- Work on changing the things that you can change. For example, you can ask for contact lenses if you don't like wearing eyeglasses.
- Make peace with yourself and the people from whom you inherited these traits.
- Learn how to continuously enhance or improve yourself—physically, emotionally, academically, and socially.

When trying to understand who you are, you also need to consider your self-image. How you see yourself is your *self-image*. If you have a positive self-image, you have the confidence and inner strength to propel yourself to greater heights of character and leadership. A lack of confidence and inner strength can prevent you from projecting the special qualities you possess. Your self-image can positively or negatively affect your attitude and personality.

Impact of Attitude and Personality

Your interaction with family and friends helps to shape your attitude and personality. These two traits affect how you see yourself as well as how others see you. Likewise, the way you view yourself will have a great impact on your attitude and personality.

Attitude

The way you deal with and treat yourself and other people is your **attitude**. Do you have a positive or negative attitude about yourself and others—physically, emotionally, or academically? Do you see the glass as being half empty or half full? Do you give yourself the benefit of the doubt? Do you send out positive verbal and mental messages about yourself? Do you speak positive words about yourself, such as "I am confident of my skills" and "I am smart enough to be in this class"? Or are you always speaking negatively, such as "I am dumb, and I cannot do that" or "I am not attractive, and I do not like my body, hair, height, or weight"? The more you say these things about yourself, the more you believe them and the more others believe and accept these descriptions of you.

Usually, your attitude is reflected in the words you choose to describe yourself. It is exhibited by the way you behave when interacting with others. If you want to test whether your attitude is positive or negative, start at home by observing how your family members react to the way you behave and treat them. Attitude begins at home. Are you respectful toward them, or do you always demand to have your needs met before theirs? Are you considerate of their needs and their possessions? Are you honest? Do you always tell the truth—even if it means sometimes getting into trouble? Do you apologize when you have done something wrong or inappropriate? Are you careful to use an appropriate tone of voice that does not exhibit "attitude"?

Your attitude plays an important part in helping others decide if they want to spend time with you and accept you as a member of their group. Is your leadership potential and success being hidden behind or overshadowed by your negative attitude? If so, reflect on those times when you felt you were overlooked to be the team leader or not chosen for participation on certain teams and clubs. If these memories still bring up hurtful feelings and images, let that be a clue to your current need to develop a defense mechanism—your negative attitude—to protect your feelings.

Reflect on times in your past and remember some of the positive victories. Identifying events that produced positive feelings helps to establish a sense of acceptance, victory, and affirmation in you. As you send these messages to yourself, it becomes easier to send the same or similar messages to others for things that they do. A healthy dose of self-awareness and self-esteem goes a long way toward creating a positive attitude. Check your attitude—starting now!

Personality

Understanding your personality type or style is important to your growth and development. Personality is mostly influenced by your family and the environment in which you were raised. Some of the ways you behave, treat other people, and view and judge behaviors are a direct result of your family environment. Your personality has also been influenced by the friends you have socialized with throughout your life. You have also been influenced in other environments, such as school, church, and other places where you may spend time with people other than your family. In these places, you sometimes may display a different personality than the one you usually exhibit at home and away from school. In an attempt to fit in, you sometimes make adjustments to your personality. You make these adjustments because you recognize that certain personality traits are more appropriate at different times.

Your **personality type** indicates how you deal with the different situations and experiences in your life. It also helps you identify your

TEACH
Ask students how they can tell whether a person has a positive or a negative attitude. List their answers on opposite sides of the board. Have students review the lists. Do they see their own attitudes more on the positive or the negative side of the board?

TEACH
Ask students if they have ever encountered someone who acted differently around different groups of people. Why do they think people sometimes adjust their personality in different environments?

TEACHING STRATEGIES
Visual Learners
Auditory Learners
Have students draw pictures representing the personalities they display at home, at school, and in other groups to which they belong. Have students share their drawings and discuss the differences, if any, in their personalities.

A **TEAM** *Effort*

People tend to be one of two personality types—introvert or extrovert. Work as a team to develop a questionnaire or checklist that can be used by others to help determine if they are an introvert or extrovert. It may be helpful to use the Internet to research introvert and extrovert characteristics.

THINK *CRITICALLY*

Do you think people can have behaviors that represent both personality types and not have one dominant style? Could this be revealed in your questionnaire or checklist? Explain how.

TEACH
Ask students how they think knowing your personality style can help you become a better or more effective leader. Point out that the more you know about yourself, the better you will be able to find the right "fit" for you.

A TEAM EFFORT
In creating their questionnaires or checklists, students may want to search the Internet using "Myers-Briggs Type Indicator" as a search phrase. Students should understand that being an introvert or extrovert refers to a person's "preferred" style. Individuals often will have some characteristics of both styles.

Think Critically Answers
Answers will vary.

TEACHING STRATEGIES
Gifted Students
The Myers-Briggs Type Indicator includes four measures of personality type, of which introversion/extroversion is one. Have students conduct research on the Internet or in the library and create a PowerPoint or other visual representation of all four measures of the Myers-Briggs Type Indicator.

comfort zone—those environments in which you feel most comfortable. Your relationships with your peers, your expectations of them, and the way you communicate with them are all affected by your personality type.

People often are described as being one of two basic personality types—an introvert or an extrovert.

- An **introvert** tends to focus on inner thoughts and ideas. Introverts may be more quiet and shy, not very outgoing, and "live in their head" a lot of times. They make decisions based on thinking and analysis rather than emotion.
- An **extrovert** directs attention and interests toward the outer world of people and things. Extroverts are friendly, cheerful, and social and often are referred to as being personable and fun to be around. They like contact with other people and may prefer to discuss problems with a group before making decisions.

One personality type is not better or worse than the other. Each one is just a different way of functioning on a daily basis. If you want to get a glimpse of which personality type you think you are, start by observing your family members to see which type they seem to be. Is one of your parents more laid back? Does one of them always seem to be thinking about something? Is one of them very talkative? Which one are you most comfortable with? Whose personality style most closely matches yours? You will begin to notice that even though you and your siblings were brought up in the same household, you can be very different from one another. Being different does not mean you are ineffective in the way you deal with life's day-to-day experiences. Actually, once you can more clearly define your personality style, you can begin to better understand why you do the things you do. You will find your comfort zone and become more understanding and accepting of the way others behave.

Your increased sense of "knowing" your personality style will also help you understand how you can become a more effective leader. Not everyone can have the leading role in the school play, but leaders are also needed in stage production, lighting, and costume design. Not everyone can be class president, but someone needs to take the leadership role as the secretary, treasurer, or historian. The personality style that you exhibit will help you and others decide where you fit best into a particular group. Begin to think about your comfort zone for different activities, and you will begin to more clearly see how the right "fit" can improve your chances of success. Your success will result in more opportunities to be a leader.

 CHECKPOINT

Describe the two most common personality types.

The two most common personality types are introvert and extrovert.

SEEING AND BEING YOU

As your self-awareness and self-image increase, you will likely want to make changes to improve yourself. In order to do this, you must be able to distinguish between those things that are less significant, such as physical appearance, and those things that matter more, such as behavior.

▌Physical Appearance

You do not always get a chance to influence or decide what you wear. But the good news is that there is no particular dress code or uniform for leaders. There are many reasons people dress the way they do. What you wear can be influenced by your culture, size, religious affiliation, financial resources, and parental guidance. What you desire in the clothes you wear is a sense of comfort and presence in the way you present the "real you." Cleanliness, neatness, and a sense of style present a look of order and pride that says your appearance matters. When you constantly compare your clothes to your peers' clothes, you will be self-conscious about how you look. You may feel that you never have enough clothes to wear. Even if you have the exact same outfit as someone you envy, you may not think it looks as good on you. You may become dissatisfied with your body size, shape, and physical appearance. Feeling physically unattractive can negatively affect your inter-actions with your peers. It can also have an effect on your relationship with your parents. You may become resentful or disrespectful toward your parents if they do not buy you the clothes you want.

To avoid these negative experiences, it is helpful to take an inventory of your clothes, shoes, jewelry, and other accessories. Do this when you have time to try on things and check yourself in a mirror so you can see how you really look. If something is too small, too drab, or no

© Digital Vision/Getty Images

TEACH
Discuss the value of having a well-organized and well-matched wardrobe. Ask how many students periodically take an inventory of their clothing to make sure it fits and is in good repair.

TEACHING STRATEGIES
Tactile Learners
Have students take a physical inventory of their wardrobe—clothes, shoes, jewelry, and accessories. Have them try on clothing to make sure it fits properly and inspect items to make sure they are in good repair. Have students record their inventory and report the results.

TEACH
Ask students if they have ever been around individuals who were engaged in risky behavior, such as alcohol and drug use. How did it make them feel? Did they feel pressure to participate in order to fit in?

ONGOING ASSESSMENT
Use the Checkpoint as an opportunity to conduct ongoing assessment of student comprehension of the lesson material.

longer in style, take it out of your closet. Then match bottoms with tops, jewelry, and shoes so that when you get up in the morning you know what to wear. Get rid of the clothes that are simply taking up space in your closet. By evaluating your wardrobe needs, you can more easily justify your reasons for wanting more clothes or accessories. This inventory process can help increase your confidence in your wardrobe and allow you to focus on more important things.

Behavior

Behavior is an action caused by or a reaction to the surrounding environment. Behavior is displayed through a person's conduct, or the actions exhibited by that person. As you and your peers grow, you are exposed to many factors that can affect your behavior. These factors have the potential to increase or decrease your risk regarding inappropriate or dangerous behaviors, such as drugs, alcohol, and violence. The factors are categorized as either risk factors or protective factors. **Risk factors** include situations that could potentially increase your chances of being involved in inappropriate or dangerous behaviors. **Protective factors** include situations that could potentially decrease your chances of being involved in inappropriate or dangerous behaviors. Risk factors and protective factors usually fall into five categories: family, individual, peer group, school, and community.

Family structure, standards, and expectations in the midst of a loving and supportive environment serve as protective factors to decrease your chances of becoming involved in risky behaviors. Living and growing up in such an environment helps lay the foundation for your current behaviors. Attachment and bonding to your school and teachers are other protective factors that can improve your motivation for good attendance and participation in school.

Peer influence can be a risk factor when it involves "testing" certain behaviors, such as alcohol and drug use. Your desire to fit in and be popular sometimes can cause you to go along with whatever your friends are doing. Being well liked and accepted may sometimes seem more important than the consequences of the risky behavior. However, your positive sense of self and knowing the dangers of such behaviors can give you the courage to walk away from dangerous substances and risky behaviors.

You can draw from your personal experiences with your family, your peers, and in the school setting to help you apply behaviors that send the right message about your character. Remember, you are not yet all that you are going to become. Learn to like yourself by acting and behaving in confident and socially acceptable ways.

CHECKPOINT

Why is behavior important in dealing with others and their selection of you as a leader?

Behavior is important in dealing with others because individuals who display proper behavior are the ones who will be asked to take on leadership roles.

Follow UP

UNDERSTAND LEADERSHIP CONCEPTS

Circle the best answer for each of the following questions.

1. **The way individuals deal with and treat themselves and others is their**
   a. personality
   b. risk factor
   c. behavior
   d. attitude *(circled)*

2. **Which of the following statements about risk factors is true?**
   a. They increase a person's chances of involvement in inappropriate and dangerous behaviors.
   b. They include problems such as drugs and alcohol use and abuse.
   c. They fall into five categories.
   d. all of the above *(circled)*

THINK *CRITICALLY*

Answer the following questions as completely as possible. If necessary, use a separate sheet of paper.

3. **Why is it important to avoid comparing yourself to others?**

   You are a unique individual, but there are many things in your life over which you have no control. Self-awareness will help you understand who you are, recognize and accept the things you cannot change about yourself, and work on changing the things that you can change.

4. **Why is attitude an important factor in choosing a leader?**

   Your attitude is the way you deal with and treat yourself and others. It helps people decide if they want to spend time with you and accept you as a group member and leader. A negative attitude may prevent people from having confidence in you as a leader.

5. **To help you become more self-aware, take an inventory of your attitude, personality, physical appearance, and skills. Make a list of traits and characteristics related to each item.**

   Answers will vary.

ASSESS
Reteach
Review the goals for the lesson. Have students write one or two sentences summarizing the important points discussed for each of the goals.

Enrich
Have students give the questionnaire or checklist created in "A Team Effort" to several of their friends to complete. Are they surprised by the results?

Close
Have students think about someone they believe has a positive self-image. What qualities or characteristics make them think that the person has a positive self-image? What message is conveyed by the person's attitude and personality?

Seize the Moment

GOALS

- Describe how you can create a new vision.
- Explain the next steps toward creating your vision.

TERMS

- vision
- constructive criticism
- myths

SCHEDULE
Block 45 minutes
Regular 1 class period

FOCUS
Ask students how they think individuals can begin making changes in their life. What action steps are required?

TEACH
Discuss the definition of a vision. Ask students how they feel about creating a new vision for their life.

NEW VISION

You have had a chance to reflect back over your life's experiences and opportunities. As you have examined those experiences and the traits you possess, hopefully you have recognized that you are special. You have had many opportunities to lead, even though you may not have identified them as such. Now you are beginning to see the leader in you more clearly. You have taken an inventory of your physical self, emotional stability, attitude, personality, and skills. You have cleaned out your closet—or at least you have given it some thought. You are at the point where you want to make changes in your behavior. A new vision is beginning to appear. A **vision** is an idea or a project that you imagine turning into reality by undergoing some type of change.

Your inventory made you aware of where your different characteristics—from physical to emotional to social—come from. You are also aware that your attitude, behavior, and personality are all grounded in your connection to your parents, family, and home environment. Your acceptance and understanding of your characteristics should be growing.

It is now time for you to seize the moment and declare a new level of maturity, personal satisfaction, academic achievement, and confidence. *Seize* means to grab hold or take charge of something or someone, such as a dream, goal, or desire. It is time to view your life from a different perspective to gain a new and clearer vision of the leader in you. You will become empowered as you set new goals and work to fulfill this new vision. *Empowerment* influences and enables you to take action. It is now your turn to assert yourself in more positive ways that will demonstrate that you are capable of doing and being so much more.

© SW Productions/Photodisc/Getty Images

CHECKPOINT

What is a vision?

A vision is an idea or a project that you imagine turning into reality by undergoing some type of change.

NEXT STEPS

Where do you go from here? What do you do next with this enhanced "you"? You may have to go outside of your comfort zone. You may have to take more positive risks. You may have to shake off peers who do not want to go and grow in this new way with you. Old negative habits and traits must be replaced with positive factors that will support you through this period of change. Rely on family and trusted friends to be there for you through this journey when things seem overwhelming.

Consider the following steps to help you fulfill your new vision.

- **Make a decision to figure out what you really want to do and be right now.** What you want to do and be will change as you mature and experiment with different interests. Your interest in and passion for a particular thing will help you figure out what it is that you really want to participate in at this particular time. It must be something that you truly want to accomplish so that you will continue to work hard even when things get tough. What you feel passionate about on the inside must match your behaviors on the outside. You need to share what is important to you and what you believe in as a leader with the people who choose to support you.

- **Make a plan so that you can set and reach your goals.** As has been said in the past, "if you don't plan your work, you cannot work your plan." For some of you, goal setting sounds like a huge task. To avoid being overwhelmed, set only a few goals in the beginning. Having one or two goals that you will work toward is more important than having a list of goals and not knowing how to reach them. If goal setting is new to you, start small. Maybe your goal will be to get your homework done before you watch TV at night or to get it done by a certain time. Another goal could be to make your bed every day before leaving for school because it helps your attitude and mindset when you walk into a room that is neat. Maybe

COMMUNICATE

Goal setting and planning help people make decisions about the direction to take in their lives. If you are new to goal setting, you may want to get started by using a to-do list and checking off your accomplishments as you complete each one. As you gain confidence in completing the list, you will want to commit to completing even bigger goals. Keep in mind that you will need a more detailed plan to support your efforts in reaching bigger goals. Success in your personal goal setting can set the stage for goal setting as a leader in your group.

THINK *CRITICALLY*

Explain how setting goals can help you in school. How can setting goals help you be a better leader?

© Ken Usami/Photodisc/Getty Images

your goal is to drink only one soda a day to gain the health benefits of less sugar. Getting into the habit of setting goals and planning is important so that you can meet challenges of increased responsibility as you progress through school and toward the world of work.

- **Improve your organizational skills.** Become more organized, orderly, and clean. This will help you change old habits and prioritize your activities. Getting organized helps to clear your mind. It gives you a sense of knowing where things are and how things should be done. Being organized helps you use your time wisely, and it enables you to enjoy newfound freedom and peace. Others will see you as being more responsible and capable. They will view your organizational skills as a positive trait for being a leader. They sense that you can bring or restore order to a situation, idea, or program. The benefits of organization extend beyond you as you begin to influence others.

- **Overcome the negatives of your past.** Overcoming negative experiences of your past is one of the more difficult things to do. It sometimes means forgiving people who have hurt you in some way. They may have rejected you, denied you your rights, spoken lies about you, stolen your things, or broken your heart and your spirit.

First, seek support and encouragement from your family. This step sometimes calls for special help from your school counselor or other professionals. Your favorite teacher or another trusted adult may be able to act as a go-between or provide guidance. The anger and hurt resulting from these situations go deep and can prevent you from growing in an emotionally healthy way. It can cause you to lose interest in other parts of your life. A leader who is feeling hurt or angry because of past negative experiences may be unable to lead others in the right direction. Learning how to overcome your past is important to your success as a leader.

- **Increase your level of readiness.** You must be ready and willing to learn new skills. They can energize you and increase your self-worth. In order to increase your readiness level, it is sometimes necessary to do a skill assessment to determine those areas in which you need to improve. The skills can range from physical or social to technical or decision making. Taking a class is not always necessary to learn a new skill. Seeking and being able to accept feedback and encouragement from family and friends can be one way of learning a new skill. You might be pleasantly surprised to learn that your parents actually know a lot about many things. Remember, they used to be teenagers themselves at one time. Another way would be to consult with one of your favorite teachers or school counselors for direction and support. For some students, consulting a spiritual

TEACH

Ask students how they feel when their room at home or their locker at school is a mess. Do they have trouble finding the things they need? How do they feel when things are neat and orderly?

Ask students if they have ever been angry or upset with someone and "held a grudge" against the person. How did that make them feel? Do they think it was helpful or productive? Point out that they need to overcome past hurts and move forward in order to be effective leaders.

TEACHING STRATEGIES
Print Learners

Have students list any negative experiences in their past that they have not yet been able to overcome. Next to each item, have students list a way that they think they might be able to overcome the negative experience or someone they think may be able to help them.

© Scott T Baxter/Photodisc/Getty Images

TEACH
Write the word *criticism* on the board. Ask students how criticism makes them feel. Does it have a negative or positive feeling? Then ask them what they think *constructive criticism* means. Explain that constructive criticism is positive feedback and encouragement to help them improve a particular skill.

TEACH
Have students name some of the myths about leaders that they now realize are not true.

leader is another possible source for help. A change in attitude may be necessary to increase your level of readiness. It is important to be open and willing to accept constructive criticism as you reach out to others for support. **Constructive criticism** is feedback that encourages improvement and is given in a positive way. The amazing thing about learning new skills is the sense of accomplishment and joy it brings to your life. The benefits for you are increased enthusiasm, energy, and empowerment. As your readiness level increases, so do your chances of being chosen as someone to lead others into new areas.

- **Validate others.** Give attention, affirmation, encouragement, and feedback to others. If you follow this approach, your family, friends, and peers will respond positively to you and appreciate your support of them. In turn, they are likely to support you in a leadership role.

Debunking Myths about Leaders

Many of the things you previously may have thought about leaders are simply **myths**, which are fictional or unproven beliefs. Leaders come in all sizes, shapes, and colors, with different personality styles and attitudes. There is no official "look" or wardrobe or attitude for a leader. There are preferred styles in each of these areas depending upon the situation. The challenge is to be the best you can be so that you can begin to see the leader in you in any given situation.

LEADERSHIP *Tip*

Knowing what you are passionate about can help you direct your energy toward work that is rewarding and satisfying. Your enthusiasm then begins to rub off on others around you.

LEADERSHIP TIP
Divide students into small groups. Within each group, ask students to describe the things that they are most passionate about right now. Have other group members suggest the type of work that might be rewarding and satisfying for each student in the group.

ONGOING ASSESSMENT
Use the Checkpoint as an opportunity to conduct ongoing assessment of student comprehension of the lesson material.

CHECKPOINT

Describe one of the "next steps" in fulfilling a new vision.

Next steps include figuring out what you want to do and be now, making a plan to reach your goals, improving organizational skills, overcoming negatives in your past, increasing your level of readiness, and validating others.

Follow UP

UNDERSTAND LEADERSHIP CONCEPTS

Circle the best answer for each of the following questions.

1. Which of the following is a myth about leaders?
   a. They must always have a high grade point average.
   b. They must have good communication skills.
   c. They must be truthful and honest.
   d. all of the above

2. What should you consider when making a plan to set and reach a goal?
   a. Start with high expectations so you can work hard to meet them.
   b. Ask your friends to suggest a goal for you.
   c. Set a few goals and start small.
   d. Never let anyone know your goals in case you do not reach them.

THINK *CRITICALLY*

Answer the following questions as completely as possible. If necessary, use a separate sheet of paper.

3. Why is it important for people to overcome the negative experiences they may have had in their lives?

Unless they can overcome the negative experiences they have had in life, people

cannot grow in an emotionally healthy way. They may lose interest in other parts of

their life. Leaders also may not be able to lead others in the right direction.

4. Why is it important for a leader to have organizational skills?

People view leaders with organizational skills as being more responsible and capable.

They consider organizational skills as a positive trait for a leader and feel that the

leader will be able to bring order to a situation, idea, or program.

5. Discuss how learning a new skill can improve a person's attitude.

Learning a new skill energizes a person and increases his or her self-worth. It provides a

sense of accomplishment as well as increased enthusiasm, energy, and empowerment.

ASSESS
Reteach
Have students review the "next steps" for fulfilling their new vision. Have them write one or two sentences summarizing the key points in each step.

Enrich
Have students select a leader, either current or historical, and conduct research about that leader. Did the person have a clear vision? Did he or she have a plan to reach goals? Was the person organized and ready to accept the responsibility of leadership? Have students report their findings.

Close
Ask students to explain the value of readiness. Ask if they think a person can be an effective leader if he or she is not prepared and ready to assume a leadership role.

Chapter Assessment

REVIEW *LEADERSHIP CONCEPTS*

TEACHING RESOURCES
Exam*View*® **CD**, Ch. 1

Write the letter of the term that matches each definition. Some terms will not be used.

___h___ 1. Someone with the ability to guide others toward accomplishing a goal

___j___ 2. Indicates how you deal with the different situations in your life

___b___ 3. The way you deal with and treat yourself and other people

___l___ 4. Situations that could potentially increase the chances of being involved in inappropriate and sometimes dangerous behavior

___m___ 5. A learned ability or strength that allows an individual to do something well

___o___ 6. An idea or a project that you imagine turning into reality by undergoing some type of change

___c___ 7. An action or reaction caused by the surrounding environment

___d___ 8. The ability to find acceptable solutions to problems and experiences to benefit both you and the others involved

___f___ 9. Someone who directs attention and interests toward the outer world of people and things

___a___ 10. To agree with, validate, or confirm the actions or behaviors of others

a. affirmation
b. attitude
c. behavior
d. conflict resolution
e. constructive criticism
f. extrovert
g. introvert
h. leader
i. myth
j. personality type
k. protective factors
l. risk factors
m. skill
n. skill level
o. vision

Circle the best answer.

11. How you accept, treat, and view yourself and others is an indication of your
    a. academic ability
    b. decision-making skills
    c. emotional stability
    d. communication skills

12. Which of the following is a category for risk and protective factors?
    a. family
    b. individual
    c. peer group
    d. all of the above

13. Your personality and behaviors are more greatly influenced by your
    a. school
    b. youth group
    c. family
    d. peer group

ASSESS

Reteach
Give students a list of the key terms from the chapter and have them use each one in a sentence to demonstrate their understanding of the terms.

Enrich
Invite a professional organizer to speak to the class about how they can become better organized. (You may find professional organizers in your community in the Yellow Pages or on the web site of the National Association of Professional Organizers.)

CLOSE
Ask students to explain how knowing more about yourself can help you become a good leader.

14. *Do you agree with this statement—"Leaders are born, and others cannot be taught the skills of leadership"? Explain your answer.*

Answers will vary. Students should recognize that leadership skills can be learned.

_____

_____

_____

_____

_____

15. *Discuss two personal qualities that were used to select you as a leader now or in the past.*

Answers will vary but may include physical size, physical attractiveness, skill level,

academic ability, emotional stability, honesty and truthfulness, or treatment of others.

_____

_____

_____

16. *Besides the leadership qualities discussed in this chapter, describe another quality you believe is important for a leader to have.*

Answers will vary.

_____

_____

_____

_____

_____

17. *Why are feedback and encouragement important to your growth and development?*

Feedback and encouragement are the major components of constructive criticism.

They are important to your growth and development because they offer opportunities

for improvement in a positive way.

_____

_____

18. *Why is it important to assess and know your traits for leadership?*

Assessing and knowing your traits for leadership will help you become more

self-aware and better able to understand who you are. It will help you understand

how you can become a more effective leader.

_____

19. **Reading**   Select a song by a recording artist whose music you like. Use available resources, such as a CD cover sheet or the actual CD, to read the lyrics. Describe how these lyrics affect your behavior or your attitude.

Answers will vary depending on the song selected. Song lyrics can be inspirational and

provide incentive to make changes in one's life or behavior.

_____

_____

_____

_____

_____

20. **Research**   It is commonly believed that athletes should be leaders both on and off the playing field. Use available resources, such as the Internet, library, or magazines, to gather information on an athlete of your choice. Identify some behaviors and attitudes that your chosen athlete exhibits to show his or her leadership skills.

Answers will vary depending on the athlete selected.

_____

_____

_____

_____

_____

_____

21. **Creative Thinking**   In column format, list three groups or teams that are active in your school. Write the name of the group at the top of each column. Under each column, write a list of skills required for membership in that group or team. Then, use a highlighter to highlight the similarities in skills needed in all three groups. Using a different colored highlighter, highlight the skills that are not the same. Write one or two paragraphs describing the reasons for the similarities and differences.

Answers will vary depending on the groups or teams selected.

_____

_____

_____

_____

_____

_____

22. **Problem Solving**   Think about the habits you would like to change or acquire, either at home or at school, and list two of these habits. Then list the actions you believe you need to take to change your habits. Assign a time period for making these changes, such as two weeks. Share a copy of your list of actions and deadlines with a classmate. Then commit to checking in with your classmate each day and reporting your behavior. Your partner will record your behavior next to the date on your list. You are to become one another's accountability partner. At the end of the time period, share with the class how, or if, your behavior changed and how you felt after going through this process.

Answers will vary.

_____

_____

_____

_____

_____

_____

_____

_____

23. **Technology**   Organizational skills are important for a leader. Use the Internet to learn about a specific type of technology that can help you get organized. Describe it and explain why it would be useful.

Answers will vary. There are many electronic daily planners and calendars that can help

individuals get organized.

_____

_____

_____

_____

_____

_____

_____

24. **Communication**   Using the Internet, conduct research on a well-known business leader, such as Oprah Winfrey or Wendy's Dave Thomas. Write a one- to two-page paper describing the obstacles this person had to overcome to become a great leader.

Answers will vary depending on the business leader selected.

_____

_____

_____

_____

_____

_____

_____

LEARNING TO LEAD

FOCUS

Learn about your career and technical education student organization.

DESCRIPTION

Participation in student organization activities and leadership roles is an effective way to improve your teamwork and leadership skills. Three national organizations serve students enrolled in business courses—Business Professionals of America (www.bpa.org), DECA (www.deca.org), and Future Business Leaders of America - Phi Beta Lambda (www.fbla.org). While there are many student organization opportunities available to students in their schools and communities, these three student business organizations are integrated with the courses students are taking. The focus of all three organizations is on career preparation and leadership development.

Select the career and technical education student organization that has a local chapter in your school and is most closely related to the business courses you are currently taking and that you plan to take in the future. Locate the national and state organizations' web sites and talk to the teacher who is the student organization adviser in your school to learn about the organization's structure.

ACTIVITIES

1. *Identify the official organization name, location of the national office, and the names of the national executive director or chief executive and the state adviser for your state. Identify the names of all of the organization's divisions and who each division serves. Identify the names and home states of the national officers for your division. Identify the names and the home town of the state officers for your division.*

2. *Identify the requirements for being a member in the organization's high school division.*

3. *Read about the organization's official purpose or mission.*

4. *Research three important historical facts about the organization.*

5. *Describe three different types of leadership opportunities and leadership development activities that are offered by the organization.*

6. *Identify the name of the local chapter adviser for your school and the classes that he or she teaches. Identify the names of the local chapter officers for your school.*

7. *Determine the meeting schedule for your local chapter.*

SHARE YOUR RESULTS

1. *Develop a two-page written summary of the information you gathered.*
2. *Prepare a brief oral presentation to give to other students that describes the student organization you selected and the benefits of membership for students who are seeking to improve their leadership abilities.*

ACCEPTING THE CHALLENGE

CASE STUDY 1—WRITING PERSONAL GOALS

As you learned in the opening scenario, What Would You Do?, *Becky was elected as a classroom officer. This experience helped her develop leadership skills. One of the most important skills that she learned as a leader was goal setting. She came to realize that goals helped her stay on track and follow through with her plans. However, goal setting took practice. In the beginning, Becky was not setting realistic and precise goals, which often led her to give up. She soon learned to develop SMART goals. SMART goals are*

S M A R T

Specific – *Goals should be specific about what you want to accomplish.*

Measurable – *Goals should state how you will measure your progress.*

Attainable – *Goals should not be too far out of your reach.*

Realistic – *Goals should represent things you are able and willing to do.*

Timely – *Goals should have target dates or deadlines.*

ACCEPTING THE CHALLENGE
Case Study 1
Write Becky's first goal on the board ("I will get to know more of my class-mates.") Ask students if they think this is a well-written goal, and have them explain their answers.

Review each of the steps in setting SMART goals. Then ask students to rewrite the goal on the board using the SMART process. Have several students present their answers. How do their SMART goals compare to Becky's rewritten goal?

As a new student and class officer, Becky developed the following goal:

I will get to know more of my classmates.

After learning how to write SMART goals, she revised the goal as follows:

I will work to build relationships by introducing myself to one new classmate each week and learn about some of his or her interests.

The first goal provides no direction, while the second goal is SMART. Becky also learned that writing SMART goals was only part of what she needed to do to succeed. She also needed someone to support her in reaching her goals. She found that by involving a friend, teacher, or family member as a goal-setting partner, she had someone to motivate her. Becky checked in periodically with her partner to report her progress. Her partner often helped her work through any obstacles so Becky could get back on track and achieve her goals.

THINK CRITICALLY

1. *Explain how the second goal above meets the SMART criteria.*

The first goal is too broad and general. The second goal meets each of the SMART

requirements. It is specific, measurable, attainable, realistic, and timely.

2. *How do the steps involved in writing SMART goals make goals easier to achieve?*

When goals are written in broad, general terms, they are too easy to ignore or

overlook. SMART goals are written in specific language so that you know exactly what

action must be completed by a specific deadline.

APPLY *WHAT YOU HAVE LEARNED–Personal Qualities*

DIRECTIONS: *Below is a list of personal qualities that often provide opportunities to lead. You can complete this activity on the lines below or on the Student Activity CD included with this textbook. Enter a personal goal for improving each of the qualities below in order to enhance the leader in you. Be sure the goals are SMART (specific, measurable, attainable, realistic, and timely). Select one goal that you would most like to achieve and set a completion date for it. Choose a goal-setting partner to help you reach your goal. Use a monthly calendar (provided on the CD or your own) to enter your selected goal. Enter your comments, ideas, and discussions related to your goal in a journal (provided on the CD or your own) to help plan and track your progress.*

1. Physical size

_____

_____

_____

2. Physical attractiveness

_____

_____

_____

3. Skill level (social, communication, decision-making, self-control, or technical/mechanical)

_____

_____

_____

4. Academic ability

_____

_____

_____

5. Emotional stability

_____

_____

_____

6. Honesty and truthfulness

_____

_____

_____

7. Treatment of others

_____

_____

_____

Apply What You Have Learned—Personal Qualities

Note that students can complete this part of the *Accepting the Challenge* activity in the book or on the Student CD. Instructions are provided on the CD.

Throughout the text, students will have opportunities to complete goal-writing activities. Setting and achieving goals will help students develop the skills to become better leaders.

A goal-setting partner can add an element of accountability and offer positive feedback to help students stay on track to achieve goals.

Have students write a SMART goal related to each of the personal qualities listed. Then students should select the one goal they most want to achieve. Instruct students to set a completion date for the goal and have them enter their goal on a monthly calendar. Students can use the calendars on the Student CD that accompanies this textbook or their own calendar. Explain to students that they may also use weekly calendar pages (on the CD or their own) to plan activities that will help them achieve their goals. Finally, direct students to use a journal (on the CD or their own) to track and evaluate their progress in achieving their goal.

Students should be given the opportunity to reflect on the progress they have made toward achieving their goal. To do this, students can complete the *Evaluate Your Progress* activity on the Student CD. Stress to students that it is important to complete this activity on the original target completion date even if they have not met their goal at that time.

Chapter 2

Understanding the Characteristics of Leadership

© Jim Arbogast/Photodisc/Getty Images

2.1 *Leadership Characteristics*

2.2 *Leadership Skills*

2.3 *Social Intelligence and Communication*

What would **YOU** do?

JOHN'S DREAMS AND ASPIRATIONS

John Bruce, a sports enthusiast, always wanted to attend the University of North Carolina (UNC) at Chapel Hill and play basketball for its legendary coach. He was a good student in high school with a high GPA. He was enrolled in college prep courses, inducted into the National Honor Society, and belonged to the school's Quill and Scroll chapter. He was also a member of his high school's varsity basketball team, but he was not a starter or a scholarship athlete. Yet he knew the story of Michael Jordan. Jordan once was cut from his high school varsity basketball team. Later he became a great player at UNC at Chapel Hill and in the National Basketball Association.

John knew that pursuing his dream would not be easy. It would take commitment and dedication on his part. He carefully considered what he should do. John took his first step toward his goal while attending UNC. Although he had not been recruited to play basketball for the university, John decided to try out for the team as a walk-on player for the junior varsity basketball team. His determination paid off, and he made the team. He eventually became a starter. After two years of fun and glory, he served as a student-assistant basketball coach of the JV team. During his senior year at the university, he became one of the managers of the women's basketball team. That team went on to win the NCAA championship and was invited to the White House to meet the President of the United States.

After graduating from UNC at Chapel Hill, John once again considered what to do next. He set a new goal for himself. He wanted to become a successful college basketball coach. His first coaching opportunity was at a private high school as the head coach of the girls JV basketball team. He taught and mentored his players. He challenged them to work hard to improve their skills. Through determination, they became one of the two best teams in their school's league.

Today, John is a successful head basketball coach at a small private college in South Carolina.

THINK *CRITICALLY*

1. What leadership characteristics do you think John demonstrated? Explain why. How can leadership skills help you fulfill goals?

2. What have you learned by reading John's story? Are you willing to commit to pursuing your dream like John did?

Think Critically Answers
1. Answers will vary but may include personal integrity, commitment and dedication, optimism, and courage as well as being a forward thinker. Leadership skills help you stay focused on the steps necessary to fulfill your goals.
2. Answers will vary.

TEACHING RESOURCES
Instructor's Resource CD
Lesson Plans, Ch. 2
PowerPoint Slides, Ch. 2
Student Activity CD, Ch. 2
thomsonedu.com/school/
leading
Crossword puzzle, Ch. 2
Flash Cards, Ch. 2
Exam*View*® **CD**, Ch. 2

CHAPTER OVERVIEW
Chapter 2 discusses the characteristics of leadership, leadership styles and skills, and the importance of good communication skills.

Lesson 2.1
Identifies the characteristics of a leader and describes different leadership styles.

Lesson 2.2
Explains how to develop leadership skills and describes common mistakes made by leaders.

Lesson 2.3
Explains the value of communication as part of social intelligence and describes the communication process.

WHAT WOULD YOU DO?
Describe how John set specific goals and worked to fulfill those goals. Ask students if they think John would have been as successful if he had not set goals and had the commitment to stay focused and work toward those goals.

Leadership Characteristics

SCHEDULE
Block 45 minutes
Regular 1 class period

FOCUS
Ask students to think of someone whom they view as a leader. What characteristics do they identify with that person?

TEACH
Review the definition of leadership. Ask students to think of a group or an activity in which they participated that helped develop their leadership skills.

DEVELOPING AS A LEADER

Leadership is the ability to influence others to achieve a common goal. Leadership skills usually begin early in life. You may have begun developing as a leader by participating in community activities such as the Girl Scouts or Boy Scouts. You may have participated in athletics or other activities at your church or school. Becoming a leader begins with dreams, aspirations, and the determination to be the best person, student, athlete, or citizen that you can be. Finally, you must also have the desire and ambition to become a leader.

You can become a leader if you are willing to take on the challenge of preparing yourself. Michael Jordan once said, "I've always believed that if you put in the work, the results will come. I don't do things halfheartedly because I know if I do, then I can expect halfhearted results." Accepting the challenge of leadership will help you become a role model. You will be someone who can make a difference in your school and community.

© Mel Yates/Photodisc/Getty Images

Steps in the Right Direction

Building relationships at an early age as you learn to get along with others is an important step toward leadership development. Contrary to the myth that some people are "born leaders," leaders develop their ability to influence over time by working successfully with others.

Teamwork is a vital part of leadership. Good leaders know they often need the help of others to accomplish a task or goal. Working together as a team can improve leadership skills. As you begin to develop friendships and become a member of a group in your school or community, try to listen to others more than you talk. You will be

In your history class, you have been studying the value and power of voting. A local election will take place in your community. You have decided to become involved by leading a group that will develop campaign flyers and posters that communicate the importance of voting.

THINK *CRITICALLY*

1. What type of information would you include on the flyers to explain the benefits of voting in a local election?

2. How would you organize the planning process for constructing, placing, and removing posters?

amazed at how your influence will increase among the group. It has been said that the reason you have two ears and one mouth is to allow you to listen twice as much as you talk. Listening skills are invaluable for a good leader.

As you listen to others, try to be more understanding and considerate of their particular situations. Listening and caring about others will improve your effectiveness as a leader. A preferred leadership style for you to consider should be one of listening, coaching, and supporting others. Your peers will accept your leadership when your actions and words communicate that you really care about them.

CHECKPOINT

What are some important steps you can take toward leadership development?

Some important steps toward leadership development are building relationships,

working as a team, and developing good listening skills.

LEADERSHIP CHARACTERISTICS

You may have a desire to become a leader in your school, church, job, or community. Understanding the characteristics of leadership can help you develop leadership skills. These characteristics include personal integrity, dedication, congeniality, and optimism. Leaders are also forward thinkers, good listeners, good record keepers, and risk takers. Finally, good leaders should be health conscious. Some of these leadership characteristics may be debatable in terms of the order of importance but not in terms of their value.

Personal Integrity

Your personal integrity is the foundation of your character as a leader. Integrity is built on honesty and trust. You must be an honest

TEACH
Ask students if they think that some people are "born leaders." Explain that leadership abilities develop over time. Anyone can become a leader.

BUILDING COMMUNITIES
Have students brainstorm a list of reasons why it is important to vote. Ask them to review the list and then to develop a "catchy" slogan that they can use on the flyers they will distribute.

Think Critically Answers
1. Answers will vary.
2. Answers will vary.

TEACH
Have students review the leadership characteristics they identified at the beginning of the lesson. Why do they think these characteristics are important for leaders?

> If any persons seek for greatness, let them forget greatness and ask for truth, and they will find both.
>
> — *Thomas Mann*

and trustworthy person to be an effective leader. More importantly, your teachers, friends, family, and members of your community should recognize these characteristics in you.

Dedication

Loyalty and commitment are essential components of dedication. Showing dedication to your team members and to your goals earns you respect. In turn, those that you lead will develop the same sense of dedication toward you.

Congeniality

Leaders are friendly people who enjoy being around others. Remember that a person you do not know is just a friend that you have not yet met. Reach out to others in a friendly manner. Being friendly can put others at ease and encourage them to communicate openly.

Optimism

Optimistic people can see the best in others. You should continue to look on the bright side and encourage others to be positive. Try not to focus on the negative. Your optimism will create a more productive environment. A positive attitude is contagious.

Forward Thinker

By offering creative ideas, leaders can lift their team or group to a higher level. Forward thinkers look for ways to improve processes to make things run more efficiently. They often have a vision of how the future should be.

Good Listener

Strengthening your listening skills will allow you to become an admired and effective leader. In many cases, your peers will want you to listen to their ideas or problems. When listening, you should focus on the message and take an interest in what the other person is saying.

Good Record Keeper

Leaders often must deal with finances. You should work closely with the treasurer of your team or group. During your fundraising activities, you should also work closely with the faculty adviser to verify that all funds are properly collected and recorded. You and the treasurer should develop a system with checks and balances to demonstrate that you both are good record keepers of the group's finances.

Courage/Risk Taker

When necessary, you should be a risk taker. Risks often lead to opportunities. Your ability to demonstrate courage does not mean that there is an absence of fear. It actually is your control of a situation in spite of your fear. Through determination, you can overcome your fears. Avoid taking foolish dares or participating in dangerous acts to prove your courage. Differentiate between good and bad risks.

TEACHING STRATEGIES
Visual Learners
Have students create a collage representing the characteristics of a leader. They might use newspaper clippings, photos, postcards, greeting cards, or pictures cut from magazines to create their collages. Display their artwork in the classroom.

ONGOING ASSESSMENT
Use the Checkpoint as an opportunity to conduct ongoing assessment of student comprehension of the lesson material.

TEACH
List the four different types of leadership styles on the board. Ask students how they think a person's personality and level of comfort working with others can affect his or her leadership style.

Ask students why they think the authoritarian leadership style might work well in the military. Why do they think it might not be as effective in other settings?

Health Conscious

Good leaders are concerned about their own mental and physical health as well as that of other group members. You should maintain a healthy and active lifestyle. This will reduce stress and increase your performance. If you are not mentally and physically healthy, you will not be able to focus your efforts on your leadership duties.

 CHECKPOINT

Name the characteristics of an effective leader.

Effective leaders have integrity, dedication, congeniality, and optimism. They are forward

thinkers, good listeners, good record keepers, risk takers and are health conscious.

TYPES OF LEADERSHIP

The way a leader works with others is an indication of his or her leadership style. Your leadership style, to an extent, will depend on your personality and your level of comfort working with others. You may need to adapt your leadership style to fit the setting in which you are working. Different types of leadership styles include authoritarian, transactional, transformational, and joint leadership.

Authoritarian Leadership

Authoritarian leadership uses a top-down approach in working with members of the group, team, or organization. In the *top-down approach*, the person in charge gives direct instructions for the group to follow without asking for input from group members. This particular style of leadership works well in the military services and to some extent in athletics. It is not as effective in other settings. This leadership style could be used when you need to make a quick decision and have all the information needed to do so.

© Janis Christie/Photodisc/Getty Images

Transactional Leadership

Transactional leadership is based on an exchange of rewards for the accomplishment of tasks or goals. Group members working under this style of leadership understand that they will be rewarded for completing a task successfully. The rewards act as a motivational tool. The leader assigns tasks to the group members but allows them to work in their own way as long as tasks are completed and goals are met. The leader may not have any further involement unless a problem occurs.

Transformational Leadership

Transformational leadership works to persuade others to commit to a vision in order to enhance the performance or reach the goal of the group. Transformational leadership encourages others to take on leadership roles and make decisions affecting the day-to-day activities of the group. The transformational leadership style uses a *bottom-up approach*. With this approach, the opinions of others are taken into consideration to help solve problems. A transformational leader takes an active role by listening, encouraging, and supporting the members of the group.

Joint Leadership

Joint leadership often is referred to as *team leadership*. Currently, it is the style most frequently used in schools and communities. Leaders agree to take joint control of the group. Each person's role is clearly defined. Sharing the leadership role as co-captain of your high school soccer team or cheering squad is an example of joint leadership. The advantage of joint leadership is having two or more people to help guide and manage a group. The disadvantage is that the co-leaders may disagree on the purpose of the group or the direction to take to meet goals.

 CHECKPOINT

Describe the difference between a top-down leadership approach and a bottom-up leadership approach.

In a top-down approach, the leader gives instructions to be followed without asking for

input. In a bottom-up approach, others are encouraged to make decisions themselves.

TEACH
Ask students to think of any groups or activities in which they participate that use the transactional leadership style. (An example might be the exchange of an allowance or extra privileges for the completion of chores at home.)

Discuss the meaning of *bottom-up approach*. Ask students what advantages they think might come from sharing the decision-making function in a group.

Ask students to name the advantages and disadvantages of joint leadership. Have they ever been a joint leader with someone else (such as a co-captain on a team)? Did they have a positive experience?

Follow UP

UNDERSTAND LEADERSHIP CONCEPTS

Circle the best answer for each of the following questions.

1. **Which of the following is not an important characteristic of leadership?**
   a. listening skills
   b. appearance
   c. commitment
   d. friendliness

2. **Which leadership style persuades others to follow a vision?**
   a. authoritarian leadership
   b. transactional leadership
   c. joint leadership
   d. transformational leadership

THINK *CRITICALLY*

Answer the following questions as completely as possible. If necessary, use a separate sheet of paper.

3. **Why is it important for a leader to include others in the decision-making process?**

   By including others in the decision-making process, the leader can receive input from a

   number of different people. This team approach enhances the performance of the

   group and encourages others to commit to a shared vision.

4. **What leadership characteristics do you believe you possess that will improve your effectiveness as a leader in your school or community?**

   Answers will vary.

5. **Describe the differences between transactional leadership and transformational leadership. Which style would you prefer? Explain why.**

   Transactional leaders assign tasks to group members and reward them for successfully

   completing the tasks. Transformational leaders allow others to participate in the day-

   to-day decision making. They listen, encourage, and support members of the group.

ASSESS
Reteach
Have students list the characteristics of leadership discussed in the lesson and write one or two sentences explaining each characteristic.

Enrich
Have students research the leadership style of a well-known leader (either past or present). Have them orally report to the class whether the leader used an authoritarian, transactional, transformational, or joint leadership style. They should support their position with evidence from their research.

Close
Ask students to compare and contrast the four leadership styles discussed in the lesson. Have them explain how each style could be effective in certain situations.

Leadership Skills

SCHEDULE
Block 45 minutes
Regular 1 class period

FOCUS
Ask students if they have ever learned an important lesson from a mistake they have made. Do they think leaders also can learn from their mistakes? Have them explain their answers.

DEVELOPING LEADERSHIP SKILLS

A hidden gem is a precious stone that is a little rough around the edges. However, with some work, it may become a diamond of beauty and value. You may be a hidden gem with a desire to engage in leadership, but you may feel unworthy because you lack leadership skills. You must begin to see yourself as a leader with the self-esteem and motivation to accept the challenge of learning, improving, and developing your leadership skills.

Accepting the Challenge

Your development as a leader may not be the same as others', and it should not be. By focusing on your own abilities, you will be successful in meeting the leadership challenge. If you are ready to accept the challenge, you should take this leadership pledge:

I (say your name), pledge my best effort to be a leader with good character in my school and community.

Now you are ready to learn about the twelve-point plan for development of leadership skills. The twelve points are: (1) ethical behavior, (2) decision making, (3) teamwork, (4) motivation, (5) peer-mentoring, (6) visionary, (7) conflict resolution, (8) goal setting, (9) emotional stability, (10) interpersonal relations, (11) communication, and (12) time management.

Ethical Behavior

As a leader, your ability to demonstrate ethical behavior will make you a role model for others. Your actions are based on your personal values and your belief in doing the right thing, even when no one is watching. These actions may be referred to as ethical behavior. Leading by example will show others your true character. It will demonstrate to members of your school and community that you are a leader who is guided by ethics.

© Digital Vision/Getty Images

A TEAM Effort

You have been assigned the responsibility of organizing a weekend camping trip at Lake Happy Valley for the 12 members of your high school basketball team. Some of your team members have indicated to you that they cannot swim and are fearful about going to the lake. You have acknowledged their concerns, but you have not shared the information with the team coaches.

THINK *CRITICALLY*

Why would you not share the information about your team members' concerns with the coaches? Do you think that the camping trip is a wonderful opportunity for the team to bond as a group even though some team members are fearful? Explain your answer.

Decision Making

Making choices based on information and knowledge that you have is your decision-making ability. A good leader will carefully evaluate all choices before making a final decision. You may feel more comfortable discussing the problem with others and getting a *consensus,* or reaching an agreement, before making a decision. In many cases, this is the best way to make decisions. At other times, you will have to make your own decisions without the input of others. As you gain experience as a leader, your ability to make decisions will improve.

Teamwork

Your willingness to work as part of a team to achieve goals will attract others to follow you. The development of unity and cooperation among members of the group is very important. As you involve others in various activities, they will accept you more as their leader. Your success as a leader is based on your ability to get members of your group to work together as one unit. The slogan "all for one and one for all" conveys the real meaning of teamwork.

Motivation

Leaders should inspire feelings of excitement and positive energy in others. To do this, they must motivate others. **Motivation** is the driving force that persuades individuals to take action. As a leader, you should learn what motivates members of your group. Talk with them and involve them in setting up a rewards system. When you recognize individuals for a job well done, they will put forth their best effort.

Peer-Mentoring

A **peer-mentor** is someone who serves as a role model and provides motivation and encouragement to others. At times, you may be called upon to share your words of wisdom and give advice to some of your peers. At other times, being a peer-mentor simply requires you to be a good listener. As a leader, you are a peer-mentor, and your opinions and support are important to members of your group.

TEACH
Have students review the leadership pledge. Point out that they should take the pledge only if they are willing to accept the challenge of developing their leadership skills.

A TEAM EFFORT
Ask students how they would feel if they were one of the team members that could not swim. Do they think the team member who is organizing the camping trip is exhibiting good leadership skills? Why or why not?

Think Critically Answers
Answers will vary.

LEADERSHIP TIP
Have students brainstorm a list of ways that a leader can build relationships with others. Discuss why it is important to build relationships before making changes.

LEADERSHIP *Tip*

As a leader, you should build relationships with others before attempting to make major changes in your school or community.

Discuss the meaning of
esprit de corps. Ask students
if they have belonged to
groups that had a strong
team spirit. How was conflict
dealt with in those groups in
order to maintain positive
group morale?

Ask students whether they
set goals for themselves.
Discuss why setting goals is
important for a leader.

Ask students to think about
how they feel when others
show appreciation and support for their accomplishments. Ask students to
provide examples of ways to
improve interpersonal relations skills. Can they think of
ways (other than those already discussed in the text)
to show group members
that they are valued?

Visionary

Your ability to communicate a vision or idea to others shows that you are a forward thinker. It also demonstrates your belief in the ability of others to carry out your vision and reach a higher level of success. Your vision should be explained in such a way that others can see it and want to embrace it. You should allow members of the group to express their thoughts and concerns, both positive and negative.

Conflict Resolution

Jealousy and bitterness among members of a group will lower their morale and performance. Your role as a leader includes building a welcoming climate where people can express their ideas and concerns without fear of being attacked by others. You may need to meet privately with the individuals involved to discuss their differences in order to reach a positive solution. Both people must be willing to resolve the conflict to maintain *esprit de corps,* which is a common spirit of enthusiasm and devotion to a cause among members of a group.

Goal Setting

Setting goals for yourself is good practice. Your personal success in setting and achieving goals can help prepare you to lead and motivate others to do the same. Your ability to set reachable goals for your group will show that you are leading them in the right direction. When setting goals, you should try to involve all members. Focus on realistic goals that are based on the purpose of the group and that can be accomplished within a specific time period, such as the end of the semester or school year.

Emotional Stability

As a leader, you should remain calm during tense situations. This will show others that you have the emotional stability to move forward even when things are not going as planned. Others will see that you are confident and secure in your abilities as a leader. By avoiding hurtful criticisms during disagreements, you will show others that you can handle situations in a mature manner.

© Digital Vision/Getty Images

Interpersonal Relations

To a large extent, your success as a leader will not be based on how high your grade point average is but on how well you get along with people. Your ability to demonstrate interpersonal relations skills will show others that you value them. Recognize members of your group for their accomplishments. Speak words of support and encouragement to show your appreciation. Be a good listener and allow others to share their ideas.

Communication

You may have to speak publicly about the mission or purpose of your group. If you are nervous about speaking in front of large groups, consider joining the debate team or drama club to develop your public speaking skills. Practice, practice, practice, and your nervousness will begin to disappear as you gain more experience. In many cases, your leadership in high school will be measured by your presentation skills during your class discussions and projects, school assemblies, club meetings, concerts, and other public activities.

Written communication skills are also important. As a leader, you will most likely have to write letters and prepare reports that will be read by many people. To be effective, all written communications should contain proper grammar and correct spelling.

Time Management

Demonstrating time management skills will show others that you are serious about meeting deadlines and conducting meetings and other activities in a timely manner. Planning is an important component of time management. A plan gives you direction and saves you time. When conducting your meetings, an *agenda*, or a plan that outlines the topics to be discussed, can help you keep them brief, pleasant, and meaningful. This shows others that you value their time and commitment.

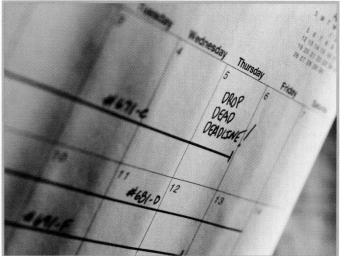

© Steve Cole/Photodisc/Getty Images

 CHECKPOINT

Identify two leadership skills that would improve your effectiveness as a leader in your school.

Answers will vary but may include any of the points in the twelve-point plan for

development of leadership skills.

MISTAKES MADE BY LEADERS

As you take on leadership roles, you will make mistakes occasionally along the way. This is part of the learning experience. Mistakes help you learn what to do differently in the future. There are seven common mistakes made by leaders, which include the following:

1. *Uncaring attitude.* A leader must genuinely care about a group's purpose as well as its members. An uncaring attitude can spread to others, and the group's mission will be defeated.
2. *Avoidance of situations.* Leaders will have to deal with unpleasant situations. Perhaps the group is not meeting its goals or one of the group members is performing poorly. Avoiding these situations is not the answer. They should be met head on and resolved as quickly as possible to keep things moving forward.
3. *Lack of character.* A leader shows character through personal traits such as honesty, fairness, loyalty, and maturity. When leaders show a lack of character in dealing with others, they will not earn the respect needed to carry out their plans.

TEACHING STRATEGIES
Kinesthetic Learners
Have students write a brief speech about the mission or purpose of a group to which they belong. After students have practiced their speech, have them deliver it to the class.

ONGOING ASSESSMENT
Use the Checkpoint as an opportunity to conduct ongoing assessment of student comprehension of the lesson material.

TEACH
Point out to students that leaders are not perfect individuals. They make mistakes like everyone else, but they use those mistakes to continue learning and improving their leadership skills.

© Jeff Maloney/Photodisc/Getty Images

4. *Lack of vision.* All leaders must have a vision of what they want to accomplish and how they plan to accomplish it. Without a vision, the leader will have trouble finding a purpose for the group. The leader will struggle to gain control and will eventually fail.

5. *Showing favoritism.* In order for a leader to succeed, he or she must be fair when dealing with others. If one or more members of the group believe the leader is showing favoritism toward another member, the group will not function effectively. All group members must feel valued.

6. *Failure to hold members of the group accountable.* Being **accountable** means accepting responsibility for your actions. If someone does not perform as expected and makes excuses, blames others, or covers up the problem, that person is not being accountable. The leader should stress to group members that because their actions affect many other people, they will be held accountable for their decisions.

7. *Poor communication and interpersonal skills.* Communication is the key to being a good leader. Leaders must keep group members informed and listen to their ideas and concerns. It is also very important to get along well with others. This makes it easier to get things accomplished. Leaders with poor communication and interpersonal skills will not succeed in leading others.

If you are challenged in any of these areas, you should seek help from a peer-mentor, family member, or one of your teachers. Admitting that you have some leadership areas that need improvement is the first step toward strengthening your leadership skills.

 CHECKPOINT

What are the seven most common mistakes made by leaders?

Uncaring attitude, avoidance of situations, lack of character, lack of vision, showing favoritism, not holding members accountable, poor communication and interpersonal skills

Follow UP

UNDERSTAND LEADERSHIP CONCEPTS

Circle the best answer for each of the following questions.

1. **Leaders can improve their interpersonal relations skills by**
   a. being a good listener
   b. recognizing the accomplishments of others
   c. speaking words of encouragement
   d. all of the above

2. **Esprit de corps is a**
   a. time management program
   b. common spirit of devotion to a cause
   c. lack of emotional stability
   d. common mistake made by leaders

THINK *CRITICALLY*

Answer the following questions as completely as possible. If necessary, use a separate sheet of paper.

3. **Explain the function of a peer-mentor in the twelve-point plan for acquiring leadership development skills.**

   A peer-mentor is a role model. The peer-mentor provides motivation and

   encouragement to others and supports the members of the group. Effective leaders

   are peer-mentors.

4. **Identify one or more common leadership mistakes that you have made. How can you avoid making these mistakes in the future?**

   Answers will vary but may include one or more of the seven common mistakes

   discussed in the lesson.

5. **What does the slogan "all for one and one for all" mean? How does it apply to teamwork?**

   The slogan "all for one and one for all" means that group members support one

   another and work together as a team for the good of the entire group.

ASSESS
Reteach
Have students list the 12 points of the 12-point plan for development of leadership skills. Have them write one or two key points for each item in the 12-point plan.

Enrich
Have students create a classroom bulletin board, poster, or other visual representation of the 12-point plan for development of leadership skills.

Close
Have students review the seven most common mistakes leaders make. Have students list at least one way that a leader could avoid making each mistake.

Social Intelligence and Communication

SCHEDULE
Block 45 minutes
Regular 1 class period

FOCUS
Ask students to think of a time when someone might have misunderstood a message they were trying to convey. What do they think caused the communication problem?

TEACH
Discuss the meaning of social intelligence. Ask students how they think improving their social intelligence can help them become more effective leaders.

WHAT IS SOCIAL INTELLIGENCE?

Social intelligence is a new science for successful leadership. Your success as a leader will be based not on how smart you are but on how well you get along with other people. Specifically, **social intelligence** focuses on your communication skills—both verbal and non-verbal—and your interaction with members of your family, school, and community. Being sensitive to the needs and interests of others is the core of social intelligence. Understanding its importance will improve your performance as a leader in your school and community.

Importance of Social Intelligence

© Pando Hall/Photodisc/Getty Images

Today's world focuses more on people and their interpersonal behaviors than their technical skills. It is important for you to understand the value of social intelligence and how it affects the accomplishments of people in your home, school, or community. People perform far better in a pleasant and accepting environment than in a hostile and unwelcoming setting. Resentment or hostility among members of your team or group will lower group morale and decrease performance.

Reflect on your past experiences as a member of a school or athletic team. Try to recall a time when members of the group did not get along. Did it affect your performance? How did you recover from that particular experience? What role did social intelligence play in resolving the situation?

Verbal Language

Verbal language communicates a spoken message to others. It lets them know if you are sensitive to their needs and interests. You may know people whose verbal language is inappropriate when meeting someone for the first time. They may say things that are insensitive. Certain topics of conversation may be inappropriate for you to comment on unless you are asked to do so. Even then, you should proceed with caution. A good response to their request for your opinion might be "no comment." You could follow up your "no comment" response by saying that you value and respect the person and would prefer not to express your opinion until you have become better acquainted. Your comment will convey the message that you are a sensitive and caring person.

There are times when "silence is golden," especially when you do not have positive comments to offer or when you do not have all the facts to form an opinion. Being silent at the appropriate time can be a good thing. For example, if you are present when a friend is being disciplined by a parent, it would not be a good time for you to offer your viewpoint, because it does not involve you. It would be best to excuse yourself and walk away.

When the time is right, your verbal language can communicate a message of encouragement to others that will create a pleasant and welcoming environment. Remember that the words you speak can build others up or tear them down. Let your words become "seeds" to help others grow and develop.

Non-Verbal Language

Body language is the combination of gestures, movements, and physical mannerisms that you use to communicate to others. It is a non-verbal language. Non-verbal body language can be more revealing than verbal language. For example, your body language can indicate if you are being open and friendly or angry and upset by the way you fold your arms or by the look on your face.

Your body language is capable of communicating a wide range of emotions and attitudes without you speaking a word. But cultural differences do exist. For example, eye contact is a part of the American culture. Eye contact acknowledges that you

© Barbara Penoyar/Photodisc/Getty Images

Ask students what they think the saying "silence is golden" means. Have they ever said something they wished they could "take back"? Discuss how strong verbal language skills can benefit a leader.

Show students some pictures of people displaying different facial expressions. Ask students what these facial expressions communicate to them. Point out to students that, when communicating with others, it is important to consider the culture when interpreting the message being sent.

TEACHING STRATEGIES
Limited English Proficiency (LEP) Students
Have students share with the class any cultural differences from their home countries that would affect either verbal or non-verbal communication.

are paying attention, listening, and connecting with the other person. In the Asian culture, however, prolonged eye contact is viewed as a sign of disrespect.

Another example of cultural differences in body language involves the way in which we greet others. In the American culture, it is acceptable for men and women to shake hands with each other. In the Middle Eastern culture, men typically do not shake the hands of women, especially during their religious holiday season.

Written Language

Another major form of communication is written language. Written language can include such things as homework, e-mail, text messages, and letters. Written language can convey both positive and negative messages. Because the message will be in writing and may be seen by many people, you want it to represent you in a positive manner. You should carefully compose all written communications. Poor grammar and spelling are evident in written documents and will reflect poorly on your communications skills.

Language Barrier

If you understand the way the body "speaks," then you can become a leader who communicates well both verbally and non-verbally. Sometimes your verbal language can contradict the message that your body language is communicating. For example, telling someone that you are not angry may be difficult for that person to believe if your arms are folded and you have a scowl on your face.

Leaders should become skilled in handling social situations by gaining a clear understanding of the impact of body language and the message it conveys. Learn how to use movement, posture, and gestures to get your point across to others. Be aware of when, where, and how to communicate using eye contact, facial expressions, or posture.

Written language is usually less confusing because body language is not involved. However, even written language can cause problems if the words used are misunderstood by others. Using clear, simple language is the best way to communicate.

COMMUNICATE

In your school, have you ever noticed that some of your classmates cannot seem to connect with certain groups? Your classmates who are insensitive to the needs and interests of others are considered to be lacking in social intelligence. If you encounter this as a leader, the best way to deal with it is through communication. You should address the situation by doing the following:

- schedule a separate meeting with the person to discuss his or her situation
- share your observations in confidence
- discuss ways to improve the situation and provide follow-up sessions, if necessary

THINK *CRITICALLY*

Why is communication the best way to deal with group members who are having problems connecting or fitting in with the group?

CHECKPOINT

Describe two reasons why social intelligence is important.

Social intelligence is important because it will improve your performance as a leader.

Also, people perform better in a pleasant and accepting environment.

THE COMMUNICATION PROCESS

Whether you are using verbal, non-verbal, or written language, you are attempting to communicate a message to others. The idea or information you want to send is the *message*. Conveying a clear message to others should not be taken lightly. Understanding the communication process may assist you in establishing better communication with your classmates, friends, family members, and others. In addition, effectively using the communication process can enhance your leadership development. To understand the communication process, you must learn about the components involved, which include the following:

- Sending the message
- Receiving the message
- Encoding the message
- Choosing a communication channel
- Decoding the message
- Giving feedback

TEACH
Review the components of the communication process. Ask students how they think that understanding the communication process can affect their success as a leader.

Point out to students that sometimes they are the sender, and at other times they are the receiver. In a conversation with someone, they typically would assume both roles.

Ask students to name different ways that the message they are trying to convey could be encoded. Do they think the message would be more easily understood if they used more than one form?

Sending and Receiving the Message

In the communication process, the *sender* is the source of the message or information to be transmitted to another person. The *receiver* is the person to whom the message is being directed. The role of the sender is to start the communication process and transmit a clear and concise message to the receiver. If you are running for student council and are writing an article for your school newspaper to promote your candidacy, you are the sender of information, and your classmates are the receivers of your message.

Encoding the Message

Putting the message into a form that is understood by the receiver is called **encoding**. The form of the message may be in words, symbols, or even pictures. When encoding a message, it is important that you use language that is familiar to the receiver. For example, if you are giving a campaign

© F64/Photodisc/Getty Images

TEACH
Ask students to think of the various communication channels that they use on a regular basis. These might include things like text messaging and instant messaging with friends.

Ask students if they have ever had difficulty understanding what was being said by someone because of noise or distractions around them. What effect do they think noise and distractions can have on the communication process?

Explain to students that the communication process can be thought of as a continuous loop. Once the message has been received and interpreted, feedback goes back to the sender. The sender then can correct for misunderstandings by re-sending the message and encoding it in a different way to help the receiver understand it more clearly.

TEACHING STRATEGIES
Visual Learners
To illustrate how a message can be conveyed in forms other than verbal language, have students convey simple messages using a game format such as Pictionary.

TEACHING STRATEGIES
Specific Learning Disability Students
Have students draw a diagram illustrating the communication process.

ONGOING ASSESSMENT
Use the Checkpoint as an opportunity to conduct ongoing assessment of student comprehension of the lesson material.

speech as a student council candidate, you should use clear language. If you are using visual aids, such as posters, use images that are easily identifiable by your audience and that will capture its attention.

Choosing a Communication Channel

A *communication channel* is the method used by the sender to relay the message. Selecting a communication channel depends on what needs to be communicated to your audience. If your message is interactive or conversational, you might consider using e-mail, text messages, or a telephone. On the other hand, if your message is more impersonal and requires no response, you might consider writing a letter, memo, or an article in your school newspaper. Keep in mind that certain channels work better for certain messages. For example, if you want to get your campaign message out to a large group of people, the telephone is probably not the best method for communication. Knowing the communication preferences of your audience or receiver will also help you choose the most appropriate communication channel.

Decoding the Message

Interpretation or translation of a message by the receiver is called **decoding**. Decoding is a critical stage in the communication process because the receiver's perception of the message may not be the same as the sender's intended message. Decoding is affected by the receiver's knowledge, value system, and biases. For example, your classmates may interpret your campaign promises differently based on their backgrounds and experiences. Noise, or distractions, can also interfere with your message. If some group members are talking while you are giving a speech, others may not hear you clearly and decode your message incorrectly. As a leader, you must strive to reduce or eliminate distractions.

Giving Feedback

How was the message received and understood by those to whom it was sent? Feedback can help you answer this question. **Feedback** is the receiver's response to the sender's message. The effectiveness of your message can be measured by the feedback you receive. It enables you to determine whether the message was interpreted correctly. There will be times when you have to ask for feedback. Feedback allows the sender to take corrective action if the message has been misinterpreted by the receiver. If one of your classmates does not understand how you will fulfill one of your campaign promises, you could try encoding the message in another way to get your point across.

 CHECKPOINT

Explain why an impersonal message might require a different communication channel than an interactive message.

An impersonal message requiring no response could use a less personal channel, such as a letter or memo, but an interactive message is more conversational.

Follow UP

UNDERSTAND LEADERSHIP CONCEPTS

Circle the best answer for each of the following questions.

1. Body language is which form of communication?
   a. verbal language
   b. written language
   (c.) non-verbal language
   d. none of the above

2. The components of the communication process include
   a. sending the message
   b. giving feedback
   c. receiving the message
   (d.) all of the above

THINK *CRITICALLY*

Answer the following questions as completely as possible. If necessary, use a separate sheet of paper.

3. Explain how sometimes your spoken words can contradict the message that your body language is communicating.

Body language is non-verbal communication that consists of gestures, movements, and

physical mannerisms. It can communicate a wide range of emotions and attitudes.

Regardless of your spoken words, your body language can reveal if you are being open

and friendly or angry and upset by the way you fold your arms or by the look on your face.

4. List several different types of communication channels you could use as a leader of a group.

Answers will vary but may include telephone, e-mail, letter, or article in the school

newspaper.

5. Explain why feedback is important to the communication process.

Feedback is important to let the sender know if the message has been correctly

interpreted by the receiver. If the message has been misunderstood, the sender can

then take corrective action to clarify the message.

ASSESS
Reteach
Review the goals for the lesson. Have students list the key points discussed in the lesson for each of the goals.

Enrich
Have students choose another country or culture and conduct research on the differences in non-verbal communication in that culture. Have students report their findings to the class.

Close
Have students explain how social intelligence contributes to an individual's success as a leader.

Chapter Assessment

TEACHING RESOURCES
ExamView® CD, Ch. 2

REVIEW *LEADERSHIP CONCEPTS*

Write the letter of the term that matches each definition. Some terms will not be used.

a. accountable
b. authoritarian leadership
c. body language
d. decoding
e. encoding
f. feedback
g. joint leadership
h. leadership
i. motivation
j. peer-mentor
k. social intelligence
l. transactional leadership
m. transformational leadership

__b__ 1. Uses a top-down approach in working with members of the group

__g__ 2. Often called team leadership

__h__ 3. The ability to influence others to achieve a common goal

__j__ 4. Someone who serves as a role model and provides motivation

__k__ 5. Focuses on communication skills and interactions with others

__c__ 6. Gestures, movements, and physical mannerisms

__e__ 7. Putting a message in a form that is understood by the receiver

__m__ 8. Works to persuade others to commit to a vision

__i__ 9. The driving force that persuades individuals to take action

__l__ 10. Based on the exchange of rewards for accomplishments

Circle the best answer.

11. Understanding the importance of social intelligence will do which of the following?
    a. decrease your performance as a leader
    b. have no effect on your performance as a leader
    c. improve your performance as a leader
    d. none of the above

12. Offering creative ideas and having a vision of the future is known as being
    a. congenial
    b. a forward thinker
    c. dedicated
    d. an optimist

13. All of the following are common mistakes made by leaders except
    a. working as part of a team
    b. avoiding situations
    c. showing favoritism
    d. failing to hold group members accountable

14. In a military setting, which type of leadership would be most effective?
    a. joint
    b. transformational
    c. authoritarian
    d. none of the above

ASSESS
Reteach
Assign students to work with a partner. Have the partners take turns quizzing each other on the meanings of the terms in the chapter.

Enrich
Have students work in groups to create a multimedia presentation on leadership skills that can be presented to other groups in your school. Have groups practice their presentation skills in class.

CLOSE
Have students list the four types of leadership. Ask them to decide which leadership skills would be most beneficial for each leadership style.

THINK *CRITICALLY*

15. *Identify your leadership style and explain how it has changed over time.*

Answers will vary but should relate to one of the four leadership styles discussed in the

chapter—authoritarian, transactional, transformational, or joint leadership.

_____

_____

_____

16. *What could a leader do to motivate members of the group who may be reluctant to put forth their best effort to complete a given project?*

Answers will vary but may include various types of recognition or rewards systems.

_____

_____

_____

_____

17. *Why is it important to provide potential leaders with the opportunity to practice the leadership skills they have learned?*

Practice leads to improvement. Potential leaders will make mistakes, but by learning

from their mistakes, they can become better, more effective leaders.

_____

_____

_____

18. *What do you think is the most important skill for a leader to possess? Explain your answer.*

Answers will vary but may include any of the skills in the twelve-point plan: ethical

behavior, decision making, teamwork, motivation, peer-mentoring, visionary, conflict

resolution, goal setting, emotional stability, interpersonal relations, communication,

and time management.

_____

19. *What are some advantages and disadvantages of a top-down versus a bottom-up approach to leadership?*

An advantage of the top-down approach is that decisions can be made quickly because

they are made only by the leader. A disadvantage of the top-down approach is that it

does not consider the opinions of others to help solve problems. Group members do

not have an active role in decision making like they do in the bottom-up approach.

_____

_____

20. **Research** Leaders are often thought of as risk takers. Use the Internet to research a well-known leader. Describe a risk(s) this individual took that helped pave the way to his or her role as a leader.

Answers will vary depending on the leader selected.

_____

_____

_____

_____

21. **Problem Solving** Time management skills are essential for a leader. Analyze how you use your time. For three days, record everything you do during the course of the day. Be sure to include start and stop times for each activity. At the end of the three days, write a summary of how you use your time. Explain how you could use your time more efficiently.

Answers will vary.

_____

_____

_____

_____

_____

22. **Communication** You are campaigning for the office of class treasurer at your school. Prepare a speech that could be presented to the student body that will persuade them that you are the best candidate for the job.

Answers will vary.

_____

_____

_____

_____

_____

23. **Teamwork** You are coordinating the car wash fundraising project to generate money for the junior/senior prom. The activity requires organizing, planning, scheduling, and motivating your classmates. As a part of your plan, outline how you will motivate the members of your group to participate in the fundraising.

Answers will vary.

_____

_____

_____

_____

_____

LEARNING TO LEAD

FOCUS

Learn about the types of leadership opportunities available through student organizations.

DESCRIPTION

To become an effective leader you must study leadership, participate in leadership training activities, and practice your leadership skills by accepting leadership roles. BPA, DECA, and FBLA are student organizations devoted to developing student leaders and offer a variety of activities and opportunities to fit your interests, current abilities, and time commitments.

Review your student organization to understand the types of leadership programs, the variety of activities, and how members can choose and become involved in the programs. Gather information by using the national and state organizations' web sites and printed materials and asking questions of your local chapter adviser, officers, and experienced members.

LEARNING TO LEAD
This project is written for use with student organizations such as BPA, DECA, and FBLA. Student organizations can help students prepare for key leadership roles. After students complete the activities, discuss what they learned about their student organization.

Activities
Answers will vary based on the student organization and the activities and leadership opportunities identified.

ACTIVITIES

1. Identify the major national, regional, and state conferences that members can attend. List the purpose of each meeting and at least two leadership development opportunities offered at each.

2. Identify specific programs and workshops that offer leadership training. Write one or two sentences describing each program and workshop and explain how members can qualify to participate.

3. Describe the purpose of the competitive events program offered by the organization. List at least two individual competitive events and one team competitive event that interest you.

4. Identify how local chapters can be recognized for community service and business partnership projects.

5. Identify two forms of individual recognition available to members and two forms of chapter recognition.

6. List the titles and brief descriptions of the organization's member publications.

SHARE YOUR RESULTS

1. Identify one leadership development opportunity that is of greatest interest to you and that you believe would contribute to the success of your local chapter. Discuss with your chapter adviser or a chapter officer what you need to do to prepare for this opportunity.
2. Compile a list of the three most important activities you need to complete. Develop a plan, including a timeline, for completing all activities.
3. Prepare a report that describes the leadership development opportunity and outlines your strategy for meeting this challenge.

Share Your Results
1. Answers will vary. Students should be prepared to explain why they think this leadership opportunity would contribute to the success of their local chapter.
2. Answers will vary. To help students develop a timeline, suggest that they begin with the deadline for having all activities completed and work backwards to make sure they have allowed enough time for the successful completion of all three activities.
3. Answers will vary.

ACCEPTING THE
CHALLENGE
Case Study 2
Ask students if they have
ever had conflicts between
school assignments and
other obligations, such as a
team sport. How did they
resolve the conflict. Discuss
John Bruce's leadership
characteristics that helped
him work through the
conflict to succeed both
academically and as a college basketball coach.

ACCEPTING THE CHALLENGE

CASE STUDY 2—LEADERSHIP CHARACTERISTICS

As indicated in the opening scenario, What Would You Do?, John Bruce was always up for a challenge. He always put forth the extra effort to be the best he could be. During high school, John took several college prep classes in addition to playing on the school basketball team. He often found that his homework assignments and basketball obligations conflicted with one another. He could easily have given up by quitting the basketball team or letting his grades slide. Instead, because of John's positive attitude, courage, and dedication to his long-term goal of playing and coaching college basketball, he pushed forward. He remained optimistic that he could be both a good student and a good basketball player. He succeeded and went on to become a successful college basketball coach who, in turn, encouraged his players to be the best they could be.

THINK CRITICALLY

1. *Describe John's attitude and personality.*

John has a positive attitude and a congenial, optimistic personality.

2. *Even though John's true love was basketball, why do you think it was important to him to succeed academically as well?*

Answers will vary. Leaders strive to succeed in all areas of their life. John had a positive

attitude and dedication to both goals, and he knew that quitting was not a good

choice in the long-run.

3. *What characteristics does John possess that helped him achieve his long-term career goal of leading a college basketball team?*

John's leadership characteristics include a positive attitude, courage, and dedication.

John also is a forward thinker.

4. *What lessons can you learn from John?*

Answers will vary but may include maintaining a positive attitude, setting goals and

being dedicated and committed to fulfilling those goals, and being courageous and

willing to take a risk to accomplish your goals.

APPLY *WHAT YOU HAVE LEARNED–Take an Inventory*

DIRECTIONS: *Now it is time to learn more about your leadership characteristics. Do an inventory of your characteristics by completing the list below or on your Student Activity CD.*

1. *Describe your personal integrity.*

_____

_____

2. *Describe your dedication.*

_____

_____

3. *Describe your congeniality.*

_____

_____

4. *Describe your optimism.*

_____

_____

5. *Describe your ability to be a forward thinker.*

_____

_____

6. *Describe your listening skills.*

_____

_____

7. *Describe your thoughts on taking risks.*

_____

_____

8. *Develop a plan to address any weaknesses. Select the characteristic that you think you need to improve upon the most. On the lines below or on the Student Activity CD, create a SMART goal (including a completion date) that will help you strengthen the characteristic you have chosen to improve. Enter your goal in a monthly calendar (on the CD or your own). Then enter your thoughts, ideas, and discussions related to your goal in a journal (on the CD or your own) to help you plan and track your progress. Remember to select a goal-setting partner to help you achieve your goal.*

_____

_____

_____

_____

ACCEPTING THE CHALLENGE

Apply What You Have Learned—Take an Inventory

Note that students can complete this part of the *Accepting the Challenge* activity in the book or on the Student Activity CD. Instructions are provided on the CD.

Have students complete the inventory of their leadership characteristics. After they have chosen one characteristic that they want to improve have them write a SMART goal, including a date for completion.

Ask students to enter their goal on a monthly calendar (on the Student Activity CD or their own). Remind them that they may also use weekly calendar pages (on the Student Activity CD or their own) to plan activities and tasks that must be completed to help them achieve their goals. Finally, direct students to use a journal (on the Student Activity CD or their own) to track and evaluate their progress in achieving their goal.

Students should work with a goal-setting partner who can add an element of accountability and can offer positive feedback to help students stay on track to achieve their goals.

Students should be given the opportunity to reflect on the progress they have made toward achieving their goal. To do this, students can complete the *Evaluate Your Progress* activity on the Student Activity CD. Stress to students that it is important to complete this activity on the original target completion date even if they have not met their goal at that time.

Character Matters

© Jacobs Stock Photography/Photodisc/Getty Images

3.1 *What Is Character?*

3.2 *When Character Is Missing*

3.3 *Acting Ethically*

JERLYN'S DECISION

Jerlyn closed her laptop and slid it into her backpack. She was glad she stayed after class to talk with Ms. Berstine even though it meant she would not be able to visit with her friends at lunch. She had been struggling with the assigned homework problems, but the ten-minute discussion now made it more understandable. It would mean less frustration and less time when she got home tonight.

As Jerlyn walked toward the door, she noticed something on the floor under a desk. She reached down, picked it up, and saw that it was folded money. As she began to unfold it, she saw that it was a $20 bill. She looked toward the teacher's desk but saw that Ms. Berstine had her back turned.

Jerlyn felt lucky. She could always use $20, and right now her finances were in pretty bad shape. But as she walked out, she got a vision of her friends from class. What if one of them had lost the money? She knew how disappointed she would be if it had been her money that was lost. But how could she find the person who lost the money even if she wanted to? She decided she had to try.

Jerlyn asked Ms. Berstine for advice. When she explained the situation, Ms. Berstine said, "I saw you pick up the money, and I was curious to see what you would do with it. You did the right thing. Tomorrow, I'll ask the students if anyone lost something in class. If someone is able to identify the folded money, you can return it to them."

Before the day was over, Jerico approached Ms. Berstine and asked her if anyone had found some money. He had folded a $20 bill and placed it in his sock before school. He needed it to make the last payment on his class ring. He thought it might have fallen out during one of his classes. Jerlyn did not know Jerico well, but she could relate to how difficult it had been to earn the money for her own class ring. She had mixed feelings when she returned the money to him, but his big smile and "thank you" made her feel better about how she handled the situation.

THINK *CRITICALLY*

1. Do you think the amount of money influenced Jerlyn's decision? What if it had been $5? What if it was a $100 bill?

2. Do you think the fact that Jerlyn did not know Jerico well affected her feelings about her decision? Why or why not?

TEACHING RESOURCES
Instructor's Resource CD
Lesson Plans, Ch. 3
PowerPoint Slides, Ch. 3

Student Activity CD, Ch. 3

thomsonedu.com/school/ leading
Crossword puzzle, Ch. 3
Flash Cards, Ch. 3

Exam*View*® **CD**, Ch. 3

CHAPTER OVERVIEW
Chapter 3 discusses the value of good character and ethical behavior.

Lesson 3.1
Defines character and its two main components and describes how to recognize evidence of a person's character.

Lesson 3.2
Discusses the importance of character and the effects of poor character.

Lesson 3.3
Explains the importance of having a code of ethics.

WHAT WOULD YOU DO?
Discuss Jerlyn's decision to try to find the person who lost the money. Ask students how they would feel if they lost the money they had saved to pay for something important like a class ring. What would they want the person who found it to do?

Think Critically Answers
1. Answers will vary. Doing the right thing should not depend on the amount of money.
2. Answers will vary. Initially Jerlyn had mixed feelings since she did not know Jerico well. In the end, she knew she made the right decision.

What Is Character?

GOALS

- Define character and its two major components.
- Recognize evidence of a person's character.

TERMS

- reputation
- character
- personal characteristics
- relationships
- value

WHAT IS CHARACTER?

Character—you hear about it every day. Adults talk about the importance of character. Yet you see examples in business, politics, and even among family and friends where it seems evident that some people have forgotten about its importance. You sometimes study character in your classes, but it often seems difficult to discuss. So what is character?

From Simple to Complicated

Maybe the simplest description of character is a person's reputation. **Reputation** is how a person is viewed by most other people. You may say that a person has a good or bad reputation. Some people are known for their honesty or for being trustworthy, while others are not. Some people generally treat others well, while others seem to look out for only themselves.

Your reputation develops over time based on your day-to-day actions with many people. While you might act in a different way from time to

© Photodisc/Getty Images

Your friend has an after-school job and missed the only bus connection that will get him to work on time. You have driven to school today because your mother asked you to pick up your younger sister from her daycare on your way home. Your friend begs you to drive him to his job so that he will not be late. It is in the opposite direction you need to travel and will probably make you late to pick up your sister. You know your mom does not approve of having friends in your car.

THINK *CRITICALLY*

1. How would you respond to your friend's request for help? Why did you make that decision?

2. Is there a way to respect your friendship and still be responsible to your mother and sister?

time when in unique settings or with certain people, in general, your behavior becomes fairly consistent. You are viewed by most people as a person with either a good reputation or a poor reputation.

While reputation is a simple description, the meaning of character is really more complicated. A more complete definition of **character** is the combination of qualities and attributes (traits) that makes one person different from others. With that definition, character is categorized as neither good nor bad. You should be concerned about developing good character, so you must be aware of the attributes and qualities that are viewed as positive by most people. Good character means a good reputation.

Character is complex. It is more than what you think or even what you say. Good character is demonstrated when you find yourself in difficult situations, when you are forced to choose, or when you think your actions won't really make a difference. Character is demonstrated by your actions. Occasionally, you may do something that you regret or that you are not proud of. But good character means recognizing those wrong decisions and wrong actions, making up for them if possible, and learning from them. Your character is built over time from your actions. If you continue to make the wrong choices, you will be known for your poor reputation. If you strive to take positive actions time after time, even when faced with difficult choices, it will result in good character.

The Components of Character

Just as character is not easy to define, the attributes and qualities that make up character are also complex. The attributes of good character may not be the same in different countries, different cultures, or even different families.

Some qualities are viewed as more or less important and may receive greater attention at certain times. For example, if a politician takes a large bribe or if a business executive is caught making an unethical decision that harms customers or competitors, more attention may be focused on those issues. There is general agreement on two components

TEACH
Discuss the definition of character. Point out that character is demonstrated by your actions. Good character leads to a good reputation.

Explain to students that good character may mean different things in different countries, cultures, or even families. But generally, character is made up of personal characteristics and your relationships with others.

WHAT ABOUT ME?
Good character involves making good decisions, even when faced with difficult choices. When others see that you are responsible and make good decisions, they know they can trust you and depend on you.

Think Critically Answers
1. Answers will vary. Students will need to weigh their family responsibilities against their desire to help a friend. Ask students if they would typically make this type of decision quickly or give it a lot of thought.
2. Answers will vary. Students might suggest phoning their mother to discuss options or helping their friend find another person to drive.

that make up character—personal characteristics and relationships with others.

Personal Characteristics

The individual attributes that make up your personality and guide your actions are **personal characteristics**. The personal characteristics that are related to good character are

- honesty and truthfulness
- reliability and responsibility
- self-discipline

Relationships with Others

Your **relationships** are the ways you interact and deal with others. There are many types of relationships, including family, friendships, and business or professional connections. Relationships can be life-long or very brief. No matter the circumstances, the way you interact with others will demonstrate your character. The important characteristics of effective relationships with others are

- respect and fairness
- trust, loyalty, and caring
- good citizenship

 CHECKPOINT

Describe the two components that make up your character.

The two components that make up your character are your personal characteristics and your relationships with others.

HOW DO YOU RECOGNIZE CHARACTER?

When you first meet someone, it is not easy to determine that person's character. What do people do to demonstrate to you that they are honest, trustworthy, loyal, and fair? What makes you cautious about a person, believing that he or she may not have the best character traits?

■ Developing Character

People are not born with good or bad character. The elements of character develop over a long time. Character can change from good to bad and bad to good based on a person's experiences, needs, and relationships.

© Doug Menuez/Photodisc/Getty Images

© S Meltzer/PhotoLink/Getty Images

TEACH
As you discuss the characteristics that are important in relationships with others, ask students for specific examples of how they have seen these characteristics exhibited.

TEACH
Ask students how they try to determine a person's character. What actions would make them think that a person had good character? (Possible answers include honesty, loyalty, fairness, and trustworthiness.) What actions would make them think that a person had poor character? (Possible answers include dishonesty, unreliability, and lack of caring.)

Discuss the meaning of individual values and explain how values develop over time from childhood rules. Ask students to name personal values and the rules from which they may have developed. (For example, if you were taught to always tell the truth, you may value honesty.)

TEACHING STRATEGIES
Kinesthetic Learners
Have students cut pictures from old magazines or other sources to create a collage that illustrates the components of good character.

Young children are neither honest nor dishonest. They do not know how to treat others with respect or how to exercise self-discipline. They must learn those behaviors from others—usually their parents, brothers and sisters, or other adults with whom they spend time. At first, they learn simple words like "yes" and "no" that tell them what they can and cannot do. Then they are given rules that are designed to protect them and guide their behavior.

Don't cross the street without an adult.

Don't talk to strangers.

Share your toys with your playmates.

Young children usually will follow the rules if they remember them or if they believe they are going to be rewarded or punished. However, the rules may conflict with something that is more important at the moment. *Someone is attempting to play with my favorite toy. I don't know him, but he has a cute puppy.* In those cases, they may forget the importance of the rules. They may not share their toys, or they may approach a stranger. This does not mean that they are bad children or that they have poor character.

With time and experience, children begin to understand that their decisions and actions affect their relationships with others and their personal happiness and safety. They begin to develop values. A **value** is a strongly held belief that guides individual action. If you value your safety, you may not need a rule to tell you not to talk to strangers. If you value friendship, you may be willing to share things of importance to you with family and friends. While rules will still be needed for specific situations, many rules will be consistent with your values, so it will be easy for you to follow those rules. It is what you would do anyway because of your values.

With age and experience as well as guidance from important adults in your life, your values continue to develop. Not everyone has the same set of experiences or is taught the same values. Some values are more strongly held than others. It is not unusual for a person to have conflicting values. It is also possible, due to lack of guidance, poor examples, regular punishment, or other factors, that a child or adult will develop values that result in poor character.

Evidence of Character

Typically you want to associate with people who have good character. It is difficult to be around people who are dishonest, disrespectful, or unreliable. If you associate with people with those characteristics, others may begin to believe that you approve of those actions or share those values. You will find it personally difficult and often disappointing when someone you are associated with displays unpredictable behavior that affects you in a negative way.

You can get some idea of people's characters by talking with them and finding out what is important to them. As people develop friendships or close working relationships, they often share their beliefs and values. However, as is often said, "Actions speak louder than words." True character is not evident until a person faces a situation that requires action. When your choice of actions challenges your beliefs and values, your true character will usually come through. Will you be honest or dishonest? Can people trust you or not? Do you have respect for other people, or will your actions demonstrate prejudices that you hold? When it comes to your actions, people will see the important components of your character. In turn, you will see character in the actions of others. Those actions may confirm what you believe, or they may surprise you.

 CHECKPOINT

Why are a person's actions the best evidence of character?

Actions speak louder than words. A person's true character usually comes through when he or she is faced with a choice of actions that challenges his or her beliefs and values.

© Digital Vision/Getty Images

Follow UP

UNDERSTAND LEADERSHIP CONCEPTS

Circle the best answer for each of the following questions.

1. **How a person is viewed by other people is that person's**
   a. character
   b. values
   c. actions
   d. reputation *(circled)*

2. **Which of the following statements about character is true?**
   a. Everyone agrees on the elements of good character.
   b. People are born with most of their character elements.
   c. Character can best be demonstrated through a person's actions. *(circled)*
   d. all of the above

THINK CRITICALLY

Answer the following questions as completely as possible. If necessary, use a separate sheet of paper.

3. **Why is the character of students in a class important to the teacher? Why is it important to other students?**

The teacher needs to know if students have positive personal characteristics such as

honesty, truthfulness, and responsibility that will contribute positively to the class.

Character is important to other students as they develop friendships in the class.

Effective relationships require mutual respect and fairness, trust, loyalty, and caring.

4. **Why do long-time friends often have similar values and beliefs?**

To maintain a long-term friendship, you usually have certain characteristics in

common, and you generally approve of the other person's actions and share his or her

values and beliefs.

5. **What personal characteristics are related to good character?**

Personal characteristics related to good character include honesty and truthfulness,

reliability and responsibility, and self-discipline.

ASSESS
Reteach
List the key terms from the lesson on the board. Have students write a definition for each term.

Enrich
Divide the class into groups of three or four. Have each group develop a scenario in which a student would have to choose a course of action that would demonstrate the student's character. Have each group role play its scenario for the class and discuss the choice the student had to make.

Close
Ask students for examples of how a person's values can affect his or her character, either positively or negatively.

When Character Is Missing

GOALS

- Identify situations in your life when character is important.
- Discuss the effects poor character has on people.

TERMS

- social group
- citizenship
- career track

SCHEDULE
Block 45 minutes
Regular 1 class period

FOCUS
Ask students why character matters. How do they think an individual's poor character can affect other people?

THE IMPORTANCE OF CHARACTER

Does character really matter? On a day-to-day basis, you probably do not think a lot about character. When you meet new people, you won't know much about their reputation or character. As you choose where to go or what to do, you do not usually stop to consider the relationship between your decision and your values and beliefs. Yet, even though you typically are not consciously thinking about character, it does affect you in many important settings and relationships. Everyone is a member of several social groups. A **social group** is a group of people that depend on each other for their well-being. Three important social groups are family and friends, school, and work.

Family and Friends

© Ryan McVay/Photodisc/Getty Images

Because you spend most of your time with family and friends, you do not knowingly consider how character affects those relationships. Yet you will share more values and beliefs with family members and close friends than with anyone else. Family members and friends are your support network. They are the people you can count on when you have problems, and they are the ones with whom you want to share your successes and the things you enjoy.

Family is the first social group to which you belong. Your family is one of the most important influences on your activities, interests, and values. Even if you are separated from family members for short or long periods of time, you have connections with parents, brothers and sisters, and often grandparents, aunts, uncles, and cousins.

You value positive experiences with family members more than with most other people. You can also be very disappointed by family members when they do not meet your expectations.

Long-time, close friends can almost seem like family members. When you have known a person for a number of years and have shared many experiences, you might develop a relationship that is different from your relationship with casual friends or acquaintances. You talk

TEACH
Ask students to name the social groups they belong to. Did they remember to name their family as a social group? Point out that three important social groups are family and friends, school, and work.

A (TEAM) Effort

A person's character influences decisions and actions. Yet sometimes people make different decisions and act in different ways depending on where they are or whom they are with. Form a group and discuss the reasons why some students might act differently in school or on the job than they would when they are with their parents or other family members. What, if anything, does that say about their character?

THINK *CRITICALLY*

Do you think people can have both good and bad character that changes based on the circumstances? Defend your answer.

---

more frequently and share information with close friends that you would not be comfortable telling others. You share each other's happiness and sadness with more understanding than others. You are pleased with each other's success rather than being jealous, and you are disappointed and supportive when close friends do not achieve goals that are important to them.

The relationships with family and close friends matter more than almost any other relationships in your life. These relationships help develop your character. When someone close to you does something that conflicts with your beliefs or is the opposite of what you expect, you will usually be disappointed and upset. But because the person is special to you, you will usually try to understand and help if you can.

School

From the age of five, you have been in school. If you attended pre-school, you started even younger. Many of you will continue beyond high school to college. Your school experience will contribute a great deal to your character. It also will provide many opportunities for you to demonstrate your character.

Many of the people you meet in school and the activities you are involved in at school will not be as important to you as your family. There may be many teachers and students in your school that you will never know or will get to know only briefly through a class, activity, or school function. With the exception of a few people, your relationships at school will be short-term and related to a class, an extracurricular activity, or an event. They will not be particularly personal. You may develop some good friendships for a semester or a year, and some of those friendships may continue if you have common interests or enjoy each other's company. However, only a few relationships started in school will develop into long-term friendships.

Are you concerned about the character of the many people in school with whom you are not close friends? For the most part, it won't be important to you. However, the character of individuals ultimately can affect the organizations in which you participate. If there are even a few students in a class who are unmotivated and disruptive, they will affect the entire class atmosphere and interfere with the opportunities of others to learn. If some students do not respect school property, school

TEACH
Point out to students that family is the first social group to which they belong. Introduce ways in which their family has a major influence on their activities, interests, and values.

Ask students how their relationship with their closest friends differs from their relationship with casual friends or acquaintances. Why do they think there is a difference?

A TEAM EFFORT
Some students may act differently because they are trying to please other people or "fit in" with a certain group. Their character may not be strong enough yet for them to support their values and beliefs regardless of what others think.

Think Critically Answers
Answers will vary.

TEACH
Ask students if they are concerned about the poor character or disruptive actions of others in their school. Discuss how the poor character of a few people can affect the entire atmosphere of the school.

TEACH
Ask students what it means
to be a good citizen. Ask
them to name some ways
they have seen students demonstrate good citizenship
in their school.

TEACHING STRATEGIES
Visual Learners
Have students create a
poster or bulletin board
display that represents the
importance of character in
the three social groups—
family and friends, school,
and work.

TEACH
Ask how many students
have or have had a part-time
job. Ask students how the
character of their supervisors, coworkers, and even
their customers can affect
how they feel about their
job.

Ask students to name some
things that employees and
managers do that demon-
strate good character at
work. Ask students how they
might have to adjust their
work style because of someone else's character.

TEACHING STRATEGIES
Print Learners
Have students conduct re-
search in the library or on
the Internet about a career
in which they are interested.
Have them learn the educational requirements and
career track for their chosen
profession. Encourage them
to consider how their values
and beliefs may affect their
career choices.

© S Meltzer/PhotoLink/Photodisc/Getty Images

rules, or other students who are different from them, conflicts will occur with those who have different attitudes and beliefs. While the rela-tionships you have with those students will likely not be close, their character and their actions based on their character will have an effect on you and the others who are a part of the school community.

There is an expectation of good citizenship in school. **Citizenship** means participating effectively in an organization, supporting its goals, and contributing to its success. In a school setting, good citizenship produces a positive learning environment for everyone. A student's citizenship reveals a lot about his or her character.

▌ Work

You will have many jobs in your lifetime. You likely have already worked briefly and may hold a regular part-time job. People's first jobs usually are selected to provide needed funds or to gain experience. Later in life, jobs will be chosen as part of a career track. A **career track** is a series of related jobs ranging from entry-level to advanced positions that help fulfill career goals. You will have a different interest in jobs that are part of your career track. You will choose these jobs because they use your education and skills, provide interesting work, and lead to advanced jobs with greater responsibility and higher earnings.

No matter what the job, you will be affected by the people working around you. You will have a group of coworkers who work closely with you as well as other employees with whom you may have only limited contact. You will have a direct supervisor as well as other managers who have authority over employees and control of the business. Often you will need to work with customers. Customers will have expectations about the level of service and the quality of the products they purchase from the company.

As you interact with all of these different people, you will likely find that each one has unique character, which may affect your job. You may have to make changes to your work style because of someone else's character. Your values and beliefs as well as those of the other people associated with the business will affect the amount and quality of the completed work, the working atmosphere, and the success of the business. If the job is an important part of your career track, you will want your work to be interesting, enjoyable, and successful. Others may not have that same level of commitment. The actions of others, including employees, managers, and customers, can interfere with your job success if they act inappropriately or unethically.

 CHECKPOINT

List three important social groups in which character is important.

Three important social groups in which character is important are family and friends, school, and work.

THE RESULTS OF POOR CHARACTER

What happens when people forget about character or believe it is not important? How does their poor character affect you and others in your family, in school, and on the job? Their poor character will have a greater effect on them and on others around them than many people realize.

The Effect on You

When you are constantly exposed to people with poor character, it can have many negative effects on you. Those effects are both emotional and physical. What happens when you are around family members or friends who are not honest, are disrespectful to others, or do not demonstrate self-discipline? Sometimes you may find these people to be unpredictable. You are not sure what they will do next, but you expect that they may create problems. When you are with them in social situations or in school, you expect that you might be embarrassed by something they do or say. If problems occur as a result of their actions, you will have to determine whether or not to be involved. Do you support them and risk having others view you in the same way? Do you try to ignore their actions and hope the problem will go away? Or do you confront them and try to get them to do the right thing?

More often, the person with poor character will be someone who is not close to you. You may not be personally involved in the inappropriate behavior, but you may well be affected by it. What happens to other students in your school if one student cheats on a major test or assignment or disrespects a teacher or another student? In the workplace, will other employees be affected if a few employees are dishonest or the supervisor attempts to violate safety rules in a business? How might these situations affect you?

When you are around people who frequently create problems by acting inappropriately, you will be uncomfortable. You will be on edge wondering what is going to happen, whether you will be their

ONGOING ASSESSMENT
Use the Checkpoint as an opportunity to conduct on-going assessment of student comprehension of the lesson material.

TEACH
Ask students to think of a time when someone they know forgot about character and behaved badly. What effect did his or her actions have on the family or close friends? What effect did it have on others in the school or on the job?

Discuss the negative effects (physical and emotional) that can occur from being constantly exposed to people who behave badly. Explain why others may try to avoid being around these individuals.

TEACHING STRATEGIES
Attention Deficit Disorder (ADD) Students
Have students keep a journal, noting situations where they were negatively affected by the poor decisions or behavior of others. Have them indicate how they were affected, such as being embarrassed or uncomfortable or losing privileges because of someone else's actions.

TEACH
Ask students how they feel when they are around people who are behaving badly. Do they trust those individuals, or do they try to avoid them? Explain that when people exhibit poor behavior, it makes others uncomfortable, and they do not want to be around them.

Discuss how good character contributes to positive mental and physical health. Point out that when you feel good about yourself, get along with others, and engage in interesting activities at home, school, and work, you actually have fewer physical and mental health issues.

TEACHING STRATEGIES
Auditory Learners
Have students brainstorm a list of ways to exhibit good character at home, school, and work. From the list, have each student select one item that they believe would make the biggest difference in the way they feel, both physically and mentally.

ONGOING ASSESSMENT
Use the Checkpoint as an opportunity to conduct ongoing assessment of student comprehension of the lesson material.

target, or whether you will be affected. You cannot feel secure and happy when others around you demonstrate poor character.

The Effect on Others

How do your actions affect others? If you regularly demonstrate poor character, others will not trust you. They will not want to be associated with you and will avoid you whenever possible. Your friendships will be limited to others who approve of your poor behavior because they have the same character qualities.

You may believe that others are not affected by your actions and should not be concerned about what you do. But over time, with repeated examples of your poor character, most people will go out of their way to avoid you. Your actions make them uncomfortable, and they do not want to be with people or in situations where problems may occur. With continued displays of poor behavior, you will find yourself excluded from activities and relationships with your family, friends, school, and work.

Character Matters

While you may not think about character every day, it is apparent that most of your decisions and actions affect your character and how others view you. Character affects your mental and physical health. You can feel good about yourself, get along well with most people, and be involved in interesting activities at home, at school, and at your job. Good character and good citizenship contribute a great deal to your current happiness and future success.

 CHECKPOINT

How can your character affect your mental and physical health?

Good character contributes to your happiness and success at home, school, and work, which helps keep you mentally and physically healthy.

Follow UP

UNDERSTAND LEADERSHIP CONCEPTS

Circle the best answer for each of the following questions.

1. **A group of people that depend on each other for their well-being is known as**
   a. a social group
   b. citizens
   c. a club
   d. none of the above

2. **Jobs that are a part of your career track**
   a. are all high paying
   b. are more interesting to you
   c. require a college degree
   d. are difficult to obtain

THINK *CRITICALLY*

Answer the following questions as completely as possible. If necessary, use a separate sheet of paper.

3. **In what situations would the character of a person you just met be very important to you? Why?**

   The character of a person you just met would be important to you if that person is a member of a social group to which you also belong, such as a student in your school or a customer or an employee at your workplace. That person's character could have either a positive or a negative effect on you and your ability to succeed.

4. **How does the character of one family member affect other family members?**

   Because family is the first social group to which you belonged and is one of the most important influences on your life, the character of each member can affect the physical and emotional wellbeing of the other members. If a family member behaves badly, it can embarrass you or make you uncomfortable.

5. **How can good or poor citizenship affect the atmosphere of a school?**

   Good citizenship in school creates a positive learning environment for everyone. Students who are unmotivated or disruptive or who do not respect school property, school rules, or other students create a negative atmosphere in school.

ASSESS
Reteach
Review the goals for the lesson. Have students write one or two sentences summarizing the important points discussed for each of the goals.

Enrich
Have students create a chart with columns for each of the three social groups—family and friends, school, and work. Each column should be further divided into two columns—positive and negative. Have students list both the positive and negative effects of character on relationships in each social group. Have students work with a partner to compare their answers.

Close
Have students list the positive characteristics they admire in another person. How does that person's character positively affect them and others?

Acting Ethically

SCHEDULE
Block 45 minutes
Regular 1 class period

FOCUS
Ask students if they think it is possible to ignore a rule or break a law and still be behaving ethically.

WHAT IS ETHICS?

If someone intentionally damaged school property and you know who did it, should you report it? Should you tell only if you are asked? Would it matter if the person were your friend rather than someone you did not like? What if the damage was accidental rather than intentional?

If you were the parent of a very sick child and could not afford the medicine that would save the child's life, what would you do? If you were unable to find anyone who would provide the money for the medicine, would you resort to stealing it? Would it be worth going to jail to provide medicine for your child?

Both of these situations present a very difficult decision between right and wrong. The first appears to be less serious, with fewer consequences. The second deals with breaking the law and the possible death of a child. Both decisions are very serious. But each situation describes a decision involving ethics.

Right Versus Wrong

Ethics describes the decisions and actions of individuals and groups based on an understanding of right and wrong. You have learned that values are strongly held beliefs that guide individual action. Ethics are closely related to your values. Ethical decisions and actions are based on what you believe is right and wrong. If you do not think carefully about important decisions, you may

© Digital Vision/Getty Images

end up doing something that you will later regret. Decisions may be difficult, but if you base them on your values, you usually will feel good about the actions you take.

Rules and Procedures

Because of differences in background and culture, people may not share the same values and ethical beliefs. Some people may also not have learned the importance of ethical behavior. These people may not think carefully about decisions and consider whether their actions are right or wrong.

To make sure that people understand what behavior is acceptable or unacceptable, groups and organizations develop rules. Your family has rules that you must follow, and so does your school. If you participate in sports, you know that each sport has a specific set of rules that everyone is expected to follow. Your coaches may have developed rules they expect team members to follow when training, participating in practice, or traveling to other schools for competition. A **rule** is a written statement of appropriate action that people are expected to follow. Rules describe acceptable and unacceptable behavior for a group or organization. They may not always be based on values, but rules are developed to keep order and to organize the actions of the group.

© Geoff Manasse/Photodisc/Getty Images

In addition to rules, organizations also develop procedures to guide actions. **Procedures** are a series of steps and actions that must be followed to complete an activity. Your teachers may have given you a set of procedures they expect you to follow each day at the beginning or end of class. If you have a fire drill at your school, everyone must know the procedure to follow to evacuate the building rapidly and move to a safe location. Businesses develop procedures for their employees to follow when they are unable to attend work due to an illness or when operating a piece of equipment.

Procedures are more specific than rules. They tell people exactly what they are expected to do to complete a task successfully. Rules provide guidelines for actions based on what is right and wrong. But the most important guidance for determining right from wrong is a person's ethics. Ethics are not just written statements that must be followed. Ethics are deeply held beliefs and values. If you feel strongly about what is right and wrong, you usually will base your actions on those beliefs. You will want to do what is right and avoid doing what is wrong. You will feel bad when you do something that goes against your values and beliefs.

CHECKPOINT

Why do groups and organizations develop rules?

Groups and organizations develop rules to make sure that people understand what behavior is acceptable or unacceptable.

LEADERSHIP *Tip*

Leaders must set ethical examples for the people they are leading. If group members see their leader acting unethically, they no longer have respect for the leader, or they may believe it is acceptable for them to act unethically as well.

TEACH
Explain what a code of
ethics is. Ask students why
they think groups and organizations need to have a
code of ethics. Codes of
ethics may vary based on the
group or organization for
which they are written.
However, all codes of ethics
should be easy to under-
stand and should convey
what is most important to
the group or organization.

COMMUNICATE
Have students review the list
of things to do when planning and preparing rules.
Discuss the importance of
each point.

A CODE OF ETHICS

Individuals and families have their own values and beliefs. Usually the values and beliefs of one family member are very similar to those of other family members. Family members spend time together and talk about what they believe is right or wrong. They also talk about their values and beliefs. Often, those values and beliefs have been passed down from one generation to another, or they are part of the family's culture. They may also develop from religious or spiritual beliefs.

Other groups and organizations do not automatically have a shared set of values and beliefs. The members of the group or organization may not have always been together. Some are new to the group while others have been there a long time. They may have different back-grounds and experiences. Yet the groups and organizations will not operate effectively unless members agree on and support some basic values that guide their decisions and actions.

Groups and organizations can develop rules and procedures for people to fol-low. However, if people do not under-stand why the rules and procedures were developed or if they do not value and respect the organization they work for or the people they work with, it may be difficult to enforce the rules and proce-dures. Developing shared values that reflect the beliefs of the people in the group will encourage people to make ethical decisions and do the right thing.

Many groups and organizations develop a code of ethics. A **code of ethics** is a written statement of the beliefs and values that should guide the actions of a specific group or organization. The code of ethics provides a statement of what is expected of those who are a part of the organization in terms of right and wrong actions. When people join a group or organization, they must agree to follow the code of ethics. A code of ethics also informs those people who may deal with the organization that it believes in honesty and integrity. **Integrity** is a com-mitment to following a set of values and is often associated with ethics.

Individuals can also develop their own code of ethics, or *code of conduct.* A code of conduct is a set of rules to help guide personal behavior and decisions.

COMMUNICATE

Rules help members of a group or organization under-stand what is expected of them. The rules must be understand-able and communicated in a way that group members want to support the rules. If you are one of the leaders of a new group, you may have to develop rules for membership, meetings, and activities. When planning and preparing rules, you should

- Have a small number of rules. Too many rules can be overwhelming.

- Develop rules that you believe are impor-tant to make the organization operate effectively.

- Make sure the rules are understandable and specific. State the rules using positive rather than negative language.

- Communicate the rules to members so that they recognize why the rules are needed and how the rules will contribute to a more effective organization.

THINK CRITICALLY

List one rule for a group to which you belong. Does the rule meet all of the requirements discussed above? Explain why or why not.

Think Critically Answers
Answers will vary.

Sample Codes of Ethics

A code of ethics should be meaningful and understandable. It also should communicate what is important to the organization. Codes of ethics range from long and detailed to short and concise. The activities of some professionals, such as accountants and lawyers, are guided by numerous laws and regulations. Their ethical codes outline responsible practices that are both ethical and legal. Others, such as physicians and religious leaders, have significant moral obligations that are the basis for their codes of ethics. Many businesses have developed basic ethical guidelines that identify the importance they attach to ethical behavior for managers, employees, and customers. A sample code of ethics for businesses is shown in Figure 3.1. A code of ethics for athletes used by many high schools is shown in Figure 3.2.

TEACH

Ask students to compare the terms *integrity* and *ethics*. How do students view them as being related, and how do they view them as being different?

Review the two sample codes of ethics shown. Note that each code of ethics provides a clear statement of the values and beliefs of the organization that members are expected to follow. Ask students to describe what they believe the values and beliefs of each group are after reading each code of ethics.

FIGURE 3.1   *An Ethics Statement for a Business*

OUR BELIEFS, OUR VALUES

We believe who we are says much more about us than what we achieve. As a business we want to be known for the actions we take, the decisions we make, and the relationships we have with others. We believe a business can be built on values and that those values will determine what is right and what is wrong. The choice between right and wrong is not always the easiest decision and not always the most profitable. However, it is the choice that will make us feel right about what we do and will result in the right outcomes and the type of success we are seeking.

Our core values are honesty, integrity, fair play, objectivity, and respect for ourselves and others. We express our values and practice our beliefs in the way we treat each other, our expectations of everyone, and our interactions with those with whom we do business. We work to base our decisions and actions on those beliefs and values and are committed to improve when we fall short. We want to be known for ethical leadership in our community, our industry, and in the view of all who know us.

FIGURE 3.2   *Athletes' Code of Ethics*

As an athlete, I understand that it is my responsibility to:

- Place academic achievement as the highest priority.
- Show respect for teammates, opponents, officials, and coaches.
- Respect the integrity and judgment of game officials.
- Exhibit fair play, sportsmanship, and proper conduct on and off the playing field.
- Maintain a high level of safety awareness.
- Refrain from the use of profanity, vulgarity, and other offensive language and gestures.

- Adhere to the established rules and standards of the game to be played.
- Respect all equipment and use it safely and appropriately.
- Refrain from the use of alcohol, tobacco, illegal and non-prescription drugs, anabolic steroids, or any substance to increase physical development.
- Know and follow all state, section, and school athletic rules and regulations as they pertain to eligibility and sports participation.
- Win with character; lose with dignity.

© F64/Photodisc/Getty Images

▌ Character and Ethics

An organization's code of ethics is often developed to meet the needs of that particular group and to respond to the types of ethical situations that are most often encountered by the group members. That is why many codes of ethics are quite detailed and contain statements unique to the business and organization. However, acting ethically on a daily basis does not require that people memorize a specific code of ethics or the laws and regulations that guide a type of business or a profession. In general, ethical actions are drawn from the elements of good character. If you are concerned about your actions and about how they will affect others, you will exhibit ethical behavior. If you think carefully about decisions you are making and whether they are the types of actions you would want family and friends to know about, your decisions and actions will be ethical.

Use the checklist in Figure 3.3 to help determine whether you have the elements of good character. The checklist can also help you determine if your decisions and actions are ethical.

TEACHING STRATEGIES
Gifted Students
Have students search the Internet for the code of ethics of other groups and organizations. Have students share several examples with the class and discuss the values and beliefs that seem to be communicated in the statements.

TEACH
Review the questions in the checklist entitled "Do You Have Good Character?" Then have students complete the checklist. Ask them to describe how each of the questions is a reflection of good character and ethical behavior.

ONGOING ASSESSMENT
Use the Checkpoint as an opportunity to conduct ongoing assessment of student comprehension of the lesson material.

FIGURE 3.3	*Character Checklist*

DO YOU HAVE GOOD CHARACTER?
Personal Characteristics

☐ Are you honest and truthful in your dealings with others?

☐ Can people count on you? Do they view you as reliable and responsible?

☐ Do you exercise self-discipline rather than take unsafe risks?

Relationships with Others

☐ Do you respect others and treat them fairly?

☐ Do you exhibit loyalty and trust to family, friends, and others? Do you genuinely care about others and their feelings?

☐ Are you a good citizen of each group and organization in which you participate? Do you support its purpose, care for its resources, and help it to be successful?

 CHECKPOINT

What is a code of ethics and why is it needed?

A code of ethics is a written statement of the beliefs and values that should guide the actions of a specific group or organization.

Follow UP

UNDERSTAND LEADERSHIP CONCEPTS

Circle the best answer for each of the following questions.

1. The decisions and actions of individuals and groups based on an understanding of right and wrong is
a. ethics
b. values
c. character
d. judgment

2. Acceptable and unacceptable behavior in an organization is described in its
a. procedures
b. rules
c. bylaws
d. principles

THINK *CRITICALLY*

Answer the following questions as completely as possible. If necessary, use a separate sheet of paper.

3. How is ethics different from and similar to character?

Character is made up of the qualities and traits that make one person different from another. Character can be either good or bad. Ethical decisions, on the other hand, are based on what you believe is right and wrong. Generally, a person who has good character will also have good values or beliefs that guide his or her actions, and, therefore, will make good ethical decisions.

4. Do you think your school should have a code of ethics for its students, teachers, administrators, and staff members? Why or why not?

Answers will vary.

ASSESS
Reteach
Review the terms and answers to the Checkpoint questions to make sure that students understand the key concepts in the lesson.

Enrich
Divide the class into groups of three or four. Have each group write a code of ethics for the classroom. Compare the completed codes of ethics and have students select one that they would recommend as a classroom code of ethics.

Close
If your school has a code of ethics or list of rules for student conduct, review them with the class and discuss the reason for each statement or rule.

Chapter Assessment

TEACHING RESOURCES
ExamView® CD, Ch. 3

REVIEW *LEADERSHIP CONCEPTS*

Write the letter of the term that matches each definition. Some terms will not be used.

a. career track
b. character
c. citizenship
d. code of ethics
e. ethics
f. integrity
g. personal characteristics
h. procedures
i. relationships
j. reputation
k. rule
l. social group
m. value

___k___ 1. A written statement of action that people are expected to follow

___m___ 2. A strongly held belief that guides individual action

___b___ 3. Qualities and attributes that make one person different from others

___j___ 4. How a person is viewed by others

___d___ 5. A written statement of the beliefs and values that should guide the actions of a group or organization

___c___ 6. Participating effectively in an organization, supporting its goals, and contributing to its success

___i___ 7. The ways you interact with others

___g___ 8. Attributes that make up your personality and guide your actions

___l___ 9. A group of people that depend on each other for their well-being

___e___ 10. The decisions and actions of individuals and groups based on an understanding of right and wrong

Circle the best answer.

11. The two components that make up character are
    a. actions and attributes
    b. personal characteristics and relationships with others
    c. rules and procedures
    d. decisions and beliefs

12. The first important social group for individuals is
    a. family
    b. close friends
    c. pre-school or daycare
    d. their first job

13. Ethical decisions and actions are based on
    a. rules and laws
    b. past illegal and inappropriate actions
    c. the behavior of leaders
    d. what you believe is right and wrong

14. _____ are more specific than rules and tell people exactly what they are supposed to do to complete a task successfully.
    a. Policies
    b. Procedures
    c. Decisions
    d. Codes of ethics

ASSESS

Reteach
Divide the class into two teams and have them stand and face each other, spelling-bee style. In turn, ask each student to define a key term or answer a Checkpoint or Follow-up question from the chapter. If a student misses a question, he or she must sit down, and the next student is given the same question to answer. The last person standing is the winner.

Enrich
Have students make a list of rules that they are expected to follow at home, at school, on a team or organization to which they belong, or in their work-place. Ask students to write the purpose of each rule.

CLOSE
Ask students to explain how your character relates to your reputation. What can a person do to improve a bad reputation?

THINK *CRITICALLY*

15. *What are some examples in school of personal characteristics related to good character? What are examples from work?*

Answers will vary but may include: School — showing respect for teachers,

administrators, and classmates, completing all assigned work honestly and responsibly,

and taking care of school property. Work — arriving on time, being reliable,

completing all work assigned, and treating coworkers, supervisors, and customers with

respect.

16. *"Character can change from good to bad and bad to good based on a person's experiences, needs, and relationships." Do you agree or disagree with this statement? Explain your answer.*

Answers will vary. Character is built over time, so it is possible to make a wrong

decision. But good character means that you recognize that you made a bad choice,

you try to make up for it, and you learn from it.

17. *Provide an example of the negative effects on individuals and groups when they are exposed to people with poor character.*

Answers will vary but may include both emotional and physical effects, such as being

embarrassed, feeling uncomfortable, or feeling stressed.

18. *How are your ethics similar to and different from your behavior?*

Your behavior is generally affected by your ethics. Ethics involve the decisions you

make and actions you take based on your understanding of right and wrong.

However, you could do something against your ethics—something that you know is

wrong—because of peer pressure or a desire to "fit in" with a group.

19. *If you were the manager of a large business, would you want to develop a code of ethics for that business? Why or why not?*

Answers will vary. A code of ethics would let your employees know what the company

stands for and what is expected of them in terms of right and wrong actions.

20. **History**   *Select one person from history that you believe is an example of someone with good character. Use the library or Internet to learn about the person's life. Write a two-paragraph description of the person's beliefs and actions that provide evidence of his or her character.*

Answers will vary depending on the person selected.

_____

_____

_____

21. **Research**   *The culture in which a person is raised plays a very important role in the person's values. Use the Internet or library to gather information on a culture that is different from yours. Identify two values from that culture that you believe are different from your values and two values that you believe are similar.*

Answers will vary based on the culture selected.

_____

_____

_____

_____

22. **Creative Thinking**   *List five different social groups to which you belong. Think carefully about each group and decide how similar or different each group is from the others in terms of values and beliefs. Using a blank sheet of paper, draw a circle to represent each of the social groups you identified. The more similar the values and beliefs of a group are to another group, the more those two circles should intersect. The more different the values and beliefs of a group are from another group, the less those two circles should intersect. After all five circles are drawn, look at the diagram and consider the similarities and differences. Write a paragraph describing what the illustration demonstrates about your social groups and your values and beliefs.*

Answers will vary.

_____

_____

_____

_____

23. **Communication**   *Use the checklist of the elements of good character as well as the sample codes of ethics in Lesson 3.3 as guidelines to help you write your own personal code of ethics, or code of conduct.*

Answers will vary.

_____

_____

_____

_____

LEARNING TO LEAD

FOCUS

Develop a plan to become actively involved in your local student organization chapter.

DESCRIPTION

Some people want to be leaders but do not recognize the work needed to become an effective and respected leader in an organization. To be accepted as a leader requires getting to know other members and letting them become comfortable with you. You need to be active in the organization, take on your share of the work, be an effective team member, and let others see that you have the best interests of the organization in mind. Taking on small and short-term leadership assignments and doing well prepares you for key leadership roles in your local chapter and possibly for state and national leadership in the future.

Become familiar with the program of work and activities of your local student organization chapter. Identify the ways you can apply your current abilities and interests to support the chapter's work and to develop into an effective member and leader.

LEARNING TO LEAD

This project is written for use with student organizations such as BPA, DECA, and FBLA. Student organizations can help students prepare for key leadership roles. After students complete the activities, discuss what they learned about their student organization.

Activities

1. Discuss some of the monthly and yearly calendar of activities of the student organization.
2. Discuss the member expectations of the student organization.

ACTIVITIES

1. Obtain all printed information available to members that describes the local chapter of your student organization. If there is a local web site, familiarize yourself with the member information provided. Review the chapter's monthly and yearly calendar of activities if it is available.

2. Meet with a local chapter officer or experienced member and discuss the operation of the chapter and the expectations for members. Determine if there is a code of ethics or code of conduct for members. Acquire information on meetings and other activities. Learn how information is communicated to members so you can stay well informed.

3. Identify all committees and groups that have leadership responsibilities for chapter activities. Make notes on each committee and group and the work required of members and leaders. Identify the current chairperson or team leader of each committee.

4. Identify the officers and duties of each office for the local chapter leadership team. Make sure you know each of the current officers. Interview one officer to learn the path he or she followed to become an effective member and officer.

3. Describe the various committees or groups and the work required by their members.
4. Describe the path taken by one officer to become a group member or leader.

Share Your Results

1. Answers will vary. Students should explain how their selection matches their interests, skills, and future leadership goals.
2. Answers will vary. Share some of the student posters with the class.

SHARE YOUR RESULTS

1. *Identify three ways that you could become an active member in your local student organization this year. Write a brief description of why each choice is appropriate based on your interests, current abilities, and future leadership goals.*
2. *Prepare a poster or some other kind of visual aid that represents your interests, abilities, and leadership goals.*

CASE STUDY 3—CHARACTER AND ETHICS

In the opening scenario, What Would You Do?*, Jerlyn found and helped return some money to its rightful owner. She did the right thing. This was not the first time that Jerlyn faced an ethical dilemma. Jerlyn worked after school a few days a week and on weekends as a sales clerk at one of the large department stores in the local mall. There, she and several coworkers had access to the money in the cash register as well as the merchandise in the cosmetics department in which they worked. As she and her coworker Isabella were closing up one night, she saw Isabella slip a bottle of perfume in her purse. Isabella said that the store would never miss one bottle of perfume. She also justified it by saying, "Other employees do the same thing, so why shouldn't I?" Jerlyn knew it was wrong to steal from her employer.*

THINK *CRITICALLY*

1. Given what you know about Jerlyn from the opening scenario and the case study, what is your opinion of Jerlyn's character?

Answers will vary. Jerlyn's character is generally good because she returned the money and knows that stealing from her employer is wrong. However, her character may still be developing since she hesitated and considered keeping the money.

2. What is your opinion of Isabella's character?

Isabella's character is poor. She is stealing from her employer and justifying her actions by saying that "other employees do the same thing."

3. What ethical dilemma does Jerlyn face at work?

Jerlyn must decide whether to report Isabella to her supervisor for stealing the bottle of perfume or whether to not say anything to avoid conflict with Isabella.

4. How would you advise Jerlyn to handle this dilemma?

Answers will vary. Jerlyn might talk to Isabella first and give her the opportunity to put the perfume back before reporting her to the supervisor.

APPLY *WHAT YOU HAVE LEARNED–Character Survey*

DIRECTIONS: *Your character greatly influences the way others view you. Learn more about your character by completing the Character Survey below or on your Student Activity CD. Rate yourself by placing an **X** on the appropriate line next to each character trait. Then ask a parent, sibling, friend, teacher, or classmate to rate you on these same traits. Do not let him or her see your ratings.*

CHARACTER SURVEY

	Never	Some of the Time	Most of the Time	Always
Personal Characteristics				
Honesty	_____	_____	_____	_____
Truthfulness	_____	_____	_____	_____
Reliability	_____	_____	_____	_____
Responsibility	_____	_____	_____	_____
Self-Discipline	_____	_____	_____	_____
Relationships with Others				
Respect	_____	_____	_____	_____
Fairness	_____	_____	_____	_____
Trust	_____	_____	_____	_____
Loyalty	_____	_____	_____	_____
Caring	_____	_____	_____	_____

Upon completion of the survey by you and one other person, use a blank survey form to combine the scores. If the marks are the same on both surveys, make a mark under the same column on the new survey form. When the marks are different on both surveys, transfer the lowest rating to the new survey form. Use the new survey to evaluate your character. If the majority of the marks fall under the Most of the Time *and* Always *columns, you are living a life of character that will benefit you and others. If there are marks in the* Some of the Time *column, you need to consider making improvements in these areas. If you have any marks in the* Never *column, there is definite need for reflection and change in these areas.*

Select a trait (from the Never *or* Some of the Time *columns) and create a SMART goal (including a completion date) to help you make the needed changes to improve your character. Enter the goal on the lines below or on the Student Activity CD. Enter the goal in a monthly calendar (on the CD or your own). Then enter your thoughts, ideas, and discussions related to your goal in a journal (on the CD or your own) to help you plan and track your progress. Ask the person who completed your survey to be your goal-setting partner to help you achieve your goal.*

_____

_____

_____

_____

ACCEPTING THE CHALLENGE
Apply What You Have Learned—Character Survey
Note that students can complete this part of the *Accepting the Challenge* activity in the book or on the Student Activity CD. Instructions are provided on the CD.

Discuss how character influences others' view of an individual. Discuss the results of the Character Survey. Ask students whether they were surprised about any of their survey results.

Instruct students to write a SMART goal (including a completion date) related to a character trait they would like to improve. Have them enter their goal on a monthly calendar. Students can use the monthly calendar on the Student Activity CD or their own calendar. Explain to students that they may also use weekly calendar pages (on the CD or their own) to plan activities and tasks that will help them achieve their goals. Finally, direct students to use a journal (on the CD or their own) to track and evaluate their progress in achieving their goal.

A goal-setting partner can add an element of accountability and can offer positive feedback to help students stay on track to achieve their goals.

Students should be given the opportunity to reflect on the progress they have made toward achieving their goal. To do this, students can complete the *Evaluate Your Progress* activity on the Student CD. Stress to students that it is important to complete this activity on the original target completion date even if they have not met their goal at that time.

Becoming a Leader: Developing Your Personal Plan

© Doug Menuez/Photodisc/Getty Images

4.1	Being a Leader in Your School and Community
4.2	Creating a Sense of Community within Your School
4.3	Planning for Servant Leadership

What would **YOU** do?

IAN'S PERSONAL PLAN

Ian Wilson began his leadership development during the fifth grade. He was president of the student body at Port Royal Elementary School, located in a large southern community. His teacher and his parents supported Ian's desire to become a leader. Because Ian was friendly and likable, his fifth-grade teacher compared him to Bill Cosby. She suggested that Cosby would be a good role model for Ian. But Ian's parents encouraged him to focus on local role models. They explained that role models should come from your community, not from television. His parents wanted Ian to know that television personalities are actors, but role models in your community are "real people" whom you see on a regular basis. In many cases, they are willing to be mentors.

In middle school, Ian became involved in Student Council and began participating in youth leadership training activities. He also joined the school's basketball and soccer teams. Ian was also a good student and was enrolled in gifted courses.

Ian's leadership training in middle school set the stage for his later success. In high school, he became president of the student council at the state level. Ian was thrilled with the success he had achieved and began thinking about how he could put his leadership skills to work. He remembered his parents' advice—role models come from the community and often become mentors. Ian decided that he wanted to be a role model in his community and school and help others succeed as he had. But how could he do this?

His participation in national conferences for student council as well as in school plays helped Ian develop excellent communication skills. He decided to put those skills to good use as a public speaker. He became a youth speaker for several churches and for a community organization called ACTS—Academic, Counseling and Training Sessions—whose motto is "Do your best." He hoped that he could provide inspiration and motivation for others to do their best.

THINK *CRITICALLY*

1. Do you agree that role models should come from within the community and not from TV or movies? Explain why or why not.

2. How did Ian prepare himself to help others to do their best?

3. How would you use your leadership abilities to help others?

TEACHING RESOURCES
Instructor's Resource CD
Lesson Plans, Ch. 4
PowerPoint Slides, Ch. 4

Student Activity CD, Ch. 4

thomsonedu.com/school/ leading
Crossword Puzzle, Ch. 4
Flash Cards, Ch. 4

Exam*View*® **CD,** Ch. 4

CHAPTER OVERVIEW
Chapter 4 discusses the development of a personal plan for leadership in your school and community.

Lesson 4.1
Describes a personal leadership plan and ways to develop as a community leader.

Lesson 4.2
Explains the benefits of a sense of community within a school and identifies strategies to create a caring school climate.

Lesson 4.3
Explains the major challenges and primary components of servant leadership.

WHAT WOULD YOU DO?
Ask students to name some role models in their community who could serve as mentors to help them develop leadership skills. (Role models might include a teacher, coach, counselor, religious leader, or an adviser in a youth organization.)

Think Critically Answers
1. Answers will vary.
2. Ian developed excellent communication skills through his participation in national student council conferences. Those skills helped him as a youth speaker for several churches and a community organization.
3. Answers will vary.

Becoming a Leader: Developing Your Personal Plan   Chapter 4   **83**

Being a Leader in Your School and Community

- Describe the strong points included in your personal leadership plan.
- Explain the importance of maintaining a positive attitude in school and community activities.
- Discuss various ways to develop as a leader in your community.

- personal plan
- practical experience
- networking

SCHEDULE
Block 45 minutes
Regular 1 class period

FOCUS
Have students name some ways that they can begin now to develop their leadership skills in their school and community.

IDENTIFY YOUR STRONG POINTS

To be a leader in your school and community, you should consider developing a personal plan. Your **personal plan** serves as a foundation and guide to enhance your leadership development.

Your personal plan should include a self-evaluation of your strengths and weaknesses. You should identify those areas in which you have excelled. Although you need to accept your weaknesses or areas that need improvement, do not focus on them. Instead, focus on the things that you do best. Sometimes individuals tend to focus more on the things that they cannot do rather than on those things that they can do.

As you develop your personal plan, strive to make leadership skills one of your strong points. You can do this by gaining practical experience, networking with others, displaying a positive attitude, and taking action to get things done.

© Digital Vision/Getty Images

Practical Experience

Increasing your knowledge and skills by applying them in an area in which you are interested will provide you with useful or **practical experience**. Gaining practical experience will increase your self-confidence. It will also improve your leadership development. In gaining practical experience, your goal is to learn more about and become more skilled in something that interests you. For example, if you like writing short stories, poems, rap lyrics, or letters, you should consider serving on the school's newspaper. As a reporter on the newspaper, you could start a "Did You Know?" or "Have You Heard the Latest?" column.

Your high school is preparing for election of the Student Government Association (SGA) officers for the upcoming school year. Several of your classmates have suggested that you run for president of the SGA. Your past leadership experiences have been successful. You have served as secretary and vice-president in your sophomore and junior years. Becoming president of the SGA would be quite an honor for you. You are aware that it will take a team effort for you to win. You need the help of good friends and supporters to run your campaign. Your two best friends have stepped up to help, but both want to be your campaign manager. Besides campaign manager, you have many other positions to fill on your team. The time to submit your campaign papers and organize your team is fast approaching, and you need to make some decisions.

THINK *CRITICALLY*

1. *What process will you use to choose which friend will be your campaign manager?*
2. *How will you organize your campaign to win the election? What will be the roles and responsibilities of your team members?*

You could interview your classmates and publish their responses. Your interviewing approach would probably generate interest and increase the readership of the student newspaper. Your classmates would enjoy seeing their names in the newspaper. You would be amazed by the excitement you could create throughout your school. The practical experience you gain as a school reporter would help you improve your writing skills, which, in turn, would give you the confidence and ability to seek other leadership opportunities.

As you gain practical experience, the knowledge that you gain is reinforced and stored in your memory to be used again at the appropriate time. Building a strong foundation of practical experience and applying your knowledge helps you develop as a leader. If you dream of one day becoming president of your Student Government Association (SGA) but you are afraid to speak in public, consider joining the school's drama club. Remember that most of the stars in Hollywood started with small parts to gain practical experience before becoming the superstars that they are today. For example, Clint Eastwood got his first acting experience when a teacher assigned him a part in a school play to help him become less introverted. He gained many years of practical acting experience before winning the Academy Award for directing and producing *Million Dollar Baby*.

Another way you can obtain practical experience is by volunteering. Community service organizations like your local YWCA or YMCA are always looking for volunteers to help with their after-school tutorial and peer-mentor programs. You could also volunteer as a peer-tutor to help your classmates with their homework. As you teach others, your knowledge also increases.

Your personal plan for leadership development should include getting as much practical experience as you can. Leaders are aware that learning is an ongoing process.

TEACH
Have students begin working on their personal plan by listing their strengths—areas in which they feel they excel.

Explain the meaning of *practical experience* and discuss how practical experience can improve leadership skills.

Have students review their list of strengths to determine what type of practical experience they might be able to gain. (For example, if a student has strong technical skills, he or she might gain practical experience by working in the school's audiovisual department.)

A TEAM EFFORT
Ask students if they know anyone who has run for an elected office. How were members of the campaign team selected?

Think Critically Answers
1. Answers will vary. Students should consider whether friendship alone is enough of a "skill" or if they should use some other method to select the best person for the job.
2. Answers will vary.

© Photodisc/Getty Images

■ Networking with Others

Networking involves interacting with others and developing beneficial relationships. Throughout your life, you will meet and interact with many people. Contacts you make with others can prove to be beneficial. Perhaps you met someone from your volunteering efforts who would be an excellent resource for an upcoming class project. Maybe your best friend's older sister who served on high school student council could give you advice on running for office. Networking gives you the opportunity to meet people who can answer your questions and help guide you in making decisions.

Whenever you meet someone new, you are expanding your network. Networking provides you with a number of people resources that can offer experience and knowledge. Networking also helps you improve your interpersonal and social skills. Equipped with excellent interpersonal skills and a network of people willing to lend a hand, you will be ready to take on the challenges of being a leader in your school and community. Networking will allow you to achieve more with others than you could do by yourself.

 CHECKPOINT

Why is practical experience important in your leadership development?

Practical experience allows you to learn more about and become more skilled in areas

that interest you. That foundation of practical experience helps you develop as a leader.

MAINTAIN A POSITIVE ATTITUDE

A positive attitude is one of the major characteristics that will serve you well in being a leader in your school and community. Maintaining a positive attitude means focusing on positive expectations more than negative ones. It is said that people who expect more out of life tend to get more and that those who expect less tend to get less. When you participate in competitive activities in your school and community, take on a positive attitude by getting excited and having high expectations for success. For example, if you are trying out for the leading role in your school play, a positive attitude can boost your self-confidence. Positive attitudes are needed for positive results.

TEACHING STRATEGIES
Kinesthetic Learners
Have students research a person they admire, such as a business leader, athlete, or entertainer, to determine what practical experience the person gained prior to becoming well known. How do they think that practical experience contributed to the person's later success?

TEACH
Have students name some ways that they might be able to expand their network of contacts. Ask them how they think networking can enhance their leadership skills.

ONGOING ASSESSMENT
Use the Checkpoint as an opportunity to conduct ongoing assessment of student comprehension of the lesson material.

© Photodisc/Getty Images

People with a positive attitude are contagious. Their enthusiasm can spread throughout your school. Creating a positive atmosphere in your school is easier to do with positive-thinking classmates. They are like magnets and are drawn to each other. Team sports in high schools are more about a winning attitude than ability. There have been times when the team with the most ability did not win the game because the opponent refused to lose. A positive attitude can accomplish amazing results. It can influence your *achievement altitude*, or how high you go in life.

▌Put a Stop to Negative Attitudes

A negative attitude is easy to acquire. Criticism and finger pointing are often used by others to escape blame. You may know a few classmates who have a negative attitude. They may seem frustrated about something most of the time. Avoid spending time with people who have a negative attitude, because they can "bring you down" or damage your reputation. Be aware of their influence. Just as positive attitudes can be contagious, so can negative attitudes. They must be dealt with in order to stop the spread of disruptive behavior throughout the group and school.

As a leader in your school, it may be helpful to understand the source of the negative attitude. Some causes of negative attitudes may be miscommunication, misinterpretation, or misunderstanding of a message or situation. If this is the case, better communication may lead to improved attitudes. In many cases, people with a poor self-image have a negative outlook. As a leader, you may want to help others in your group improve their self-image. Perhaps you could lead a "Be Good to Yourself" after-school program for interested students. The program could focus on fitness for the body and mind. Members would be encouraged to focus on their personal best by developing individualized health fitness programs. Individualized plans would make the program less competitive because members would strive to meet personal goals. The group would offer support to all members. As members reach their goals, their self-image and attitude would improve. The success of one member would affect the others in the group.

TEACH
Ask students if they know any individuals who are always putting things off—those who talk about completing a task but who do not take action. Do they think of those people as good leaders? Why or why not?

ONGOING ASSESSMENT
Use the Checkpoint as an opportunity to conduct ongoing assessment of student comprehension of the lesson material.

TEACH
Ask students to name some of the major issues in their local community. How familiar are they with the people and issues in their own neighborhoods?

Have students name some ways that they can become knowledgeable about issues in their community. In addition to reading the local newspaper and watching local news channels, students might consider attending a city council or town hall meeting.

■ Actions Speak Louder Than Words

Some of your friends and classmates have the ability and discipline to get things done. They do more than just talk about their plans—they actually carry out their plans. These are the people who are usually selected to complete various tasks because they are dependable. There are other people whom you may know as "feet draggers." They have the ability to put off almost any major task. They always have time to do it later, but they never have time to do it now. Their actions speak more loudly than their words.

As a leader in your school, you should make your classmates aware that individuals are judged more by their actions than by the words they speak. Connecting your words to your actions and completing a task will reveal to others the strength of your leadership in terms of dependability, consistency, and maturity. Keep in mind that your actions are also connected to your attitude, whether it is positive or negative. A "can do" attitude is a positive attitude.

 CHECKPOINT

As a leader in your school, explain the importance of maintaining a positive attitude.

Your positive attitude can boost your self-confidence and lead to positive results.

Others will be drawn to you because of your winning attitude. It can affect how far you go in life.

COMMUNITY LEADERSHIP

Being a leader in your community begins with an understanding of the people and issues in your neighborhood. It may also require you to build relationships with your neighbors and to demonstrate your ability to organize resources. How well do you know the people in your community? Are you concerned about some of the major community issues? Are there summer jobs for youth and programs that address drug abuse, teen pregnancy, violence, and other community issues?

■ Knowledge of Your Community

Understanding people and issues in your community is similar to understanding your classmates and the issues in your school. You have to be informed and aware of what is going on in your community just as you are in your school. Remember that knowledge is power. Read the local newspapers and magazines and watch the local news channels to stay abreast of the issues in your community. Discuss some of the major community issues with your parents and friends to see if their views are similar to yours.

■ Building Relationships

Building relationships in your community is all about how well you get along with people and your attitude toward helping others. How close is your relationship with your neighbors? As part of your leadership development, you need to take steps to get to know people in your community who can help you get things done. Remember that building relationships starts in your neighborhood and extends throughout your community. Use the relationship with your family to make connections to other adults in the community. You can also rely on friends to connect you to their families and local organizations. You will discover that building relationships with people in your community can be a rewarding experience. You will take pride in helping others, which will make you feel good about yourself. You will start to be recognized by others as a community leader.

▌ Organizing Resources

Organizing resources is not always about money or fundraising. Organizing human resources is also an important part of community leadership. It involves your ability to organize people in support of a community issue. It can be about requesting votes for a political decision in your community. For example, school improvements and funding may be controversial in your community, and the need to rally voters for support of the school board can become a focal point.

Organizing people and persuading them to support your position requires a person with a pleasant personality. Some people have a special gift for organizing others. Their personality attracts others who enjoy being around them. They are people on a mission to serve their communities. Your ability to organize resources, including human resources, will enhance your efforts to be a leader in your community.

CHECKPOINT

Being a leader in your community begins with two things. Describe one of them.

Being a leader in your community begins with acquiring knowledge about the issues in your community and building relationships with the people in your neighborhood.

TEACH
Discuss the importance of building relationships with your neighbors. Have students write the names of at least two people in their neighborhood. Beside each name, have them write at least one way that they can build a closer relationship with that person.

Ask students how they think the ability to organize people and persuade them to support a certain position relates to a person's personality and attitude. Can they think of someone in their school or community who is especially skilled at organizing others to support a school or community issue? What kind of personality or attitude does that person have?

ONGOING ASSESSMENT
Use the Checkpoint as an opportunity to conduct ongoing assessment of student comprehension of the lesson material.

© S Meltzer/PhotoLink/Photodisc/Getty Images

Follow **UP**

UNDERSTAND LEADERSHIP CONCEPTS

Circle the best answer for each of the following questions.

1. Your personal plan should
   a. serve as a foundation for leadership development
   b. serve as a guide for leadership development
   c. include a self-evaluation of your strengths and weaknesses
   d. all of the above

2. A focal point in your personal plan should include
   a. your appearance
   b. your hobbies
   c. your attitude
   d. none of the above

THINK *CRITICALLY*

Answer the following questions as completely as possible. If necessary, use a separate sheet of paper.

3. What kind of practical experience would you like to gain? Explain why it is an important part of your personal plan.

Answers will vary based on students' interests.

4. Why is it important to network with others to become a leader in your school and community?

Networking with others provides you with resources to gain knowledge and experience. It also helps you improve your interpersonal and social skills. With this increased knowledge and experience as well as improved interpersonal and social skills, you will be better equipped to become a more effective leader.

5. Describe two major issues in your community. Discuss the importance of these issues with your classmates.

Answers will vary.

ASSESS
Reteach
Have students create a table with the following three column headings: *Gaining Knowledge of the Community*, *Building Relationships*, and *Organizing Resources*. Under each heading, have students list several ways that they can achieve that particular goal.

Enrich
Have students organize a "campaign" to create a more positive attitude among students in your school. As part of the campaign, they might create a "catchy" slogan, make posters, or organize a "positive attitude" student rally.

Close
Ask students to name some ways that they can become better disciplined at putting their actions into words. Some suggestions might include improving time management and organizational skills.

Creating a Sense of Community within Your School

A CARING CLIMATE

The interaction between students and teachers is the basis for creating a sense of community and a caring climate in your school. The **climate** is the physical comfort and positive relationships within your school in which students and teachers can work and learn. The climate is set when students and teachers respect and support everyone, including visitors to the school. There are many benefits of a school that has a positive climate and strong sense of community, including the following:

- Absenteeism is lower because students are excited about learning. They do not want to miss school activities.
- Students' grades are better in a nurturing environment rather than a stressful environment.
- Students and teachers display a sense of pride in and commitment to their school.
- Parents become more involved when their children are excited about school and learning.
- Teachers work as a team. Students are encouraged to model this behavior.
- There are fewer discipline problems because students have a stronger interest in learning.
- Dropout rates are lower because students have a feeling of belonging and ownership.

© Digital Vision/Getty Images

A family just moved into your neighborhood with two students who will be attending your high school. You were excited about meeting new friends, but they made it clear that they were unhappy about moving to a new neighborhood and going to a new school. You tried to share information with them about your school and community, but they seemed to have no interest in what you had to say. They were only interested in talking about their old school and neighborhood. You were very disappointed because you had hoped with your help they would want to get involved in school and community activities.

THINK *CRITICALLY*

What are some ways you could improve communication between you and your new neighbors to make them reconsider getting involved in the school and community?

- Administrators, teachers, students, and parents work together. The environment encourages learning and enjoyment.
- Administrators and teachers know all of the students in their school.
- Teachers and students understand and respect the values of others.

Because of the many benefits of a school with a strong sense of community, administrators, teachers, parents, and students should work to create a caring climate. It requires an effort on everyone's part. Suggestions for creating a caring climate include the following:

- relationship development sessions
- learning contracts between parents, students, and teachers
- involvement of local employers
- a zero-tolerance discipline policy
- focus group sessions
- a one-by-five plan

▮ Relationship Development

Relationship development is a discussion session designed by teachers and students to explore ways to positively relate to each other. The sessions use **vignettes**, short theatrical scenes performed by student-actors. These vignettes include motivating stories of how teachers and students work together to create a sense of community in their school. They show how the pros and cons of a situation can affect the climate in your school.

The relationship development sessions are limited only by your imagination. Try to think "outside the box." Explore ways to show that your school is a caring community that provides a total approach to learning and life. For example, in your relationship development sessions you can explore ways to encourage classmates to become involved in academic, athletic, and social groups, because participation in school activities often leads to commitment and pride. Relationship development sessions will give students a feeling of acceptance and belonging. They show a commitment to creating a strong sense of community.

▮ Learning Contract

The **learning contract** is a written agreement between parents, students, and teachers. It reinforces the learning process. Your parents agree to work with the teacher as an extension of the classroom. They actively supervise your homework assignments and review your work. They set aside quality time to listen to you explain the assignment and the outcome. It is not important that your parents understand the details of your assignment. You need only to discuss the overall concepts of the assignment. The learning contract is not a legal document. It is a positive way to include parents in the learning process. It shows the importance of having parents' support in maintaining higher student achievement.

An example of a learning contract is shown in Figure 4.1. It is usually a one-page document containing several major components, including the following:

- title of lesson
- purpose of the homework assignment
- due date for completion of the assignment
- evidence of discussion of the assignment with parents
- student's comments on the importance of the assignment
- signatures of the student, parent, and teacher

| FIGURE 4.1 | *Learning Contract for a Homework Assignment* |

Title of Lesson: _____
_____

Purpose of Assignment:
(What can you learn from this particular activity?)
_____
_____
_____

Due Date for Completion of Assignment: _____

Evidence of Discussion with Parents:
(a brief description of 50 words)
_____
_____
_____

Student's Comments on Importance of Assignment:
(a statement of 50 words)
_____
_____
_____

Signature of Student: _____ **Date:** _____
Signature of Parent(s): _____ **Date:** _____
                          _____   _____
Signature of Teacher: _____ **Date:** _____

TEACH
Have students work in small groups to create a vignette that demonstrates how various situations can affect the climate of the school either positively or negatively. Have each group share its vignette with the class.

TEACH
Discuss the purpose of a learning contract. Have students review the sample learning contract in Figure 4.1 and discuss the major components. Are there other components that students think should be added to the learning contract? Ask students if they think the use of a learning contract would help them with their school work. Have them explain their answers.

TEACHING STRATEGIES
Attention Deficit Disorder Students
Have students prepare a learning contract for several upcoming homework assignments. Have them take the learning contracts home for their parents to review.

© Russell Illig/Photodisc/Getty Images

Employers' Involvement

Involving local employers in the school curriculum provides a broad learning approach and a sense of community. Employers provide a connection between school and work. Because employers are in touch with the skills needed in the workplace, they can provide valuable information regarding the education and training needed to help students succeed. Involving employers brings a real-world component to education. You will discover that many of the issues that occur in the workplace also apply to the classroom. Common work and school-related issues might include the following:

- **Employer-employee relations** are similar to teacher-student relations. You should discuss this issue with your teacher to determine what is considered appropriate behavior.
- **Appropriate dress for work** is similar to proper attire for school. Your school may not have a dress code, but what you wear on the outside says a lot about who you are on the inside.
- **Customer relations** are similar to your relationships with classmates, particularly if you are in a leadership role. For example, if you work on your school newspaper, you should talk to your classmates and get their input to make sure you are producing a product (newspaper) that is satisfactory. In a sense, your classmates who read the newspaper are your customers.
- **Communicating when you will be late or when you cannot report to work** is similar to communicating with your school when you will be tardy or cannot attend class. Unexcused tardies or absences do not provide a positive image of you. You should notify your school and employer when you cannot attend or will be late and provide an explanation why.

Zero Tolerance Discipline Policies

A school with a sense of community is one in which students and teachers feel safe and secure from danger. Although you sometimes may take discipline for granted, there are times when a zero tolerance discipline policy is necessary. **Zero tolerance** discipline policies are developed to protect schools from acts of violence, drug abuse, weapons, and disruptive behaviors. They help to create a climate where students know what to expect and know that everyone will be treated in the same way. They may be necessary to protect students and teachers while maintaining a positive learning environment.

As a member of the school and community, you should work with your teachers to maintain a safe, positive, and supportive learning environment. For example, you could help establish an extended day or after-school program for those students who want to work to improve their behavior. The entire community benefits when students are involved in positive, supervised learning activities.

 CHECKPOINT

List three issues that are common at both school and work.

Common issues could include employer–employee relations, appropriate dress,

customer relations, and communication of absences.

TEACH
Explain the meaning of the term *zero tolerance*. If your school has a zero tolerance discipline policy, share it with the students.

ONGOING ASSESSMENT
Use the Checkpoint as an opportunity to conduct on-going assessment of student comprehension of the lesson material.

TEACH
Ask students to name some ways that they can create a caring climate in their school.

Discuss the purpose of a focus group. Divide students into small groups, and assign one student in each group to act as the group leader. Have each group address the question "What can we do to have more of a sense of community in our school?"

OTHER STRATEGIES TO CREATE A CARING CLIMATE IN SCHOOL

As a leader in your school, you should look for creative ways to encourage a sense of community. All students need to feel welcome and accepted at school. There are many ways to create a caring climate within your school. Two suggestions include conducting focus groups and using a one-by-five plan.

Focus Groups

A **focus group** is a listening session in the classroom. These sessions involve a small group of seven to ten students. Under the supervision of your teacher, students are encouraged to express their attitudes, experiences, beliefs, feelings, and opinions about an issue or situation. The purpose of the focus group is to listen to students' concerns about issues in their school and community and to develop possible solutions.

© Digital Vision/Getty Images

Your role as the leader of a focus group is to ask your classmates a focusing question and listen to their responses: For example, *"What can we do to have more of a sense of community in our school?"*

In a typical classroom with 25 to 30 students, there can be three focus group sessions going on at the same time. As a group leader, you are responsible for keeping your group on task, taking notes, and sharing the results with your teacher and classmates. The listening and sharing sessions are a wonderful opportunity for you as a leader to hear the voices of the students in your school.

One-by-Five Plan

The one-by-five plan is another strategy for creating a sense of community in your school. The **one-by-five plan** encourages a leader to spend more time with his or her classmates by giving them individualized attention—one minute per day for five consecutive days. The goal is to get to know your classmates slowly rather than rapidly

© Doug Menuez/Photodisc/Getty Images

firing questions at them in passing conversation. For example, after meeting them for the first time, you might share how you got your first name and ask them to do the same. If your classmates do not know how they got their first name, you may challenge them to find out by asking someone in their family. Hopefully, this suggestion will provide a bonding exercise for the student at home and at school to enhance a sense of community.

The one-by-five plan might be done in several mini-interview sessions so that you can spend quality time with each of your classmates. Keep in mind that quality time is not measured in minutes. It is measured in the richness of the conversation and sharing during the session.

The one-by-five plan gives you an opportunity to personally meet and welcome your classmates and to set the tone for a sense of community. It is designed to be a win-win situation for everyone involved.

 CHECKPOINT

Explain the purpose of the one-by-five plan.

The purpose of the one-by-five plan is to meet and learn more about your classmates

by giving them individualized attention—one minute a day for five consecutive days.

Follow UP

UNDERSTAND LEADERSHIP CONCEPTS

Circle the best answer for each of the following questions.

1. **Creating a sense of community and a caring climate in your school**
   a. begins with a focus group
   b. begins with the interaction between students and teachers *(circled)*
   c. begins with a learning contract with parents
   d. none of the above

2. **Relationship development sessions are designed to**
   a. explore ways to positively relate to each other
   b. show how teachers and students can work together
   c. get students to think outside the box
   d. all of the above *(circled)*

THINK CRITICALLY

Answer the following questions as completely as possible. If necessary, use a separate sheet of paper.

3. **What is the role of parents in the learning contract agreement for homework assignments?**

   In the learning contract agreement, parents work with the teacher as an extension of
   the classroom. They actively supervise their student's homework assignments and set
   aside time to listen to the student explain the assignment and the outcome.

4. **Describe two school- or community-related issues that you personally have experienced and would like to discuss in a focus group.**

   Answers will vary.

5. **What is your opinion of zero tolerance discipline policies? Do you think they are a good idea or a bad idea? Explain why.**

   Answers will vary.

ASSESS
Reteach
Have students list the strategies for creating a welcoming and accepting climate.

Enrich
Have students conduct research to locate examples of other schools throughout the country that have achieved success in creating a sense of community in their schools. Have students discuss some of the techniques these schools are using.

Close
Have students create a presentation, including visual aids, that highlights the benefits of a school with a strong sense of community and suggests ways to create a caring climate in your school. Have students share their presentation with groups in your school.

Planning for Servant Leadership

SCHEDULE
Block 45 minutes
Regular 1 class period

FOCUS
Ask students to think about how they feel when they help a person in need or volunteer for a worthy cause. Point out that many worthwhile organizations could not survive without the help of volunteers.

© Mel Curtis/Photodisc/Getty Images

TEACH
Define the term *servant leadership*. Ask students to name some volunteer opportunities in their school or community.

WHAT IS SERVANT LEADERSHIP?

Are you a community volunteer? More importantly, do you have a commitment for service to others? These questions should be considered if you are planning to become a servant leader. **Servant leadership** involves making a personal commitment to serve the needs of others. Keep in mind that the power of persuasion is very important to a servant leader. To become a servant leader, you will have to deal with social woes, social responsibilities, and qualities of the heart and head.

Social Woes

Some *social woes* or social problems that currently exist in schools might prevent you and your classmates from enjoying a safe and supporting learning environment. These problems are challenging to teachers and administrators as well as to students interested in servant leadership. They may include the following:

- Bullying
- Latch-key children
- Parental custody disputes
- Social rejection
- Eating disorders
- Depression
- Gang activity
- Teen pregnancy
- Teen drinking and substance abuse
- Physical and emotional abuse

A major challenge for you and your classmates is to work with your teachers and administrators to eliminate some of the social woes that face your school and community. For example, you might consider joining the fight against teenage drinking and substance abuse by organizing a Students Against Destructive Decisions organization (SADD) if one does not already exist. If it does exist, then work with the group as well as with other existing organizations, such as Mothers Against Drunk Driving (MADD).

A Habitat for Humanity chapter has started in your community with a call for volunteers. You and two of your friends decide to participate even though you do not have any skills in residential construction. All of you are excited about building a house. However, since neither you nor your friends have experience with this type of work, the construction supervisor has asked all three of you to work with the laborers or non-skilled persons who assist the more highly skilled construction crew. This means your involvement in the actual construction of the house will be more limited than you had hoped. Your two friends are disappointed and want to leave the site.

THINK *CRITICALLY*

How will you react to your friends' decision to leave the site? If they decide to quit, will you leave as well? How can you turn this into a positive experience for all?

Social woes in your community can be just as challenging as those in your school. In fact, problems in your school are often a sign of problems in your community. They may include poverty and other economic problems for some students and their families. Some of your classmates may live in poor housing or shelters. Others may come to school unprepared to learn because of difficult family issues. These problems often disrupt the learning process. Your role, as a servant leader, is not to look down on students with social woes but to work with your teacher and classmates to make everyone feel accepted, respected, and supported.

Social Responsibility

Social responsibility is the duty to respond in positive ways to the needs you see around you. You have a responsibility to your school, community, society, and other people, including yourself. Your understanding of social responsibility will fuel your desire to help others.

Some of your classmates have the desire to help others, and some do not for various reasons. Sharing your experiences of helping others in need will encourage others to do the same. Your greatest joy may occur when you reach out to help someone and they respond with heartfelt appreciation.

The personal satisfaction you receive from helping others is one of the benefits of social responsibility. Providing a role model is another benefit. Some of your classmates may think that one person cannot possibly make a difference in your school or community. Your positive behavior serves as a role model and demonstrates to those in doubt that they can make a difference in the lives of others.

Responding to the needs of your school and community can be demonstrated through volunteering. There are many volunteering opportunities, including the following:

TEACH
Discuss the list of social problems. Ask students how they think these problems affect the climate in their school.

Ask students to name ways that they can help eliminate some of these social problems in their school or community.

BUILDING COMMUNITIES
Have students name some of the benefits of working on a Habitat for Humanity house. Answers may include helping with a worthwhile community project, learning new skills, and making new friends.

Think Critically Answers
Answers will vary. You might point out to your friends that you all made a commitment to the project. It can become a positive experience as you learn new skills and make new friends.

TEACH
Ask students to think of a time when they reached out to help someone in need. Did they view it as a duty or responsibility? How did it make them feel?

- **Clean-up campaigns**—Adopt a road or street in your neighborhood and pick up litter.
- **Summer camp counselor**—Share your knowledge and advice with elementary and middle-school students.
- **Community conservation projects**—Work with your local parks and recreation department to beautify your community.
- **Big Brothers/Big Sisters**—Serve as a peer-mentor, role model, and friend to an underprivileged child.
- **Homeless shelters**—Work in a soup kitchen to feed the homeless.
- **Retirement or nursing homes**—Chat with elderly residents or just listen to them talk about the "good old days."

Look around your neighborhood for other volunteering opportunities. Your school may be able to provide you with a list of various organizations that need the help of volunteers.

Qualities of the Heart and Head

Qualities of the heart relate to your passion, creativity, and spirit. On the other hand, qualities of the head relate to gaining and sharing knowledge. Your role as an effective servant leader is to combine qualities of both the heart and head.

Your success as a servant leader may depend on your ability to understand issues and balance your response with actions from your heart and your head. In other words, your heart and head should be in agreement with your response to a given situation. Sometimes, your response may be misinterpreted by others. In these cases, your heart may be in the right place, but you did not use your head to think about your actions before responding.

Your focus should always be on doing the right thing so that others will know where your heart is even though they may not understand where your head is on a given issue. Doing the right thing does not mean that you will always do everything right, but at least others will recognize your heartfelt qualities. Connecting with the hearts of your classmates can provide lifelong friendships and relationships.

Describe a major challenge for someone planning to become a servant leader.

Major challenges for someone planning to become a servant leader are dealing with social woes, social responsibilities, and qualities of the heart and head.

COMPONENTS OF SERVANT LEADERSHIP

The components of servant leadership have been around for many years. The results continue to be effective for individuals planning for this style of leadership. Field experience and peer evaluation are two methods that you and your classmates should consider to increase your ability as a servant leader.

Field Experience

A **field experience** allows you to gain practical experience by working in a service organization. A field experience for servant leadership could include working in a mission field or volunteering as a summer camp counselor to help at-risk children. You might even consider volunteering for a humanity service project with your local Red Cross chapter. You could provide assistance in its blood drive or food distribution in your community.

The duration of your field experience can vary, but a minimum amount of time should be determined before volunteering. You might consider serving a minimum of two hours per session three times a week. Keeping a journal of your experience should be a requirement. This enables you to reflect upon and learn from your experiences.

© Doug Menuez/Photodisc/Getty Images

> "Life is a place of service. Joy can be real only if people look upon their life as a service and have a definite object in life outside themselves and their personal happiness."
> —*Leo Tolstoy*

TEACH
Ask students to read the quotation and reflect on its meaning. Do they agree with Tolstoy? Why or why not?

ONGOING ASSESSMENT
Use the Checkpoint as an opportunity to conduct ongoing assessment of student comprehension of the lesson material.

TEACH
Point out that in order to become effective servant leaders, students need to gain practical experience and solicit constructive feedback to help them improve leadership skills.

Ask students to name some of the benefits they think could be gained from field experience. Have several students who have had practical experience as a volunteer share their experiences with the class.

TEACHING STRATEGIES
Tactile Learners
Have students create a bulletin board display of information about various volunteer opportunities that provide field experience. Examples might include organizations such as Habitat for Humanity, the American Red Cross, the Salvation Army, or a local homeless shelter.

Many schools now require students to participate in volunteer or community activities. Students must accumulate a certain number of service hours as part of their graduation requirements. Field experience would be a good way to develop leadership skills while meeting those graduation requirements. In addition, the experience you gain and the people you meet while completing your field experience can benefit you beyond high school as you strive to meet your personal and career goals.

Peer Evaluation

Constructive feedback from your classmates or peers concerning your leadership performance is referred to as **peer evaluation**. Observations and comments from your peers can help you make improvements to develop as a successful servant leader. The peer evaluation process may be formal, with written guidelines to follow. It may also be completed informally through casual conversation with classmates.

A creative way to evaluate your leadership performance is with a *360–degree feedback appraisal,* which represents the circle of individuals who have observed and experienced your leadership abilities. Several individuals, such as teachers, administrators, coaches, classmates, and others, will provide feedback on your performance as a leader. The 360-degree feedback appraisal may touch upon your ability to communicate clearly with others and your responsiveness to their questions and concerns.

CHECKPOINT

Explain the importance of a field experience as a component of servant leadership.

Field experience is a major component of servant leadership. It allows you to gain valuable practical experience by volunteering with a non-profit organization.

© Jeff Maloney/Photodisc/Getty Images

Follow UP

UNDERSTAND LEADERSHIP CONCEPTS

Circle the best answer for each of the following questions.

1. Social woes in schools are challenging and may include
a. parental custody disputes
b. eating disorders
c. teen drinking and substance abuse
(d.) all of the above

2. The highest priority of a servant leader is to
a. make lots of money
(b.) provide service to others
c. speak out against social rejection
d. none of the above

THINK *CRITICALLY*

Answer the following questions as completely as possible. If necessary, use a separate sheet of paper.

3. Describe three problems or social woes that currently exist in your school.

Answers will vary but may include bullying, latch-key children, parental custody

disputes, social rejection, eating disorders, depression, gang activity, teen pregnancy,

teen drinking and substance abuse, and physical and emotional abuse.

4. Explain the connection between social responsibility and servant leadership.

Social responsibility is a duty to respond to the needs of others at school and in your

community. Servant leadership also considers it a high priority to serve the needs of

others.

5. How can peer evaluations and 360-degree feedback appraisals help you develop as a servant leader?

Through peer evaluation and 360-degree feedback appraisal, you will receive

constructive feedback on your leadership performance that will help you make

improvements in your leadership skills.

Chapter Assessment

TEACHING RESOURCES
ExamView® CD, Ch. 4

a. climate
b. field experience
c. focus group
d. learning contract
e. networking
f. one-by-five plan
g. peer evaluation
h. personal plan
i. practical experience
j. relationship development
k. servant leadership
l. social responsibility
m. vignettes
n. zero tolerance

REVIEW *LEADERSHIP CONCEPTS*

Write the letter of the term that matches each definition. Some terms will not be used.

__i__ 1. Increasing knowledge and skills by applying them to your areas of interest

__a__ 2. Physical comfort and positive relationships within your school

__m__ 3. Short theatrical scenes performed by student-actors about an issue

__d__ 4. A written agreement to reinforce the learning process

__n__ 5. Discipline policies to protect schools from acts of violence and disruptive behaviors

__c__ 6. A listening session conducted by a small group of students

__k__ 7. A commitment to serve the needs of others

__l__ 8. A duty to respond to the needs of others

__e__ 9. Interacting with others and developing beneficial relationships

__g__ 10. Constructive feedback from classmates

Circle the best answer.

11. Improving your interpersonal and social skills through interaction with others is part of
    a. developing a learning contract
    b. being a servant leader
    (c.) networking with others
    d. none of the above

12. Being a leader in your community begins with
    a. your fundraising efforts
    b. an evaluation of your personal needs
    c. both a and b
    (d.) none of the above

13. A strategy for spending more time with your classmates by giving them individualized attention is called a
    a. focus group
    (b.) one-by-five plan
    c. personal plan
    d. vignette

14. A field experience
    a. could include volunteering
    b. should include keeping a journal
    c. should have a designated minimum amount of time assigned to it
    (d.) all of the above

ASSESS

Reteach
Have students write several quiz questions for each lesson in the chapter. Then have students trade papers with a classmate and answer the questions. Partners should check each other's answers for accuracy.

Enrich
To help students develop a greater sense of community and get to know their classmates better, have them create a visual display that includes photos, artwork, and items that represent all the students and cultures in your class.

CLOSE

Have students review the personal plan that they began developing at the beginning of the chapter. Have them make any changes or additions to the plan that they think will help them further develop their leadership skills.

15. *What are the advantages of the one-by-five plan as a strategy to demonstrate that your school has a sense of community?*

The goal of the one-by-five plan is to become better acquainted with your classmates by spending time with them individually over five consecutive days. The one-by-five plan helps to create a bond among students that enhances the sense of community in school.

16. *How can gaining practical experience help you develop as a leader?*

Gaining practical experience can help you develop as a leader by exposing you to a variety of situations with many different types of people. It helps you learn new skills as well as develop your interpersonal, communication, and organizational skills.

17. *What suggestions would you make to create a welcoming and caring climate in your school?*

Answers will vary but may include relationship development sessions, learning contracts, involvement of local employers, a zero-tolerance discipline policy, focus group sessions, and a one-by-five plan.

18. *What are five benefits of a school with a strong sense of community?*

A school with a strong sense of community has lower absenteeism, better student grades, a sense of school pride, more parental involvement, teamwork among teachers, fewer discipline problems, lower dropout rates, a cooperative environment, and an understanding and respect for the values of others.

19. *What suggestions can you give to a classmate to change his or her negative attitude to a positive one?*

Answers will vary but may include developing better communication skills and working to improve self-image.

20. **Problem Solving**   *The climate in your school is rather "chilly" toward students from other cultures. You have accepted the challenge to create a more welcoming environment. Analyze the situation and then describe the process you will use to change the climate into a caring community.*

Answers will vary but may include implementing a one-by-five plan to help students

get to know each other better. Relationship development sessions could also be used to

give the students from other cultures a feeling of acceptance and belonging.

21. **Research**   *Throughout the United States, there are many excellent volunteer programs. Use the Internet to find three of the best ones. Select the program that interests you most and explain why.*

Answers will vary.

22. **Communication**   *You have been selected as the student speaker for your high school graduation. Prepare a speech to be presented to the graduating class, faculty, parents, and others. Your speech should focus on the value of servant leadership in your community.*

Answers will vary.

23. **Technology**   *Describe how you could use technology to gain knowledge about your community and help build relationships and organize resources to improve your community.*

Answers will vary but may include conducting research on the Internet to learn more

about your community and the non-profit agencies or organizations within your

community that are seeking volunteers.

LEARNING TO LEAD

FOCUS

Participate in student organization conferences.

DESCRIPTION

As an active member of a career and technical student organization, you have many opportunities to interact with other members, student leaders, and adults who share your interests and career goals. One of the most important and exciting experiences you can have as a member is participating in a student organization conference. Each student organization offers several regional, statewide, and national conferences each year. These conferences are devoted to the personal, career, and leadership development of the members. Conferences provide exciting opportunities to meet people from outside your own school and community and learn how to interact professionally and socially. You will return from the conference with creative ideas, improved confidence and enthusiasm, new friendships, and an increased commitment to your leadership development.

ACTIVITIES

1. *Review your student organization's national and state web sites and member publications. Prepare a table that lists all regional, state, and national conferences, dates and location for each conference for this school year, and the purpose of each conference.*

2. *Obtain and watch a video, CD, or other audiovisual presentation that shows highlights of a recent student organization conference.*

3. *Review and prepare a written summary of membership, code of conduct, and dress code requirements for a regional, state, or national conference.*

4. *Attend a local student organization informational meeting on an upcoming conference.*

SHARE YOUR RESULTS

1. *For each upcoming student organization conference, provide the following:*
   - *A description of what you need to do to qualify for the conference*
   - *A specific benefit of participating in the conference*
   - *One career development activity, one leadership development activity, and one social activity in which you would participate if you attend*
2. *Identify an upcoming student organization conference that you plan to attend. Working with other students who also plan to attend the same conference, prepare a 3- to 5-minute presentation to inform and recruit students from your local chapter to attend. Include at least one printed information sheet and several visuals (computer slides, posters, banners). After practicing and receiving your adviser's approval, deliver the presentation at a chapter meeting.*

ACCEPTING THE
CHALLENGE
Case Study 4
Point out to students that
because Ian had a strong
support system in his parents, teachers, and friends,
he was able to carry out his
personal plan. Now he is
supporting his students to
help them succeed in car-
rying out their own personal plans. Do they consider
Ian a good example of a
servant leader? Why or
why not?

ACCEPTING THE CHALLENGE

CASE STUDY 4—A SUPPORT SYSTEM

As you learned in the What Would You Do? *opening scenario, Ian developed a personal plan for leadership development early in his school years. Encouraged by his parents and teachers, he decided to become a role model and mentor for others. He continued to carry out his plan after graduating from high school. While in college, he and a friend started a ''Save the Children Foundation'' after visiting Zimbabwe. Ian's goal was to seek donations of books and reading materials for local libraries in Zimbabwe's rural communities. He wanted to help the children living in poverty realize their dreams and aspirations.*

Upon graduation from college, Ian became a teacher at an alternative school for at-risk students. Students in this school were at risk socially and/or academically at their traditional high schools and were enrolled in the alternative school as a last chance placement for their future success. Because Ian knew the importance of having a support system consisting of family, friends, and teachers, he became active in his students' personal lives and in the communities outside of school. He attended their sports activities, musical and art presentations, family weddings, and, unfortunately, family funerals. He made home visits to encourage parents to become involved in their children's school functions. It was important to Ian for his students to see the connection between family, school, and community. He knew that his students needed a support system to help them carry out their own personal plans and succeed in life.

THINK CRITICALLY

1. *How do you think Ian's students felt about him showing support in their personal and community activities? How would you feel if one of your teachers showed up at some of your outside school activities?*

Answers will vary. Ian's support for his students' personal and community activities

helped create a caring climate and enjoyable learning environment. His actions

demonstrated that he valued and respected each of his students.

2. *Reflecting on the personal goals you have set will help you create your personal plan. In what ways do you think your family, friends, teachers, and community can support you in achieving one or more of those goals?*

Answers will vary. Family, friends, teachers, and community can support you by

providing opportunities for practical experience and networking. They can also offer

constructive feedback in the form of peer evaluations and 360-degree feedback

appraisals to help you improve your skills.

APPLY *WHAT YOU HAVE LEARNED–Assess Your Needs*

DIRECTIONS: *To focus on the importance of having support from your family, friends, teachers, or community, respond to the Personal Needs Assessment below or on your Student Activity CD. Rate yourself by underlining either "TRUE" or "FALSE" for each statement. Then add up the number of TRUE answers and the number of FALSE answers.*

PERSONAL NEEDS ASSESSMENT

I prefer spending my free time alone and not in the company of others.	TRUE	FALSE
I do not like sharing my personal possessions (i.e., books, CDs, clothes, etc.) with others.	TRUE	FALSE
I prefer spending my free time with family or friends.	TRUE	FALSE
I prefer eating my lunch alone rather than with a large group of people.	TRUE	FALSE
I prefer not to be interrupted for any reason when I'm doing my homework.	TRUE	FALSE
I prefer staying at home when my family plans outings.	TRUE	FALSE
I like taking vacations with my family.	TRUE	FALSE
I prefer listening instead of participating by talking and providing input when in a group setting.	TRUE	FALSE
I am always willing to help my friends when they ask.	TRUE	FALSE
I don't mind asking and depending on others for help when I need it.	TRUE	FALSE
I prefer handling a task on my own even if I know I could get help.	TRUE	FALSE
I do not need a support system to help me achieve my goals.	TRUE	FALSE
I believe my family, friends, and teachers care about me and would gladly support me in my personal plan.	TRUE	FALSE

TOTAL _____ _____

If you have more TRUE answers, you may be more independent and like doing things on your own. You may not feel the need for a support system. However, a strong support system is important for everyone. Your supporters can offer encouragement and advice to help keep you focused on your personal plan. If you have more FALSE answers, you are probably outgoing and like spending time with others. Although you most likely have a great support system of family, friends, teachers, and others, there is always room to add more supporters.

On the lines below or on the Student Activity CD, create a SMART goal (including a completion date) that will help you build or expand your support system. Enter the goal in a monthly calendar (on the CD or your own). Then enter your thoughts, ideas, and discussions related to your goal in a journal (on the CD or your own) to help you plan and track your progress. Select a goal-setting partner to help you achieve your goal.

_____

_____

_____

ACCEPTING THE CHALLENGE
Apply What You Have Learned—Assess Your Needs

Note that students can complete this part of the *Accepting the Challenge* activity in the book or on the Student CD. Instructions are provided on the CD.

Instruct students to write a SMART goal (including a completion date) that will help them build or expand their support system. Have them enter their goal on a monthly calendar. Students can use the monthly calendar on the Student Activity CD or their own calendar. Explain to students that they may also use weekly calendar pages (on the Student CD or their own calendar) to plan activities and tasks that will help them achieve their goals. Finally, direct students to use a journal (on the Student Activity CD or their own) to track and evaluate their progress in achieving their goal.

A goal-setting partner can add an element of accountability and can offer positive feedback to help students stay on track to achieve their goals.

Students should be given the opportunity to reflect on the progress they have made toward achieving their goal. To do this, students can complete the *Evaluate Your Progress* activity on the Student Activity CD. Stress to students that it is important to complete this activity on the original target completion date even if they have not met their goal at that time.

Developing and Demonstrating Character

© Photodisc/Getty Images

5.1	*Your Path to Character*
5.2	*How You Demonstrate Character*
5.3	*A Path to Personal Improvement*

What would **YOU** do?

SENECA STANDS UP

Seneca grew angrier with each step he took toward his afternoon calculus class. He knew if he ran into Jerome there would be an argument. His friends, Maria and Paulie, could see Seneca's anger, and they understood his feelings. But they also did not want the problem to get bigger than it already was.

While walking back from lunch with his friends earlier in the day, Seneca had run into Alex in the school courtyard. He had first met Alex at the freshman orientation session he and other Student Council members attended in July prior to the start of the school year. Alex was small for his age and used a wheelchair due to a childhood illness. Seneca helped Alex participate in several of the orientation activities. He found Alex to be friendly, but he was a little shy. On the first day of the school year, Seneca met Alex and showed him around the school. When he saw that Alex had a laptop computer that he used for his class work, Seneca encouraged him to get involved in the computer club.

When Seneca saw Alex sitting in the school courtyard, he could see that Alex was upset. Alex told Seneca that Jerome regularly teased him, but today it went further. Jerome told Alex that if he came to the lunch room, Jerome and his friends would embarrass him in front of everyone. To avoid any problems, Alex did not go to lunch. Seneca knew that Jerome was immature. He seemed to enjoy picking on other students who would not fight back. Seneca was tired of that type of behavior, especially when it meant that Alex could not enjoy his lunch break. Seneca felt that the only way to get Jerome's attention was to threaten him physically.

Maria and Paulie tried to calm Seneca down. "Even though you are doing it for the right reasons, you will only get into trouble if you start a fight with Jerome," said Paulie. "You've done a lot for this school. Other students look up to you." Marie pleaded, "Don't throw all that away by losing your temper and breaking the rules. If we work together, we can think of a way to support Alex and stop Jerome's teasing."

THINK *CRITICALLY*

1. Does anger affect the way you attempt to solve problems? How can you channel anger into positive rather than negative actions?

2. What are some positive ways Seneca and his friends could help Alex and change Jerome's behavior?

TEACHING RESOURCES
Instructor's Resource CD
Lesson Plans, Ch. 5
PowerPoint Slides, Ch. 5

Student Activity CD, Ch. 5

thomsonedu.com/school/leading
Crossword Puzzle, Ch. 5
Flash Cards, Ch. 5

Exam*View*® CD, Ch. 5

CHAPTER OVERVIEW
Chapter 5 discusses how to develop and demonstrate character.

Lesson 5.1
Explains how character begins to develop in children and the relationship between values and behavior.

Lesson 5.2
Describes how character is demonstrated in relationships with others.

Lesson 5.3
Describes how to plan for personal improvement and character development.

WHAT WOULD YOU DO?
Ask students to think of a time when they or someone they know may have broken a rule for what they thought was a good reason. What was the result?

Think Critically Answers
1. Answers will vary.
2. Answers will vary. Seneca and his friends could speak privately to Jerome. They could also make sure Alex has friends to accompany him to the lunchroom each day. They should alert an administrator, teacher, or counselor of the problem.

Your Path to Character

- Explain how children develop an understanding of positive and negative behavior.
- Identify the sources of values and the relationship between values and behavior.

- personality
- media
- belief

SCHEDULE
Block 45 minutes
Regular 1 class period

FOCUS
Have students think about their behavior. Do they always act in a way that is consistent with their values and beliefs? Are there things about themselves that they would like to change?

TEACH
Ask students if they can usually predict how their best friends will act in certain situations. Why do they think they are or are not able to accurately predict this behavior? Explain that while a person's character may predict how he or she will act, character continues to develop and change until adulthood.

Ask how many students have taken care of a baby or young child, perhaps as a babysitter for a younger sibling or neighbor. What behaviors did they notice in the child? How did the child's personality develop and change in response to the people around him or her?

THE BEGINNING OF CHARACTER

People are born neither good nor bad. Yet over time, every individual develops character. That character is a tendency to act in particular ways. As you get to know people well, you can reasonably predict how they will act in certain situations. A person's character can result in more negative than positive actions or in more positive than negative actions. However, it is not likely that every person will be consistently good or bad. A person's character continues to change and develop. New experiences and circumstances affect a person's actions and character.

People change from the time when they are infants with no specific character traits until as adults they have a well-developed character that is generally consistent and predictable. As you examine how character develops, it may help you understand your current character and what you can do to develop into the person you want to be.

© PhotoLink/Photodisc/Getty Images

Babies and Behavior

From the first weeks and months of life, infants begin to recognize the people who regularly care for, hold, feed, and comfort them and provide for their security and safety. They also start to understand that their actions can affect how their caretaker treats them. If the baby smiles, people will lean over, smile, and talk to the baby. If the baby cries, someone will come to pick up, hold, and hug the baby, change a diaper, or provide food.

Unless there are physical problems, infants develop somewhat constant behavior within the first year in response to the actions of caretakers. They begin to understand whether positive or negative behavior receives the most attention. They begin to behave in ways that get the results they want. A beginning personality starts to take shape. **Personality** is the total set of emotions, traits, and behaviors that makes each person unique. If you have regular contact with a new baby, you can see firsthand how behavior changes and personality develops. The actions and responses of the people closest to the baby play an important role in shaping that personality.

© PhotoLink/Photodisc/Getty Images

During the first several years of a baby's life, development occurs rapidly. Within the first year, memory begins to form. The baby starts to gain control of arms and legs and pay attention to language. By holding objects or pushing them away, the baby can demonstrate likes and dislikes. The baby will reach toward someone to be picked up or will squirm to be put down. Words like "yes" and "no" start to have meaning and will at least get the baby's attention if not always change the behavior. Getting rewarded through smiles, praise, food, and attention will usually result in positive actions. Punishments in the form of frowning, using negative words, taking away a favorite toy, or ignoring the baby will usually result in crying or other negative behavior.

Learning Right and Wrong

A child develops physically, mentally, and emotionally during the preschool years of ages 1 through 5. Youngsters gain greater control over their behavior and recognize that behavior can influence the actions of others. Language skills improve, and children see that the right choice of words can get positive or negative reactions from others.

Young children seek the approval of those who are important to them. Parents, family members, and others with whom they have

TEACH
Have students read the quote from Mr. Rogers. Then have them discuss the meaning of the expression "walk the talk." Ask students why they think it is important to set a good example (walk the talk) when teaching children right from wrong.

"
I doubt that we can ever successfully impose values on our children by threat, guilt, or punishment. But I do believe they can be built on trust, example, talk, and caring.
—*Mr. Rogers, children's TV personality*
"

TEACH
Ask students to reflect on their behavior when they were young children. Whose approval did they seek the most (parent, grandparent, sibling)? How did that person's actions and words shape the students' behavior?

Have students think about the last time they may have broken a rule that their parents or another adult imposed on them. Why did they break the rule? What reward did they feel they received (attention, approval of peers, etc.)?

TEACHING STRATEGIES
Limited English Proficiency Students
Ask students to compile a list of rules that have been established by their parents or guardians. Have LEP students share some of their rules with the class and compare them to the rules in families of other cultures. How are they similar? How are they different?

© PhotoLink/Photodisc/Getty Images

regular contact influence young people by their words and actions. At first, children do not really understand right and wrong. They just respond the way they believe those in authority want them to. They also rely on their memory of what happened in the past when they acted in a particular way. "No" and "Don't do that" communicate disapproval. "Atta boy" and "You're a good girl" let the child know that he or she did the right thing.

Do you remember all of the times as a young child you sought the approval of Mom, Grandpa, or big brother? "Watch me," "I picked up all my toys," and "I remembered to brush my teeth" were efforts to get the attention and approval of people who were important to you. If they disapproved of something you did, you felt bad and tried to find a way to change their opinion of you. Your beliefs about right and wrong as well as your good and bad behavior were shaped by their actions and words.

The Meaning of Rules

Children begin to learn at an early age that rules guide behavior. At first, there are simple rules. *You must be in bed by 7 p.m. You can't go out to play until you have finished your meal. Don't go near a hot stove.* Young children don't question the rules. They have learned that consequences, including rewards and punishments, are attached to most rules. If young children do not follow the rules, it is usually because they forgot or do not recognize that a particular rule applies to the situation they are in. They also may not follow the rules if no consequences are attached to the rules or the consequences are not clear.

As children get older, their views of rules begin to change. They recognize that rules are not as simple as they once believed. They also recognize that rules are not always applied in the same way and that consequences may change. Children begin to express independence. They want to show their control over some situations. They may be willing to go against a rule just to show that they can do it. The reward of violating the rule and showing that they are in control may seem better than the punishment they may suffer as a result of breaking the rule.

There is no longer just a small group of adults to whom the youngster looks for support. Friends, brothers, sisters, and other young people whom the youngster looks up to and wants to impress become more important. Behavior may be guided more by a desire for attention and approval from these people than from the adults who make the rules.

A Broader Set of Influences

As you get older, your family and close friends still provide the greatest influence on your beliefs and behavior. However, you begin to meet more people. You have a wider range of experiences and are exposed to the ideas and beliefs of other people. Those experiences may include attending a daycare center or preschool, participating in youth clubs and sports teams, and taking part in religious and spiritual development. Each experience introduces you to new ideas, principles, and beliefs as well as to more adult influences, including teachers, coaches, and religious leaders.

In addition to your expanding participation in groups and organizations outside your home, you are also increasingly exposed to a variety of popular media. **Media** are the channels of communication in a society. They include radio, television, music, movies, the Internet, and even more traditional forms such as books, newspapers, and magazines. Some media reinforce the beliefs and values of the people who have been your most important influences. However, media also introduce you to new ideas, beliefs, and values that may conflict with your current views.

© Cohen/Ostrow/Digital Vision/Getty Images

As your experiences and contacts expand, you may see other people who appear to have interesting and exciting lives, different from your own. They may be young people who are a bit older than you but who are leaders in groups or activities with which you identify or to which you want to belong. You may also be attracted to national or international celebrities, such as entertainers, athletes, or others receiving media attention. Those people may influence the way you dress, talk, and act even if your parents object. Those actions and influences may be short-lived, or they may result in long-term changes in your behavior and even some of your beliefs. At the time, however, they are very important to you.

From infancy to the teenage years, many people and experiences influence the development of character, as shown in Figure 5.1. Young people experience and experiment, listen to others and view their behavior, and make decisions about the beliefs and values that influence the way they will act. Character is not yet fully developed and is

TEACH
Ask students how much time they spend each day watching television, listening to popular music, or surfing the Internet. How much influence do they think these media have on their beliefs and values?

TEACHING STRATEGIES
Auditory Learners
Have students brainstorm a list of the people and things that influence their values and beliefs as well as the way they dress, talk, and act. The list may include family, friends, teachers, coaches, and other adults in leadership roles as well as entertainers, athletes, movies, music, the Internet, and other forms of media. Discuss the positive and negative effects that each person or thing can have on beliefs and behavior.

FIGURE 5.1   *Influences on Your Character*

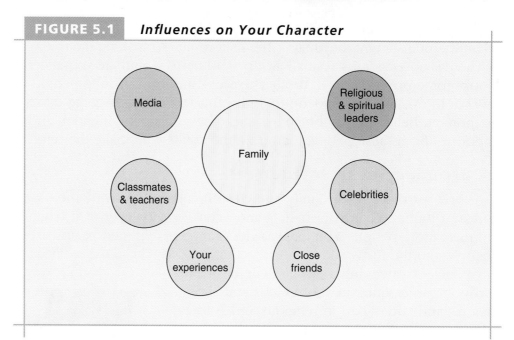

usually still not good or bad. But it is beginning to shape each person's personality. Other people will begin to make judgments about the language, decisions, and actions of another person and decide whether the person is someone they trust, respect, and want as a friend.

 CHECKPOINT

Are infants born with character? Why or why not?

Infants are born with no specific character traits. Character is a tendency to act in

particular ways, and it develops in individuals over time as they grow and mature.

BELIEFS, VALUES, AND BEHAVIOR

As you have gone from being an infant to becoming a teenager, you have gone through a lot of changes that have shaped your personality and character. You have assumed more individual responsibility for your decisions and actions. Your character has begun to take form based on the people with which you most closely identify, your positive and negative experiences, your developing self-image, and how you want others to view you.

More complex factors are now shaping your character. Much of your daily behavior is being guided by beliefs and values. A **belief** is something you accept as true. Important beliefs that guide actions become your *values*. However, those beliefs and values are not always obvious and will continue to strengthen and even change as you get older.

▌ What Are Your Values?

By the time you are a teenager, you have values that influence your decisions and actions. Values are strongly held beliefs that guide your actions. Values develop from the principles and beliefs expressed by the people who have had the greatest influence on you. Values also come from the knowledge you have developed. That knowledge comes from your experience and from reading, listening, studying, and thinking. It is presented by people, such as your parents, teachers, and organization leaders. It also comes from media, such as books, music, and movies.

Values are not always easy to identify. If you had to list the three most important values that shape your decisions and actions, what would they be? You probably can recall some important values that have been passed on to you by parents and grandparents. *Respect your elders. If you are going to do it, do it right. Be considerate of the feelings of others. It is better to give than to receive.*

Other values come from religious or spiritual development. Many of the world's religions have similar statements of values. For example, the well-known Golden Rule states, "Treat others as you want to be treated." The Golden Rule is consistent with values expressed in several major religions:

Hinduism	"Do naught unto others which would cause you pain if done to you." (Mahabharata 5:1517)
Confucianism	"What you do not want others to do to you, do not do to others." (Confucius)
Christianity	"Do to others as you would have them do to you." (Luke 6:31)
Islam	"No one of you is a believer until he desires for his brother that which he desires for himself." (Sunnah)
Judaism	"What is hateful to you, do not to your fellow man. This is the law: all the rest is commentary." (Talmud, Shabbat 31a)

Finally, your values are shaped by your experiences. If you have positive interactions with people from a variety of cultures and backgrounds, you will learn to respect and value those differences. Successful participation in athletics will increase your value of personal health and fitness and the importance of teamwork and competition. Involvement in drama, music, and art will cause you to value creativity, self-expression, and self-confidence. As you progress through school and earn good grades, you will value the effort needed to succeed academically and the benefits of earning a high school diploma and continuing on to higher education.

All people do not have the same experiences, or their experiences are not as positive. This results in different sets of values about individual differences, healthy lifestyles, teamwork, and academic success.

▌ Values versus Behavior

Your *behavior* involves the actions you take in a particular situation. As values become a greater part of your personality, those values will guide most of your important decisions and behavior. But values are

TEACH
Discuss the Golden Rule and how it is expressed in most major religions. Ask students to name some other important values that have been passed on to them by their parents or grandparents. (Examples may include values dealing with honesty, forgiveness, generosity, compassion, etc.)

TEACHING STRATEGIES
Print Learners
Have students list the three most important values that they feel influence their decisions and their behavior. What experiences can they identify that have shaped their values? (For example, experiencing early success in school may have helped shape a student's value of education and achieving good grades.)

Often friends influence the actions and behaviors of each other. That influence can cause you to do something you otherwise would not do. However, it can also keep you from doing something you might later regret. Work as a team to identify situations in which the actions of friends had a positive or negative influence on other people in a group.

Then discuss what happened in each situation that changed the behavior in either a positive or negative way.

THINK *CRITICALLY*

What are some things friends can do for each other when they see that an action or behavior will likely have negative consequences?

TEACH
Have students think of an action they may have taken that they later regretted. Have them reflect on why they chose that action at the time. Ask them what they would do differently now that they have had time to reflect on their actions.

A TEAM EFFORT
Point out to students that often, people are too close to a situation to clearly see the consequences of their actions. Friends who have similar values can help each other avoid making poor decisions if they look out for each other.

Think Critically Answer
Answers will vary.

ONGOING ASSESSMENT
Use the Checkpoint as an opportunity to conduct ongoing assessment of student comprehension of the lesson material.

strongly held beliefs, not actions. Your day-to-day behavior may not always match your values.

Can you recall an action you took that you later regretted? Maybe it was something that embarrassed you, hurt someone's feelings, or caused your parents to believe they could not trust you. When you think about that inappropriate behavior, you can remember that it seemed like the right thing to do at the time. It might have seemed exciting or fun. It might have been designed to get attention or impress others. As you think back and consider the results, you can now see that the behavior does not really reflect your values.

If you could always see the consequences of your behavior, you might do things differently. If you always had the chance to consider how your values related to possible actions, your behavior would more closely match your values. However, you often have to make a decision and act quickly without considering the consequences. You may be influenced by things that seem more important at the time than your values. They may cause you to act in ways that result in problems.

Your actions may not always be consistent with your beliefs and values. However, if your values are strong and you are committed to good character, you learn from those mistakes. You apologize to those whom you have harmed, find ways to make up for problems you have caused, and make sure you do not repeat the same negative behavior.

You may believe that a few inappropriate actions really do not make a difference. But your character develops based on your experiences. The views others have of you come from their experiences with you and the ways they are affected by your actions. Inappropriate behavior over time will shape your beliefs and values just as positive actions will reinforce and strengthen your values.

CHECKPOINT

Why do behaviors not always match values?

People often make decisions and act quickly without considering the consequences.

They may be influenced at the time by things that seem more important than values.

Follow UP

UNDERSTAND LEADERSHIP CONCEPTS

Circle the best answer for each of the following questions.

1. **Which statement about the development of character in children is true?**
   a. Babies are born with an understanding of right and wrong.
   b. Other children have a greater influence on the behavior of young children than their parents do.
   c. Young children follow rules without questioning them.
   d. all of the above

2. **What is the relationship between values and beliefs?**
   a. A value is a strongly held belief.
   b. With experience, values develop into beliefs.
   c. Beliefs, not values, guide behavior.
   d. There is no relationship between values and beliefs.

THINK *CRITICALLY*

Answer the following questions as completely as possible. If necessary, use a separate sheet of paper.

3. **What childhood memories do you have that demonstrate how your values developed?**

Answers will vary.

4. **Why do parents and close friends usually have a greater influence on a person's values than media or celebrities do?**

Parents and close friends are involved in your life on a consistent, daily basis and generally are the most important influences in your life. Therefore, they can affect your values more than media or celebrities with whom you do not have a personal relationship.

5. **As children get older, how do their views of rules begin to change?**

As children get older, they recognize that rules are not always applied in the same way and that consequences may change. They realize that rules are not as simple as they had thought when they were younger.

ASSESS
Reteach
Have students review the goals for the lesson and list the important points for each goal.

Enrich
Have students create a chart similar to Figure 5.1, illustrating the various influences on their character. For each circle (family, close friends, media, etc.) have students fill in the names and specific details of the people and things that have the greatest influence on their character.

Close
Have students define *personality* and explain how personality develops in young children.

How You Demonstrate Character

SCHEDULE
Block 45 minutes
Regular 1 class period

BEHAVIOR RATHER THAN BELIEF

Actions speak louder than words. Don't just talk the talk. Walk the walk. What you do speaks so loudly that I can't hear what you say.

© Photodisc/Getty Images

All of these well-known sayings suggest that your beliefs and values will have little meaning to others if they are not reflected in your actions. Everyone knows people who are willing to make loud and powerful statements about their beliefs and values. Yet when they are called on to act on those values, they do not always follow through.

Have you found yourself in situations where you believed you would act one way but you ended up doing something different? You believe that you treat everyone with respect, yet when you hear some of your friends making demeaning statements about another student or a teacher, you do not say anything. You feel that you won't cheat in school or help others cheat to get a better grade, yet when a friend says he had to work late and did not get his homework finished, you let him borrow your completed assignment to copy.

On the other hand, you may have surprised yourself by making a difficult decision or taking an unpopular stand that demonstrates a value that is important to you. You and your friends find another student's cell phone, and your friends suggest you make some long-distance phone calls since it won't cost you anything. You won't participate and advise them not to either because the student will probably get in trouble with her parents and she or her parents will have to pay for the calls. Your class has a new student teacher who is having difficulty with discipline. Several of the class members sit in the back of the room and make inappropriate comments, laugh, and refuse to follow the new teacher's instructions. Outside of class, you and some friends decide you will talk to the disruptive students and ask them to cooperate. The class is important to you and your friends to meet graduation requirements, and you do not want anything to happen that may affect your grade. You also believe the student teacher is trying hard and deserves a chance.

Consistency Is the Key

Character is not complete until it is consistent. To be **consistent**, your actions, behaviors, and beliefs must be the same time after time. With a consistent character, you will act the same way no matter what group or circumstance you find yourself in despite the consequences you face. It is not possible to be absolutely consistent in every situation. But, when you have confidence in how you will act and others who know you can usually rely on your behavior, your character is becoming well-developed. How confident are you in your character? How do others view your character in their relationships with you?

Character and Self-Concept

Your **self-concept** is your full set of beliefs and feelings about yourself at a particular time. Your self-concept develops over a period of time and is based on your experiences and how you see others responding to you. Self-concept consists of self-image and self-esteem. Your **self-image** is the mental picture you have of yourself. Do you see yourself as attractive or plain, physically fit or out of shape, friendly and outgoing or more of an introvert? With a positive self-image, you generally feel good about yourself, your appearance, and your abilities. **Self-esteem** is the general feeling of value you have about yourself. Do you have a more positive or negative view of yourself? Do you feel more liked or disliked? With positive self-esteem, you view yourself as a good, well-liked person. A person with a strong self-concept is usually one who demonstrates good character.

COMMUNICATE

Whether you are participating in a team meeting at work, a class discussion, or a conversation with friends, there often will be a point where people disagree. Being able to disagree and still have a positive conversation is an important communication skill. Here are some pointers:

Do not overlook the difference of opinion just to get along. Be willing to discuss differences.

Do not attack the person's character. Keep the focus on the issue.

Do not make statements that indicate your position is right and the other position is wrong, which limits the chance for further discussion.

Explain your views and identify differences in a positive way. "You might be right, but my view is...." "A reason I disagree with you is...."

Let others have a chance to express their views.

Be willing to listen and learn more about the other person's views.

THINK *CRITICALLY*

Do you think all disagreements have to be resolved in order for team members to work together effectively? Explain your answer.

Have students think of a time when their actions spoke louder than their words. Are they proud of what their actions said about them?

Explain the importance of being consistent in your actions, behaviors, and beliefs. Ask students how they think other people view their character in their relationships with them. Do they think others consider their character to be consistent?

Ask students to think of some ways that a person with low self-esteem can develop a more positive view of himself or herself. (An example might include joining a group or participating in an activity in which the person may excel and make new friends.)

Review Figure 5.2 with students and discuss how personal characteristics demonstrate good character. Ask students if they think it is okay to tell a "little white lie" if it will spare someone's feelings. Have them explain their answers.

TEACHING STRATEGIES
Attention Deficit Disorder Students
Ask students to review the column in Figure 5.2 that indicates how each positive personal characteristic is demonstrated. Have students select one or two items that they feel they need to improve. Then have them write an action statement describing how they will work toward improvement.

ONGOING ASSESSMENT
Use the Checkpoint as an opportunity to conduct ongoing assessment of student comprehension of the lesson material.

FIGURE 5.2	*How Personal Characteristics Demonstrate Good Character*

Personal characteristic	Is demonstrated by
Honesty and truthfulness	■ being honest and truthful in both actions and communications
	■ not withholding information when it is important for others to know
	■ being sincere and not being misleading by providing false information or half-truths or remaining silent
	■ understanding and following the rules without using trickery or cheating
	■ avoiding even small lies told to prevent personal problems or embarrassment
Reliability and responsibility	■ keeping promises and commitments
	■ avoiding promises and commitments that are inappropriate or cannot be fulfilled
	■ using extra effort, if necessary, to meet obligations
	■ not making excuses or rationalizing why you did not meet commitments
	■ being consistent in actions and the quality of your work
Self-discipline	■ doing your best and finishing what you start
	■ looking for ways to learn from mistakes and make improvements
	■ exercising self-control
	■ taking personal responsibility rather than passing it off on others

Figure 5.2 illustrates actions that show how good character is demonstrated through positive personal characteristics. It is not easy to consistently demonstrate each of these personal characteristics. If you make a mistake or fail in an effort, it won't be a problem as long as you recognize what happened, learn from it, and attempt to improve. When you find yourself taking the actions described in Figure 5.2, it will contribute to a positive self-concept and a growing confidence in your character.

 CHECKPOINT

What personal characteristics demonstrate good character?

Personal characteristics that demonstrate good character include honesty and truthfulness, reliability and responsibility, and self-discipline.

RELATIONS WITH OTHERS

In addition to personal characteristics, character is made up of effective interpersonal relations. **Interpersonal relations** are connections, interactions, or affiliations between two or more people. These relationships come in many forms. Relationships exist among family and friends as well as among members of work teams, school clubs, and student organizations. Some relationships develop based on common interests, such as hobbies. Other relationships develop when people are brought together to accomplish a task or goal. For example, you might be assigned to work with a group to complete a class project.

Figure 5.3 offers examples of how good character is demonstrated through positive relationships with others.

LEADERSHIP *Tip*

Being elected to an office of an organization does not assure that a person will be viewed as a leader by the members. Remember that leadership is granted to officers who are respected by the members and who value the success of the organization more then their individual power.

FIGURE 5.3	*How Good Character Is Shown in Relationships*

Characteristic of effective relationships with others	Is demonstrated by
Respect and fairness	▪ being courteous and well-mannered ▪ not taking advantage of others ▪ being tolerant of differences ▪ respecting others' ideas, values, and possessions ▪ being objective and unbiased ▪ following rules and procedures
Trust, loyalty, and caring	▪ showing confidence in others ▪ valuing and maintaining friendships ▪ keeping commitments ▪ giving credit to others ▪ looking out for the interests of others ▪ keeping confidences ▪ showing concern for others
Good citizenship	▪ being a positive member of a group and contributing to its success ▪ respecting and supporting the rules, values, and beliefs of the group ▪ volunteering and doing a fair share of the work ▪ setting a positive example for others ▪ working to solve problems

TEACH
Ask students to think about the different relationships they have. How were they formed?

LEADERSHIP TIP
Ask students if they can think of an officer in an organization to which they belong whom they do not view as a leader. Have them identify the reason(s) that this person is not respected by members as a leader.

ONGOING ASSESSMENT
Use the Checkpoint as an opportunity to conduct ongoing assessment of student comprehension of the lesson material.

 ## CHECKPOINT

Name some positive characteristics that can be found in effective interpersonal relationships.

Examples of positive characteristics include respect, fairness, trust, loyalty, caring, and good citizenship.

Follow UP

UNDERSTAND LEADERSHIP CONCEPTS

Circle the best answer for each of the following questions.

1. **If there is a difference in your beliefs, actions, and behavior from time to time, you are not being**
   a. fair
   b. honest
   c. consistent
   d. accurate

2. **The mental picture you have of yourself is your**
   a. self-concept
   b. self-image
   c. self-respect
   d. self-esteem

THINK *CRITICALLY*

Answer the following questions as completely as possible. If necessary, use a separate sheet of paper.

3. **Why is it sometimes very difficult to behave in the way that reflects your beliefs and values?**

   It sometimes is difficult to behave in a way that reflects your beliefs and values

   because you may be influenced by other people or by complex situations. Your

   character may not yet be consistent so that your behavior is the same time after time.

4. **What is self-concept and how does it develop?**

   Self-concept is your full set of beliefs and feelings about yourself at a particular time. It

   develops over time and consists of your self-image and self-esteem. Your self-concept

   is based on your experiences and how you see others responding to you.

5. **Can you have good interpersonal relationships if you have a poor self-concept? Why or why not?**

   Interpersonal relationships are connections with other people. It is difficult to connect

   in a positive way with others if you have a negative image of yourself and view

   yourself as a person who is not friendly, outgoing, or well-liked.

ASSESS

Reteach
Have students list and define each of the terms in the lesson. Then have students write one key concept from the lesson that relates to each term.

Enrich
Have students create a poster or bulletin board display that illustrates ways to demonstrate character. They may use sayings ("Actions speak louder than words") or pictures illustrating positive character traits (respect, responsibility, trustworthiness, etc.).

Close
Have students write one or two paragraphs assessing their self-concept. They should identify their self-image (how they view themselves) and their level of self-esteem (how they feel about themselves). Do they feel that any part of their self-concept is preventing them from being an effective leader?

A Path to Personal Improvement

- Analyze your character and what you want to improve
- Describe the steps to follow in developing your character

- priority
- mental practice

SCHEDULE
Block 45 minutes
Regular 1 class period

FOCUS
Ask students how proud they are of the way they behave at home, at school, and on the job. How do they think others view their behavior?

TEACH
Ask students to think about how their behavior has changed from the time they were young children to the present time. As children, they most likely did not think about how their actions affected others. As teenagers, they are more aware of the effect their behavior can have on others, and they consider others more often when making decisions. Their actions indicate their developing character.

YOUR DEVELOPING CHARACTER

A person's character develops over time just as each person develops physically and mentally. Most people do not think much about character until they are presented with a moral or ethical issue.

Very young children act in a particular way because the adults who are important in their life tell them how to act. They follow rules they have been taught, and they begin to understand the difference between right and wrong. Older children begin to think for themselves more frequently. They make decisions that demonstrate their independence, that are designed to get the attention and approval of friends and peers, and that reflect their developing values and beliefs.

As a teenager you are now at a more advanced stage of personality and character development. You have a clearer understanding of right and wrong. You have seen examples of good and poor behavior. You recognize that decisions are often complex and that not everyone views things in the same way you do or has the same set of values as you and your family. You have also seen that your actions affect others. What appears good to you may not be good for others. More and more frequently, you make decisions based on how your actions will affect others and what is best for the group rather than just your own best interests. Even though you do not think a lot about it, you are developing your character, and your decisions and actions reflect that character.

▌Are You Satisfied?

Do you have the character that you want, that pleases those who are important to you, and that will help you achieve future personal, educational, and career goals? This is a

© Digital Vision/Getty Images

good time to examine how your character is affecting your life because your character can still be changed. Answer the following questions to determine if you are satisfied with your character.

1. Are you generally happy with yourself and your life?
2. Do you feel good about your appearance and health?
3. Do you have accomplishments and achievements that make you proud?
4. Do you believe you have a good chance to be successful with most things you attempt?
5. Are you comfortable in most social situations and with the people you regularly have to deal with?
6. Are you generally honest and truthful?
7. Do you try to understand and follow the rules?
8. Are you careful about making commitments and then keeping those you make?
9. Do you take personal responsibility for your actions and avoid blaming others when things go wrong?
10. Can you generally maintain self-control in difficult situations?
11. Are you respectful and tolerant of others, especially when they are different from you?
12. Can people generally trust you?
13. Do people enjoy being around you and working with you?
14. Are you loyal to your family, close friends, and teammates?
15. Do you support the groups to which you belong and contribute your share to their success?

Questions 1–5 examine your feelings about your self-esteem. Questions 6–10 describe your opinion of your personal character traits. Questions 11–15 focus on your beliefs about your interpersonal relations. Now that you have answered the questions, how do you think others would answer these questions about you? Do you believe your parents, friends, teachers, classmates, and others would have the same answers?

What Would You Change?

Thinking about your character and how you feel about specific character traits is important. It is difficult to make changes without understanding your strengths and the areas needing improvement. But having opinions about your character is not enough to really understand it. Your character is demonstrated by your actions, not by your beliefs alone. You need to think about the things you do and how those actions affect you and others. Ask yourself the following questions about your behavior.

1. Do I have regular arguments and disagreements with my parents and other family members? Do I sometimes feel embarrassed by who they are and what they do?

2. Do I frequently have difficulty with adult leaders, teachers, and other people in authority? Do they have to spend more time with me than with others because of those problems?

3. Am I often punished for disobeying rules or not following procedures?

4. Have I been caught frequently not telling the truth or making excuses for my actions?

5. Do I often rush into decisions that I later regret or that create problems for me and others?

6. Do many of the people I associate with have problems getting along with others, or are they viewed as troublemakers?

7. When given choices of team members or people to work with, do others often avoid selecting me?

8. Do I often express biases and prejudices about others, their beliefs, and behaviors?

9. Do I have problems accepting responsibility, completing the things I start, and doing things the right way?

10. Do I tend to disrupt a group or distract them so that they cannot focus on what they are supposed to accomplish?

These ten questions identify common character problems faced by teens. The behavior in each question is not unusual and does not present a serious problem if it occurs infrequently. However, if any of the negative behaviors occur frequently, it can be evidence of poor character that will stand in the way of friendships, personal satisfaction, and future success.

 CHECKPOINT

What do teenagers do that show they are at an advanced stage of character development?

Teenagers more frequently make decisions based on how their actions will affect

others and what is best for the group rather than just for their own best interests.

A PLAN FOR CHARACTER DEVELOPMENT

Star athletes, leading actors, or top-selling musicians can make their performances appear effortless. It is easy to believe that they are naturally gifted. Others do not see the hours of practice or the problems they have encountered and corrected. To develop their abilities, they have mastered basic skills, followed difficult practice routines, made improvements in performance, and committed to being the best they could be. Their effort is rewarded by the outstanding performances they deliver time after time, the pleasure they provide to their audiences, and their personal satisfaction.

TEACH
Write several sayings on the board such as "Look before you leap" and "Think before you speak." Ask students how these sayings relate to character. Lead a class discussion on the importance of thinking before acting to consider how students' actions will affect them and others.

TEACHING STRATEGIES
Auditory Learners
Have students brainstorm a list of ways that their actions can affect other people, including family, friends, and coworkers. Write their answers on the board and discuss as a group.

TEACHING STRATEGIES
Kinesthetic Learners
Have students answer each of the ten questions about their behavior. For each "yes" answer, have students list a positive step they can take to improve their behavior in that area.

ONGOING ASSESSMENT
Use the Checkpoint as an opportunity to conduct ongoing assessment of student comprehension of the lesson material.

TEACH
Ask students whether they are involved in an activity that requires many hours of practice or study. Discuss the commitment and effort these activities require.

Toya had a major project due in her Web Design class but had not yet finished it. The assignment required her to create a three-page web site for a small business demonstrating the use of text, graphics, color, and animation. She knew that if she turned in what she had it would change her semester grade from a B to a C. Sitting at home the night before the assignment was due, Toya found a simple but attractive web site online. She knew she would be able to copy the programming code, make some quick changes, and turn it in. It would clearly meet the requirements for the assignment. With the changes she was making she did not believe her teacher would know that she had copied the web page. Toya rationalized that she knew how to complete all of the requirements for the assignment but that she just ran out of time. She also believed that by making some changes, she wasn't really plagiarizing, which was clearly against the rules in her class.

THINK *CRITICALLY*

1. If Toya did not finish the assignment because her mother became suddenly ill rather than because she did not allow enough time, would it make a difference?
2. Do you agree with Toya that she was not plagiarizing? Why or why not?
3. How has technology affected the way students do homework? Do you think technology can be misused? Explain how.

TECH ETHICS
Point out that by not completing the assignment until the night before it was due, Toya put herself in a situation that "tested" her character. Ask students if they think Toya passed the character test?

Think Critically Answers
1. Answers will vary. Regardless of the reason, Toya's actions were a violation of the rules.
2. Answers will vary. By copying the programming code, Toya submitted material that was not her own original work.
3. Answers will vary. The Internet provides students with quick and easy access to online resources that can easily be copied and misused.

Making the Commitment

Achieving any important goal or making a personal improvement requires the same commitment and effort of an athlete, actor, or musician. Preparing for college admission or beginning a successful career requires commitment and effort. It won't just happen. You choose to be an effective leader and to be a person with good character. Those choices require both a commitment and long-term effort to achieve your goals.

Following a Plan

Developing the character you want can be accomplished by following a five-step plan. It requires the same serious effort that athletes, musicians, or actors use to perfect their abilities. The steps are *Think, Study, Plan, Practice, and Perfect.*

Think

Do not rush into your plan. Making a change must be important to you. You need to do it for the right reasons. Why do you want to work on your character? What do you currently do well, and what do you want to improve? How will you and others that are important to you benefit if you are successful? These are all questions to consider.

Be aware that your commitment to change will require both time and effort. Change does not come easily. You will find that you will make mistakes and will not always be successful. Just as the star athlete practices for improvement, you will need to be sure that you are willing to put forth the time and effort to change your behavior.

TEACH
Prepare students for writing their personal plan for character development by reviewing the five steps. Write the steps on the board and walk the students through each one. Point out that goals cannot be achieved without proper planning and preparation.

Ask students if they have ever rushed into a project without first thinking it through. What was the outcome? Stress the importance of first thinking through the things they want to work on about their character.

After students have completed Step 1 (Think) and have set some priorities, have them make a list of the resources they will use, including the people they will talk to and observe.

To help students put their plan in writing, develop a sample plan on the board as an example and review it with students.

Have students think of adults who could review their plan and give them constructive feedback. Ask them also to think of a friend whom they could work with to provide mutual help and support. Why did they choose those individuals?

TEACHING STRATEGIES
Print Learners
Have students conduct research on their favorite musician, actor, or athlete. Have them list the education, training, and practice that the individual went through in order to become the top performer he or she is today.

What part of your character do you want to work on first? You need to prioritize your efforts. A **priority** receives more attention than alternative activities. If you have concerns about your self-image or self-concept, you will need to work on that first. Personal character traits must be strengthened before you can focus on improving interpersonal relationships.

Study

Make sure you understand the character trait on which you will focus. Experts in any area know that ability does not improve if you are working on the wrong things. Knowing what behaviors contribute to a particular character trait and the types of problems you are likely to encounter will help you develop better plans. By being knowledgeable, you will be better prepared if things do not go as you planned.

You can find a great deal of information by reading books, searching the Internet, talking to teachers, leaders, and other experts, and observing people who demonstrate good character. The research process will also help you identify the people and resources you can turn to for help and advice.

Plan

After you have identified what your focus will be for improving your character, it is time to develop a specific plan. While planning, questions will arise that you will have to answer. What activities will you need to complete? How much time will you be able to devote to the effort? Who will help you with your plan and activities? Put the plan in writing so that you have a record to review.

Do not make your plan too complicated, and do not develop a plan that will take too long to complete. A few important activities completed over several weeks or months will give you a feeling of accomplishment. You can then extend your plan if needed.

© Doug Menuez/Photodisc/Getty Images

Discuss your plan with adults who are willing to give you guidance and support. Ask them if they will be willing to review your progress and provide feedback for you as you work on the plan. It is also helpful to have a close friend who is committed to the same type of change so that you can support each other.

Practice

Just as athletes, actors, or musicians practice to improve their performance, you must also practice the behaviors that are a part of the character trait you are trying to improve. You might practice by yourself, work with a friend, or complete mental practice. **Mental practice** is imagining yourself completing each of the steps of an activity correctly. If you can visualize yourself performing an activity, you will begin to believe that you can do it. You can identify situations at home, school, work, or in an organization to practice the behaviors.

Practice may not always go smoothly. Expect to make mistakes. You might forget and fall back on your old behaviors from time to time. But keep trying and maintain your commitment. You will find yourself getting better.

Perfect

By following your plan, maintaining your commitment, and getting the support of others, you will experience success. Soon the behavior will become part of your everyday routine. People will notice the difference in you, and you will be proud of your accomplishment. The character trait will now become part of your personality, and you can then focus on other aspects of self-improvement.

While the behavior will become routine, you cannot totally forget about its importance. You may be confronted with a problem or situation that you have not previously considered that may test your character. In such situations, remember your beliefs and values. Thinking carefully about your behavior usually will result in the correct decision and appropriate action.

 **CHECKPOINT**

What are the five steps in a character development plan?

The five steps in a character development plan are think, study, plan, practice, and

perfect.

Follow UP

UNDERSTAND LEADERSHIP CONCEPTS

Circle the best answer for each of the following questions.

1. Young children are more likely than teenagers to
   a. follow rules *(circled)*
   b. question their parents
   c. make decisions based on how their actions will affect others
   d. have positive character traits

2. When developing a plan to improve your character, you should
   a. work on one trait at a time
   b. prepare a simple plan for a short period of time
   c. use mental practice as a way to change your behavior
   d. all of the above *(circled)*

THINK CRITICALLY

Answer the following questions as completely as possible. If necessary, use a separate sheet of paper.

3. Do you think most people have the same perception of their own character as others have of their character? Explain your answer.

Answers will vary.

4. Do you believe that people who consistently demonstrate good character think a lot about their behavior or that it just comes naturally to them?

Answers will vary. Character is demonstrated by actions. People who consistently demonstrate good character think about their actions and how those actions affect themselves and others.

5. When developing a plan for character improvement, why is it important that the plan not cover a long period of time?

If the plan covers a long period of time, you may become discouraged and lose sight of your goal. By completing a few important activities over several weeks or months, you will get a feeling of accomplishment.

ASSESS
Reteach
Have students list the five steps in the plan for character development. Ask students to write one or two sentences explaining each step.

Enrich
Have students create an electronic presentation to illustrate how excuses, justifications, and rationalizations can harm character development. Students may start with a graphic of a trash can and "toss" in excuses, justifications, and rationalizations (such as "Everybody does it").

Close
Have students continue working on their personal character development plans.

Chapter Assessment

REVIEW *LEADERSHIP CONCEPTS*

Write the letter of the term that matches each definition.

a. belief
b. consistent
c. interpersonal relations
d. media
e. mental practice
f. personality
g. priority
h. self-concept
i. self-esteem
j. self-image

_c_ 1. Connections, interactions, or affiliations between two or more people

_j_ 2. The mental picture you have of yourself

_g_ 3. An activity that receives more attention than alternative activities

_f_ 4. The total set of emotions, traits, and behaviors that makes each person unique

_i_ 5. The general feeling of value you have about yourself

_e_ 6. Imagining yourself completing each of the steps of an activity correctly

_b_ 7. Actions, behaviors, and beliefs that are the same time after time

_a_ 8. Something you accept as true

_h_ 9. Your full set of beliefs and feelings about yourself at a particular time

_d_ 10. The channels of communication in a society

Circle the best answer.

11. Which of the following statements is *not* true about character?
    a. People are born neither good nor bad.
    b. Even with people you know well, you are usually unable to predict how they will act.
    c. A person's character continues to change and develop.
    d. New experiences affect a person's character.

12. How do children's views of rules change as they get older?
    a. They view all rules as either right or wrong.
    b. They do not agree with most rules they are expected to follow.
    c. They recognize that rules are not as simple as they once believed.
    d. They are afraid of the consequences of violating a rule.

13. Character is not complete until it is
    a. consistent
    b. practiced for many years
    c. approved by your parents and teachers
    d. related to your beliefs

14. Which of the following is the first step in planning to develop the character you want?
    a. perfect
    b. study
    c. think
    d. practice

THINK CRITICALLY

15. *Why do very young children usually follow rules while older children may break the rules from time to time?*

Very young children usually do not question rules. They have learned that

consequences are attached to most rules. Older children want to express their

independence and show that they have control over some situations. They recognize

that rules are not always applied in the same way and that consequences may change.

16. *How do you feel about people who express strongly held beliefs about something yet their actions say something different? Why do you believe some people are very vocal about beliefs that they do not hold strongly?*

Answers will vary. People who express strongly held beliefs but act differently do not

yet have consistent character. Their character may still be developing, and they may

not yet be confident in their character.

17. *If you have a good friend who seems to have a low self-concept, what could you do to help improve your friend's personal views?*

Answers will vary. Because self-concept is based on a person's experiences, you could

encourage your friend to join a group or participate in an activity that would provide

some positive experiences and interactions with other people.

18. *Do you believe that by the time people near the end of their teenage years their character is pretty well set? Explain your answer and provide examples to support your ideas.*

Answers will vary. As people grow, their character becomes more fully developed. By

the time they are teenagers, they have developed some strong beliefs and values that

guide their actions. But character is not really complete until it is consistent—actions,

behaviors, and beliefs are the same time after time.

19. *As you get to know people, what are the aspects of their character that are most important to you in developing a friendship? What aspects of character are not very important to you?*

Answers will vary. Aspects of character to consider may include honesty and truth-

fulness, reliability and responsibility, and self-discipline.

20. **Research** *Use library resources to study the following three terms:* beliefs, values, *and* ethics. *Write a short paper that compares the similarities and differences among the terms.*

Answers will vary.

_____

_____

_____

_____

21. **Communication** *Ask the following question of three people—a young child, a teenager, and an adult: "Why should people follow rules?" Compare their answers. Based on the differences in their ages, what do you think their answers say about their understanding of why we have rules? Discuss your results with other classmates.*

Answers will vary based on interview responses.

_____

_____

_____

_____

22. **Technology** *Create a three-column table. Use the Internet to locate a reference book that contains quotations. Find five quotations about character and copy them into the first column of the table. Make sure that you identify the name of the person who is the source of each quotation. In the second column, identify whether you agree or disagree with each of the quotations. In the last column, write one or two sentences describing why you agree or disagree.*

Answers will vary.

_____

_____

_____

_____

_____

23. **Problem Solving** *Identify one character trait that interests you. Use the school library to locate two books that contain information about that character trait. Prepare three questions for which you would like to find answers through your reading.*

Answers will vary.

_____

_____

_____

_____

_____

LEARNING TO *LEAD*

FOCUS

Study and select specific leadership training programs.

DESCRIPTION

You may already have some of the traits of a leader and even have undertaken some leadership roles. However, even the best and most effective leaders continue to study and learn more about leadership. They seek out opportunities to participate in leadership development activities, conferences, and training programs. If you want to be the best leader you can be, you, too, need to plan for your leadership development.

Identify the types of formal leadership training programs offered by your student organization. Each organization offers training programs at the state and national levels and often within your local chapter. Your goal is to study the leadership training programs offered, determine eligibility requirements, and develop a specific plan for your participation this year and in future years as you undertake more challenging leadership roles.

LEARNING TO LEAD
This project is written for use with student organizations such as BPA, DECA, and FBLA. Student organizations can help students prepare for key leadership roles. After students complete the activities, discuss what they learned about their student organization.

Activities
1. Before they begin this activity, suggest that students make a list of all available resources to help them plan a more thorough and efficient search.

ACTIVITIES

1. *Ask the adviser of your local student organization chapter to identify any leadership training programs (other than officer training) available to members from the national and state offices. Visit web sites, read articles, and review recent publications and newsletters from your national and state organizations about the training programs.*

2. *Identify a student from your local chapter who has participated in one of the training programs. Interview the student to learn more about his or her experience and the benefits of participation.*

3. *Identify the dates of all training programs that will be offered this school year, the purpose and goals of each, the requirements for applying and participating, and the costs.*

2. Prior to conducting the interview, students should prepare a list of questions they want to ask to help them stay organized and focused during the interview.
3. It may be helpful for students to create a table to organize the information about each available training program.

SHARE YOUR RESULTS

1. *Select one leadership training program that you believe would be of immediate benefit to you this year and one that would be of greater benefit in a future school year.*
2. *Write a short statement describing how your personal leadership development would benefit from participating in each training program you selected. Describe how you plan to use the leadership skills you develop this year and in future years to benefit your local student organization and your school.*
3. *Working with your adviser, prepare a written outline of the steps you need to take to apply for and, if selected, participate in the training program you have chosen for this year. Create a timeline for completing each step.*

Share Your Results
1. Answers will vary.
2. Answers will vary.
3. Answers will vary.

ACCEPTING THE
CHALLENGE
Case Study 5
Ask students to think of
ways that respect for all
students is encouraged in
their school. Do they see
any areas where improve-
ment is needed? Do they
think that a "Respect
Committee" might work
well in their school? Why
or why not?

ACCEPTING THE CHALLENGE

CASE STUDY 5—IMPROVING RELATIONS

In the What Would You Do? *opening scenario, Seneca was quite angry because of Jerome's bullying behavior toward Alex. After he calmed down, Seneca reflected on past situations in which his anger flared because of some of his peers' misbehavior or mistreatment of others. He came to realize that his anger could not change the behavior of others—it only affected his own behavior. Seneca was concerned that the school's climate did not encourage the safety and nurturing of others. As a respected school leader, he decided to seek the help and collaboration of the school's guidance counselor and representatives from other school clubs and organizations to create a "Respect Committee." He realized it was crucial to include representatives from different "cliques" and groups who felt disconnected from their school and peers. The purpose of the committee would be to emphasize the importance of positive interpersonal relations with others in the school. The committee would sponsor speakers, workshops, and other activities that stress good character and positive relationships. Members of the committee could also act as peer mediators to help students work out problems they may be having with other students.*

THINK CRITICALLY

1. *Describe a situation in which you have been angered or frustrated by someone else's behavior toward you or others. How did you react?*

Answers will vary.

_____

_____

_____

2. *Explain how someone else's negative behavior toward you has changed your opinion of that person's character.*

Answers will vary.

_____

_____

_____

3. *Is there a particular group of students in your school who seem to get picked on or bullied by others? If so, what could you and others do to support that group or prevent the abusive behaviors toward them?*

Answers will vary but may include speaking to an adult, such as an administrator,

teacher, or counselor; speaking directly to the students doing the bullying; involving

the students being picked on in activities with other school groups; or organizing a

"respect" committee as Seneca did.

APPLY *WHAT YOU HAVE LEARNED—Assess Your Home Climate*

DIRECTIONS: *In shaping your character, it is important to realize that your training begins at home with your family. The patterns of behavior that we exhibit have been ''copied'' or emulated from those who have been influential in our lives. If someone close to you is a bully, your chances of being a bully are greater. If someone close to you exhibits strength and confidence, you stand a very good chance of exhibiting these traits as well. Take the* Home Climate Survey *below or on your Student Activity CD to learn more about your home environment. Underline either ''TRUE'' or ''FALSE'' for each statement.*

HOME CLIMATE SURVEY

1. I am encouraged to make my own decisions.	TRUE	FALSE
2. I am encouraged to try new things and supported even if I fail.	TRUE	FALSE
3. I feel loved, nurtured, and comfortable in my home.	TRUE	FALSE
4. I like the way my parents/guardians treat me and others.	TRUE	FALSE
5. I respect my siblings and their things and do not use their things without asking.	TRUE	FALSE
6. I believe my parents/guardians are honest and truthful.	TRUE	FALSE
7. I am not allowed to make decisions without input from my parents/guardians.	TRUE	FALSE
8. I am punished if I fail in my attempt to try something new.	TRUE	FALSE
9. I feel anxious, nervous, and uneasy in my home.	TRUE	FALSE
10. I do not like bringing friends to my house because my parents'/guardians' behavior is unpredictable.	TRUE	FALSE
11. I borrow things from my siblings without asking, and they do the same.	TRUE	FALSE
12. I do not believe my parents/guardians always handle situations in an honest and truthful manner.	TRUE	FALSE

If you have more TRUE answers for Numbers 1–6 than you do for Numbers 7–12, then you most likely have a nurturing home climate that demonstrates positive behavior and good character. If you have more TRUE answers for Numbers 7–12, your home climate may not offer a positive role model for building good character. Regardless of the type of home climate you have, there are probably things you would like to change about it.

On the lines below or on the Student Activity CD, create a SMART goal (including a completion date) that expresses your desire to make improvements in your home climate. Then enter your thoughts, ideas, and discussions related to your goal in a journal (on the CD or your own) to help you plan and track your progress. Select a goal-setting partner, such as a family member or friend, to support you as you work toward your goal.

_____

_____

_____

_____

Teams and Teamwork

© Don Tremain/Photodisc/Getty Images

6.1 *The Need for Teams and Teamwork*

6.2 *Character of Teams and Team Members*

6.3 *Making Teams Work*

What would **YOU** do?

MARISSA'S HISTORY LESSON

Marissa Lopez had been the cheerleading captain in her former middle school, located in a Hispanic community. She looked forward to trying out for the cheerleading squad at the high school for the upcoming school year. Marissa knew the competition would be tough because three other middle schools in her district were also a part of the same high school. When tryouts started, she noticed that none of the girls from her old school were there to compete, but with her skill and experience, Marissa easily made the squad.

As the season progressed, the squad not only practiced at school but often got together after practice. Because none of Marissa's former squad members were on the team, she usually did not go out after practice with the squad. Marissa was always on time for practice, worked hard, and showed her support at the games. But she noticed that after the games, squad members often went out together, but they did not invite her. She also noticed during the game that her suggestions for cheers were often voted down. Marissa wondered if she was being treated badly because she was the only Hispanic member on the team.

The cheerleading coach sensed the tension between the girls. She knew that some of the girls had developed a "history" from knowing one another during years of cheering together in middle school. She had a team meeting after practice to discuss their lack of teamwork. The girls sat quietly for a while. Then one of the girls finally stated that some team members acted unfriendly and did not want to be friends beyond practice and games. Marissa knew that comment was directed at her. She was surprised because she did not consider herself to be unfriendly. Another team member admitted that she had never been on a squad with people of a different race and ethnicity, and she did not know how to treat them.

To become a better team, the girls agreed to share some of their "history" with each other. All of the team members agreed to do a better job of listening to one another and accepting differences. By working as a team, they could help others see that learning a person's "history" is an important part of creating a sense of acceptance and belonging.

THINK _CRITICALLY_

1. Why is it important to know other people's personal "history" when establishing friendships and relationships?

2. How might team-building activities improve team unity?

TEACHING RESOURCES
Instructor's Resource CD
Lesson Plans, Ch. 6
PowerPoint Slides, Ch. 6

Student Activity CD, Ch. 6

thomsonedu.com/school/leading
Crossword Puzzle, Ch. 6
Flash Cards, Ch. 6
Exam*View* ® CD, Ch. 6

CHAPTER OVERVIEW
Chapter 6 discusses various aspects of teams, teamwork, and team membership.

Lesson 6.1
Explains the importance of working in teams and describes how teams function.

Lesson 6.2
Describes the character traits of successful teams and team members.

Lesson 6.3
Describes the roles of team members and identifies the characteristics of effective and ineffective teams.

WHAT WOULD YOU DO?
Some students in class may have a long "history" with one another from elementary and middle school while others may feel like outsiders. Ask students what they can do to make everyone feel accepted as a member of the class.

Think Critically Answers
1. Answers will vary. Knowing other people's personal "history" helps create a sense of acceptance and belonging.
2. Answers will vary. Team-building activities bring people together for a common purpose or goal.

The Need for Teams and Teamwork

GOALS
- Explain the importance of working in teams to complete tasks and accomplish goals.
- Describe the various levels at which teams function.

TERMS
- independent
- interdependent
- collaborating

MANY HANDS MAKE WORK LIGHT

When people relied more on farming for a living, it was important for families to have lots of children so that there would be enough family members to work in the fields and tend to the animals. Because farms usually occupied many acres, families typically lived great distances

© D Falconer/Photolink/Photodisc/Getty Images

apart from other families. Although they lived farther apart, it was important for survival for families in the same community to work together to harvest their crops and build barns and family homes. That type of teamwork still exists today in Amish communities as well as in some community organizations such as Habitat for Humanity. That spirit of teamwork also comes into your homes through television shows like *Extreme Makeover: Home Edition* and *Trading Spaces.* On these shows, it would be impossible to complete the enormous amount of work being done to change the homes and lives of families if it were not for the extraordinary teamwork that is displayed.

Even closer to home is your own family. Think about the upkeep of your home and all of the things that your parents or guardians work to provide for your family. You may help out by babysitting younger siblings, cleaning your room or other areas of the house, working in the yard, and doing well in school. All members of the family need to work in harmony with one another for the good of the group.

Families that work together as teams are personal examples of the need for teams and teamwork. You may have seen some of your friends' families that do not work closely together. You can see how difficult it is on their relationships and the successful running of their homes.

There Is No "I" in Team

There are times when teams are not needed to get the job done. For example, at your age, no one is going to help you brush your teeth or feed and dress you. Unless you are disabled, you can do those things yourself. You are also capable of doing your homework, selecting the clothes to wear to school, and making many other daily decisions on your own.

On the other hand, there are times when teams are necessary because a group of people working together toward a common goal can more successfully achieve that goal than an individual working alone. Individuals working together toward a common goal or task use their collective strengths, personalities, talents, and skills to create something larger than any one of them could accomplish alone. The saying "together we stand; divided we fall" applies to those crucial times when only teamwork can make the difference between success and failure.

COMMUNICATE

As you grow and mature, you will begin to notice how difficult it sometimes can be to communicate with your parents because you think they do not understand how things work in your world. Ask your parents or guardians to set aside a time when you can talk to them about getting the family to work together as a team. Let them know that you are interested in becoming a more effective team member since you are an important part of your family. Be sure to listen to, as well as hear, what they share with you. Then ask them how they think you can become a better team member, starting with one or two suggestions for making improvements.

THINK CRITICALLY

How do you think this sort of conversation can open the lines of communication between you and your parents or guardians? How can it improve interactions with other members of your "family team"?

Transitioning from Individual to Group to Team

As people work together, they can move from being individuals to being part of a group or a team. Individuals move from being **independent**, operating individually, to being **interdependent**, depending on the help of others. Interdependence involves a connection with others.

Many individuals become part of a group because of what they may need or have in common with others. These groups are called by different names such as families, friends, relatives, neighbors, churches, choirs, bands, gangs, and communities. When these groups work together toward common goals or tasks, they have the potential to become a team.

Although a team is a group of people, all groups are not teams. As you sit in each of your classes, you are part of a group of students in that class. However, your class is not considered a team unless certain roles are clearly defined and you are working together toward the same goal. All of your classmates are probably individually working toward getting an "A" in that particular subject, but you are not focused as a team on ensuring that everyone in the class gets an "A." There are times when you work on a group project for which you get a group grade. With these types of projects, you can become a team because you are working together, with tasks assigned to each

© Doug Menuez/Photodisc/Getty Images

student, toward a common goal to produce a product for the good of the group so that your team gets an "A."

You can tell whether or not the group you are in is a team by the way individuals work together. For example, when your parents or guardians tell you that they are planning a family vacation, do you brainstorm together to decide on a location for the vacation? Do you and your siblings work together to save your allowance to purchase your parents an anniversary gift? Do you and your classmates participate in a fundraiser to help a fellow student whose family has a special need? Do you and your fellow musicians join together to become a band and display your talents at a party or talent show? These are all collaborative efforts toward some common goal that would be impossible to achieve alone. **Collaborating** involves cooperating and working together in a joint effort.

Teams collaborate, discuss, and have a shared understanding of their mission. Team members get to know one another and discover each other's strengths and preferred ways of getting things done. Teams set timelines and meet to discuss their progress. Team members are committed to the team's purpose and goals.

✓ CHECKPOINT

Why are teams not always necessary to get things done?

For certain routine, daily tasks, teams are not needed to get the job done. Doing your homework, choosing what to wear, and doing other daily tasks do not require a team.

HOW TEAMS FUNCTION

In order for teams to work effectively, the leader must recognize that teams function at different levels. These levels include the individual level, the group level, the goal/task level, and the school/community impact level. The working environment, which in turn affects how goals are accomplished, is different at each level. The leader, working independently and interdependently with others, must somehow guide the team through the individual level and group level to reach the goal/task level and school/community impact level. Teams functioning at the last two levels can produce benefits that extend beyond the team. A team's success is measured by how well it serves others.

Individual Level

When a team first forms, it most likely will function on an individual level. The personalities, attitudes, needs, strengths, and personal agendas that each person brings to the team are exposed at this level. It is human nature that individuals want to have their needs met and to be considered valuable and worthwhile in the eyes of others. People who have a good sense of self-awareness and self-esteem can accept who they are and what they bring to relationships with others. These people are often considered to be "low maintenance" because they are self-confident and do not feel the need to be the center of attention. Then there are individuals who are more "needy" and need confirmation from others that what they say or do is okay. They are usually considered "high maintenance." All team members should have a sense of acceptance and belonging before the team can move to the next level—the group level.

Group Level

The group level of functioning is greatly affected by how people's needs were met at the individual level. In order for the team to work toward a goal or complete a task, there must be a sense that the whole is greater than the sum of its parts. Team members must recognize the benefits of teamwork. They must work on social and interpersonal skills, put their own personal agendas aside, and come together to work as a group. Team-building activities may be used to help team members get to know one another, discourage competition among team members, resolve conflicts, and build trust.

During this time, you will discover that other people have some of the same skills and talents that you have. You see that your peers are just as creative and smart as you. Instead of becoming jealous and competitive, you should share what each of you knows and blend your skills to achieve even greater results. Individuals must be able to see the big picture and determine how they fit into it for the good of the group.

© Photolink/Photodisc/Getty Images

Goal/Task Level

At the goal/task level, team members come together and begin working as a team. When a team is functioning at this level, team members understand the goal or task and commit to achieving it. No matter how difficult it might be, team members are willing to make sacrifices of time, energy, talent, and resources to get the job done. At this level, all team members are focused on the mission of the team. Team members collaborate and make the best use of everyone's skills to accomplish the task at hand.

School/Community Impact Level

The school/community impact level is based on the school's or community's perception of how useful or important your team is. You may have noticed that some teams have more visibility, necessity, usefulness, and popularity than others. Membership in these teams is often highly desired. The football or basketball team may get more attention than the golf or hockey team. Unfortunately, some of the highly visible and popular teams have limited membership and require certain types of skills. Fortunately, there are many other teams that need a variety of strengths and skills that many individuals have to offer.

All teams should consider the kind of impact they have on their school or community. If your school and community place a high value on your team, you should strive to meet their expectations. They may be depending on your team to create a plan, provide recommendations, complete a task, or solve a problem. Teams that are working at the school/community impact level recognize that their efforts can potentially benefit others.

 CHECKPOINT

Which team level do you think is the most effective? Why?

Answers will vary. Teams that function at the school/community impact level not only help the team and its members but also benefit others in the school or community.

© Photolink/Photodisc/Getty Images

Follow UP

UNDERSTAND LEADERSHIP CONCEPTS

Circle the best answer for each of the following questions.

1. Which statement about teams is true?
a. It is not necessary to assign roles to team members.
b. It is always better to work on a project with a team rather than by yourself.
c. Members should be committed to the goal.
d. There is never a limit to the number of members allowed.

2. Functioning at the group level requires you to
a. see the big picture and how you fit into it
b. recognize that others may have similar skills and talents as you
c. personally and socially interact with others who are similar to and different from you
d. all of the above

THINK *CRITICALLY*

Answer the following questions as completely as possible. If necessary, use a separate sheet of paper.

3. Why is it sometimes necessary to work with a team to accomplish a goal or complete a task?

By working toward a common goal, individuals use their collective strengths,

personalities, talents, and skills to create something larger than any one of them could

accomplish alone.

4. How does your sense of self-awareness and self-esteem impact your ability to function as part of a team?

People with a good sense of self-awareness and self-esteem accept who they are and

what they bring to relationships with others. These "low maintenance" members are

self-confident and do not need to be the center of attention. Individuals who need

confirmation from others that what they say or do is okay are considered "high

maintenance." These people may cause delays and conflicts.

5. Why must teams move from the individual level to the goal/task level?

Teams need to move to the goal/task level because that is one of the levels that can

produce benefits to others. A team's success is measured by how well it serves others.

ASSESS
Reteach
Have students list the benefits of working as a team to complete tasks and accomplish goals.

Enrich
Have students create a chart illustrating the differences between the four levels of team functioning. Students should have a column heading for each of the four levels—individual, group, goal/task, and school/ community impact.

Close
Ask students to think about their family. At which level does their "home team" function? What, if anything, do they think they can do to move their family team to the next level?

Character of Teams and Team Members

CHARACTER OF TEAMS

Just as people have certain character traits, a team—which is made up of people—also has character traits. The character of the individuals who make up the team will have a great impact on how effectively the team functions. The character of the team will be no better than the character of its members and how well they work together to accomplish team goals. In order for a team to be successful and have an accepted place in your school or community, it must exhibit certain traits. Your team must

- **Have a good reputation.** When the name of your team is mentioned in conversation, it is important that people react positively. Your team should be known and respected for its accomplishments.
- **Be respectful of its team members, other teams, and the school or community.** Team members must treat one another with respect. In a large group of people, tempers can flare and personalities can clash. To function, team members must learn to work together for the good of the team. Teams must be respectful in their everyday dealings with other teams or individuals in the school or community. Teams must give respect to earn respect.

© Flying Colours Ltd/Digital Vision/Getty Images

- **Exhibit appropriate behavior.** Team behavior is noticed and discussed by others. Word gets around if the baseball team was rude to the opposing team during the playoff games. What team members do and how they behave reflects on the entire team. That may not seem fair, especially when you cannot personally choose every member of your team. While the team cannot make someone else behave appropriately, the leader can discuss the problem to try to stop the inappropriate behavior. If the bad behavior continues, the team's reputation is at stake. The last resort when a person's behavior continues to cause problems for the team is to dismiss him or her from the team.

- **Be responsible and live up to the team's purpose and goals.** When attempting to attract new people to join your team, you may be asked, "What does your team do?" If the team is living up to its purpose, you will be able to proudly answer that question by describing what your team has achieved and how it has served others.

- **Contribute in a positive way to the improvement, enhancement, or growth of the community.** Student Council is supposed to be the "voice" for students. The team of council members represents the student body and its concerns. It should not be a clique made up of students who just want to win school-wide approval and popularity. The council's job is to make sure that student issues are put before the student body and the administration. Student council should work as a team to make improvements and enhancements that will benefit all students in the school.

- **Understand and accept diversity.** Keep in mind that everyone does not look, act, feel, and believe the same way. Teams often will be made up of a diverse group of people. **Diversity** is often thought of in terms of race, gender, or age, but it includes many other elements, such as ideas, opinions, values, belief systems, and experiences. Not everyone has to be alike to get along. Instead of viewing diversity as a problem, teams should view it in a positive way. Differing viewpoints can lead to new and unique approaches to solving problems.

- **Care for team resources—human, material, and financial.** The materials, finances, and people needed to run an organization or team are called **resources**. Individuals should not misuse resources such as school property, money, or even other people. When a team demonstrates that it cares about the resources provided to it, school administrators will willingly offer additional resources to help the team meet its goals. It is a give-and-take relationship, just as in your home and community. When others recognize that your team handles resources responsibly, they will gladly lend a hand to help.

✔ CHECKPOINT

Why is it important for a team to have a good reputation?

Your team should be respected in your school and community for its accomplishments.

A team with a good reputation can have a positive influence on others.

CHARACTER OF TEAM MEMBERS

The character of a team is affected by the character of its members. A team is no better or worse than its team members. The things that you do and say can reflect on the team. It is almost like speaking with "one voice." Even though you are your own person, you are also a representative of your team. It is the same way in your family. How many times have you been told by your parents that you represent them no matter where you are and what you do? Have you ever been

TEACH
Have students brainstorm a list of character traits that they think a team should have. Have them compare their list to the points made in the text. How closely does their list match?

Ask students what they think when they hear the word *diversity*. Do they think that diversity of ideas, opinions, values, beliefs, and experiences is good or bad for a team? Have them explain their answers.

Ask students what happens at home when they do not take good care of the things their parents have provided for them. (They most likely are not given more things until they begin to behave more responsibly.) Explain that the same thing applies to teams that misuse the resources they are given.

TEACHING STRATEGIES
Print Learners
Have students draft a code of conduct that could be adopted by the various teams in your school. The code of conduct should include guidelines for individual behavior that will reflect positively on the team's reputation.

ONGOING ASSESSMENT
Use the Checkpoint as an opportunity to conduct ongoing assessment of student comprehension of the lesson material.

You have been selected as a member of the community outreach team at your school. The purpose of this team is to select and organize a community project and recruit student volunteers to work on it. From the start, the team ran into problems. The team leader is very demanding and does not listen to other people's opinions or ideas. Some team members are always late to team meetings, while some do not show up at all. During meetings, team members cannot reach agreement on how to best use the team's resources. Your team has not met any of its goals, and the principal is becoming concerned.

THINK *CRITICALLY*

1. Your principal has asked you why your team is having difficulties. What will you say?

2. What changes would you recommend to improve the way the team and team members operate?

TEACH
Ask students if they are familiar with the saying "a chain is no stronger than its weakest link." How does this saying relate to the relationship between team members and teams?

WHAT ABOUT ME?
Ask students if they have ever been a member of this type of dysfunctional team. If so, how were problems resolved?

Think Critically Answers
1. Answers will vary. If you answer the principal honestly, he or she may be able to offer some advice or suggestions to help build a more cohesive team.
2. Answers will vary. Team-building activities may help the team members become more cohesive and committed to achieving the team goals.

proud to let people know that your sister won the lead in the school play? Have you ever tried to deny that you were related to your brother because he is always in trouble? People often attach labels to individuals based on their connections with others and assume that they all think, act, and behave the same way.

Being a team member carries a lot of responsibility. You want to be a positive representative of the team. You also want your team to have a positive reputation that makes you proud to be a member. The character of the team and the character of the team members are so closely related that they share the same character traits. Team members must

- **Create and have a good reputation.** You have probably heard from your parents and friends throughout your lifetime how important it is to develop and maintain a good reputation. Some young people, though, have followed the crowd or have been influenced by other people or situations to take part in negative behaviors and activities. When these individuals attempt to rebuild their reputation, they will need forgiveness and support. Participating as a valuable, productive team member can help individuals build or rebuild a good reputation.

- **Be respectful of other members, teams, and the school and community.** If you are respectful in your everyday dealings with others, that trait will also be exhibited when you are in a group. If you are not respectful in your dealings with others, from your family to your peers to your friends, you may have a difficult time getting along with a large group of people. You must make an effort to respect others' opinions and actions, unless they are completely inappropriate. Treat others as you want to be treated. Go out of your way to compliment others for something they have done well.

- **Exhibit appropriate behavior.** You must be able to control your personal feelings and emotions to avoid inappropriate behavior that will reflect poorly on your team. A member of the math club must treat the opposing team respectfully even if he thinks the opposing team is cheating. Then, when it is more appropriate, he can speak with the person in charge of the event. You must recognize the appropriate way to take action. Remember, you are a representative of your team and school. You should always be on your best behavior.

- **Be responsible and live up to the team's purpose and goals.** As a representative of your team, it is not fair for you to speak negatively about the purpose and goals of your team to anyone outside of your team. This will damage the credibility of the team. If you are unhappy with the team, you should share your concerns with the team leader or in a team meeting so that the problem can be resolved. If you cannot resolve the problem and you are still in disagreement with the team's purpose or goals, you may need to consider leaving the team.

- **Contribute in a positive way.** Teams function better when members speak and act in a positive manner. This does not mean you cannot voice your opinion or feelings. But everything you say and do should not be negative or mean-spirited. If you feel that there is no process in place for sharing and giving feedback that would be helpful to the team, then approach the leader and suggest ways that it can be done in a climate of trust and support. Individuals need to be able to express themselves without being shut down or shut out. You will be more effective if you approach your role on the team with a positive attitude.

- **Understand and accept diversity.** Just because people are different from you does not mean that everything they say or do is wrong. Be careful not to mistreat, judge, or deny others access to some of the same opportunities that you have. People can be negatively different from you or positively different from you. Those who are positively different may have different viewpoints, but they are still respectful and pleasant to be around. Those who are negatively different often have an unpleasant attitude and are unwilling to compromise or listen to others' opinions. You do not have to like everything that is different about another person, but you should try to find some common ground that allows you to work together for the good of the team.

- **Care for team resources—human, material, and financial.** As a team member, you will have access to many of the team's resources. You must use these resources responsibly. If your team has been assigned a designated space in the building, you need to help take care of it and keep it clean. If you belong to a team that has a uniform, it is important that you take proper care of it. If your team role is to manage the team's finances, you should always keep the team's money separate from your own money. Always operate honestly, report all money transactions to the treasurer, and get a receipt when necessary. By respecting your team's resources, you will earn the reputation as a trustworthy, responsible individual.

 CHECKPOINT

Why are character traits the same for both the team and its members?

Character traits are the same for both the team and its members because they are so

closely related. Everything team members do and say reflects directly on the team.

> The biggest job in getting any movement off the ground is to keep together the people who form it. This task requires more than a common aim. It demands a philosophy that wins and holds the people's allegiance, and it depends upon open channels of communication between the people and their leaders.
>
> —*Martin Luther King, Jr.*

TEACH
Ask students what they think should be done when a team member speaks negatively about the team to others outside of the team. How can this member's behavior damage the entire team?

TEACHING STRATEGIES
Auditory Learners
Have students brainstorm a list of ways that team members who are very different can find common ground in order to work together for the good of the team. Write their answers on the board for discussion.

TEACH
Ask students for their thoughts on the quote in the margin. Have students conduct research on Martin Luther King, Jr. What leadership skills did he possess that helped him get the civil rights movement off the ground and hold the allegiance of the people?

ONGOING ASSESSMENT
Use the Checkpoint as an opportunity to conduct ongoing assessment of student comprehension of the lesson material.

Follow UP

UNDERSTAND LEADERSHIP CONCEPTS

Circle the best answer for each of the following questions.

1. If a team has a good reputation, which of the following is likely to occur?
a. Others will offer additional resources to help the team meet its goal.
b. The team's influence will grow.
c. The team will earn respect in the school and community.
d. all of the above

2. Having an understanding and acceptance of diversity means that you
a. accept everything that is different about another person
b. recognize that diversity covers race, gender, age, ideas, opinions, values, beliefs, and experiences
c. see yourself as being better than others
d. none of the above

THINK *CRITICALLY*

Answer the following questions as completely as possible. If necessary, use a separate sheet of paper.

3. Why is it important to care for a team's human resources?

The team's human resources are its people. When a team misuses or abuses its people, it loses the respect of its members and of other teams and individuals in the school and community.

4. Why is diversity in ideas necessary for a team?

Diversity in ideas helps a team look at situations in different ways. Different ideas can lead to new, unique approaches to solving problems.

5. Why is it important for team members to live up to the goals and purpose of the team?

A team is only as good as its members. If team members do not live up to the goals and purpose of the team, the team will be ineffective and will not succeed.

ASSESS

Reteach
Have students list the character traits of both teams and team members. Have them explain the reason that both lists contain the same character traits.

Enrich
Invite an outside speaker to talk to the class about the benefits of diversity in building a strong team. The talk should include the benefits of diversity not only in race, gender, or age but also in ideas, opinions, values, beliefs, and experiences.

Close
Have students discuss what is meant by the expression that being a member of a team is like "speaking with one voice."

Making Teams Work

IDENTIFYING TEAM ROLES

By observing the different teams in your school, you may have noticed that some of them seem to operate more successfully than others. But the reasons why some teams are successful while others are not may not always be clear. Teams do not always work well because of the human factor. Teams are made up of people with different personalities, attitudes, work ethics, needs, and character traits. So how do you bring them all together for the good of the team?

In order for a team to operate effectively, the strengths, talents, and creativity of each member should be identified to help define each member's role on the team. This process is known as **role identification**. Roles may be formal or informal. *Formal roles* are assigned, while *informal roles* are ones that members take on themselves. The leader is a formal role. Examples of informal roles include nurturers/caretakers, worker bees, challengers/confronters, analyzers, and mediators.

Leader

The person who assumes the role of leader is usually selected because of his or her ability to work effectively with people to get things done. As the task or goal changes, the person serving as the leader may also change because another person may have the strengths or skills needed to accomplish the new task or goal. Some teams have built-in goals, such as an athletic team whose goal is to win every game. Other teams have specific tasks, such as completing a float for the homecoming parade. Still other teams are formed around a leader's vision or passion, such as fundraising for hurricane victims.

Nurturers/Caregivers

Individuals who are **nurturers/caregivers** are concerned about the feelings and emotions of other team members.

© Digital Vision/Getty Images

Your role on a team can change based on the talent, creativity, skills, and personality that you possess. Working in a small group, make a list of the different team roles that have been discussed. Then add to the list any other roles you have observed or have taken on as a member of a team. Individually, select at least two roles in which you think you would comfortably fit. Then select at least one role in which you definitely would not fit. Compare and discuss your lists with other members of your group.

THINK *CRITICALLY*

What roles did you select that surprised your group members? What roles did they select that surprised you? After all members have explained their choices, share with one another your opinions about the roles you would have selected for each member. Explain your choices.

TEACH
On the board, list different types of teams, such as athletic, academic, artistic, technical, financial/fundraising, and student government. Ask students to name the traits that they think are most important for the leader of each type of team. Have them explain their answers.

TEACHING STRATEGIES
Tactile Learners
Have students create a collage representing the different types of roles members may have on a team. Display the collages in your classroom.

A TEAM EFFORT
In selecting the roles in which they would or would not comfortably fit, students should compare the descriptions of team roles in the lesson to their own talents, skills, and personality.

Think Critically Answers
Answers will vary.

Individuals assuming this role will often hide their own feelings and emotions to avoid conflict with others. The nurturer/caregiver will offer praise and support to other team members.

Worker Bees

Members who are **worker bees** do whatever it takes to get the job done. Once the task or goal has been identified and the need has been communicated, they jump right in and get started. These members may need to learn to be patient and include other team members when working on tasks and making decisions. Other team members know they can count on the worker bees to get things done.

Challengers/Confronters

Some team members may take on the role of a challenger or confronter. **Challengers/confronters** often try to keep the leader honest and committed to the team's goal. Their challenges and confrontations should not always be seen as negative. There are times when they force the leader and the team to rethink a direction or decision that may not be right. The leader of the team should avoid conflict with these individuals and make them feel that they are contributing members of the team.

Analyzers

Members that listen and then offer a solid response based on what they believe is the right direction, goal, or task for the team are **analyzers**. They often summarize what has been said or done to make sure they fully understand the situation. Analyzers bring reasoning and logic to team discussions and help keep members focused and on track.

Mediators

When there is a conflict or a breakdown in communication among team members, **mediators** will work to find a solution or an acceptable compromise. Individuals in this role usually have a high level of emotional stability. They keep a cool head when others are losing their tempers or are failing to accept the diversity among the members.

 CHECKPOINT

Why is it important for team members to identify their roles on a team?

For a team to operate effectively, the strengths, talents, and creativity of each member should be identified to help define each member's role on the team.

CHARACTERISTICS OF EFFECTIVE AND INEFFECTIVE TEAMS

Even if you have not participated on many teams, you know that an effective team is one that wins the game, accomplishes the goal, or completes the task. However, you probably have seen teams that are not effective. What characteristics determine if a team is effective or ineffective?

Effective Teams

Effective teams succeed in meeting their goals. But what makes a team effective? What is the difference between a team that succeeds and one that fails? There are several characteristics of an effective team.

Strong Leader

Selection of the leader should not be a popularity contest. The leader should be selected for his or her strong leadership skills. The leader must also be committed to the team's purpose and goals. Other members must know and trust that the leader can get the team to work together toward the goal, purpose, or task at hand.

Committed Team Members

Sometimes people join teams for the wrong reasons. Individuals may join because the team is highly popular or because their friends are members. In order to have team unity, a member's values, passion, and commitment must be in alignment with the team's goals. There is a difference between "knowing" the goals and actually "buying into" them. Team members who are committed to the team's goals will be willing to rise to the challenge.

Process-Oriented

The team's **process** defines how the team gets things done. Teams must determine how goals and tasks will be identified and agreed upon, how information will be communicated to the members, and how roles and responsibilities will be assigned. Does the leader set the goals or purpose? Is there shared leadership in establishing goals? When making decisions, do all team members have to agree, or does the majority vote win? A team will not be effective if it does not have a process in place to get things done.

ONGOING ASSESSMENT
Use the Checkpoint as an opportunity to conduct ongoing assessment of student comprehension of the lesson material.

TEACH
Ask students if they have ever been a member of a winning athletic team or some other type of team that succeeded in accomplishing its goals. What characteristics of their team made it effective?

Point out to students that the first two characteristics of an effective team relate to individuals—the team leader and team members. Both must be committed to the team's purpose and goals.

Ask students if they have ever joined a team just because they thought it was popular or because their friends were members. How do they feel about their decision to join that particular team? Do they think it was a good choice?

Ask students why they think it is important for a team to have a specific process in place in order for the team to accomplish its goals. To be effective, do they think that the process needs to be in writing?

TEACHING STRATEGIES
Gifted Students
Have students interview the leader and several members in different types of teams within their school. They should ask questions such as, "What do you think makes your team effective?" "What do you feel are your team's greatest weaknesses and how could you strengthen them?" and "What is your team's process for accomplishing goals?" Have students compile the responses and share them with the class.

Good Resources—Human, Material, and Financial

Usually, when people think of resources, they think of material things, such as computers, paper, and books, or financial resources, such as money. But team members are also resources. They make up the human resource pool from which the talent, skills, and creativity comes. The resource that is most in need at any given time can change. For example, a team may need to find an auditorium (material resource) to give a presentation. The team may also need money (financial resource) to make copies of handouts for the presentation. Finally, the team will need members (human resources) with the skills to create and give the presentation. In order for a team to be effective, it needs the right resources.

Defined Team Member Roles

Team members must understand their formal roles on the team and the responsibilities attached to their roles. When roles are clearly defined, team members will know what is expected of them. This will lead to more effective interactions among them.

Diverse Membership

Team members must realize that diversity is expressed in many ways other than race, ethnicity, gender, or culture. There is diversity in belief systems and value systems and in how people process information and interact within a social group. There is also diversity in skill level, talent, and creativity. Each team member also has diverse life experiences, or **personal history**. A team that has a diverse group of people is a team that can offer well-rounded, valuable opinions, thoughts, and solutions. By bringing together these different characteristics, a team is better equipped to serve the diverse needs of its members and community.

© Ryan McVay/Photodisc/Getty Images

Skilled Team Members

Does the debate team need the same kind of expertise that the chess team needs? Does the soccer team demand the same athletic skills as the volleyball team? Does the dance team use the same kind of steps as the football team? The type of team and its purpose and goals will determine the kinds of skills needed to get the job done. Without the right set of skills, a team cannot function effectively.

Good Communication

Strong communication skills are at the core of a successful team. Communication involves speaking, writing, and listening. People must not only listen to what is being said, but they must also hear the emotion, concern, or feelings that are being expressed. Observe people's body language. It can tell you a lot about a person's emotions. The team leader and team members need to communicate with each other and respond appropriately. Team members that believe they are being heard will feel valued and want to contribute to the success of the team.

Climate of Trust

As a member of a team, your behavior helps to create the climate in which your meetings and activities take place. The more accepting you are of others, the more others will trust what you say and do. Do you sit in the meeting and whisper to your friends while the leader is giving directions or asking for feedback? If so, it may appear that you are talking about someone in the room. Do you snicker when a challenger confronts the leader about his or her decisions? If so, you are creating an environment that does not feel safe for others to freely express their opinions or feelings. Once this negativity spreads, it is difficult to restore the spirit of trust and teamwork.

Strong Work Ethic

All members of a team need to have a strong work ethic. The worker bees cannot be the only members who work toward reaching the team's goals. This means that you need to do the work assigned to you to the best of your ability, whether it is answering the phone, taking meeting notes, or fundraising. A strong work ethic will give you the commitment needed to see a task through to completion.

▌Ineffective Teams

Trying to determine whether ineffective team members create ineffective teams or whether ineffective teams create ineffective team members is like trying to figure out which came first—the chicken or the egg. Any of the following characteristics of ineffective teams can relate to individual team members or to the team as a whole.

Poor Leadership and Direction

When the leader is uncertain and struggling, it is difficult for the team to function effectively. For many reasons, a leader may become overwhelmed when faced with the challenges of leading. There may not be enough available resources or support from team members. There may be too few members on the team to accomplish the task. Whatever the reason for the lack of leadership and direction, not having a talented leader in this role is a problem for the team. Decision making also becomes a problem when no one seems to be in charge of guiding the team toward completion of the task or goal.

Dissatisfied Team Members

Members become dissatisfied for many reasons. If there seems to be a lack of leadership or direction, members will become frustrated and stop participating in the team process. Members will also become discouraged if they do not feel a sense of acceptance. People join teams for many reasons, but one of the most important reasons is to belong to a group that adds purpose to their lives. If this need is not met, team members will no longer want to be a part of the team.

LEADERSHIP *Tip*

People will sometimes leave one team and move to another because they do not think a particular team is successful or popular. Your team is only as effective as its members make it. So be an effective team member or leader and help make your team the best it can be.

LEADERSHIP TIP
Ask students if they have ever left a team or "switched" to another team. If so, have several students explain why they left. Ask students to brainstorm a list of ways that teams can retain their current members while also attracting new members.

TEACH
Discuss the importance of developing listening skills as part of good communication. Explain that listening is more than hearing. It is an active process in which the listener focuses not only on what is being said but also on how it is being expressed.

Have students name some positive actions they can take to help create a climate of trust in the teams to which they belong.

Ask students if they have ever been a member of a team that could not "get it together." Why do they think the team did not accomplish its goals or complete its tasks?

Lack of Clear Purpose and Goals

When people commit their time, energy, and talent, they want to feel that it is for a clearly defined purpose or goal. If the leader does not communicate a vision or goal, team members will become confused about what to do. Team members may carry out tasks assigned by the leader, but without knowing the purpose, they will eventually lose interest and may leave the team.

Breakdown in Communication and Information Flow

If team members feel that they are out of the information loop, they become dissatisfied and disconnected. When a communication breakdown occurs, people often avoid their responsibilities and become more confrontational. Communication keeps the team moving forward and helps team members build a bond with one another.

Lack of Skill, Talent, and Creativity

Good intentions and team commitment do not necessarily guarantee that a team member has the talent, skill, or creativity to do a particular task. Individuals who want to be part of the team need to select the role that best fits their skills and talents. When selecting members for some teams, such as athletic teams, leaders must look for individuals that demonstrate a certain level of skill. In other teams, the type and level of skills, talents, and creativity needed is not as restrictive.

Lack of Trust

When trust is broken or lost, it is damaging to any kind of relationship. When others do not keep their word or do what they promise to do, they let others down and cause a breakdown in the completion of the task. Once this occurs, there may be a distrust of certain team members. This may affect the way the team operates. If team members feel they cannot depend on one another, they will not work together as a group to achieve the goal.

Lack of Resources

Some teams have no difficulty getting the resources they need because of the team's value or necessity within the school. They sometimes have booster clubs and community support. Other teams may have difficulty securing the resources they need to successfully function. They may not have enough team members with the right kind of skills and talents. Teams may not have the equipment they need or the money they need to buy the equipment. It becomes difficult to carry on with little or no support. It feels as if the purpose or goal of the team is not valued or necessary.

 CHECKPOINT

How is an effective team different from an ineffective team in the way it communicates?

On effective teams, members feel valued because they believe they are being heard. On ineffective teams, members feel out of the information loop, and they become dissatisfied.

Follow UP

UNDERSTAND LEADERSHIP CONCEPTS

Circle the best answer for each of the following questions.

1. **Team member roles include**
   a. nurturer/caregiver
   b. analyzer
   c. leader
   d. all of the above

2. **All of the following are characteristics of an effective team except**
   a. it is process-oriented
   b. team membership is limited in order to exclude certain people
   c. team roles are clearly defined
   d. it has a strong work ethic

THINK *CRITICALLY*

Answer the following questions as completely as possible. If necessary, use a separate sheet of paper.

3. **Why do some teams operate more successfully than others?**

Some teams operate more successfully than others because they are process-oriented and they have strong leadership, good resources, a diverse membership, team members who are skilled and committed, defined team member roles, good communication, a climate of trust, and a strong work ethic.

4. **Do you think a team member can take on more than one role? Explain why or why not.**

Answers will vary. Roles are based on a member's strengths, talents, and creativity, so it is possible for a member to have skills that quality him or her for more than one role. Also, members may be assigned a formal role while taking on one or more informal roles.

5. **Select one of the teams in your school and describe the resources—human, material, and financial—that you think it utilizes to function effectively.**

Answers will vary.

ASSESS
Reteach
Have students review the goals for the lesson and list the key points for each goal.

Enrich
Have students observe one or more team meetings to try to identify the various roles (formal and informal) that team members assume. Have them share their observations with the class.

Close
Have students explain how the team leader can contribute to a team being either effective or ineffective.

Chapter Assessment

TEACHING RESOURCES
ExamView® CD, Ch. 6

REVIEW *LEADERSHIP CONCEPTS*

Write the letter of the term that matches each definition. Some terms will not be used.

a. analyzers
b. challengers/
   confronters
c. collaborating
d. diversity
e. independent
f. interdependent
g. mediators
h. nurturers/
   caregivers
i. personal history
j. process
k. resources
l. role
   identification
m. worker bees

___i___   1. A person's life experiences

___f___   2. Depending on the help of others

___k___   3. Materials, finances, and people needed to run a team

___m___   4. Team members who do whatever it takes to get the job done

___b___   5. Team members who try to keep the leader honest and committed to team goals

___g___   6. Team members who seek a solution or a compromise to a problem

___l___   7. Identifying a person's strengths, talents, and creativity

___h___   8. Team members who are concerned with the feelings and emotions of others

___c___   9. Cooperating and working together in a joint effort

___d___   10. Includes areas such as ideas and values and belief systems in addition to race, gender, and age

Circle the best answer.

11. Understanding the difference between a group and a team will help you realize that
    (a.) although a team is a group of people, all groups are not teams
    b. teams and groups always work the same way
    c. groups do not need leaders
    d. none of the above

12. The person serving as the leader
    a. always remains in that position until the team dissolves
    b. is always selected by a majority vote
    c. does not need to communicate his or her vision with others
    (d.) none of the above

13. An individual who serves as a mediator
    a. should decide what is right and wrong
    (b.) must have emotional stability and the ability to keep a cool head
    c. is also the leader of the team
    d. none of the above

14. Teams may be ineffective for all of the following reasons except
    a. lack of communication
    b. lack of trust
    (c.) too many resources
    d. poor leadership

ASSESS
Reteach
Have students work with a partner to review the chapter terms. Students should take turns quizzing each other on the definitions.

Enrich
Have students work in groups to learn about team roles (formal and informal) other than those discussed in the chapter. Have each group report its findings to the class.

CLOSE
Have students review the characteristics of effective and ineffective teams as discussed in the chapter.

THINK CRITICALLY

15. *Describe a task that could be completed more effectively by a team instead of an individual. Then describe a task that could be completed more effectively by an individual.*

Answers will vary. Tasks that could be completed more effectively by an individual should include routine, daily tasks. Tasks that could be completed more effectively by a team are tasks that require individuals to work together toward a common goal, using their collective strengths, personalities, talents, and skills.

16. *Explain why the team leader role may need to pass from one person to another.*

As the task or goal of the team changes, the team leader role may need to pass from one person to another because another person may have the strengths or skills needed to accomplish the new task or goal.

17. *Other than the leader, which team member role do you think is the most important? Why?*

Answers will vary. Each team member role is important in order to have a successful and effective team.

18. *Think about the teams in your school. Select one team that you think operates effectively. Explain why you selected this team.*

Answers will vary.

19. *Select a team in your school that you think operates ineffectively. Explain why you selected this team.*

Answers will vary.

20. **Research**   Reflect on the different types of teams that exist in your community. Select one whose purpose/goals appeal to your area of interest. Interview at least one member of that team to discover why he or she is involved. Describe the person you interviewed and the reasons for the team's effectiveness in your community.

Answers will vary.

_____

_____

_____

_____

_____

_____

_____

21. **Problem Solving**   Think about a change that you would like to see made or a problem that you would like to see solved at your school. Write a proposal for assembling a team to help carry out your vision. Describe the purpose and goal of the team, the skills and talents needed on the team, and the resources needed to achieve the goal. Provide any other details about the team that you believe are important. Submit this proposal to your teacher.

Answers will vary.

_____

_____

_____

_____

_____

_____

22. **Communication**   You are impressed with the behavior of your school's basketball team, whether it wins or loses. Write a letter to the coach sharing how you think the team effectively represents the school and its student population. (If, however, you are disappointed in the team's behavior, write a letter to the coach stating your disapproval of the behavior and express how poorly the team represents the school.) Turn in your letter to your teacher.

Answers will vary.

_____

_____

_____

_____

_____

_____

_____

LEARNING TO LEAD

FOCUS

Participate in a community service project as a part of a team.

DESCRIPTION

Business leaders recognize that they have a responsibility to their communities. Most businesses provide financial resources when asked, but more importantly, they offer the time and talents of managers and employees as volunteers to "give back" to their communities. Business student organizations are also committed to community service. Each year students from across the nation volunteer in many important community service projects. When you become a part of one of these projects, your work in the organization contributes to making your community a great place to live. You can see firsthand how effective teamwork can be personally rewarding.

LEARNING TO LEAD
This project is written for use with student organizations such as BPA, DECA, and FBLA. Student organizations can help students prepare for key leadership roles. After students complete the activities, discuss what they learned about their student organization.

Activities
1. Answers will vary depending on the project.

ACTIVITIES

1. Obtain and study the information on the community service project guidelines provided by your national student organization office. Ask your chapter adviser and officers if a community service project has been identified for your chapter this year. If so, learn how you can become involved in the project. If not, obtain and review the written report your chapter prepared on a previous community service project.

2. Locate local media reports of community service projects that are currently being supported by businesses in your area. Identify the ways that businesses are providing money, volunteers, and other types of resources for the projects.

3. Interview a manager or an employee from a local business who is active in community service work to learn why he or she became involved. Determine how this person benefits personally and how the business benefits as a result of his or her efforts.

2. Answers will vary. Students may find their local community newspapers helpful in locating this information.
3. Answers will vary. Students should contact the interviewee to schedule a time for the interview and should prepare a list of questions in advance of the interview.

Share Your Results
1. Answers will vary depending on the volunteer project and the students' role. They should maintain detailed records of their volunteer service, especially if their school requires community service for graduation.
2. Answers will vary. Students may submit their publicity pieces to their school newspaper as part of their volunteer service.
3. Answers will vary based on the project selected.

SHARE YOUR RESULTS

1. *Volunteer for a local community service project sponsored by your student organization or another group in your school or community. Choose an individual role that makes the best use of your skills and allows you to contribute effectively to the team. Prepare a calendar and complete a weekly schedule of your community service responsibilities.*
2. *Prepare two publicity pieces for the project. The first will recruit volunteers for the community service project and the second will inform the community about the project and its benefits to the community.*
3. *Following the guidelines of your national organization, prepare a two-page proposal for a community service project that your organization can complete next year. Describe the purpose, the activities that will need to be completed, the resources required, and the reasons you believe the project is important for your student group and the community.*

ACCEPTING THE **CHALLENGE**

ACCEPTING THE
CHALLENGE
Case Study 6
Have students think about
the various groups within
their school. Are there too
many cliques of students
who perhaps have a
shared "history"? Do they
think other students may
be uncomfortable or may
feel like "outsiders"? Ask
students to suggest ways
that students in their
school can "expand" their
history like Marissa did.

CASE STUDY 6—REWRITING "HISTORY"

As you learned in the opening scenario, What Would You Do?, *Marissa usually made excuses to avoid spending time with the cheerleading squad after practice or games because she did not feel comfortable with them. Many of the members of the cheerleading squad had known each other since elementary school. They often talked about experiences they had shared while growing up together. Marissa lacked a sense of acceptance and belonging, and it was having a negative impact on her and the team.*

After the coach had the team members discuss their feelings, Marissa realized that her lack of "history" with the others made her feel like an outsider. She did not socialize with her team because it was much easier to stick with the people she already knew (her history) than to try to get to know new people. From that point on, Marissa made an effort to learn about her teammates' history. She took on a leadership role and organized weekly get-togethers. She developed team-building activities that would help everyone become better acquainted. She decided it was time to "expand" her history by creating new experiences with new people.

THINK *CRITICALLY*

1. *Do you think the cheerleading squad is more effective as a team now? Explain why or why not.*

The cheerleading squad should be more effective as a team now that the members

have become better acquainted and have learned more about each others' history. The

team-building activities also should help them become a more cohesive group.

2. *Describe an experience in which you were the one who was "different" from others. How did it make you feel?*

Answers will vary.

3. *Is there someone at school with whom you have difficulty communicating? How do you feel when you are around this person? Could not having "history" with the person be part of the problem? Explain.*

Answers will vary.

APPLY *WHAT YOU HAVE LEARNED–What Is Your Team Character?*

DIRECTIONS: *To be an effective team member, you need to be able to interact, socialize, and effectively work with others. Rate yourself on the following collaborative behaviors to see how you prefer to work with others. Using the survey below or on your Student Activity CD, enter the word YES or NO to reflect how you see yourself.*

COLLABORATION SURVEY

_____ 1. I like working on class group projects.

_____ 2. I prefer working on class projects alone.

_____ 3. I like sharing my ideas with my classmates and peers.

_____ 4. I am comfortable receiving feedback on my work from others.

_____ 5. I am comfortable giving feedback to others about their work.

_____ 6. I prefer working with students who are my friends and who are similar to me.

_____ 7. I am comfortable working with students who are not my friends and who are different from me.

_____ 8. I like sharing the leadership role with others depending on our strengths and skills.

_____ 9. I am comfortable having my ideas challenged by others.

_____ 10. I am comfortable sharing my "history" with others.

_____ 11. I prefer to work with classmates who keep their personal "history" to themselves.

_____ 12. I am comfortable supporting someone else's idea or vision even though my ideas and vision may be different.

_____ 13. I prefer classmates who let me express my feelings without passing judgment.

If you have more YES answers, you most likely feel very comfortable collaborating with others to complete tasks and accomplish goals. If you have more NO answers, you likely prefer working alone and may find it challenging to work with others. In either case, there is always room to make improvements to become a more effective team member. Review your answers above and the list of character traits for team members in Lesson 6.2.

On the lines below or on the Student Activity CD, create a SMART goal (including a completion date) that will help you become a more effective team member. Enter the goal in a monthly calendar (on the CD or your own). Then enter your thoughts, ideas, and discussions related to your goal in a journal (on the CD or your own) to help you plan and track your progress. Ask one of your teammates to be your goal-setting partner by providing feedback about your team behavior and interactions.

_____

_____

_____

_____

_____

_____

_____

ACCEPTING THE CHALLENGE
Apply What You Have Learned—What Is Your Team Character?
Note that students can complete this part of the *Accepting the Challenge* activity in the book or on the Student Activity CD. Instructions are provided on the CD.

After students have completed the Collaboration Survey, instruct them to write a SMART goal (including a completion date) that will help them become a more effective team member. Have them enter their goal on a monthly calendar. Students can use the monthly calendar on the Student Activity CD or their own calendar. Explain to students that they may also use weekly calendar pages (on the Student Activity CD or their own calendar) to plan activities and tasks that will help them achieve their goals. Finally, direct students to use a journal (on the Student Activity CD or their own) to track and evaluate their progress in achieving their goal.

A goal-setting partner can add an element of accountability and can offer positive feedback to help students stay on track to achieve their goals.

Students should be given the opportunity to reflect on the progress they have made toward achieving their goal. To do this, students can complete the *Evaluate Your Progress* activity on the Student Activity CD. Stress to students that it is important to complete this activity on the original target completion date even if they have not met their goal at that time.

Effective Groups and Organizations

© Patricia Clark/Photodisc/Getty Images

7.1 *Understanding Groups*

7.2 *Followership in Support of Leadership*

7.3 *The Changing Work Ethic*

What would **YOU** do?

SHOULD ARTHUR JOIN A GROUP?

Most people hope to join a certain group or belong to a popular organization in their school and community. Arthur Wiggins, a friendly high school student with a positive attitude, was interested in giving back to his community in some way. Arthur's father was his role model and the current commissioner of the little league football program in his community. Arthur was a high school football player. After graduation he wanted to give back to his community by following in his father's footsteps as the football commissioner.

Arthur had heard about the Jaycees organization. He knew it was a national organization that was active in community service projects such as Habitat for Humanity, Special Olympics, and homeless shelters. Arthur thought that he could fulfill his need to serve the community by joining the Jaycees. He discussed his interest with members of the Jaycees. They encouraged him to attend one of their membership meetings after he graduated from high school.

Arthur took their advice and attended a Jaycees' meeting shortly after graduating. He learned more about the members' roles and responsibilities related to the community service projects. Arthur became excited about the group's mission and purpose. The group members encouraged Arthur to join the Jaycees.

Arthur was torn. He had always planned on becoming the commissioner of the little league football program. He knew that in order to become the football commissioner, he would first have to gain experience as a little league football coach. He was concerned that if he joined the Jaycees, he would not have enough time to devote to the Jaycees' projects and the little league. Arthur knew he needed to give this careful consideration before making a final decision to join the organization.

THINK *CRITICALLY*

1. Why should Arthur take his time before making a final decision about joining the Jaycees even though he is excited about joining the organization?

2. Do you think there is a way that Arthur could combine his interests so that he could do both?

3. What advice would you give Arthur to help him make a decision?

TEACHING RESOURCES
Instructor's Resource CD
Lesson Plans, Ch. 7
PowerPoint Slides, Ch. 7

Student Activity CD, Ch. 7

thomsonedu.com/school/ leading
Crossword Puzzle, Ch. 7
Flash Cards, Ch. 7

Exam*View*® **CD**, Ch. 7

CHAPTER OVERVIEW
Chapter 7 discusses effective groups and organizations, the roles of followers, and the changing work ethic.

Lesson 7.1
Identifies types of groups and organizations and explains the importance of joining the group that is right for you.

Lesson 7.2
Explains the value of followership and identifies the roles of followers.

Lesson 7.3
Explains the value of work ethic and describes ways to stop its decline.

WHAT WOULD YOU DO?
Ask students if they have ever had to choose between two organizations or activities, both of which they wanted to do. How did they resolve the problem?

Think Critically Answers
1. Answers will vary. Arthur should take time to decide if this group meets his needs.
2. Answers will vary. Arthur could possibly combine his interests if the Jaycees were involved in a local little league football league.
3. Answers will vary. Arthur should consider his interests, skills, and abilities, and decide what is best for him to achieve his personal goals.

Understanding Groups

GOALS

- Identify the different types of groups and organizations in most schools.
- Explain the importance of joining a group that is right for you.

TERMS

- social dynamics
- supportive climate
- culture
- stereotype

SCHEDULE
Block 45 minutes
Regular 1 class period

FOCUS
Ask students how they decide whether or not to join a particular group or organization. What types of things do they consider and what questions do they ask themselves?

TEACH
Have students think of some of the groups and organizations in their school and community that seem to be effective. What traits do they have in common?

TYPES OF GROUPS

Why are some groups and organizations more effective than others? More important, what are the characteristics that make them effective? As you think about these two questions, try to focus on some of the groups and organizations in your school and community that seem to be effective. Their purpose may be different, but they all have some common traits of effectiveness. One common trait among groups that are effective is **social dynamics**, or good interpersonal relationships among group members. Other common traits include open communication and respect for each other. There are many different types of groups and organizations in most schools, but the most common categories include the following:

- academic groups
- service clubs/organizations
- athletic teams/groups
- career-oriented groups

Other Traits of Effective Groups

Having a supportive climate is another trait of an effective group or organization. A **supportive climate** is an environment that encourages

© Russell Illig/Photodisc/Getty Images

creativity among group members in a noncompetitive way. Other common traits of a supportive climate are (1) diversity among members, (2) strong commitment and participation by group members, (3) a clear purpose or message that is understood by all members, (4) a focus on future trends, and (5) general agreement among group members in most cases. These common traits may appear to be simple. But because group members have different personalities, it can be quite a challenge for them to work together effectively.

The size of a group may also play a part in how effective it is. A small group may include from three to five members. A large group can be more than ten or twelve members. If a group is too small, there may not be enough members to complete all of the tasks. If a group is too large, it may be hard to manage. The best size for a team depends on the task at hand. A small group may be able to handle a simple task, while a larger group may be needed to handle a task that requires a larger set of skills.

© Jeff Maloney/Photodisc/Getty Images

Academic Groups

Some examples of high school academic groups and organizations are technology clubs, debate teams, science clubs, National Honor Society, and French, German, and Spanish clubs. Often, students in these groups have a reputation for being smart and getting good grades.

The roles and responsibilities of leaders in academic groups are similar to those of other groups in your school. The leader should communicate the group's purpose and be in charge of group activities. It is the leader's responsibility to uphold the high standards of the academic group. Additional responsibilities for members of academic groups include the following:

- Participate in academic projects and presentations
- Share expertise with others by serving as peer-tutors
- Provide advice and encouragement to new members
- Support activities of the group and its officers
- Serve as a student representative on school committees

Service Clubs/Organizations

Students who have a desire for serving and helping others may be in your school's service clubs such as Peer Discovery, Key Club, Students Against Destructive Decisions (SADD), and other similar organizations. Members of these groups are focused on helping others by providing valuable services. They may be called service-providers. They are often admired by others because of their commitment to serve. Responsibilities of service organization members may include the following:

- Be a good listener with empathy for others' feelings, concerns, or situations and offer your support

TEACH
Have students review the common traits of a supportive climate. Ask them to think of the groups and organizations to which they belong. Do they have a supportive climate? Have several students provide examples.

Have students name the groups or clubs in their school that they consider to be academic groups. What similarities, if any, do they see in these groups?

Ask students to think about the groups in their school or community that are service clubs/organizations. What are some of the services they provide or the events they sponsor to help others?

TEACHING STRATEGIES
Gifted Students
Have students choose a service club or organization in their school or community and interview one of its members. Questions should include what the group does to help others, what the requirements are to join the group, and why the person joined this particular group. Have students report their findings to the class.

- Serve as a peer-mediator to resolve student conflicts
- Learn about and collaborate with other service providers or organizations in your school or community
- Refer people to other service organizations that can provide them with the help they need

Athletic Teams/Groups

The athletes may be considered the most popular people at your school. They are sometimes referred to as "jocks." Their popular image gains them many friends and supporters. Athletic teams are similar to other school groups, but they often have more public support. The role of team captain is similar to the role of other group leaders. The selection of the team captain is partly based on the athletic skill of the athlete. Other considerations include the person's character and ability to get along with others. Team members will not follow the lead of someone they do not respect. The responsibilities of members in athletic groups may include the following:

- Promote and enhance the school's image, values, and spirit
- Know and understand the academic requirements for maintaining athletic eligibility
- Participate in academic study group assignments
- Maintain personal health and fitness
- Be a good role model by displaying good sportsmanship and good behavior on and off the field

Career-Oriented Groups

Most members of career and technical student organizations (CTSOs) are interested in exploring and preparing for careers. They are also interested in leadership development in their career area. Career-oriented groups may promote careers in areas such as agriculture, business and marketing, family and consumer science, health, and technology.

Students who are interested in jobs and careers in agriculture might want to consider membership in the National FFA Organization. The

© Rim Light/Photodisc/Getty Images

Darnell's student organization is preparing for its annual fundraising event. Several members have decided to use their writing and computer skills to develop term papers to sell on the Internet. At first, Darnell thought they were joking, but he soon learned that they were serious. He voiced his concerns about their fundraising plan but was overruled. The other members said that their idea was not illegal and that they were fulfilling a need to help others complete their homework or research assignments. Darnell soon began to question his own beliefs and ethics. Was the service the others were providing really unethical? As he thought about their point of view, he asked himself, "What should I do?"

THINK *CRITICALLY*

1. What would you do if you were Darnell?
2. Even though their fundraising scheme is not illegal, what advice would you share with the group? Explain your reasoning to the group.

National FFA Organization prepares students for careers including horticulture, agricultural sales, agribusiness, forestry, and other agriculture-related jobs.

Students interested in careers in business and marketing should consider membership in Business Professionals of America (BPA), DECA, or Future Business Leaders of America-Phi Beta Lambda (FBLA-PBL). Members of these organizations receive training in economic and business principles, retailing, merchandising, advertising, management, public speaking, technology, and other business-related occupations.

Students could become members of Family, Career and Community Leaders of America (FCCLA) to learn more about family and child development, family services, and consumer education. The Health Occupations Students of America (HOSA) organization focuses on careers in health care and promotes quality health care for all people. Students with an interest in nursing, radiology, emergency medical services, and other health-related careers can join the HOSA organization.

The SkillsUSA organization is designed for students who are interested in industrial and technical careers, such as those in computer technology, electronics, cabinetmaking, construction, air conditioning and refrigeration, and other technical skill occupations.

No matter what your career interests are, there is most likely a student organization that supports it. By joining one of these organizations, you can develop your skills and prepare for a career.

TECH ETHICS
Discuss Darnell's ethical dilemma in terms of your school's code of ethics or code of conduct to help students decide what Darnell should do. Regardless of its legality, ask students if they think this fundraising activity will reflect positively on the student organization.

Think Critically Answers
1. Answers will vary.
2. Answers will vary. The group should consider how this activity will reflect on its reputation in the school and community.

ONGOING ASSESSMENT
Use the Checkpoint as an opportunity to conduct ongoing assessment of student comprehension of the lesson material.

CHECKPOINT

Describe three common traits of an effective group.

Common traits of effective groups include social dynamics, open communication, respect for each other, and a supportive climate.

UNDERSTANDING GROUP CULTURE

© Ryan McVay/Photodisc/Getty Images

Culture may be described as the beliefs, values, language, and dress that are characteristic of a certain group of people. You may gain a better understanding of a group in your school by learning more about its culture. You can learn more about a group's culture by taking a close look at its members. What kind of reputation do the group members have? What is their appearance like? What is their socioeconomic status, gender, and ethnicity? Answers to these questions may lead to new questions about the group's culture. For example, if the group does not have a diverse membership, or if its members are mostly male, you may want to find out why. If the group does not value diversity but you do, then your culture will conflict with the group's culture. Be careful not to **stereotype**, or pass judgment on a group based only on your experiences with one member. You must look at the group as a whole.

TEACH

Discuss the meaning of culture as it relates to groups within a school or community. Then ask students to think about a group to which they belong. How would they describe the group's culture?

Ask students if they have ever joined a group and then discovered that the group's purpose, issues, or concerns conflicted with their own. Would asking questions before they joined have helped them make the right decision?

ONGOING ASSESSMENT

Use the Checkpoint as an opportunity to conduct ongoing assessment of student comprehension of the lesson material.

■ Ask Questions Before Joining a Group

Before joining a group in your school or community, you should ask several questions to avoid joining the wrong group. You should talk with group members to learn more about the group's purpose and goals. As you talk with them, listen to your "inner voice" regarding your feelings and concerns about the group. You should also consider talking to individuals who are not members of the group that you want to join. Getting opinions from people outside the group can help you see the pros and cons of particular groups or organizations. Finally, you should ask yourself the following questions to help you decide if you are making the right choice.

- Why am I interested in joining this particular group?
- How does the group make me feel about myself?
- What level of commitment can I offer the group?
- What are my expectations of the group?
- Do I clearly understand the purpose of the group?
- Do I have some of the same concerns or same issues as the group?
- Does the group's purpose conflict with my beliefs and values?

 CHECKPOINT

Describe what culture means to you.

Culture encompasses the beliefs, values, language, and dress that are characteristic of a certain group of people.

Follow UP

UNDERSTAND LEADERSHIP CONCEPTS

Circle the best answer for each of the following questions.

1. Which of the following is a common trait found in effective groups?
   a. all group members share the same beliefs and values
   b. the group does not focus on future trends
   (c.) there is open communication among group members
   d. all of the above

2. The desirable number of members for an effective group is
   a. 6–8 persons
   b. 9–10 persons
   c. 10–12 persons
   (d.) group size can vary

THINK *CRITICALLY*

Answer the following questions as completely as possible. If necessary, use a separate sheet of paper.

3. Describe the four types of groups and organizations in most schools.

The four types of groups and organizations in most schools are academic groups,

service clubs/organizations, athletic teams/groups, and career-oriented groups.

_____

_____

_____

4. How would you describe the role of a student leader in an academic organization?

The leader in an academic organization should communicate the group's purpose and

be in charge of group activities. The leader also is responsible for upholding the high

standards of the academic group.

_____

_____

5. Explain the importance of understanding the culture of an organization, group, or team.

It is important to understand a group's culture in order to avoid joining a group whose

values and beliefs conflict with your own.

_____

_____

_____

ASSESS
Reteach
Ask students to list the common traits of a supportive climate. Have students write one or two sentences explaining how each trait contributes to a supportive climate and to the effectiveness of the group.

Enrich
Have students create a checklist of things to do and questions to ask before joining a group. The checklist should provide an easy-to-follow format to help students evaluate a group before joining.

Close
Have students explain the meaning of stereotyping. Ask several students to provide examples.

Followership in Support of Leadership

- Explain why followership is an important part of leadership.
- Identify the various roles of followers.

- followership
- gatekeeper

LEADERS AND FOLLOWERS NEED EACH OTHER

The saying "together we can accomplish more" describes the importance of collaboration between leaders and followers. Both groups need each other to be successful. They must work together to ensure the success of the group, team, or organization. Sometimes their roles are similar because leaders are also followers. Leaders usually have to report to a person with higher authority. For example, the team captain of the football team reports to the team's coach. The DECA student organization president reports to the faculty adviser of the organization.

Reasons for Becoming a Follower

Followership is the act of following a leader's guidance and direction. Although there are many reasons why people follow a leader, four common reasons are based on characteristics of a leader, including (1) personal integrity, (2) forward-thinking, (3) dedication, and (4) congeniality. Followers want leaders who have integrity and are trustworthy. They also want leaders who are forward-thinking with creative ideas for solving problems and reaching goals. Followers are looking for leaders who are committed to the mission of the group. Finally, followers want leaders who have a congenial, friendly personality that appeals to others and gives them a sense of acceptance and belonging. A smile, a pat on the back, or an encouraging word from a dedicated leader to a follower sends a message of encouragement and inspiration.

© Digital Vision/Getty Images

■ Following for the Wrong Reasons

Sometimes people follow a leader for the wrong reasons. They may go along with the group leader even though they are uncomfortable with the leader's actions because they fear losing friends or being left out of a popular group. They hide or put aside their own feelings. Sometimes people go along just to get along with others. Another reason some people choose to be a follower is because it lets them stay in their comfort zone. It is less risky to let others take the lead. Leaders have more responsibilities and often have to take the blame if things go wrong. But with time, followers can gain the confidence needed to overcome their fears and become outstanding leaders.

CHECKPOINT

Why do people choose to follow a leader?

Many people become followers based on the leader's characteristics, including

personal integrity, forward-thinking, dedication, and congeniality.

TYPES OF FOLLOWERS

There are many types of followers in your groups who assume different roles and responsibilities. For example, some followers have the role of gatekeeper and work closely with the leader. A **gatekeeper** closely monitors the daily operations and activities of the group. In many cases, gatekeepers develop leadership skills and become leaders in their group or in other groups. Because gatekeepers work closely with other group members, they must have some of the same characteristics as leaders. For example, they must be congenial and dedicated. Other roles and responsibilities of followers may include

- active followers
- passive followers
- courageous followers
- situational followers
- negative followers

Active Followers

People who think on their own and who are willing to take responsibility for their own actions are *active followers*. This type of follower is self-motivated and supportive of the leader and the purpose and mission of the group. Active followers are sometimes difficult to work with. They mean well, but in their eagerness to get things done, they often fail to consider the thoughts and opinions of others. The leader needs to determine how to manage active followers without damaging their spirit or weakening their support.

Passive Followers

People who are dependent on the leader for constant direction and supervision are known as *passive followers*. As the leader, your job is to

> Followers tend to focus on doing things right while leaders tend to focus on doing the right things.
>
> —*Stephen R. Covey, A. Roger Merrill, and Rebecca R. Merrill*

TEACH

Ask students why an effective group needs both leaders and followers. Do they think that a leader alone can accomplish the group's goals?

Ask students why they think the characteristics of the leader are important in an individual's decision to become a follower. What do they think might happen to the followers if a leader lacked these common characteristics?

Ask students what they think is meant by the quotation in the margin. Point out that followers focus more on completing tasks while leaders focus on setting and achieving goals that will accomplish the group's purpose.

Ask students if they have ever joined a group or organization for the wrong reason. What was the outcome?

ONGOING ASSESSMENT

Use the Checkpoint as an opportunity to conduct ongoing assessment of student comprehension of the lesson material.

© Photodisc/Getty Images

encourage them to take a more active role in the group. Your words of encouragement might motivate them to complete a task. Recognizing their accomplishments may motivate them even more. You could also try giving them more responsibility to show your confidence in their abilities. Since passive followers are not risk takers, you should remind them that they will not be punished for making a mistake. Ensure them that you will provide help if needed.

Courageous Followers

Most groups have courageous followers who are good at getting things done because they work well with others. *Courageous followers* are self-starters and serve as role models for other followers in the group. They are considered the MVPs (most valuable people) of the group because of their good interpersonal skills. They are considered risk takers and are willing to take on more responsibility. They are also willing to accept responsibility if things go wrong. Although they may question the leader's actions, they do it in a respectful manner while still showing support for the group's mission. Courageous followers are often considered for leadership opportunities because of their ability to work well with others.

Situational Followers

You may know of cases where a classmate or teammate has made the change from follower to leader because of a given situation. These individuals are *situational followers*. After Hurricane Katrina, students who were followers felt the need to step up to the plate and take the lead in serving the needs of others. Many students took on leadership roles in various service organizations and went to New Orleans to help storm victims. Consider also the story of former National Basketball Association (NBA) player Scottie Pippen. Pippen was a trainer and manager for his college basketball team at the University of Central Arkansas until one day he had to fill in as a replacement player for an injured teammate. The rest is history as Scottie Pippen went on to help lead the Chicago Bulls to six NBA championships.

Negative Followers

Do you know people in your group who are smart, independent thinkers but who seem to distance themselves from others? These people may be referred to as *negative followers* because of their negative and untrusting attitudes. Negative followers often prefer to work alone and do not want others' advice or help. Their negative attitude may be due to disappointment or lack of trust in the leader. As a leader, your challenge for negative followers is to build their trust and persuade them to work more cooperatively with others in the

TEACH
Discuss each of the types of followers found in groups and organizations. Have students think of the organizations to which they belong. Do they assume different roles and responsibilities in different groups? Are there other individuals in their groups that fit these roles?

TEACHING STRATEGIES
At-Risk Students
Ask students to create a table or chart of the different types of followers. Have them list the types of followers in the first column and a description of each type of follower in the second column.

George was selected as the school's new drum major. He was extremely happy and excited to be leading the marching band. He decided to conduct a meeting with his section leaders to discuss some new creative routines for the band. During the meeting, two of the section leaders said they had no interest in learning new routines. They argued that their current routines were good enough and did not see a reason to change them. George was disappointed by their reaction, but he decided to start working on new routines anyway. He was sure he could convince the others to go along with his plan.

THINK *CRITICALLY*

What type of followers do you think the two section leaders are? What kind of follower do you think George is? Do you think George is handling this in the right way? What do you think George should do to resolve this issue without causing conflict among the band members? Explain your answers.

group. Let them know that you value their opinion. Try to change their negative attitude into a positive one.

Followers Becoming Leaders

As a leader, are you helping followers become leaders? Are you speaking words of encouragement and providing leadership opportunities? The growth and success of your school and community is based on the development of future leaders. Each year, some students enter a new school, while others leave it. Experienced, older students, such as seniors, can be good mentors and role models for new students, such as freshman. A good leader will prepare followers to take over leadership positions. It is important to have new leaders who will continue to carry out the mission of the outgoing leaders. To help followers become leaders, work closely with them to determine what they do best. Encourage them to use this skill or talent to create leadership opportunities. Other things you can do to help followers become leaders include the following:

- Provide a supportive climate that promotes creativity and growth
- Speak words of encouragement and inspiration often
- Listen and give advice when asked
- Share books and articles that are good learning tools
- Provide challenging leadership opportunities
- Serve as a mentor or recommend a peer-mentor who will keep them focused on becoming a leader

CHECKPOINT

Name the different types of followers found in most groups.

The types of followers found in most groups include gatekeepers, active followers,

passive followers, courageous followers, situational followers, and negative followers.

A TEAM EFFORT
Ask students why they think the two section leaders may have reacted the way they did to George's suggestion about new routines. Do they think that George should begin working on new routines before resolving the problem?

Think Critically Answers
Answers will vary. The two section leaders are negative followers. Although George is now a leader, his behavior is indicative of an active follower because in his eagerness to create new routines, he is failing to consider the opinions of others. George needs to find out why the section leaders are so opposed to new routines and resolve that issue in a calm and respectful manner before he alienates others on his team.

ONGOING ASSESSMENT
Use the Checkpoint as an opportunity to conduct ongoing assessment of student comprehension of the lesson material.

Follow UP

UNDERSTAND LEADERSHIP CONCEPTS

Circle the best answer for each of the following questions.

1. People often follow a leader because of his or her
  a. personal integrity
  b. forward thinking
  c. congeniality
  (d.) all of the above

2. A group member who works well with others is a(n)
  a. active follower
  b. passive follower
  (c.) courageous follower
  d. situational follower

THINK *CRITICALLY*

Answer the following questions as completely as possible. If necessary, use a separate sheet of paper.

3. Identify the type of follower that best describes your role and responsibility in a group or organization to which you belong. It may include an informal group, such as friends, or a formal group, such as a club.
Answers will vary but may include gatekeeper, active follower, passive follower,
courageous follower, situational follower, or negative follower.

4. Explain the difference between active and passive followers.
Active followers think on their own and are willing to take responsibility for their own
actions. However, in their eagerness to get things done, they may fail to consider the
opinions of others. Passive followers are dependent on the leader for constant direction
and supervision. They are not risk takers.

5. Describe three activities that you can do to help followers become future leaders.
To help followers become future leaders, you can work with them to determine what
they do best, encourage them to use their skill or talent to create leadership opportunities,
provide a supportive climate, speak words of encouragement, listen and give advice, share
books and articles, provide challenging leadership opportunities, and serve as a mentor or
recommend a peer-mentor who will keep them focused on becoming a leader.

The Changing Work Ethic

GOALS

- Understand the meaning and value of work ethic.
- Describe how you can stop the decline of the work ethic.

TERMS

- work ethic
- compensation

MEANING AND VALUE OF WORK ETHIC

What does the saying "doing a good day's work for a good day's pay" mean to you? More important, does the term *work ethic* have any meaning in your life? **Work ethic** refers to a person's character, values, beliefs, and behavior as related to work, which may be paid or unpaid employment.

Historically, the term *work ethic* in the United States can be traced back to the sixteenth century. The Protestant work ethic emphasized the importance of work as a benefit to society. During that time, it was a cultural expectation that people would do meaningful work. During the Industrial Revolution of the late eighteenth and early nineteenth centuries, work ethic became even more important as the nation moved away from agricultural jobs to manufacturing jobs.

Because the types of work have continued to change throughout the years, from farming to manufacturing and currently to service and information technology, the way people think about work has also changed. In the past, most people left home to go to a job that was physically demanding. Today, many people do not even leave the comfort of their homes because they can do their work on their home computers.

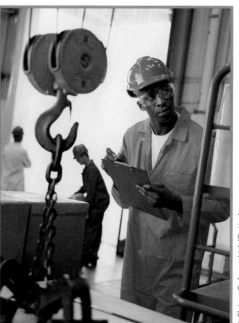
© Flying Colours Ltd./Getty Images

We are now working in the Information Age, and it has brought about a new meaning and understanding of the work ethic. Instead of the traditional work schedule of 9:00 to 5:00, more people are working flexible hours. They can often perform their job by working on a schedule that best meets their needs.

SCHEDULE
Block 45 minutes
Regular 1 class period

FOCUS
Write the term *work ethic* on the board and ask students what they think it means. Do they think you have to be a paid employee to have a good work ethic? How does work ethic apply to other areas in their lives?

TEACH
Discuss how "work" has changed over the years. Ask students for examples of agricultural, manufacturing, service, and information technology jobs.

Ask students if they know people who telecommute or work from their home computer. What do they think are the advantages and disadvantages of telecommuting? Ask students whether they would like to work from home. Why or why not?

Changes in the work environment also include the location of the job. More than ever before, people are working out of their homes and in other non-traditional locations. Because of these and other changes in the work environment, the work ethic of the twenty-first century has a different meaning to people than in past years.

What Work Looks Like Now

Today, many people have a new attitude about work ethic. Many people work because they enjoy it, not because they feel an obligation to society. Because of the change in work ethic, people are creating their own businesses based on what they enjoy doing. How many people do you know who have created jobs and businesses based on their interests? In the service industry, jobs are being created daily, such as web site designer, personal shopper, landscaper, musician or singer, babysitter, pet sitter, and many others.

What is the work environment like in your community? Are there more manufacturing jobs or service jobs in your community? What observations have you made of your parents, teachers, or neighbors regarding their attitudes toward work? You and your friends will have a different image of the work ethic than people in earlier generations. This image is not good or bad—just different. As the work environment changes, the way in which people work also changes. Business is becoming more global, which may also affect the work ethic.

 CHECKPOINT

Explain the term work ethic *and its meaning in your personal life.*

The term *work ethic* refers to an individual's character, values, beliefs, and behavior related to both paid and unpaid employment.

© Digital Vision/Getty Images

A GOOD DAY'S WORK

Many people believe that work ethic is not as strong today as it was in the past. This may be due to a change in attitudes. In past generations, people were more focused on helping others. Today, people seem to be more focused on themselves and how others can help them. When you accept a job or task, do you put forth your best effort to accomplish it, or do you first want to know how it will benefit you? Maybe you want to know your **compensation**, or what you will receive in return for completing the task. At your job, your compensation is usually in the form of money, or wages paid, for work done. Some people believe that work ethic is closely tied to compensation. If this were true, it would mean that workers would have a stronger work ethic if they were paid more money. However, work ethic is actually more closely tied to personal integrity than to how much money you will receive. Work that is meaningful and enjoyable results in a stronger work ethic.

"Show me the money" should not be your attitude about work. You should focus on doing a good job to serve the needs of others. If you believe that your job has a purpose, you more likely will be committed to it and want to do a good job.

Volunteer workers and unpaid interns are good examples of the connection between work ethic and personal integrity. These individuals provide quality services for no pay. Your attitude toward work should be one of pride and accountability for doing a good job. This attitude will help rebuild a strong work ethic in our society.

Your attitudes and values toward work as well as your respect for authority begin at home. What is your attitude about chores and other tasks you have to do around the house? You should take pride in the fact that you are contributing to the household. Your work ethic also begins at school. Do you make an effort to turn in quality work on time? If so, you are aware of the value of work and have a strong work ethic. These qualities will serve you well throughout life.

Work Ethic Is an Invisible Honor Code

The Boy Scout's oath, "On my honor, I will try to do my best," is an example of an invisible honor code to follow to help improve your

COMMUNICATE

Audrey is the president of the student organization Students Against Destructive Decisions (SADD) at her high school. She is concerned about the behavior of two members of her organization. Audrey has learned that they are "hanging out" with the wrong crowd and are often drinking on weekends at parties. She confronted them and explained that their behavior was unacceptable for members of the SADD organization. The discussion with them did not go well. They felt that Audrey was lecturing them and told her that their behavior after school was not her concern. Audrey was trying to communicate to them that their actions could hurt the image of the organization.

THINK *CRITICALLY*

What advice would you give Audrey on how to handle this situation? Do you think there is a better way for Audrey to communicate her concerns to these two members? How might she get her point across to them without making them feel unwelcome in the organization?

The new work ethic concerns a labor of love. Find a job that you enjoy and love doing, and you will never "work" another day in your life.

TEACH
Provide students will a complete copy of the Boy Scout's oath as a sample of an invisible honor code. Then have them write an honor code for themselves, expressing the qualities and work ethic that they personally stand for.

CHARACTER BUILDER
Have students think about a class they love at school. Do they look forward to it? Does the time fly when they are there? Explain that finding a job you love feels the same way.

ONGOING ASSESSMENT
Use the Checkpoint as an opportunity to conduct ongoing assessment of student comprehension of the lesson material.

work ethic. An invisible honor code motivates you to do your best and to do the right thing even when no one is watching you. You will gain self-respect by following your personal code of ethics. This will set you apart from others as a leader. Followers admire leaders who behave ethically and who have a commitment to their tasks. An invisible honor code and work ethic are closely related. Personal qualities and traits that should be part of both your honor code and work ethic include the following:

- Good attendance—Attend work, school, group meetings, and other obligations as expected. Let someone know if you are going to be late or absent.
- Respect for peers—Learn to work well with others. Be cooperative and willing to listen to others' thoughts and opinions.
- Positive attitude—Enjoy what you are doing. Determine how you can be of help and assist others in getting the job done.
- Good personal appearance—Try to dress appropriately and stay healthy and fit to feel better about yourself.
- Open communicator—Share your thoughts and opinions with others. Communicate openly and identify problems that, if not resolved, could affect your work ethic.
- Quality performance—Work to the best of your abilities in order to accomplish the purpose and mission of the group or organization.

CHECKPOINT

List one personal quality or trait associated with work ethic and explain why it is important.

Qualities associated with work ethic include good attendance, respect for peers, positive

attitude, good personal appearance, open communication, and quality performance.

© Photodisc/Getty Images

Follow UP

UNDERSTAND LEADERSHIP CONCEPTS

Circle the best answer for each of the following questions.

1. Work ethic is directly related to
  a. how much money a person earns
  (b.) a person's values, beliefs, and behavior regarding work
  c. the Information Age
  d. none of the above

2. All of the following personal qualities and traits are related to work ethic except
  a. positive attitude
  b. respect for peers
  c. good personal appearance
  (d.) ethnic background

THINK *CRITICALLY*

Answer the following questions as completely as possible. If necessary, use a separate sheet of paper.

3. Describe how work and the workplace have changed throughout the years in the United States.
The Protestant work ethic of the sixteenth century emphasized work as a benefit to society. People were expected to do meaningful work. During the late eighteen and early nineteenth centuries, work in the United States moved from agricultural jobs to manufacturing jobs. Currently, work relates more to service and information technology, and more people are able to work from home on their home computers.

4. How do you think the work ethic of employees affects our society?
Many employees focus on themselves and how others can help them instead of how their work can help their employer, coworkers, and society in general. Their emphasis is on how much money they are being paid, and their work ethic is tied to compensation.

5. What suggestions can you make to improve your personal work ethic?
Answers will vary.

ASSESS
Reteach
Have students list the personal qualities and traits discussed in the lesson that should be part of their honor code and work ethic. For each item listed, have students indicate one thing they can do personally to achieve that specific quality or trait.

Enrich
Have students draw a time line that illustrates the changing face of work in America, beginning with the Protestant work ethic and continuing through the Information Age.

Close
Ask students what they can do at home and at school to maintain a strong work ethic.

Chapter Assessment

TEACHING RESOURCES
ExamView® CD, Ch. 7

REVIEW *LEADERSHIP CONCEPTS*

Write the letter of the term that matches each definition.

> a. compensation
> b. culture
> c. followership
> d. gatekeeper
> e. social dynamics
> f. stereotype
> g. supportive climate
> h. work ethic

__f__ 1. Pass judgment on a group based only on experiences with one group member

__b__ 2. Beliefs, values, language, and dress that are characteristic of a certain group of people

__a__ 3. What you receive in return for completing a task

__d__ 4. A group member who closely monitors the daily operations and activities of the group

__c__ 5. Act of following a leader's guidance and direction

__h__ 6. Personal character, values, beliefs, and behavior as related to work

__g__ 7. Environment that encourages creativity among group members in a noncompetitive way

__e__ 8. Good interpersonal relationships among group members

Circle the best answer.

9. Most student members of a career and technical student organization (CTSO) are interested in
   a. career exploration
   b. leadership development
   c. career preparation
   (d.) all of the above

10. A supportive climate has all of the following traits except
    a. a diverse membership
    b. a commitment by group members
    (c.) a focus on competition
    d. a clear purpose or mission

11. Before joining a group, you should consider
    a. whether or not your friends belong to the group
    (b.) why you are interested in joining
    c. what kind of follower you are
    d. none of the above

12. A good leader has
    a. a good work ethic
    b. an understanding of the group's culture
    c. the ability to prepare others for leadership roles
    (d.) all of the above

ASSESS
Reteach
Review the key terms, goals, and Checkpoint questions in the chapter by using a game format such as Jeopardy.

Enrich
Have students review the classified job ads in their local newspaper to determine what types of jobs are available in their community. Have them report whether there are more manufacturing, service, or information technology jobs. Also have them note if they found telecommuting opportunities and ads offering flexible working arrangements.

CLOSE
Ask students to predict future changes in the ways people work. Do they think these future changes will have an effect on the work ethic?

THINK *CRITICALLY*

13. *What are two questions you should consider asking yourself before joining a particular group or organization?*

Before joining a group, you should ask yourself why you are interested in joining, how the group makes you feel about yourself, what level of commitment you can offer the group, what your expectations are of the group, whether you clearly understand the group's purpose, if you have the same concerns or issues as the group, and if the group's purpose conflicts with your beliefs and values.

14. *Review the career-oriented groups discussed in this chapter. Which one of the groups most closely matches your career interests? Do you think it would be helpful to join this group? Explain why or why not.*

Answers will vary.

15. *Explain two reasons why some groups or organizations are more successful than others.*

Common traits among effective groups are open communication, respect for each other, and social dynamics, which includes diversity among members, strong commitment and participation by members, a clear purpose or message, a focus on future trends, and general agreement among group members.

16. *Describe the difference between negative and courageous followers. Do you know of individuals in these categories?*

Courageous followers work well with others. They are self-starters and good role models, and everyone enjoys working with them. Negative followers, on the other hand, are negative and have untrusting attitudes. They often prefer to work alone and do not want the advice or help of others.

17. *Why is it important for followers to become future leaders?*

The success of the organization depends on the development of future leaders. As older, more experienced members eventually leave the group, it is important to have new leaders ready to step in and continue to carry out the mission of the outgoing leaders.

18. **Research**   *Understanding the importance of culture is necessary to break down stereotypes that students may have of others who are different from them. Use the Internet, newspapers, and magazines to gather information about culture. Create a colorful collage of the different cultures represented in your school and community.*

Answers will vary.

_____

_____

_____

_____

19. **Problem Solving**   *Review the different groups and organizations in your school. Determine the purpose and mission of the one that most interests you. Identify the group or organization as academic, service-oriented, athletic, or career-oriented. Describe the culture of the group. Decide if you would be interested in joining the group or organization. Explain why or why not.*

Answers will vary.

_____

_____

_____

_____

20. **Communication**   *You are the president of the Student Government Association (SGA) at your school. One of your challenges for the next school year is to communicate to the student body how to choose and join a student organization. Write a one-page article to be published in your school's newspaper to share tips and advice with your fellow students. Your article should be entitled "Look Before You Leap."*

Answers will vary.

_____

_____

_____

_____

21. **History**   *Research the Industrial Revolution. What were some of the inventions during that time? How do you think these inventions may have affected the work ethic of people working during that time period?*

Answers will vary.

_____

_____

_____

_____

LEARNING TO LEAD

FOCUS

Learn strategies to improve the effectiveness of your student organization.

DESCRIPTION

You may be a part of a club or group that seems to have no purpose or focus and struggles to keep its members interested and involved. You may also be involved in clubs and groups that everyone wants to join and that always seem to be doing something fun and exciting. What makes the difference? You have learned a lot about what makes a group effective. Whether you are a member or the leader of a club or other organization, you want to make sure it is fun, meaningful, and successful.

Apply your knowledge of effective groups to your local student organization. You will learn about tools and resources that can be used to make groups more effective and, in turn, more successful.

LEARNING TO LEAD
This project is written for use with student organizations such as BPA, DECA, and FBLA. Student organizations can help students prepare for key leadership roles. After students complete the activities, discuss what they learned about their student organization.

ACTIVITIES

1. *Study the web site of your national student organization to locate information and resources on topics designed to improve the effectiveness of local chapters. Locate "how to develop a chapter program of work" and "how to conduct a chapter meeting." Read articles about successful local chapter activities in the national magazine for your organization.*

2. *Interview five students about their experiences with various clubs and student organizations. Identify what they do and do not like and what they believe makes an effective organization that people want to join.*

3. *Use the Internet to find articles on effective and ineffective groups. Summarize the articles to help you in future group leadership roles.*

SHARE YOUR RESULTS

1. *Use the information you gathered from your national student organization's web site to develop a monthly calendar of activities for your local chapter.*
2. *List and briefly describe one or two activities for each month of the school year that you believe will be interesting to all students and keep them actively involved in the chapter. Make sure the calendar contains a variety of activities that reflect the organization's goals, including professional, social, education, and community service activities.*
3. *Work with a team of students to plan and then role play a chapter meeting for your local organization. Prepare a meeting agenda and assign each person an item on the agenda where they will take a leadership role.*
4. *If possible, videotape the meeting, review the tape, and discuss what made the meeting effective and interesting to members and how you can improve future meetings.*

Activities
1. Answers will vary. Students may want to check archived or back issues of the national magazine for information.
2. Answers will vary. Students should make an effort to interview members of different clubs and organizations.
3. Answers will vary. Students may find it helpful to list the key points from each article on 3"x5" cards for easy reference.

Share Your Results
1. Answers will vary.
2. Answers will vary.
3. Answers will vary. This may be a good opportunity to involve new or less experienced members.
4. Answers will vary.

ACCEPTING THE
CHALLENGE
Case Study 7
Ask students what they
think might happen to
Arthur if he joins a group
or becomes football com-
missioner for the wrong
reason. Do they think he
can be an effective leader
if he is not truly excited
about the group's mission?

ACCEPTING THE CHALLENGE

CASE STUDY 7—DOING THE RIGHT THING FOR THE WRONG REASON

It is quite admirable that Arthur wants to follow in his dad's footsteps and be the football commissioner, as discussed in the What Would You Do? *opening scenario. However, his dad thinks Arthur wants to be the football commissioner for the wrong reasons. Could it be because he knows how much being the football commissioner meant to his dad? Several years ago, Arthur joined the football team because his brother was on the team and was voted team captain. Because his brother had so much passion for the game of football, Arthur thought he should join the team too. This was another instance in which Arthur joined a team for the wrong reasons. Arthur's dad talked to him about how important it is for Arthur to have his own passion about a team or organization. His dad explained that in order to be truly dedicated and committed to a group, Arthur has to be excited about its vision and mission. Then Arthur's enthusiasm will motivate him to work hard to achieve the group's goals. His strong work ethic and dedication will most likely result in a leadership role. Arthur can then say he did the right thing for the right reason.*

THINK CRITICALLY

1. *Have you ever joined a team or group because one of your siblings or friends was a member? Were you as committed as that person?*

Answers will vary.

_____

_____

_____

_____

2. *Why do you think it is important to consider your passions before joining a group or organization?*

Answers will vary. It is important to be committed to the group's mission and

dedicated to helping the group achieve its goals. In order to do this, members need to

be passionate about the organization.

_____

_____

3. *Explain the relationship between passion and work ethic. How are these two characteristics related to leadership?*

Answers will vary. Work ethic relates to a person's values, beliefs, and behavior related

to work. When individuals are passionate about an issue or activity, they have a

positive attitude about doing whatever amount of work it takes to achieve the group's

goals.

_____

APPLY *WHAT YOU HAVE LEARNED–Is This the Group for You?*

DIRECTIONS: *To examine your commitment to the groups or teams to which you belong, you sometimes need to think about the reasons you joined them. Answer the following questions on the lines below or on your Student Activity CD to help determine whether you joined a group, or influenced others to join a group, for the right reasons.*

1. *Name and describe any group (even if it is a group of friends) either at school or in your community that you are a part of (or were once a part of) that you know you joined for the wrong reason. If you are currently a member, is there still a good reason to be a part of this group. If you are no longer a member, explain your reason for leaving the group.*

   _____

   _____

   _____

2. *List the name(s), or relationship to you (such as a friend or sister), of the person who has influenced your decision to join a group or team. Why is it important to you to please that person instead of yourself?*

   _____

   _____

   _____

3. *Describe a situation in which you have convinced someone to join a group because you did not want to join the group alone.*

   _____

   _____

   _____

4. *Describe a time when it would be acceptable to encourage others to join a group even if they have no interest or desire to be a part of it.*

   _____

   _____

   _____

5. *Select a group or team that you think you would like to join. On the lines below or on the Student Activity CD, create a SMART goal (including a completion date) to ensure that you join this group for the right reasons. Enter your goal in a monthly calendar (on the CD or your own). Then enter your thoughts, ideas, and discussions related to your goal in a journal (on the CD or your own) to help you plan and track your progress. Select a goal-setting partner to help you explore why you want to be a part of this group.*

   _____

   _____

   _____

   _____

   _____

8

Understanding and Supporting Diversity

© Jules Frazier/Photodisc/Getty Images

8.1 *Recognizing, Respecting, and Valuing Diversity*

8.2 *Working Effectively in Diverse Groups*

8.3 *Fitting in Without Fading Out*

What would **YOU** do?

REDCLOUD HOLDS ON TO HIS HERITAGE

John Redcloud has worn his hair long since he was in elementary school. His teachers and the other students have accepted it as part of his culture. John sees the length of his hair as a symbol of pride and honor for his Native-American heritage.

Throughout his educational career, John has played on various sports teams. He is also a member of the National Honor Society. At the suggestion of his social studies teacher, John also joined the debate team. He was excited when the team qualified for the state debate team competition.

When the sponsors of the state debate team competition saw John's long hair, they suggested that he be barred from participating in the competition. They said that John's appearance did not fit the image they liked students to display. John was very angry and offended by their comments. He offered to quit the team and withdraw from the competition. He felt that the sponsors of the state competition were prejudiced against him.

The sponsor of his school's debate team would not let John quit. Instead, he talked to the governing board of the state organization. He supported John's cultural right to wear his hair long. The governing board voted to accept John's participation and honored his commitment to his culture.

John's team went on to win the state competition and to participate in the national competition. If John had given up, he would have missed the opportunity not only to be part of a winning team but also to see that some people recognize and value diversity in others.

THINK *CRITICALLY*

1. What did John Redcloud learn about others' prejudice toward cultural pride?

2. John's debate team sponsor offered his support even though he had little understanding of John's culture. What do you think John learned from this?

TEACHING RESOURCES
Instructor's Resource CD
Lesson Plans, Ch. 8
PowerPoint Slides, Ch. 8

Student Activity CD, Ch. 8

thomsonedu.com/school/
leading
Crossword Puzzle, Ch. 8
Flash Cards, Ch. 8

Exam*View*ᴿ CD, Ch. 8

CHAPTER OVERVIEW
Chapter 8 discusses the advantages of diversity and ways to work with diverse groups and organizations.

Lesson 8.1
Explains the meaning of diversity and describes ways to respect and value diversity.

Lesson 8.2
Describes the benefits of diversity in groups and organizations.

Lesson 8.3
Identifies ways to fit in with diverse groups without losing your sense of self.

WHAT WOULD YOU DO?
Ask students to think of other symbols of culture that could affect an individual's image and appearance and could be misunderstood by others. (Students might mention clothing or head coverings that make some students "stand out" from the crowd.)

Think Critically Answers
1. Answers will vary. John may have learned that others were not prejudiced but that they were simply uninformed.
2. Answers will vary. John should have learned that his debate team sponsor respected his culture and supported his right to wear his hair in the tradition of his Native-American heritage.

Recognizing, Respecting, and Valuing Diversity

SCHEDULE
Block 45 minutes
Regular 1 class period

FOCUS
Ask students to explain the phrase, "stick with your own kind."

WHAT IS DIVERSITY?

When you hear the word *diversity,* you may think about race. When diversity in society was first introduced, the focus was on race because there had been much turmoil surrounding the unequal treatment of African-Americans. Since that time, the meaning of diversity has shifted. Diversity now refers to any way in which people, places, or things are different.

Differences in people could relate to their culture. *Culture* involves the values, belief systems, dress, and language that are characteristic of a particular social group. Diversity can also refer to differences in personality, attitudes, lifestyle preferences, education, talent, skills, creativity, or gender.

Differences in places may involve the neighborhood you live in or even the country where you live. Different groups of people come together to live. They develop their own society with unique characteristics.

Finally, because people have different belief and value systems, certain things are more or less important to different groups of people. For example, one person may place more value on material things, such as clothes, while another person may place more value on personal relationships, such as friendships.

It is important to look at the ways in which people, places, and things are different. This will help you gain a better understanding and acceptance of diversity.

© Monica Lau/Photodisc/Getty Images

TEACH
Write the word *diversity* on the board and ask students what comes to mind. Then have them brainstorm a list of all the ways in which people, places, or things can be diverse.

Recognizing Diversity

Recognizing that people are different is the first step in making positive changes. Awareness of these differences has resulted in laws,

A **TEAM** *Effort*

Since diversity affects everyone in one way or another, work together with your classmates to create a "Stomp Out Prejudice" campaign. Each of you should list the acts of prejudice that you have witnessed in your school. As a group, you should discuss your lists and come up with one master list. Write the acts of prejudice on a large piece of poster paper. Now, trace your shoe to create a cutout of your foot. Each of your classmates should place a cutout of a foot over a negative word or act of prejudice, replacing it with a positive word or expression. In that way, you and your classmates can begin to "stomp out" acts of prejudice that create hurtful and negative feelings in others.

THINK *CRITICALLY*

As a class, agree on one act or expression that everyone will agree not to do or say in order to show respect for one another. How could this improve relations in your school?

---

policies, and practices that have created a "level playing field" for disenfranchised groups. **Disenfranchised groups** are those whose rights and privileges have been denied on a regular and unfair basis.

The goal of diversity laws and policies is to eliminate prejudice and discrimination. **Prejudice** is a hostile and negative attitude toward people's characteristics. Sometimes these characteristics are things over which individuals have no control but which others view as negative. How many times have you teased someone who has freckles or really curly hair? How many times have you made fun of others who have a different skin color from yours? In these instances, you are demonstrating prejudice toward those people. **Discrimination** is the unfair way you favor or treat other people according to some standard that you or your group has chosen.

Recognizing diversity can lead to positive results. It can create changes in awareness, respect, behavior, attitude, acceptance, and understanding toward someone or something. Your life can be enriched by the changes you see in yourself and in others.

You may not like having to change the way you view diversity. In order to understand and accept other people, places, or things that have not been part of your comfort zone, you may need to change your belief system and your attitude. You may resent having to make emotional, psychological, and behavioral changes to embrace diversity. However, if you keep an open mind, you will see that the advantages of diversity far outweigh the disadvantages.

The Macro and Micro of Diversity

As you look at the differences among people, places, and things, you must consider the bigger issues of diversity as well as the smaller ones that affect you on a more personal level.

Macro diversity includes the larger or more global events related to diversity that are reported in the media every day. These events may include war, terrorism, and demonstrations by people who are demanding rights for specific groups of people. You may also read or

TEACH
Divide the class into two groups. Have one group brainstorm a list of the advantages of diversity. Have the other group brainstorm a list of the disadvantages of diversity. Have each group share its list and compare the results.

Ask students to name some current global events that are related to diversity. Answers may include the war on terrorism, religious differences in the Middle East, and ideological differences in places like North and South Korea.

A TEAM EFFORT
After students have completed their project, they may want to share it with other classes to help "Stomp Out Prejudice" in their entire school.

Think Critically Answers
Answers will vary. By agreeing on one act or expression to eliminate, the class will be stomping out one form of prejudice and will also be working together to value diversity.

Being open-minded and accepting of differences among others is a sign of a healthy self-awareness and self-esteem. It shows that you are able to lead and to work effectively in diverse groups.

CHARACTER BUILDER
Ask students why they think being open-minded and accepting of differences is a necessary trait for a leader. Do they think a group or organization could function effectively if the leader was not willing or able to work well with a diverse membership?

TEACHING STRATEGIES
Gifted Students
Have students research the No Child Left Behind Act. How does that law benefit individuals from diverse backgrounds? Have students discuss their findings.

ONGOING ASSESSMENT
Use the Checkpoint as an opportunity to conduct on-going assessment of student comprehension of the lesson material.

TEACH
Ask students if they have ever felt close to someone who was different from them but had had some similar experiences. (An example may be students who belong to Alateen or who have lost a loved one.)

hear about laws that affect different populations. One example is the *No Child Left Behind* Act that provides increased educational opportunities for students in different ethnic and other groups. When you see these events on the news or read about them in the newspaper, they sometimes seem to be unrelated to your everyday life. However, when diversity is discussed and supported by leaders in government and national organizations, everyone benefits.

Micro diversity takes place in your home, school, community, church, and local businesses and organizations. As you participate in any of these different groups, you must continually decide whether you will embrace or reject the diverse people, ideas, talents, skills, and creativity that surround you. You must decide if it is to your advantage or disadvantage to blend your diversity with the diversity of others.

 CHECKPOINT

What is the difference between macro and micro diversity?

Macro diversity includes the global events related to diversity. Micro diversity relates to the diversity that surrounds you in your home, school, and local community.

RESPECTING AND VALUING DIVERSITY

Have you ever been compared to one of your siblings or been told that you resemble your mother's or father's side of the family? Have you been complimented for being a better student, artist, singer, or musician than someone else in your family? Has someone important in your life ever made a comment that made you feel either good or bad about the ways in which you are different? These types of communications are often your introduction to diversity.

Now that you have begun to recognize where the diversity and differences come from in your own life, how can you begin to acknowledge and accept that some of these same differences also exist in the lives of others? How can you increase your tolerance, empathy, and celebration of yourself and others?

Tolerance is a level of acceptance or understanding of differences. It sometimes sounds negative to suggest that a person is tolerating your differences. It may feel like an insult that you and what you believe are viewed in this way. But keep in mind that tolerance is a starting point for those people who have resisted diversity.

Empathy is the ability to understand the feelings and experiences of others. Often, you feel empathy toward another person because you have had similar experiences in your own life. You begin to see others in a different way when you realize that some of the same kinds of things that happen to them have also happened to you. Their feelings of hurt, joy, sadness, happiness, and excitement become more real to you. You realize that they are just as talented, creative, smart, knowledgeable, and skillful as you are.

You will eventually realize that you have much in common with people who at first may seem much different from you. You will discover, too, that there is good in the worst of us and bad in the best of us. But we can move toward respecting and valuing the diversity in our family, friends, school, and community by looking at others with an open heart and mind.

Respecting Diversity

It may be difficult for you to accept the types of differences you have recognized in others. Some of the differences may involve the value and belief system that you have been taught by your family or the culture in which you have been raised. Other differences may relate to the unspoken community standards in your neighborhood or your socioeconomic standards that dictate much about where you live and what you have. The list goes on and on because you come from your own "space and place." You know the unwritten rules and standards that guide the daily lives of "people like you."

© Michael Matisse/Photodisc/Getty Images

Choosing to respect diversity does not suggest that you have lived a misguided life. In fact, your interest in leadership suggests that you are interested in being part of the larger community—in your home, neighborhood, and school—and in making a difference for everyone in your community. Having respect for diversity is a positive trait in a leader.

Is the Whole Greater Than the Parts?

When you talk about a group approach to leadership, the whole is greater than its parts. In the case of diversity, however, you need to consider whether the parts are greater than the whole. If you learn more about the part of a person's life that you do not fully understand, it may help you respect the ways in which that person is different from you. For example, you may focus on the way someone dresses. You may think that someone does not dress as fashionably as you and your friends do. But her family's income may not be as high as yours, or she simply may not care about "material" things. Another person may live in a neighborhood very different from yours. Does that mean you should not associate with him even though he is vice president of the National Honor Society? What about the girl who has the lead part in the school play? Should you not be her friend because her parents are not like yours? Should you refuse to participate in the play because she is in it?

Consider, too, that others may decide to exclude you from activities because you live in an affluent neighborhood, and they think you are stuck up. Or perhaps someone from a less affluent neighborhood

TEACH
Have students think about the values and beliefs that they have been taught by their family or their culture. In order to become more accepting of others, will they have to move beyond some of these values and beliefs?

Have students think about individuals in their school who are different from them in some way—the way they talk or dress or where they live. Discuss ways that they can overcome their previous way of thinking and embrace the diversity in these individuals.

is afraid to ask out someone from an affluent neighborhood because he knows the unspoken rules about "crossing the line." These and many other challenges are some of the issues you will face as you attempt to move away from your old way of thinking to embrace diversity.

Valuing Diversity

When you think of valuing someone, you most likely think of appreciating them. It is sometimes difficult to appreciate someone who is very different from you. There are several ways that you can overcome this difficulty and find a way to appreciate and value the diversity that others bring to the relationship. They include the following:

- Recognize that the ways in which people are different make each of them a unique individual.
- Realize that diversity is not limited to what you can see, such as race, age, gender, physical size, or physical or mental disability. It also relates to religion, culture, language, opinions, and experiences.
- Embrace the new level of creativity, talent, knowledge, and quality diversity brings to your school, community, workforce, and everyday world.

© Adam Crowley/Photodisc/Getty Images

- Enjoy the competitive edge that diversity brings. When you are around people who have diverse ideas and opinions, it encourages creative thinking.
- Appreciate the fact that diversity also supports the ways in which you are different, which leads to increased self-confidence and self-acceptance.

In your home, begin to see the many ways in which your family members are different from you. See them with a new level of acceptance and understanding. Recognize that your parents are doing the best they can to create home and family unity while being supportive of each family member's unique qualities.

In your school, begin to recognize the differences in your peers, friends, classmates, and teachers and learn how to better connect with them. You will realize that you have much in common with many of them, even in the midst of all the differences.

 **CHECKPOINT**

How do tolerance and empathy relate to diversity?

Tolerance involves acceptance or understanding of differences. Empathy is the ability to understand the feelings and experiences of others because of similar experiences.

Follow UP

UNDERSTAND LEADERSHIP CONCEPTS

Circle the best answer for each of the following questions.

1. **Which of the following beliefs about diversity is true?**
   a. Diversity must always be about race.
   b. Diversity can be about skills, talents, and creativity.
   c. Most students are not aware of differences among their peers.
   d. Diversity is only about the things that we can see.

2. **Diversity relates to**
   a. people
   b. places
   c. things
   d. all of the above

THINK *CRITICALLY*

Answer the following questions as completely as possible. If necessary, use a separate sheet of paper.

3. **Why is it important to recognize diversity among the members of your own family?**

   Recognizing diversity among members of your family can help you begin to view them
   with greater understanding and acceptance and to support each family member's
   uniqueness.

4. **Describe something that you think is unique or different about you. Are you proud of this quality or do you try to hide it? Explain why.**

   Answers will vary.

5. **If you saw someone of a different race being teased by some of your friends, how would you respond? Explain your answer.**

   Answers will vary.

ASSESS

Reteach
Have students review the key terms in the lesson and write a brief definition for each term. Have them work with a classmate to compare their definitions.

Enrich
Invite a representative of a different cultural group in your community to speak to the class about some of the unique customs and traditions in his or her culture.

Close
Have students list the ways they can show that they respect and value diversity in others.

Working Effectively in Diverse Groups

GOALS
- Explain the benefits of diverse groups.
- Describe ways to make diversity work in groups and organizations.

TERMS
- demographics
- homogeneity
- heterogeneous

SCHEDULE
Block 45 minutes
Regular 1 class period

FOCUS
Ask students to think of some ways that groups can benefit from diversity not only in characteristics such as age, race, ethnicity, education, and income but also in skills, talents, knowledge, and creativity.

TEACH
Ask students to think of several groups to which they belong or with which they are familiar. Are the groups more homogeneous or heterogeneous? What differences, if any, have they noticed in these two types of groups?

A BALANCING ACT

Everywhere you look today, you realize that diversity is being encouraged more than ever before. **Demographics** are the characteristics of a population, such as gender, age, race, ethnicity, and level of education and income. Demographic changes are not only taking place around the world but also happening closer to home in your own neighborhood. At one time, the world had a great sense of **homogeneity** in which everyone looked the same, believed the same, acted the same, and excluded anyone who was different. That is no longer the case. The world is more diverse, and it is important for you to learn how to work with people—in your home, school, and community—who are different from you.

Diversity has resulted in a more **heterogeneous** grouping of individuals who often are very different from one another, but who must find ways to combine their diverse skills, talents, knowledge, and creativity for the good of the group. You might think that achieving harmony among individuals with differences would not be that difficult. But you

© Jules Frazier/Photodisc/Getty Images

know from experience that "mixing" differing opinions can create a tense situation in which nothing gets done.

Why Groups Must Embrace Diversity

By taking advantage of the strengths, talents, creativity, and knowledge of each member, groups can be more effective. The leader must recognize each member's potential and put it to work for the good of the group.

When group members feel that they are understood, respected, accepted, and supported by their leader and peers, they develop a sense of belonging. This sense of belonging helps create a bond among group members. They are more willing to devote their time and effort to achieving the group's goals. Group members are motivated to do their best and will offer support to the other members. By embracing diversity, the group will be more effective in accomplishing its mission.

CHECKPOINT

Why are heterogeneous groups more effective than homogeneous groups?

Heterogeneous groups are more effective because they include individuals with diverse

skills, talents, knowledge, and creativity who work together for the good of the group.

A DOUBLE-EDGED SWORD

Diversity cuts to the core of what your belief system is about and how you treat and value other people. It also brings you face to face with how you value yourself. These two considerations guide and direct your behavior when working in groups. You must remember that groups are made up of people with differences that are visible as well as differences that are not visible.

Proving the Value of Diversity

You may begin to wonder how something that is supposed to be so positive can also be negative. Although diversity has many benefits, it can cause conflict in groups. Some individuals prefer to work in homogeneous groups because they believe that people who are alike can work together better. Their philosophy is

© David Buffington/Photodisc/Getty Images

TEACH
Ask students why they think groups need to embrace diversity. Do they think a group can be effective if it does not make good use of all the strengths, talents, creativity, and knowledge available among its members?

Ask students what they think President Kennedy meant by his quote. How do they think "we can help make the world safe for diversity"?

ONGOING ASSESSMENT
Use the Checkpoint as an opportunity to conduct on-going assessment of student comprehension of the lesson material.

TEACH
Ask students how they think diversity brings individuals face to face with how they value themselves as well as how they value other people.

Ask students if they have ever personally experienced or witnessed conflicts in a group that were caused by diversity. Have several students offer examples. How were the conflicts resolved for the good of the group?

© Doug Menuez/Photodisc/Getty Images

"birds of a feather flock together." People who think like this are not considering the value of diversity.

Embracing diversity will help you become a stronger person. Your communication skills will improve as you learn the best ways to communicate with different people. Your interpersonal skills will improve as you make new friends and learn about each other's personal history. Your problem-solving skills will improve as you listen to other group members' thoughts and ideas on how to resolve a problem. As individuals become stronger in these areas, their confidence increases, and they become more satisfied and committed group members. The value of diversity is endless.

Taking on the Challenge of Making Diversity Work

In order to do your best in your home, school, and community, you must embrace diversity. To feel valued, accepted, and safe, you must first accept the things that are different about yourself. Once you are confident enough to accept your differences, you can more easily accept the differences in others without being fearful.

There are barriers to working effectively in diverse groups that must be overcome. These barriers may include language, culture, race, ethnicity, religion, or anything that challenges what the group considers "normal." These barriers create competition and conflict. In order for groups to operate effectively, they must find ways to overcome these challenges.

The increasing number of minority students who are now in your classes represent the change that is taking place in your school—teams, clubs, groups, and student organizations. Rather than focusing on the ways in which others are different, group members should focus on working cooperatively with one another. As a leader or member of a group, you must find ways to work together. Develop principles that will guide your group and that are fair to all group members. Here is a list of principles for working effectively in diverse groups.

- Select leaders who represent the diverse makeup of your group.
- Identify an issue that is common to all group members so that you can work together toward a common goal. Each group member needs to have a clear role that uses his or her unique talents and strengths.
- Create opportunities for group members to get to know one another and share the similarities that exist among them. Share your stories and personal histories to gain appreciation for one another.
- Recognize, respect, and value individuals' strengths, such as their language, family traditions, culture, and dress.
- Celebrate one another's victories and accomplishments in the group to strengthen relationships.
- Recognize and support activities that promote fairness while developing and building relationships.
- Look to school personnel as role models for maintaining fairness and equality in relations with others.
- Seek the involvement and support from leaders of other school groups and work together toward reaching goals that will benefit all students.
- Allow group members to give feedback about the progress and efforts being made to support diversity.
- Be prepared for the changes that will take place in you and in others as a result of diversity.

CHECKPOINT

What are some of the barriers to working effectively in diverse groups?

Barriers to working effectively in diverse groups include language, culture, race, ethnicity, religions, and other things that may challenge group norms.

© Vicky Kasala/Photodisc/Getty Images

Follow UP

UNDERSTAND LEADERSHIP CONCEPTS

Circle the best answer for each of the following questions.

1. When you work with people who are different than you, it can result in
   a. greater creativity than you could achieve with people who are the same as you
   b. improved communication skills
   c. changes in people's attitudes about diversity
   d. all of the above

2. In order to work effectively in diverse groups, you should
   a. create opportunities for people to get to know one another
   b. select leaders who represent the diverse makeup of the group
   c. recognize and respect individuals' strengths
   d. all of the above

THINK *CRITICALLY*

Answer the following questions as completely as possible. If necessary, use a separate sheet of paper.

3. Why is diversity being encouraged more than ever before?
Diversity is being encouraged now more than ever before because demographic changes are taking place everywhere. The world is becoming more diverse, and it is important to learn how to work with people who are different from you.

4. Why do you think people are afraid to embrace diversity in others?
Some people may be afraid to embrace diversity in others because diversity cuts to the core of their belief system and brings them face to face with how they value themselves. Also, some people really believe that people who are alike can work better together.

5. In what area of diversity do you feel a need to be more accepting? Why?
Answers will vary.

ASSESS
Reteach
Have students review the goals for the lesson and list the key points discussed for each goal.

Enrich
Have students work in small groups to create a new reality television program that focuses on diversity. Have each group present its idea to the class and vote on the program that presents diversity in the most creative way. (If possible, have the class participate in the winning program.)

Close
In small groups, have students discuss positive things they can do to make diversity work in their school and community.

Fitting in Without Fading Out

FIND A GOOD FIT FOR YOU

Have you ever felt uncomfortable trying to fit into a particular group, whether at home or at school? Have you ever thought that you were not smart enough to fit into a particular study group? How many times have you done something as simple as changing your clothes over and over again when getting dressed for school or preparing for a special occasion? How many times have you refused to take the risk of letting others find out that you are not quite who they thought you were? **Fitting in**, or changing who you are to meet the expectations of others, can take a lot of energy and expense. The expense, or the price you pay for fitting in, may be financial or emotional.

Often you do not allow yourself to just "be" because of the pressures coming from all sides. Your family has a vision of what and who they think you should be. Your friends have an image they want you to uphold. Your teachers have certain expectations of how you should perform. And most of all, you find yourself struggling to feel comfortable and fit into the body, mind, and image you have or want to have of yourself.

Visible Differences

You may come from a different culture or race, or you may be from a different socioeconomic background. Perhaps you dress or talk differently. Trying to fit in when you have visible differences gives you no place to hide. No one has to tell you that you talk "funny"—whether it is a different language or the slang of your particular culture. You can tell by the look on people's faces when you attempt to communicate with them that they just do not understand. And if there is more than one person in the group

SCHEDULE
Block 45 minutes
Regular 1 class period

FOCUS
Ask students if they think it is possible to be true to yourself and still find a place in the groups within your school.

TEACH
Ask students what they think are some of the pressures of fitting in with various groups within their school. What do they think is the financial or emotional price, if any, of fitting in?

© Digital Vision/Getty Images

Building COMMUNITIES

The student population in your school is somewhat diverse, but you have noticed that students tend to hang out with their "own kind" during school. To help build a sense of community in your school, you suggest having a diversity fair so that students can become aware of the positive differences among their peers. In addition to helping students understand differences, you believe the fair will also show them that they are alike in many ways. Similarities between people can help build bonds and strengthen relationships. You have approached the student council for support with this activity, and they have agreed to adopt it as a school-wide project.

THINK *CRITICALLY*

How will you find the leaders of the diverse groups in your school and persuade them to be part of this project? How will you persuade them that the diversity fair will make a positive difference in the school environment and in the way people treat one another?

TEACH

Ask students if they have ever seen or heard other students being teased because they were visibly different in some way and did not fit in with the "norm." Have several students share examples. What do they think they could—or should—do when they witness this type of behavior?

Ask students if they have ever felt insecure about some trait or characteristic that made them appear different. What did they do to feel more comfortable about themselves?

BUILDING COMMUNITIES

Ask students to name some of the ways that they can use the diversity fair to make their classmates more aware of different cultures. Answers may include pictures, maps, ethnic food, clothing, and music.

Think Critically Answers

Answers will vary. The leaders need to realize that a greater understanding of diversity can lead to acceptance and respect.

listening to you, they may tease and laugh at you because your differences are outside of their comfort zone.

No one has to tell you that your style is not quite "in" because you can see other people staring at you and hear them whispering about your clothes. No one knows better than you that your style is different. It may be different because of your creativity, culture, financial situation, or lack of experience and understanding of what works for you. Or it just may be that your parents want you to wear a particular style of clothing.

No one has to tell you that you are of a different race. You already know that. So you do not need to be reminded by your peers who may make negative comments and call you inappropriate names. Trying to fit in can take a toll on your emotional and physical well-being.

It Happens to Everybody in Some Way

Every day, students get picked on for one reason or another. It happens to most everyone, regardless of race, gender, or socioeconomic background. Peers have a way of zeroing in on traits or characteristics that are different from their own. This can cause even the most popular students to have feelings of insecurity. Those students who seem to fit in everywhere with everyone may start questioning why other people want to be with them. Some of them may believe that if their true self is "found out," they will not be as popular as they are.

It would be nice if everyone could just accept the differences in others. Then you could be truly comfortable with yourself and not have to worry about trying to fit in. Unfortunately, not everyone will learn to accept people for who they are. As long as this is true, people will continue to look for ways to gain acceptance and fit in with others.

Find a Way

When fitting in is difficult, you must find a way to confront your fears. If you do not find a way, you will not be able to contribute as a leader or member of groups and organizations in your school. This may prevent you from working on something that is very important to you.

Here are some steps to help you find a way to fit in.

- Recognize and accept the diversity in yourself so that you can better recognize and accept diversity in others.
- Think about why you want to fit in with a particular group. If it is for all the wrong reasons, such as to be more popular, you are probably setting yourself up for failure. You should have a meaningful reason for wanting to be part of a group.
- Take small steps and join a team or participate in a group that interests you and represents something that you value or believe in.
- Be a people watcher. Find others who seem to react positively to your behavior and style of communication.
- Take risks and make the first move by talking to a person or joining a group. Rejection may sting a little, but the hurt will fade away. You will gain the confidence to try again.
- Ask for the help and support of a friend. There is strength in numbers.
- Find an adult supporter or role model.
- Remain focused and emotionally strong as you make changes that will allow you to embrace the differences in you and in others.

 **CHECKPOINT**

Why do you think peers pick on visible differences in others?

Peers pick on visible differences in others because those differences are outside of their

comfort zone.

DIFFERENT IS NOT WRONG

Unfortunately, some people think of the differences in themselves and others as something that is wrong with them. For example, if your hair is red and everyone else in your family has blonde hair, does that mean that there is something wrong with you? What if all of your siblings are tall, and you happen to be short? If your sister has light brown skin and straight hair while you have dark brown skin and curly hair, does that make you less attractive? Each individual is unique in their own way. This does not mean this person is wrong, just different.

▌ Words to Live By

Throughout school, you will interact with many different people. All of them will have different characteristics than you. Some of these differences may make you competitive or even jealous. But before you react negatively to these differences think about the following.

- Someone will always be prettier than you are because beauty is in the eye of the beholder.
- Someone will always be smarter than you are because their DNA supports it or because they study harder than you do.
- Someone will always be shorter, taller, thinner, fatter, and more anything you can think of than you are because that is just the way life is.

LEADERSHIP *Tip*

As a leader, recognizing, valuing, and accepting the diversity of skills, knowledge, talent, and creativity in your team members leads the way for others to follow.

LEADERSHIP TIP
Ask students if they ever played the game "Follow the Leader" as a child. Point out that in order for team members to value diversity, they must have a strong leader to follow who recognizes, accepts, and values diversity.

TEACHING STRATEGIES
Tactile Learners
Have students create a poster or bulletin board display entitled "Find Your Way." On it they should illustrate the steps that will help individuals find a way to fit in without changing who they are in order to please others.

ONGOING ASSESSMENT
Use the Checkpoint as an opportunity to conduct ongoing assessment of student comprehension of the lesson material.

TEACH
Ask students to think about the expression "Beauty is in the eye of the beholder." What do they think it means?

TEACH

Ask students to think about a time when they may have felt competitive or jealous of someone else. Was it really about the other person or were they feeling inadequate or insecure for some reason about themselves at that time?

Ask students how they think fading out can affect an individual's self-esteem. Can they think of any situation in which it would be worth fading out in order to fit in with a particular group?

TEACHING STRATEGIES
At-Risk Students

Have students begin keeping a gratitude journal. In it, they should regularly write the things about themselves that they value and appreciate and the things they have for which they are thankful, including the people in their life who accept, respect, and support them.

ONGOING ASSESSMENT

Use the Checkpoint as an opportunity to conduct ongoing assessment of student comprehension of the lesson material.

- Someone will always have more money than you do because his or her parents have different skills and talents when it comes to generating income.
- Someone will always be more athletic than you are because they have a deeper passion than you or a natural ability.
- Someone else's parents will always be more lenient than yours for any number of reasons. It might be because the parents just do not care, they have poor parenting skills, or because your friend has earned his or her parent's trust.
- Someone will always be more popular than you. Being popular might be more important to one person, while serving the school and community might be more important to another person.

Keep in mind that many of these statements work both ways. For example, many people will think you are prettier than someone else. Someone who is a better football player than you may not be able to play baseball as well as you. Even though someone may be wealthier because they have more money, you may be wealthier when it comes to having friends and family who are caring and supportive.

To survive in life, you need to learn to accept, love, cherish, appreciate, and value yourself and others. Instead of thinking about all the things you do not have, think about all of the things you do have.

Do Not Fade Out

W. E. B. DuBois, a historically well-known African-American civil rights activist and leader, cautioned African-Americans to "fit in without fading out" during a time in history when diversity was not encouraged. **Fading out** means losing your sense of self in order to fit in with a particular crowd or group. DuBois's words are still meaningful today. People will challenge what you value and believe. You should be open to making positive changes without giving up what you value most about yourself.

Discrimination is often based on things over which people have no control. How can you discriminate against someone's race or color when it is a physical trait of birth? How can you discriminate against individuals who are poor because of decisions their parents may have made? How can you discriminate against people who are handicapped in some way? People who discourage diversity or who discriminate against others usually have a closed mind. They are fearful of the unknown and would prefer it if everyone were like them. It is unfair for them to expect other people to fade out because they do not like who and what they represent. Diversity laws and training can help put a stop to discrimination and prejudices. Everyone has the right to fit in without fading out.

CHECKPOINT

Do you think discrimination is ever acceptable? Explain your answer.

Discrimination is never acceptable. It often is based on things that people cannot control, such as skin color, socioeconomic level, or physical handicaps.

Follow UP

UNDERSTAND LEADERSHIP CONCEPTS

Circle the best answer for each of the following questions.

1. **You can avoid fading out when you**
   a. follow the crowd whether or not you agree with them
   b. have a deep sense of knowing who you are and hold onto your beliefs
   c. change your style to be like your friends
   d. none of the above

2. **Which of the following is not one of the recommended steps in finding a way to fit in?**
   a. Be a people watcher.
   b. Ask for the help and support of a friend.
   c. Do not take risks and wait for someone else to make the first move.
   d. Join a group that interests you.

THINK *CRITICALLY*

Answer the following questions as completely as possible. If necessary, use a separate sheet of paper.

3. **Describe a situation in which you have seen someone discriminated against. How did it make you feel? What, if anything, did you do?**
   Answers will vary. _____
   _____
   _____
   _____

4. **Review the steps in finding a way to fit in. Decide on a change you want to make in yourself. List the action steps you will take to help make this change.**
   Answers will vary. _____
   _____
   _____
   _____

5. **Describe a situation in which you may have "faded out" in order to fit in with a particular group. What are some ways that you can be part of a group without losing your sense of self?**
   Answers will vary. _____
   _____
   _____
   _____

ASSESS
Reteach
Divide the class into two teams and review the key points in the lesson using a game format like *Family Feud*.

Enrich
Have students research the laws relating to discrimination in this country. Have them report on how and why they came about and what protection they offer all citizens.

Close
Have students think of a friend or adult supporter who can help them find a way to fit in. Have them devise a plan to ask that person for the help they need.

Chapter **Assessment**

REVIEW *LEADERSHIP CONCEPTS*

a. demographics
b. discrimination
c. disenfranchised groups
d. empathy
e. fading out
f. fitting in
g. heterogeneous
h. homogeneity
i. macro diversity
j. micro diversity
k. prejudice
l. tolerance

Write the letter of the term that matches each definition. Some terms will not be used.

__e__ 1. *Losing your sense of self in order to fit in with a particular crowd or group*

__c__ 2. *Groups whose rights and privileges have been denied on a regular and unfair basis*

__d__ 3. *Ability to understand the feelings of others because of similar experiences*

__b__ 4. *The unfair way you favor or treat others according to some standard you or your group has chosen*

__l__ 5. *Level of acceptance or understanding of differences*

__f__ 6. *Changing who you are to meet the expectations of others*

__g__ 7. *Groups of individuals who are very different from one another*

__i__ 8. *Larger or global events that are related to diversity and reported in the media every day*

__a__ 9. *Characteristics of a population*

__k__ 10. *A hostile and negative attitude toward people's characteristics*

Circle the best answer.

11. *Which of the following statements is true?*
    a. We are all different in some way.
    b. We have no control over some of the ways in which we are different.
    c. Discrimination is unfair.
    d. all of the above

12. *People who understand the feelings of others because they have had similar experiences have*
    a. empathy
    b. tolerance
    c. prejudice
    d. none of the above

13. *You are being prejudiced when*
    a. you give everyone a fair chance
    b. you persuade others not to hang out with someone because you don't think that person is popular enough
    c. you dislike a person because he said something about you that was untrue
    d. you invite only your close friends to your party

ASSESS

Reteach
Divide the class into three groups and assign each group one of the lessons in the chapter. Have the group review its assigned lesson with the class using a creative method, such as a skit, game, or other fun activity.

Enrich
Have students interview a business person in their community who is from a different culture. They should ask about the challenges that person had to overcome in order to achieve business success. What advice can the person offer about fitting in without fading out?

CLOSE
Have students think about the "unwritten rules" that guide their daily lives. Do they support diversity? If not, have students think of some things they can do to help change those "rules."

THINK *CRITICALLY*

14. Why is it sometimes important to fit in with other people?

It is important to fit in with other people because if you do not find a way to fit in, you will not be able to contribute as a leader or member of the groups and organizations in your school. This could prevent you from working on something that is important to you.

15. Discuss one physical trait about yourself that could possibly cause people to discriminate against you.

Answers will vary.

16. Choose the "Words to Live By" statement that means the most to you. Explain why.

Answers will vary.

17. List some positive ways that you can help to eliminate prejudice in your school and community.

Answers will vary. You can help to eliminate prejudice in your school and community by selecting leaders who represent the diversity in your group, respecting and valuing the talents and creativity of all members, supporting activities that promote fairness, and creating opportunities for group members to get to know and appreciate one another.

18. List two personal changes that you have made as a result of getting to know someone "different" from you.

Answers will vary.

19. **Media** Observe one of your local, state, or national politicians making a speech, either in person or on television. List any statements the person makes that could be considered prejudicial or discriminatory. Also, list any statements made that show support and respect for diversity. Share your findings with the class.

Answers will vary.

20. **Research** Use the Internet or library to research the communication styles of different cultures. Choose one culture and write a one-page report explaining the different ways this group communicates, including body language.

Answers will vary.

21. **History** Learn more about W. E. B. DuBois. What contributions did DuBois make in the areas of diversity? How did he fight discrimination and prejudice?

Answers will vary. For more than 25 years, W.E.B. DuBois was Editor-in-Chief of the NAACP publication, *The Crisis*. He was an outspoken advocate for civil rights in America.

22. **Research** Use the Internet or library to learn about the demographics in your city. Create a table listing various demographic characteristics such as gender, age, and race. (Hint: See the U.S. Census Bureau web site.)

Answers will vary.

LEARNING TO LEAD

FOCUS

Plan membership recruitment and development.

DESCRIPTION

A student organization needs to attract members who are committed to the organization and who will give time and energy to ensure its success. Membership recruitment is especially important for student organizations because each year members graduate or move to other schools. A new group of students shows up who may not be familiar with the organization and do not know how to get involved.

Build the membership of your student organization chapter using a variety of recruitment activities. Identify the importance of recruiting members with different interests, talents, and experiences to build a strong, diverse organization.

LEARNING TO LEAD
This project is written for use with student organizations such as BPA, DECA, and FBLA. Student organizations can help students prepare for key leadership roles. After students complete the activities, discuss what they learned about their student organization.

ACTIVITIES

1. Ask your local adviser to share any national, state, and local membership information and recruitment materials that are available. Visit your national student organization web site and study the information provided on membership recruitment and development.

2. Select three different membership recruitment items from those you have collected. Study them carefully to determine how effectively they represent the diversity of potential members—age, gender, ethnicity, race, physical appearance, and physical disabilities. Describe the strengths of the recruitment materials and needed improvements, if any, to attract a diverse student membership for your local chapter.

3. Identify two students who have been active members for two or more years and two new members. Discuss with these students why they joined the organization and ask for their ideas for effective membership recruitment.

SHARE YOUR RESULTS

1. Team with three or four other students to outline a two-week plan for recruiting new members for your local student organization. Recruiting would take place the week before the school year begins and the first week of classes. Incorporate materials available from your national office as appropriate. Discuss how the plan will attract the interest of a diverse group of students in your school.
2. Prepare one poster or banner that can be used as part of your membership recruitment campaign. It should contain pictures or other images that reflect student diversity and the types of activities that would interest prospective members.
3. Develop a three-minute recruitment speech your team could give at a meeting of new students to interest them in your organization. Prepare several computer slides that outline the main points of the speech.

Share Your Results
1. Answers will vary.
2. Answers will vary.
3. Answers will vary. The main points of the speech should appeal to a diverse audience.

Activities
1. Answers will vary. Students should collect and review as many different ideas as possible relating to recruitment in order to select the best methods for attracting new members.
2. Answers will vary. Students may find it helpful to create a table in which to list the strengths and weaknesses of each recruitment item.
3. Answers will vary. When conducting interviews, students should make sure they select members who represent diversity in the organization.

ACCEPTING THE
CHALLENGE
Case Study 8
Ask students what they
think John should have
done if the governing
board had not agreed to
let him continue in the
debate with his long hair.
Do they think John would
have been justified in
standing up for his rights
by quitting the competi-
tion, or would he have
been letting his team-
mates down?

ACCEPTING THE CHALLENGE

CASE STUDY 8—FITTING IN WITHOUT FADING OUT

As you learned in the opening scenario, What Would You Do?, *John Redcloud was angry when the state governing board tried to exclude him from the debate team competition because of his long hair. The board was making this decision without considering John's culture. Had John given in and cut his hair in an attempt to be accepted, he would have been going against the principle of fitting in without fading out. On the other hand, if John had quit the debate team as a way to express his cultural rights, it could have affected his team's chances of winning. There were many issues for John to consider.*

Thankfully, John's debate team sponsor stood up for John and made the governing board realize that its decision was unfair. John's teammates also supported John and his cultural rights. After this incident, John viewed his sponsor and his teammates differently. He began to see their deep commitment to respecting and valuing diversity.

THINK *CRITICALLY*

1. *Describe the issues faced by John Redcloud. How did these issues affect John, his teammates, and even his school?*

John Redcloud had to decide between standing up for his right to honor his cultural

tradition and possibly damaging his team's chance to win if he quit the competition.

Fortunately, the result was a win–win for John and his teammates.

2. *What lessons can you learn from John Redcloud about fitting in without fading out for those areas of your life where others may tease you or show prejudice toward you?*

Answers will vary. John did not fade out. He stood up for his values and beliefs, and in

the end, he was able to maintain his cultural traditions while still fitting in on the

debate team.

3. *Why do you think John's opinion of his debate team sponsor and teammates changed? How might this change his trust in other people?*

Answers will vary. By expressing their support for John to the state governing board,

the debate team sponsor and members showed that they respected John's culture. The

respect they showed John can help increase his trust in other people.

4. *How could John Redcloud use his experience to help other people embrace diversity?*

Answers will vary. By sharing his experience with others, John could encourage others

to hold fast to their values and beliefs and to find their own way to fit in without

fading out.

APPLY *WHAT YOU HAVE LEARNED–Learn to Value Diversity*

DIRECTIONS: *In an attempt to learn more about the issues related to diversity, enter answers to the following questions on the lines below or on your Student Activity CD. Answer as honestly and openly as possible.*

1. *Describe what diversity means to you.*

_____

_____

_____

2. *Describe your cultural background. How does your culture fit in with, or conflict with, the other cultures in your school?*

_____

_____

_____

_____

3. *Would you describe your classmates as tolerant or intolerant of others' differences? Explain your answer.*

_____

_____

_____

_____

4. *What does it mean to "put yourself in someone else's shoes"? How could this help you build respect for someone else?*

_____

_____

_____

_____

5. *Think about what you can do to learn more about the different cultures in your school and strengthen relationships between students. On the lines below or on the Student Activity CD, create a SMART goal (including a completion date) that will help you gain more respect for the diversity in others. Or, if you prefer, create a SMART goal that will allow you to lead others in gaining an understanding and respect of cultural differences. Enter your goal in a monthly calendar (on the CD or your own). Then enter your thoughts, ideas, and discussions related to your goal in a journal (on the CD or your own) to help you plan and track your progress. Recruit a goal-setting partner to help you put your diversity plan into action.*

_____

_____

_____

_____

ACCEPTING THE CHALLENGE
Apply What You Have Learned—Learn to Value Diversity
Note that students can complete this part of the *Accepting the Challenge* activity in the book or on the Student Activity CD. Instructions are provided on the CD.

After students have answered the questions in this activity, instruct them to write a SMART goal (including a completion date) that will help them gain more respect for the diversity in others. Have them enter their goal on a monthly calendar. Students can use the monthly calendar on the Student Activity CD or their own calendar. Explain to students that they may also use weekly calendar pages (on the Student Activity CD or their own calendar) to plan activities and tasks that will help them achieve their goals. Finally, direct students to use a journal (on the Student Activity CD or their own) to track and evaluate their progress in achieving their goal.

A goal-setting partner can add an element of accountability and can offer positive feedback to help students stay on track to achieve their goals.

Students should be given the opportunity to reflect on the progress they have made toward achieving their goal. To do this, students can complete the *Evaluate Your Progress* activity on the Student Activity CD. Stress to students that it is important to complete this activity on the original target completion date even if they have not met their goal at that time.

Personal Characteristics Build Character

© F64/Photodisc/Getty Images

9.1 *Being Honest and Truthful*

9.2 *Being Reliable and Responsible*

9.3 *Exhibiting Self-Discipline*

What would **YOU** do?

JEVONE DIDN'T MAKE IT

Jevone Taylor has always enjoyed playing the trumpet. He was inspired to start playing the instrument when he was young after hearing a CD playing on his dad's stereo. He learned that the trumpet player was Wynton Marsalis. From that time on, he spent hours on the Internet and in the bookstore reading about Mr. Marsalis. He learned that Marsalis started playing the trumpet when he could hardly hold the instrument. Marsalis was invited to play with the New Orleans Philharmonic at age 14, and he was the youngest student ever admitted to the Berkshire Music Center at the famous Tanglewood Institute.

Jevone started trumpet lessons when he was seven years old, and he spent many hours practicing. He developed his trumpeting skills rapidly and was a leader in the music department of his junior high school. He was the first chair in the junior orchestra of his city. He and his family were excited when he was admitted into the city's performing arts high school. It offered advanced music instruction and many performance opportunities. Jevone was particularly excited that the school had a jazz orchestra that had received many awards and was often invited to perform at musical events around the country.

Needless to say, Jevone was bitterly disappointed when he learned the results of the summer tryouts for the jazz orchestra. He knew that few freshmen were selected, so he had practiced hard all summer. His experience and past successes led him to believe that he would qualify for the orchestra. The selection committee commented that they were impressed with his technique. But since there was only one trumpet opening, it went to a junior who had transferred from another city with experience in a similar orchestra. Jevone did not think it was fair that the committee valued the other student's age and experience, because it was something Jevone could not control. It was the first time Jevone had not achieved what he had set out to accomplish. He went home and told his parents that he no longer wanted to go to the performing arts high school. He would be too embarrassed when others found out that he was not successful in what he had worked so hard to achieve.

THINK *CRITICALLY*

1. How do you believe Jevone's previous successes contributed to his current feelings?

2. If you were Jevone's best friend, what would you say to him when you learned the results of the orchestra tryouts?

TEACHING RESOURCES
Instructor's Resource CD
Lesson Plans, Ch. 9
PowerPoint Slides, Ch. 9
Student Activity CD, Ch. 9
thomsonedu.com/school/leading
Crossword Puzzle, Ch. 9
Flash Cards, Ch. 9
Exam*View*® CD, Ch. 9

CHAPTER OVERVIEW
Chapter 9 discusses personal characteristics that build character, such as honesty, truthfulness, reliability, responsibility, and self-discipline.

Lesson 9.1
Identifies what it means to be honest and describes how to be truthful while respecting others.

Lesson 9.2
Describes the effects of reliability on you and others and explains the difference between accepting responsibility and taking responsibility.

Lesson 9.3
Explains how self-discipline is developed and describes how to use self-discipline to achieve self-improvement goals.

WHAT WOULD YOU DO?
Ask students to think of a time when they tried out for something and they did not get it. How did they feel when they were not successful in achieving their goal?

Think Critically Answers
1. Jevone had always been successful with his music goals. He was not prepared for a failure.
2. Answers will vary. Students should consider ways to offer encouragement to Jevone so he will continue toward his goals.

Personal Characteristics Build Character   Chapter 9   *213*

Being Honest and Truthful

WHO ARE YOU AND WHO DO YOU WANT TO BE?

One of the challenges you will face as you mature is to become the person you want to be. Your character continues to develop as you make decisions, work, play, and relate to others. Your character is made up of two parts—your personal character traits and the character you demonstrate in your relationships with others. Each type of character is an important part of who you are, but your personal character traits are a basic part of your personality. They influence the way you relate to others.

You have probably watched the old television series, *Leave It to Beaver,* on Nick at Nite or TV Land. If so, you recognize Eddie Haskell as a character who brought a lot of humor to the show with his two-faced personality. He would put on an act by being overly sincere and respectful when he was around Mr. and Mrs. Cleaver. Then he would quickly go back to his arrogant, scheming, and mean-spirited personality around his friends. It is funny to watch Eddie on the television series as he tries to fool adults while he works to keep his other image among his friends. But it is not funny to deal with a person like Eddie Haskell in real life.

© Digital Vision/Getty Images

Trying to Be Two Different People

Are you an "Eddie Haskell," or do you hang out with people who are? If so, you probably know that it is not easy to keep up two very different characters. And it clearly is not fun if you have to deal with a person who acts differently around different people. Have you had any of the following experiences?

- You and your friends speak negatively about someone behind his or her back, but that person finds out what you have said.
- You tell your parents that you are going to one place, but you really have plans to go to another place that you know they would not like.
- You start dressing and acting like the "cool" group of students with hopes that they will include you. It is not the way you dressed or acted before, and it upsets your current friends because they know that is not who you really are.
- You have a teacher who you try to impress in order to get a recommendation for a student club you want to join. You go out of your way to be helpful to the teacher even though that is not your normal behavior with other teachers.

Making a Choice

Even though you may not be aware of it, other people can see the differences in your behavior. They begin to wonder what you are really like. When you try to act differently around certain people or in particular situations, you become an actor. You have to remember your "character" and your "script." You feel mental stress from trying to keep your characters straight, turning one character off and returning to the other. You also worry that people important to you may discover that you behave in ways they would not expect or respect. At some point, you will have to decide which one of the characters you are playing is your real self. Have you become someone you do not want to be? How will your character affect what you really want to do and what you really want to be?

Your personality and personal character develop over time, primarily through your actions. They are shaped by what you do more than by what you think. Over time, actions become **habitual**, meaning that you act in a certain way with little thought due to repeated behavior. So what initially was an act put on for a specific purpose can become a part of your character out of habit. As you already know, character is neither good nor bad. Sometimes, it is not even what you want it to be. It is the accumulation of your beliefs and actions. It defines who you are and how others view you. It will become a major factor in who associates with you, what opportunities are presented to you, and what you become in the future. So no matter how unimportant a particular decision or interaction seems to be right now, it is important to remember that what you choose and what you do become a part of who you are, who you want to be, and who you ultimately become.

 CHECKPOINT

What problems will people encounter when they try to act in different ways with different groups of people?

Acting in different ways with different groups of people causes mental stress from trying to

keep your "characters" straight. You also worry that people you care about will find out.

CHARACTER *Builder*

Character often is defined as doing the right thing when no one is looking. But character may be most evident when everyone is looking. When you face a conflict about what you should do, ask yourself, "How will I feel if everyone who is important to me finds out what I am about to do?"

TEACH

Ask students if they have ever had any of the experiences described in the scenarios in the text. If so, how did they feel about themselves and their behavior?

Have students think of a behavior that now has become a habit to them. Ask them if they are proud that this habitual behavior has become part of who they are or if it is something they would like to change.

CHARACTER BUILDER

Ask students if they have ever done something and then almost immediately hoped that no one would find out. What did they learn from that experience?

ONGOING ASSESSMENT

Use the Checkpoint as an opportunity to conduct ongoing assessment of student comprehension of the lesson material.

Do people believe you? Can they trust what you say? There are often sayings that express important character traits. One of those sayings is "honesty is the best policy." Yet we all know situations when people with the highest character are not totally honest. So what is honesty, and how do we demonstrate it?

The Meaning of Honesty

A person who is **honest** does not intentionally deceive or mislead. The words and actions of an honest person are based on the person's unbiased knowledge and beliefs that apply to the situation at hand. Honesty is a personal character trait. Every individual decides whether or not to be honest. You are not really honest if you feel there are situations when honesty is not necessary or if there are certain people with whom you do not feel the need to be honest. If you decide the times and places when you believe it is important to be honest and other times when you feel it is okay to deceive people, honesty is not yet a complete part of your character.

Being Honest with Yourself and Others

Honesty begins with how you feel about yourself. When you have difficult decisions and know what is in your long-term best interest, you are being dishonest with yourself if you rationalize a different choice. You might remember some times when you made excuses for poor decisions. *I don't have time to study for that exam because basketball practice ran late. I know I should save money for college, but right now I really need a new pair of shoes.* You are not being honest with yourself if you rationalize your decisions or choose to ignore information you know is important when making personal choices.

Honesty extends to our words and actions. Being truthful is the way you demonstrate honesty when you communicate with others. In addition, you are being honest in your actions when you are fair, follow the rules, and do not cheat, trick, or take advantage of others. Cheating is particularly dishonest whether playing games, competing in school, or making business decisions. When you cheat, you choose to take advantage of someone else in two ways. First, you benefit from not playing by the rules. Second, you put others at a disadvantage because they are playing by the rules you have chosen to ignore.

Recently some athletes have chosen to use illegal performance-enhancing drugs to give themselves a competitive advantage. They are doing potential harm to their bodies due to the unknown long-term effects of the

© Vicky Kasala/Photodisc/Getty Images

Online communities such as MySpace and Facebook have become a popular method of communicating with friends, meeting new people, and keeping up to date with the latest music, movies, entertainment, and fashion trends. However, they can easily be misused, causing unanticipated harm to others.

Akira, Francine, and Amy were close friends until Akira and Amy had a disagreement that led to name-calling and a vow to "get even." Akira and Francine decided to build a false profile of Amy in an online community space. They filled the profile with misleading personal information that made Amy seem like a person she really was not. They added pictures the three had taken together that were personal and that they had agreed not to share with others. They even participated in some chat rooms and blogs using Amy's identity while providing false information and answering questions in ways they knew Amy would not. They rationalized their actions by saying it really would not hurt Amy in the long run because they had made up the information, and it would be funny when everyone found out what they had done.

THINK *CRITICALLY*

1. Do you agree or disagree with Akira and Francine that Amy would not really be hurt by the online prank? Why?
2. If you were aware of what Akira and Francine had done and you were friends with all three girls, what would you do?

drugs. They are also admitting to themselves that they are unwilling or unable to compete on a level playing field with their opponents. Those competitors who choose to undergo the necessary training and preparation without using illegal substances have personal integrity and honesty. They know that their success is due to their own preparation and practice. But unknowingly, they are in an unfair competition due to the dishonesty of an opponent. Is it really worth doing anything it takes to win? How are those athletes viewed when their dishonesty is made public? How does it affect their own self-respect and the views of their family and friends? How does it affect the image of the sport in which they cheated?

You expect honesty in others and are disappointed and hurt when you find out someone has taken advantage of you through dishonesty. You look up to people who act honestly and honorably. You value their achievements because they played by the rules. You feel good about yourself when you honestly make a difficult choice and find out that you can achieve the goals you set out to accomplish.

CHECKPOINT

How does honesty affect decisions you make about yourself?

You are not being honest with yourself if you rationalize decisions or ignore

information you know is important when making personal choices.

TECH ETHICS
Harmless pranks often are not harmless. Have students discuss all of the ways that Amy could be hurt by Akira's and Francine's actions. (Answers may include embarrassment and damage to Amy's reputation as well as personal concern for how others will treat her.) Ask students how they would feel if someone did those things to them. Would they just laugh it off as a harmless prank?

Think Critically Answers
1. Answers will vary.
2. Answers will vary.

ONGOING ASSESSMENT
Use the Checkpoint as an opportunity to conduct on-going assessment of student comprehension of the lesson material.

© SW Productions/Photodisc/Getty Images

TRUTH AND RESPECT

A *fib,* a *tall tale,* or a *little white lie*—each of these words and phrases relates to truthfulness. The words suggest that some types of untruthfulness are not as bad as others. Yet there is always a difference between being truthful and being untruthful, even if we think that some untruthful statements are more acceptable than others.

Misleading Information

Being **truthful** means providing accurate and complete information while respecting the circumstances and the persons receiving the information. When you answer a question or provide an explanation, you should not try to mislead. You may typically think of being untruthful as lying or intentionally providing false information. However, it can also result from withholding information needed by others for complete understanding. If your teacher asks you, "Did you do your homework assignment by yourself?" would you be dishonest if you answered "yes" but failed to tell the teacher you had actually looked at a classmate's completed homework before starting your own? If you asked your friend, "Have you talked to Joseph?" and she answered "no," knowing that she had not directly talked to Joseph but had text-messaged him, would you think the friend had been honest with you? Each of these examples shows that honesty can be more complex and often more difficult than you might first think.

Understanding and Respect

There are times when the truth can be hurtful and even harmful to others. When telling the truth, you always should try to understand how the information will be received by others. You should ask yourself if the information may be inappropriate under the circumstances. For example, suppose a doctor has just reviewed the test results of a patient and has diagnosed a disease for which there is no realistic treatment. It would probably be inappropriate and even harmful for the doctor to immediately provide the patient with all of that information. At the same time, it would not help for the doctor to avoid any discussion of the results and act as if everything was okay. The initial conversation could begin to prepare the patient for the more difficult information to be discussed at a later time, possibly when supporting family members and friends are there to help the person deal with the bad news.

Every athletic season, students go through tryouts to make the varsity teams. Often coaches post the names of the students who did and did not make the teams in a public place in the school. It is a difficult time for those students who did not make the team to have to review the list. The information is truthful, but it may not show full respect for the students and their circumstances. Instead, the coach could meet individually with each student to talk about the student's practice and performance. The coach could also review areas of strength and areas that need improvement. While the students may still be disappointed, they will see the coach's respect for them and their efforts.

© Digital Vision/Getty Images

It is not always easy to be truthful and show respect for others. It requires you to understand other people and their circumstances. Even when your intentions are the best, it is not always possible. It is likely that you will make mistakes in trying to be honest and respectful. Sometimes you may withhold important information with the sincere belief that you are protecting the feelings of others. At other times, you may provide more information than people really need, and they will get upset. If your intentions are to be both truthful and respectful, you will be in a position to explain your actions and ask for understanding. But it is much more difficult to explain your actions when you have set out to be untruthful.

CHECKPOINT

Why is it important to show respect for others and their circumstances when being truthful?

It is important to consider others' feelings when being truthful. Sometimes the truth can be hurtful, and sometimes it can even be harmful.

TEACH
Have students think of a time when they may have received some disappointing or upsetting news. How was the news delivered? Do they feel that the person was both truthful and respectful of their feelings?

TEACHING STRATEGIES
Kinesthetic Learners
Have students talk to several of the coaches for various sports and to teacher advisers for groups or activities that require tryouts, such as the band, cheerleading squad, school plays, and debate team to determine how students are notified when they are not chosen for a position. Do they feel that the methods used are truthful while showing respect for the students and their efforts? If not, what changes would they recommend?

ONGOING ASSESSMENT
Use the Checkpoint as an opportunity to conduct ongoing assessment of student comprehension of the lesson material.

Follow UP

UNDERSTAND LEADERSHIP CONCEPTS

Circle the best answer for each of the following questions.

1. If you act in a certain way with little thought due to repeated behavior, your actions have become
a. dishonest
b. habitual
c. unimportant
d. practiced

2. A person who is truthful
a. provides all information no matter how it affects people
b. will not disclose information that might be personally embarrassing
c. shows respect for others when deciding what information to share
d. can still fib or mislead if the purpose is to be funny

THINK *CRITICALLY*

Answer the following questions as completely as possible. If necessary, use a separate sheet of paper.

3. Why are people who are two-faced not likely to be considered for leadership positions?
When people act differently around different people, others begin to see that they are acting and may wonder about their true character. Their behavior is not likely to instill the confidence and trust that a person needs to have in order to be an effective leader.

4. Do you agree that your character is shaped more by what you do than by what you think? Why do you feel this way?
Answers will vary. Character is shaped by your actions—not by your thoughts.

5. If you saw a teammate clearly cheat in a competition resulting in a victory for your team when you otherwise would have lost, how would you feel? What would you do?
Answers will vary. A good first step might be to discuss the incident with your team's coach.

Being Reliable and Responsible

GOALS

- Describe the effects of reliability on others and on you.
- Recognize the difference between accepting responsibility and taking responsibility.

TERMS

- reliability
- responsibility

THE EFFECTS OF RELIABILITY

Do you consider yourself reliable? Would your parents and close friends describe you as reliable? How about your teachers? A reliable person is dependable. A more specific definition of **reliability** is consistency in performance or behavior. In other words, a reliable person can be counted on time after time.

The Effects on Others

The most important way of being reliable is by following through on commitments. If you give your word, people expect that you will do what you say. All of us have had friends who assured us they would meet us somewhere at a particular time and either did not show up or showed up very late. If the meeting was just to go to a movie or a party, it may have been an inconvenience, and you may have felt irritated. But the same thing may have happened when a teammate did not show up to help you finish a class project the night before it was due. Or if you have a job, a coworker may have failed to come to work, creating more work for you and other workers. Failing to meet important time commitments can have a negative effect.

Meeting Time Commitments

Reliability is a character trait that seems less important to some people than many of the other traits. Failure to keep commitments often has a negative effect on others, but at least in the short run, it does not seem to affect the unreliable person in a negative way. Your friend who did not meet you for the movie may have ended up doing something else that was more important and enjoyable at the time. He knew that you would get over the inconvenience and irritation because of your friendship. The coworker who failed to show up for work recognizes work rules related to absences and knows the consequences. However, the need for additional sleep or the desire to do something more important than work makes up for the negative consequences that may be suffered when she returns to work. Of course at the time, the person

SCHEDULE
Block 45 minutes
Regular 1 class period

FOCUS
Ask students if they think there is a difference between accepting responsibility and taking responsibility. Have them explain their answers.

TEACH
Ask students to think about the people they can count on to be there for them when they need help. Are there others who have proven in the past to be unreliable? How do they feel about those individuals?

Some people may view their lack of follow-through as "no big deal." Ask students to think of all the ways that their lack of follow-through can affect others. List their answers on the board.

Ask students if they have ever failed to keep an appointment or to meet a time commitment, perhaps because something that seemed more important at the time came up. Ask them what they have done in the past to try to become more reliable about time commitments. Have those things helped or not?

People demonstrate self-discipline in many ways—how they organize their time, how orderly their work area and living space are, how they set priorities, and whether or not they set and follow goals. Work with a team to create a list of ten things you can observe about a person that would suggest a high level of self-discipline. Write the items on a sheet of paper and rate yourself on each one: high, medium, or low. Compare and discuss your ratings with those of your team members.

THINK *CRITICALLY*

Are there situations where you have a high level of self-discipline and others where your self-discipline is low? What are the differences? When you are working in a team, does your self-discipline increase or decrease? Why?

A TEAM EFFORT
The list may include being prepared, following through on commitments to others (even if something more interesting or appealing comes up), submitting assignments on time, arriving at appointments (or school or work) on time, and being willing to put off instant gratification in order to achieve long-term goals.

Think Critically Answers
Answers will vary.

TEACH
Ask students to think of a team project they worked on that went well. Then ask them to think of a team project they worked on that did not go well. What was the difference between the two projects? Students may come to realize that when they join a team and work with people who are unreliable, they may end up spending more time trying to get the team to work well together than on the project itself. Have students discuss ways that the team project experience can be improved.

does not experience the frustration you and the other people at the job are feeling as a result of having to make up for her absence.

Following Rules and Meeting Expectations

There are many other ways that you demonstrate reliability other than being on time or keeping scheduled appointments. Reliability is also shown by meeting requirements that are set by people in authority, such as parents, teachers, coaches, bosses, and team leaders. Parents count on you to follow home rules and to meet obligations for household work and chores. They expect you to be where you tell them you will be, doing what they expect you to do. Teachers expect you to attend class and participate in class activities. They also expect you to follow class and school rules and complete assignments on time to the best of your abilities. In the same way, bosses, coaches, and other adults you work with expect you to demonstrate responsible behavior and give your best to the job, sport, club, or other activities in which you have chosen to participate.

Consistent Quality and Effort

Another aspect of reliability is being consistent in the quality and amount of work and effort you put into tasks you undertake. An example is being a reliable team member. You know that if you are assigned to a team project at school the experience will not be pleasant and the results will not be successful if one or more team members are not reliable. Whether you are assigned to a team or get to choose your teammates and project, reliability requires you to work well with other team members and the team leader to plan the project and take on a reasonable part of the work load. It also requires you to complete the project on time, help other team members as needed, and give your best effort to complete a project of which all team members can be proud. You know that when you are on a team with reliable partners, the work will get done and you will enjoy the experience.

The Effects on You

Because others appear to be affected more by the unreliability of another person, it is sometimes difficult to get individuals who are not reliable to understand its importance. But being reliable or unreliable makes a big difference to an individual, both immediately and in the long run. Your reputation follows you. Being known as an unreliable person influences the way other people relate to you, interact with you, and trust you.

Loss of Trust

Have you seen the disappointment on the face of a parent, teacher, or close friend when you have failed to meet an obligation to which you had committed? While at the time you may have tried to ignore the look or not think about how you affected their feelings, you know they have a different view of you, at least for the moment. If you failed to meet a commitment for an important obligation, you may have received more than a disappointed look. It may have resulted in punishment from your parent or teacher or even a lost friendship with your close friend. That certainly has a more lasting effect on you than the expression of disappointment, but both have an effect on the future relationship you have with the other person. Even if it was not a particularly important obligation or if it was a first-time occurrence for you, other people will be a bit more cautious the next time you agree to do something for them. Each time you see them, you will feel uneasy until you can rebuild their trust.

Lack of Control

When you are unable or unwilling to meet time commitments, you may not see an immediate negative result. However, you will see changes over time in how people relate to you. You are less likely to be invited to important events or activities where being on time is important. You will also lose some personal control. Rather than allowing you to determine where and when the group will meet, people will tell you what they expect. They may also begin to tell you that they will leave without you if you are not on time.

Low Expectations from Others

When people see that they cannot count on the quality or amount of effort you are willing to put into tasks, you soon will not be a preferred team member and will not be given important assignments. In the short run, some people may consider that a positive result. They may think that they can do less work and get easier assignments but still benefit from the efforts of other team members working with them. But soon, unreliable people begin to see that they are the last to be chosen. People with whom they have worked will avoid working with them again. Their reputation for being unreliable will spread. Even when unreliable people find an exciting project to work on and want to give it their best effort, other people will expect the same low level of performance shown in the past. It will be hard for unreliable people to convince others that they now are willing to give their best effort.

> It is the responsibility of leadership to provide opportunity and the responsibility of individuals to contribute.
>
> —C. William Pollard

The Benefits of Being Reliable

It may be surprising to see the results and benefits you receive when others consider you to be reliable. Parents, teachers, and other adults will trust that you will do what you say and will keep commitments. As a result, they will not feel the need to supervise you as closely. They will allow you more choices and freedom and will give you greater responsibility over time. If you demonstrate reliability when at school or work, teachers and bosses may give you more challenging tasks and assignments. While that may seem like you are being rewarded with more work, it actually is giving you the opportunity to increase your knowledge and abilities beyond those of other students and coworkers. You will be one of the first people they will think of when recognitions, rewards, or other opportunities become available. They will be willing to provide recommendations and support when you are seeking leadership roles or development opportunities.

Your personal confidence will grow as you commit to being reliable. You know you can be counted on, you will make your best effort, and you will fulfill your obligations. Your social relationships will improve because people will see you as someone they have confidence in and can trust. Your opportunities will expand. People will offer you leadership roles and ask you to take on responsibilities that are given only to the most responsible people. Your reputation will be well-respected so that you do not always have to prove yourself to others. You will be known as a reliable and trustworthy person.

 CHECKPOINT

In what ways do people benefit when others view them as reliable?

When others view them as reliable, people are given more challenging tasks and

leadership opportunities. Others trust and respect them.

THE MEANINGS OF RESPONSIBILITY

Can you recall times when a problem occurred with a government project or a business activity that resulted in a significant cost to taxpayers or consumers? It may even have resulted in injury or loss of life to innocent people. Often a politician or a business executive is quick to step up and say, "I accept full responsibility for the problem." Yet in many instances, little is done to make up for the losses and harm. Taking responsibility involves more than just admitting a mistake.

TEACH
Ask students how they feel when their parents, teachers, and friends trust them. Do they think the benefits of being reliable are worth the effort that is required to build that reputation?

ONGOING ASSESSMENT
Use the Checkpoint as an opportunity to conduct ongoing assessment of student comprehension of the lesson material.

TEACH
Ask students to think of a time when a problem occurred in a project or activity for which they were responsible. How did they respond to the problem? Did they take responsibility and accept the consequences, or did they rationalize, make excuses, or blame others?

A **responsibility** is a duty or obligation. A responsibility is made up of two parts. When you are responsible, you have an obligation to make sure that responsibility is fulfilled. You are the one in charge. You have committed to making sure something happens. Typically, people will look to you for leadership.

The other part of responsibility is accepting the consequences that follow. If the obligation is met well, you will receive recognition from those who benefited. However, if things do not turn out as planned, people will look to you for answers because you are responsible. People enjoy responsibility when things turn out well, but they may try to look for ways to avoid responsibility when things go wrong.

Accepting Responsibility

Are you excited by a challenge? Do you like to step up and take charge? If so, you are probably someone who accepts responsibility. But accepting responsibility is more than saying you are willing to lead or make the decision. You must be committed to following through on that commitment. You need to be able to plan how to meet the obligation and take the time and effort to get things done. You also need to lead others who are helping with the activity and follow through until the obligation is met.

Louisa is the vice-president of the sophomore class and is responsible for fundraising. She knew everyone was tired of the typical candy and magazine sales, so she wanted to try something new. She talked with the other officers and a number of other students about holding a talent show and selling tickets to the community to raise money.

Everyone seemed very enthused about the new activity. However, after announcing the event, Louisa quickly ran into problems. She needed committees for planning the program, staging and operating the show, selling tickets, handling publicity, and performing several other activities. She was struggling to find good leaders and team members who would take on some of the important and time-consuming activities. People were looking forward to the show, but they did not seem to want to do the necessary work.

Louisa also knew that the event would not be successful unless the talent was good. Many people, including some of her best friends, approached her to be sure they could be part of the show. She knew not all of them were reliable, but she did not want to be the one to make the decisions. What had been an exciting idea and one that students and teachers were looking forward to was quickly turning into an uncontrollable mess. Louisa wanted to forget that she ever had the idea.

Louisa's experience shows that a great deal goes into accepting responsibility. Too often people think more about being in a position to tell others what to do and forget that there will be a great deal of work to follow. Louisa was excited about doing something that had never been done before. She felt good when others liked her idea. But then she recognized what it would take to have a successful talent show. Louisa expected that others in her class would be willing to undertake much of the work if they wanted a successful show. However, she failed to recognize that it was ultimately her responsibility to

LEADERSHIP *Tip*

If you are a leader of an organization, the organization is an extension of you. If you want the organization to be effective, you must be an effective leader. Too often, leaders who believe firmly that they are persons of good character are surprised when things go wrong in their organizations. They need to examine their leadership to learn why their personal integrity did not extend into the organization.

TEACH
Ask students how they think Louisa could have handled the situation differently. What mistakes did she make? How could they have been avoided?

TEACHING STRATEGIES
Gifted Students
Many companies have developed a plan to be followed in the event of a crisis or difficult situation, such as the recall of an unsafe product. Have students talk to business people at companies in your community to find out if they have plans in case those types of problems are encountered. Who is responsible and how do they plan to make up for the losses or harm done to the public or their customers?

LEADERSHIP TIP
Ask students why they think that things can go wrong in an organization even if there is effective leadership. Do they think that being a person of good character is enough for a leader to avoid problems?

find ways to get people involved and make sure everything was completed. Responsibility for a successful talent show was much greater than she had anticipated, but it was still her responsibility. Louisa can get help from others by organizing the committees and building enthusiasm among those who decide to help with the show. But it won't happen unless she accepts the responsibility.

Taking Responsibility

Even when you accept responsibility and put forth your best effort, things do not always turn out as planned. If the talent show goes well, Louisa will be happy to take responsibility and receive the recognition she deserves. Hopefully, she will share the spotlight with all of the others who worked hard to make the show a success.

But what happens if the show is not successful? It may be that the talent show was organized but ticket sales were low. Maybe there were technical problems with the sound and lighting or the talent was not quite as good as people expected. How would Louisa respond if people were disappointed because the talent show did not meet their expectations? It would be easy for her to place the blame on others for low ticket sales, poor publicity, or failure to plan well for the show's operations. But Louisa accepted responsibility when she decided to undertake the new fundraising event. Now she has to take responsibility for the results. While others played important roles in the event and may not have done everything as well as they could have done, final responsibility still comes back to Louisa. People with strong character take responsibility when things go wrong as well as when things go right.

Hopefully, as a good leader, Louisa worked closely with the committees. She should have checked to be sure things were going as planned to be aware of any problems. She should have worked to solve problems and to have backup plans for important things like the sound system. But no matter how hard people work and how much a leader tries to anticipate problems, there is always a chance for things to go wrong. Louisa has to take responsibility for the results.

It still is important to thank people for their efforts. If the event is unsuccessful, Louisa should talk with committee leaders, teachers, and others to try to determine what went wrong. She should share what she learns with others to help everyone learn from the activity. If the sophomore class still needs additional funds, Louisa should continue to meet her responsibility by planning additional fundraising activities. Some students may initially express disappointment with the talent show, and they may blame Louisa. But if she takes responsibility for the results and continues to work as a leader, she will regain their respect and confidence. If they see that she is willing to take responsibility in bad times as well as good times, most students will be willing to work on future projects with her.

 CHECKPOINT

What are the two parts of responsibility?

The two parts of responsibility are making sure that responsibility is fulfilled and accepting the consequences that follow.

Follow UP

UNDERSTAND LEADERSHIP CONCEPTS

Circle the best answer for each of the following questions.

1. **When you are reliable, people expect each of the following from you except**
   a. meeting time commitments
   b. following rules and meeting expectations
   c. providing consistent quality and effort
   d. achieving more than you have in the past

2. **Responsibility is**
   a. a requirement imposed by others
   b. a duty or obligation
   c. the ability to lead others
   d. none of the above

THINK *CRITICALLY*

Answer the following questions as completely as possible. If necessary, use a separate sheet of paper.

3. **How do you judge if a person is reliable or not? What happens to your relationship with others when you see that they are unreliable?**

   Reliable people can be counted on to meet time commitments, follow rules, meet

   expectations, and provide consistent quality and effort. When you see that people are

   unreliable, you lose your trust in them. You may not invite them to important events

   where being on time is important, and you have very low expectations of them.

4. **If you have been unreliable in the past, how can you rebuild others' confidence in you?**

   Answers will vary but may include being on time, following through on commitments,

   following rules, working hard to meet or exceed expectations, and providing

   consistent quality and effort. However, rebuilding others' confidence in your

   reliability will take time.

5. **Think of a time when you have accepted responsibility for an important activity and it did not turn out as planned. What did you do to take responsibility for the results? What, if anything, would you do differently if you were to accept the same responsibility again?**

   Answers will vary.

ASSESS

Reteach
Have students review the goals for the lesson and then write a paragraph that identifies the key points for each goal.

Enrich
Invite a business leader to speak to the class about the importance of being reliable and responsible in the workplace. Have students prepare questions in advance to ask the speaker after his or her presentation.

Close
Ask students to list the ways that they can demonstrate that they are reliable and responsible individuals.

9.3

Exhibiting Self-Discipline

GOALS

- Explain how self-discipline is developed.
- Describe how to use self-discipline to achieve your self-improvement goals.

TERMS

- self-control
- self-discipline
- success environment

SCHEDULE
Block 45 minutes
Regular 1 class period

FOCUS
Ask students how they feel when they are disciplined by their parents or teachers. Then ask them to consider the meaning of self-discipline. How is it different?

TEACH
Ask students if they have ever seen someone lose control or "fly off the handle" over something that someone has said or done. How do they feel when they are around that type of person?

Ask students to explain the relationship between self-discipline and achieving goals. Do they think that self-discipline is a necessary character trait for effective leaders?

Ask students to think of a baby or young child they know—perhaps a younger brother or sister. In what ways has that child already developed independence and self-control? In what ways is the child still very dependent on others?

THE MEANING OF SELF-DISCIPLINE

Having self-control and self-discipline is evidence that a person is developing responsibility and character. **Self-control** is responsibility for managing your immediate actions. When you have self-control, you can manage your emotions, desires, and actions. **Self-discipline** is the ability to forgo something that will provide immediate satisfaction in order to achieve an important, longer-term goal. It requires you to focus on how your actions will benefit you in the future. Both self-control and self-discipline are important personal characteristics that demonstrate growing maturity. It takes many years for these traits to become part of a person's character.

Developing Independence and Self-Control

If you have ever watched a baby, you know that infants have almost no control. Their physical movements, bodily functions, and sounds occur almost randomly. They must rely on others to feed and bathe them, change their clothes, and hold and comfort them. From the time children begin to gain muscle control, start to form words, and begin to understand and think, an important developmental goal is to gain personal control and independence.

If you have younger brothers or sisters or know other young children, you can see that in the years after they are babies, children develop in several ways. Even though they are sometimes awkward, they have much more physical control over muscles and movements. They are still immature emotionally, but they want to be as independent as possible. They want to do things for themselves and make their own decisions. They want to control the things that are "theirs"—their room, their toys, and their friends. They sometimes can appear to be selfish in attempting to control what they believe is rightfully theirs. With developing language skills, they become better at communicating their ideas and feelings. However, they get frustrated quickly when they cannot clearly communicate what they want or what they are feeling.

Most important, young children have almost no concept of the future. Their focus is on what is happening to them right now, and it can keep them from paying attention to anything else. Children who see a cute dog across the street may run toward it, forgetting that they should look both ways or that the animal may not be friendly. Events that are weeks or even days away are almost impossible to think about or wait for. While young children are changing and developing, they still need a lot of guidance and direction from adults. They may be frustrated when adults make decisions and do things for them. They often express that frustration with anger or tears. But in small stages, they are beginning to develop the control and independence each person seeks.

▌ Achieving Self-Discipline

Now that you are a teenager, you are developing many character traits and personal qualities of adults. You have changed from being totally focused on yourself to recognizing the importance of others. You know that to get along with others you sometimes need to forgo what is most important to you and consider the needs and interests of others. You recognize that your friends and other students in your school have different backgrounds, beliefs, and interests. To get along with them you have to find ways to adapt to differences while focusing on common interests and activities.

As a teenager, you have a great deal of independence although sometimes not as much as you would like or believe you can manage. You recognize that your parents and other adults can provide good advice and support.

You and your friends want to have fun and enjoy each day, but you also recognize that in a few short years you will leave high school and move on to college or to work. You will make your own life with a career, a home, and likely your own family. So you are thinking more and more about the future. You make plans and set goals. You are also willing to commit time and effort to things that you might not prefer to do. You recognize the benefits that activities like going to school every day, studying, and holding a part-time job will offer in the future. That shows that you are developing the important character trait of self-discipline.

© Nancy R Cohen/Photodisc/Getty Images

▌ Self-Discipline Characteristics

People who are self-disciplined are able to keep a broad and objective focus. They think carefully about the effects of their actions on themselves and their goals. They also consider how their actions will affect others. They are able to control emotions that will cause them to make decisions or take actions they will regret. They know that everyone makes mistakes from time to time no matter how carefully they plan.

TEACH
Have students list some of the ways they feel that they are achieving greater self-discipline. Have several students share their answers with the class.

TEACHING STRATEGIES
Kinesthetic Learners
Have students keep a journal for a week. In the journal, they should record things that they do each day that show self-control and self-discipline. They also should make note of things that they do that point out the need for improvement in self-control and self-discipline. At the end of the week, have students review the journals and summarize their feelings.

TEACH

Have students think of a person they know who they feel has achieved a high level of self-discipline. What characteristics do they see in the person that shows that the person has self-discipline?

ONGOING ASSESSMENT

Use the Checkpoint as an opportunity to conduct ongoing assessment of student comprehension of the lesson material.

TEACH

Ask students to think about taking a very long hike—a hike of 1,000 miles. What kind of preparation and training would they need to do before setting off on their hike? What supplies would they pack to take with them? Explain that setting a long-term goal is like planning a 1,000-mile hike. They must prepare and train by first setting smaller, more manageable goals. They also will need "supplies" like talents, skills, and abilities to take with them.

Ask students to think of a long-term goal they have set for themselves. What do they think is the "first step" that they need to take in order to reach their goal? Why should they focus on the first step as much as on the overall goal?

But they also realize that they can learn from their mistakes to avoid repeating them and to do better the next time.

People with self-discipline take on challenges that are important to them—particularly challenges that will help accomplish personal goals and lead to self-improvement. They also do their best to finish what they start. Even if they do not achieve every goal or accomplish every challenge, they do not easily give up. If they do not achieve their goals, they try to learn from their mistakes so that they can do a better job the next time. Above all, they take responsibility for their actions. They do not blame others.

Finally, self-disciplined people are future-oriented. They know that they may have to forgo some things that seem important right now and make some personal sacrifices to get where they want to be and obtain what they want to have in the future. They think carefully about their future, set goals, and work to achieve those goals.

What do you see about yourself that shows you are developing self-discipline? In what areas do you need to improve? Setting personal goals and working on self-control and self-discipline are evidence that you are preparing to achieve the independence and personal control you want.

 CHECKPOINT

What does it mean to be self-disciplined?

Being self-disciplined means being able to forgo immediate satisfaction in order to

achieve an important, longer-term goal. It requires a focus on the future.

SELF-DISCIPLINE FOR SELF-IMPROVEMENT

The Chinese philosopher Lao-Tzu said, "A journey of a thousand miles begins with a single step." Walking a thousand miles seems like a very long journey, and a single step seems like a tiny beginning. But without the beginning, the journey cannot be achieved. With the first step, the commitment is made to the journey. The single step is followed by the first yard, then the first mile. Step by step, the thousand-mile journey is achieved.

Many things go into making a journey successful. The person planning the journey must understand what is required and must be mentally and physically prepared to complete the journey. Problems will be encountered, changes may be required, and obstacles must be overcome. Only individuals who can picture what lies at the end of the journey will have the commitment to continue past the obstacles.

Identify Your Goals

You may never walk a journey of a thousand miles, but you have important personal goals to achieve, such as making the varsity team, training for a marathon, getting accepted into your favorite college, or opening your own business. Personal goals that are important and meaningful are not always easy to achieve. You may have goals that others think you cannot achieve. You, too, may have doubts. But the first part of self-discipline is deciding what you want to achieve in the future and then setting important personal goals.

Set Self-Improvement Priorities

What personal changes and improvements will you need to make to achieve your goals? Usually the requirements are greater than you first think. Making a varsity sports team requires more than just improving a specific athletic skill. You will also need to work on academic skills to meet and exceed the eligibility requirements. You will need time management skills to make sure you are able to meet all of your other commitments in addition to the practice time required for the sport. You need emotional maturity and stability to handle the pressures of competition. Many good athletes are not selected for a team because they are not effective team members. They may become easily frustrated or lose their tempers. Coaches won't select team members who are likely to cause problems.

In the same way, preparing for a successful college admission will require months and even years of effort as well as personal improvement in a number of areas. For any important goal, you must consider the changes and improvements you will need to make in the following areas:

- physical health and appearance
- self-concept and self-image
- communication skills
- specific academic abilities and study skills
- relationships with others
- time management, organizational, and planning skills
- support from parents, teachers, friends, and mentors
- emotional control and maturity
- special talents and skills

Think carefully about what is needed. Study and talk to others who have already achieved the success you desire. Carefully identify what you will need to do, and make sure you are committed not only to the goal but also to the challenges you will face. As with the journey of a thousand miles, it may seem an almost impossible challenge. However, you know that others have gone there before you successfully. Finally, you know you have the commitment and self-discipline to achieve the things that are important to you.

Create a Success Environment

What is the difference between people who overcome difficult challenges and those who do not? Often it is the environment that surrounds

TEACH
Have students list a specific change or improvement they will need to make in each of the nine areas listed in order to reach their goal. After they have completed their list, have them prioritize the items on their list so that they begin to develop a plan for self-improvement.

Ask students to think about the people, conditions, and resources in their life. Do they create a success environment that supports their efforts for self-improvement? If not, what are some positive steps they can take to create a success environment?

Have students take an honest look at the long-term goal they set earlier in the lesson. Is it really what they want to achieve, or is it a goal they set because of pressure from others, such as family or friends?

TEACHING STRATEGIES
Auditory Learners
Have students talk to someone who has achieved a major success for which they had planned. They should discuss the steps that person took in order to achieve his or her goal.

them. Those who overcome difficult challenges have a success environment. A **success environment** includes people, conditions, and resources that support rather than detract from your personal improvement efforts. Do you have friends who have long-term goals, or do they live in the moment? Do the people around you support and believe in you, or do they make fun of your ideas and discourage you? Do you have a quiet place to think, study, and relax? Do you have people to turn to when you need advice, encouragement, and help? You need to remove the negativity around you to achieve great things. Make sure that you surround yourself with support rather than distractions as you work toward your goals.

COMMUNICATE

As a leader you often will be in the position of having to persuade others to accept your point of view. Being able to give an effective persuasive speech is an important communication skill. Here are a few pointers.

1. *When you want to convince people of something, you must establish your credibility. People must believe that you understand the topic and are providing them with meaningful information.*
2. *Your ideas must make sense. Give people information they can understand and that fits with what they believe.*
3. *Be well-prepared and well-organized. People won't believe that what you are saying is important if you did not take the time to prepare for the speech. The message must be clear, specific, and logical.*
4. *Let your emotions show. People need to know you care about the topic. If you are unemotional, it may be viewed as a lack of passion and commitment to the idea.*
5. *End with reasons for their support. People need to be able to justify their support for the new idea. Give them reasons that are understandable and memorable.*

THINK *CRITICALLY*

What do you think are the differences between a persuasive speech and an informative speech? How can your body language affect your audience in a persuasive speech?

Be Honest with Yourself

It is not as easy to achieve a goal as it is to set a goal. You can make plans for personal improvement but then never accomplish those plans. A part of self-discipline is being honest with yourself. Is this really a goal you want to achieve, or are you setting it because of pressures from others? Have you really thought about the short-term sacrifices you may need to make?

It is not a sign of weakness if you do not achieve all of your goals or if you change your mind and set new goals. If you make the effort and still are not successful, you can be proud of yourself for the attempt. However, if you set unrealistic goals, constantly change them, seldom make efforts toward personal improvement, or are easily distracted from your efforts, you have not demonstrated the self-discipline and self-control needed for personal success. Many people never begin the journey and many others drop out along the way. People with maturity, dedication, self-discipline, and motivation successfully stand at the end of the thousand miles.

 **CHECKPOINT**

What are the four steps for achieving a personal goal?

The four steps for achieving a personal goal are (1) identify your goals, (2) set self-improvement priorities, (3) create a success environment, and (4) be honest with yourself.

Follow UP

UNDERSTAND LEADERSHIP CONCEPTS

Circle the best answer for each of the following questions.

1. **You can manage your emotions, desires, and actions when you have**
   a. self-confidence
   b. self-control
   c. self-discipline
   d. self-improvement

2. **All of the following are steps in achieving an important long-term personal goal except**
   a. identifying your goals
   b. setting self-improvement priorities
   c. identifying reasons you might not be successful
   d. being honest with yourself

THINK CRITICALLY

Answer the following questions as completely as possible. If necessary, use a separate sheet of paper.

3. **What are some examples you see among students in your classes that they have self-control and self-discipline? What are some examples that they have not yet developed those characteristics?**
   Answers will vary.

4. **How can role models help people successfully achieve personal improvement goals? How might they actually detract people from achieving the goals?**
   Answers will vary. Role models can help people see what can be achieved with self-discipline and a focus on setting and achieving goals. They might possibly detract people from achieving their goals if they caused them to set unrealistic goals.

5. **Describe what you believe should be part of a success environment for a student who wants to be successful academically.**
   Answers will vary. A success environment for a student who wants to be successful academically should include people who support academic excellence and offer encouragement and guidance, a quiet place to think and study, and access to resources such as libraries and the Internet as well as tutoring if it is needed.

ASSESS
Reteach
On the board, list the four steps for achieving a goal. Discuss the importance of each step.

Enrich
Have students obtain permission to observe a group of young children—in a daycare or on a playground. What can they tell about the level of independence and self-control each child exhibits? They may also want to observe a group of students in their high school and compare their observations.

Close
Ask students how they can tell whether or not a person is self-disciplined. Have them list the characteristics of self-discipline.

Chapter Assessment

TEACHING RESOURCES
ExamView® CD, Ch. 9

REVIEW *LEADERSHIP CONCEPTS*

Write the letter of the term that matches each definition.

a. habitual
b. honest
c. reliability
d. responsibility
e. self-control
f. self-discipline
g. success environment
h. truthful

__b__ 1. Not intentionally deceiving or misleading others

__h__ 2. Providing accurate and complete information while respecting the circumstances and the persons receiving the information

__g__ 3. People, conditions, and resources that support rather than detract from your personal improvement efforts

__c__ 4. Consistency in performance or behavior

__e__ 5. Managing your emotions, desires, and actions

__d__ 6. A duty or obligation

__f__ 7. The ability to forgo something that will provide immediate satisfaction to achieve an important, longer-term goal

__a__ 8. Acting in a certain way with little thought due to repeated behavior

Circle the best answer.

9. When you try to act in different ways around certain people or in particular situations, you become
   a. more mature
   b. an actor
   c. dishonest
   d. none of the above

10. Which of the following are examples of being dishonest?
    a. lying
    b. intentionally providing false information
    c. withholding information that others need
    d. all of the above

11. You are being reliable when you
    a. meet time obligations
    b. rely on others to make important decisions
    c. consistently perform the same behavior even if you are not making progress
    d. all of the above

12. A leader who demonstrates responsibility would not
    a. form teams and work with team leaders to get work done
    b. work with others to identify and solve problems quickly
    c. take responsibility for problems even if it was clearly the fault of others who worked on the project
    d. stop working on an activity or project when problems occur

ASSESS
Reteach
Have students review the answers to the Checkpoint questions. Use the questions as a lead-in discussion on the concepts covered in the chapter.

Enrich
Have students create a computer-generated (Power-Point) presentation called "Building Character" that can be shared with other groups of students. The presentation should include references to being honest, truthful, reliable, responsible, and self-disciplined.

CLOSE
Have students explain how developing the personal characteristics discussed in this lesson—honesty, truthfulness, reliability, responsibility, and self-discipline— can build character and help them become effective leaders.

THINK *CRITICALLY*

13. *Provide an example of someone who was two-faced with you. How did it make you feel about the situation and about the person? Why do you believe some people feel the need to be two-faced?*

Answers will vary. Some people may feel the need to be two-faced because they are

insecure or have low self-esteem and fear that others will not like or accept their

"real" personality.

14. *Would you feel differently about a person who unintentionally gives you incorrect information that creates a problem for you than you would about a person who intentionally lies or deceives you? Why?*

Answers will vary but students most likely would feel differently. The person who

unintentionally gives you incorrect information has simply made a mistake and is not

deliberately trying to cause a problem for you. The person who intentionally lies or

deceives you does so knowingly.

15. *Do you believe the increased availability and use of communications technology such as cell phones, text-messaging, and the Internet has changed people's views about topics such as ethics, integrity, and honesty? Why or why not?*

Answers will vary. Because electronic communications requires less personal contact,

they could possibly make it easier to "bend the truth" or withhold information.

16. *What is the difference between being reliable and being responsible? Can you have one of these character traits and not the other? Explain your answer.*

Being reliable means being consistent in your behavior. Being responsible means

making sure that a duty or obligation is fulfilled and accepting the consequences.

Because they are two separate and distinct character traits, it is possible that one trait

could be more developed than the other.

17. *Do you believe that giving children more independence will increase their self-control and self-discipline? Why or why not?*

Answers will vary. Self-control and self-discipline develop as a person matures. Each

child develops independence and self-control at his or her own rate, and giving

children more independence before they have matured enough to accept it most likely

will not increase their self-control and self-discipline.

18. **Media**   *Watch an episode of a popular television show. Make a list of the main characters in the show. For each of the characters, identify examples from the episode when they do or do not demonstrate the personal character traits discussed in the chapter. Write a three-paragraph "review" based on your observations and conclusions.*

Answers will vary.

_____

_____

_____

_____

19. **Creative Thinking**   *Think about your personal behavior and make a list of habits that you have (things you do in the same way over and over without thinking about them). Using two colors of highlighters, mark the habits that you believe are positive with one color and the habits you believe are negative with another color. Identify what you believe led to the development of the good habits and the bad habits. Make notes on differences between developing good and bad habits.*

Answers will vary.

_____

_____

_____

_____

20. **Problem Solving**   *Spend time evaluating your environment at home and at school. Identify those things that you believe contribute to your academic success and those things that detract from it. Using a sketch pad and colored pens or pencils, create an illustration of your ideas for a personal success environment. Label the parts of the environment that will contribute to your success.*

Answers will vary.

_____

_____

_____

_____

21. **Research**   *Politicians and business leaders often step forward to "accept responsibility" for events or problems. Use news reports from the Internet, newspapers, or magazines to identify one example of a public figure who "accepted responsibility" and worked to solve the problem. Describe the problem and the actions taken to resolve it.*

Answers will vary.

_____

_____

_____

_____

LEARNING TO LEAD

FOCUS

Participate in individual competitive events.

DESCRIPTION

Personal growth and improvement is an important challenge for everyone. One of the ways to demonstrate your capabilities is to participate in competition. Competition is exciting, motivating, and challenging. As a student, you have many opportunities to participate in competition. Whether your interests and abilities are in athletics, music, art, debate, chess, or another area, there are school and community teams, clubs, and organizations that offer local, regional, state, and national competitions.

Identify opportunities for participating in individual competitions offered by your student organization. Each organization offers competitions related to your interests and talents, including research and writing, speeches, demonstrations, role playing, or tests of your business knowledge. You can usually compete at the local and regional levels and, if successful, continue on to compete for state and national recognition.

ACTIVITIES

1. Go to the web site of your national student organization and locate the section that describes the competitive events. Review the information to identify the types of events and activities open to individuals.

2. Make a list of three individual events that match your interests and for which you would be eligible this year or next year. For each event, obtain descriptions of the event, the requirements for participation, and the criteria and procedures used to evaluate participants.

3. Meet with a member of your local student organization who has successfully participated in individual competition in the past. Ask that member why he or she decided to participate, the events in which he or she competed, the challenges and benefits of competition, and advice on how to prepare for an event.

SHARE YOUR RESULTS

1. Working with your adviser, select one individual competitive event. Obtain and study all of the available information on what you need to do to prepare for competition, including the dates and locations of the competitions and procedures for submitting an application.
2. If possible, identify students in your organization who are interested in the same competition to become practice partners with you.
3. Prepare a written plan and a schedule to follow to prepare and practice for the competition.
4. Identify a business mentor who will review your work and give you feedback as you prepare. Make a personal commitment to the competition, and follow your plan in order to be as well prepared as possible.

Jevone had always dis-
played confidence, but
when he wasn't chosen for
the jazz orchestra, he reacted with anger and
threatened to give up
playing the trumpet. Ask
students to think about
Jevone's behavior. Do they
think that Jevone has been
trying to be two different
people—acting one way
when he experienced suc-
cess yet acting another
way in other circumstances
when he didn't achieve
what he expected? Which
character do they think is
the "real" Jevone? Why?

ACCEPTING THE CHALLENGE

CASE STUDY 9—THE REAL YOU

As you learned in the opening scenario, What Would You Do?, Jevone was quite disappointed and distressed that he did not make the jazz orchestra. His fear of embarrassment was about to cause him to walk away from something he loved—playing the trumpet. Jevone's trumpet playing skills were well known among his friends. He had always displayed confidence in his ability to achieve whatever he set out to do. However, when Jevone's audition did not result in success, a different side of his character surfaced. He became angry and threatened to give up his dream. Perhaps the self-confidence that Jevone had displayed was only an act. By trying to imitate his highly successful role model, Wynton Marsalis, Jevone ignored the fact that success is not always possible. He was aware of Mr. Marsalis's many achievements. But he did not consider the many obstacles Mr. Marsalis faced along the way. Had he been able to personally talk with Wynton Marsalis, he might have found out that he, too, had been rejected in some of his attempts to pursue his goal of musical prominence. Jevone's drive and desire were built on the outward traits that he saw in his famous role model. His current actions were based on what he thought he should be instead of what he really wanted to be. He did not take into consideration the impact of his actions on his own goals and hopes for the future.

THINK CRITICALLY

1. *What personal characteristics do you believe Jevone failed to develop along the way as he was developing his talent for playing the trumpet?*

Jevone failed to develop self-control and self-discipline in the face of disappointment.

He became angry and was ready to give up his long-term goal of becoming a famous

trumpet player like Wynton Marsalis because he did not achieve his immediate goal of

making the jazz orchestra even after he had spent many years in preparation.

2. *What does Jevone's reaction to not being selected for the jazz orchestra say about his character?*

Jevone was disappointed and embarrassed, and he reacted with anger and frustration.

His reaction shows a level of immaturity and lack of self-control that might be

expected when a person does not achieve an important goal.

3. *What lessons can you learn from Jevone about being "caught up" in imitating the behaviors—whether positive or negative—of your chosen role model?*

Answers will vary. Jevone was so focused on becoming like his role model, Wynton

Marsalis, that he lost sight of the "big picture." He failed to realize that Mr. Marsalis

most likely had also faced disappointments before reaching his goal. He had to decide

if the goal was important enough that he could accept the current disappointment

and find other ways to work toward the goal during the next year.

APPLY *WHAT YOU HAVE LEARNED–Be Honest with Yourself and Others*

DIRECTIONS: *Some people "put on an act" when around certain people. They try to impress others by exhibiting different character traits. Assess the personal characteristics of someone you know personally, such as a parent, sibling, other family member, teacher, coach, or friend, by completing the following activity on the lines below or on your Student Activity CD.*

1. Write at least four (4) personal character traits that this person exhibits around you.

_____   _____

_____   _____

2. Write at least four (4) different *personal character traits that this person exhibits* around others.

_____   _____

_____   _____

3. Explain the difference between the two sets of character traits.

_____

_____

_____

Now, assess your personal characteristics.

1. Write at least four (4) personal character traits that you exhibit around your family or close friends.

_____   _____

_____   _____

2. Write at least four (4) different *personal character traits that you exhibit around* other people you know, such as teachers, coaches, or peers.

_____   _____

_____   _____

3. Explain the difference between the two sets of character traits.

_____

_____

_____

Examine your two different sets of personal character traits. Think about why you act differently around certain people. Ultimately, you need to be honest with yourself and others. Pretending to be something you are not can lead to problems. To improve the way you relate to others, create a SMART goal (including a completion date) to help you resolve conflicts in your character. Enter the goal in a monthly calendar (on the CD or your own). Then enter your thoughts, ideas, and discussions related to your goal in a journal (on the CD or your own) to help you plan and track your progress. Choose a goal-setting partner to help you identify positive and negative changes in your behavior when interacting with others.

_____

_____

ACCEPTING THE CHALLENGE
Apply What You Have Learned—Be Honest with Yourself and Others
Note that students can complete this part of the *Accepting the Challenge* activity in the book or on the Student Activity CD. Instructions are provided on the CD.

After students have answered the questions in this activity, instruct them to write a SMART goal (including a completion date) that will help them resolve conflicts in their character. Have them enter their goal on a monthly calendar. Students can use the monthly calendar on the Student Activity CD or their own calendar. Explain to students that they may also use weekly calendar pages (on the Student Activity CD or their own calendar) to plan activities and tasks that will help them achieve their goals. Finally, direct students to use a journal (on the Student Activity CD or their own) to track and evaluate their progress in achieving their goal.

A goal-setting partner can add an element of accountability and can offer positive feedback to help students stay on track to achieve their goals.

Students should be given the opportunity to reflect on the progress they have made toward achieving their goal. To do this, students can complete the *Evaluate Your Progress* activity on the Student Activity CD. Stress to students that it is important to complete this activity on the original target completion date even if they have not met their goal at that time.

Relationships with Others Build Character

© Doug Menuez/PhotoDisc/Getty Images

10.1   *Relationships and Character*

10.2   *Respect and Fairness*

10.3   *Trust, Loyalty, and Caring*

10.4   *Organizational and Community Citizenship*

What would **YOU** do?

CAN ASHLEY MAKE A DIFFERENCE?

The sophomore year for Ashley and her friends just did not seem to be starting out the same way as last year. Ashley had been excited when she started her freshman year at Central High School. Central High enrolled a very diverse group of students. That pleased Ashley since her friends were also quite diverse racially, economically, and even in terms of their interests in music, sports, and academics.

Ashley and her friends had a great freshman year, added new friends to their group, and were active in many school activities. They all ended the year with good academic records and were looking forward to coming back for their second year.

It was evident even before the school year started that things might be different this year. The difficult economic times and the worldwide fears of terrorism seemed to have affected the way people in the community were treating each other. While there had been no violence, there had been some verbal conflicts among groups. People seemed to be dividing along ethnic and religious lines with questions being raised about patriotism, citizenship, and even the possible relationship of some people in the community to international terrorist groups.

Those same negative attitudes and fears in the community were now spreading into the school. Some students were directly questioning whether all of the Hispanic students were legal citizens and should be able to enroll in the school. Several students who wore traditional Muslim clothing were frequently ridiculed by other students. Some students from Arabic cultures expressed fear in walking to and from school. School administrators, teachers, and student leaders were working hard to reduce the tensions, but the school was still part of the community. It was difficult to keep problems in the community from coming into the school.

Ashley and her friends wanted to find ways to help others in the school recognize that, although people had differences, they all were at the school for the same basic purpose. But they were only sophomores and represented only a small number of students in a large school. Could they really make a difference?

THINK *CRITICALLY*

1. Can a school climate really be different from the feelings and beliefs of the community around the school?

2. What do you think Ashley and her friends might be able to do to help improve the school climate? What happens if they decide that they cannot do anything?

TEACHING RESOURCES
Instructor's Resource CD
Lesson Plans, Ch. 10
PowerPoint Slides, Ch. 10

Student Activity CD, Ch. 10

thomsonedu.com/school/leading
Crossword Puzzle, Ch. 10
Flash Cards, Ch. 10

Exam*View*® CD, Ch. 10

CHAPTER OVERVIEW
Chapter 10 discusses the characteristics of respect, fairness, trust, loyalty, caring, and citizenship in relationships with others.

Lesson 10.1
Describes the variety of relationships and the characteristics of effective and ineffective relationships.

Lesson 10.2
Explains the effect of respect for people and property and describes the principle of fairness.

Lesson 10.3
Discusses the importance of trust, loyalty, and caring for others.

Lesson 10.4
Explains the meaning of organizational and community citizenship and describes citizenship responsibilities.

WHAT WOULD YOU DO?
Ask students to think about the "climate" in their school. Do the diverse groups in the school treat each other with respect or with a lack or understanding?

Think Critically Answers
1. Answers will vary. The school can have a positive influence on the community by promoting a climate that embraces diversity.
2. Answers will vary.

Relationships and Character

THE VARIETY OF RELATIONSHIPS

Your life is made up of relationships. From the time you are born, you are affected by the people around you. You also have an effect on others. If you have been around newborn babies, you are aware of the amount of attention they command. Some of that attention is required to care for the infant's basic needs. But a great deal is directed at interacting with the baby—cooing, smiling, talking, and watching the baby's reactions and responses. Over a period of just a few weeks, babies begin to recognize the people who spend the most time with them, and the first important relationships begin to form. Those first relationships are followed by others—family members, playmates, school, clubs, and long-term friendships. In many ways, those early relationships in your life will help to shape your confidence, the ways you interact with others, and what you become.

Defining Relationships

Relationships are the ways you interact and deal with others. Throughout your lifetime, you participate in many different types of relationships. Some are brief, but others last your entire lifetime. Relationships can be very personal or can be maintained on a professional level. No matter the type of relationship, your character becomes a key part of how you interact with others.

Technology has changed the nature of some relationships. **Virtual relationships** are purposeful, continuing interactions and communications between two or more people that are carried on primarily via computer networks. You have grown up with computers and the Internet, so you and your friends are comfortable with virtual communications. But some adults may have a difficult time understanding how e-mail,

© Monica Lau/Photodisc/Getty Images

instant messaging, blogs, and web pages can be used as the main means of maintaining relationships. Technology makes it easier in many ways to communicate with others, but it also presents challenges to developing and maintaining meaningful relationships.

Your relationships can be informal or formal and can last for a long time or can be quite short. **Informal relationships** occur voluntarily based on the interests people have in each other. Long-term informal relationships exist among families and close friends. Interactions with people at parties, social gatherings, or unplanned meetings are examples of short-term informal relationships. **Formal relationships** occur when people are brought together to complete an activity or achieve a goal. Long-term formal relationships develop through people's jobs and group memberships. School projects, short work assignments, and committee work in organizations are examples of short-term formal relationships.

Common Types of Relationships

Throughout your life, you will experience many different types of relationships that will help you develop effective interpersonal skills. Some of the more common types include those with your family and friends. Other relationships will develop in groups and organizations you may join in school and at work. At some time, you may also experience close, intimate relationships.

Families

Parents and their children make up the traditional family, but many people live in non-traditional families. They may live with only one parent or with grandparents, guardians, or foster parents. Some people have no brothers and sisters while others have many siblings. Extended families are common in some cultures where grandparents, aunts and uncles, and even cousins may live together or near each other.

Families are where you experience your first relationships and develop the skills needed to get along with others. You see how adults interact with each other, how decisions are made, and how conflicts are resolved. In families, you learn how to deal with both good times and bad. You develop informal communication skills, understand love and support, and know you have people you can count on if you need help. Your family is probably the most personal, important, and constant relationship in your life.

© Geostock/Photodisc/Getty Images

Friendships

The first relationships beyond your family are friendships. You continue to develop friendships throughout your life. *Friends* are people with whom you have a connection on a continuing basis because of your positive feelings, common interests, and trust. You have different levels of friendships—from the many people you know

TEACH
Have students read the quote in the margin. Ask students if they have people in their life who seem to be around when times are good but disappear when things go wrong. How do they feel about those relationships?

Ask students how they think the different types of relationships in their life help them develop effective interpersonal skills.

Ask students to think of the individuals they know, including themselves, who may live in non-traditional families. Do they think those families interact any differently from more traditional families? Have them explain their answers.

casually and see from time to time to those few people who are considered your best friends.

Some friendships do not last a long time. Opportunities to get together may decrease, or interests may change. Sometimes friendships fail as you learn more about other people and see them in a different light. A few friendships will be close and long-lasting because of strong personal feelings, shared experiences and values, and trust and support.

Groups and Organizations

Relationships are formed from participation with others in groups and organizations. Your family may have a religious affiliation, be active in neighborhood groups, or participate in the activities of a community center that offers social, cultural, or recreational opportunities. You may join a number of clubs or groups related to hobbies, interests, sports, or civic or religious activities and continue with those in which you have special interests or skills.

© Kent Knudson/Photolink/Photodisc/Getty Images

Outside of family activities, clubs and organizations are often the first activities you become involved in where participation is guided by rules and procedures. You learn to follow the rules and learn the penalties that are imposed when rules are violated. You learn that relationships in those types of organizations may be quite different from what you have experienced before due to their organizational structure, membership requirements, and activities. Personal friendships often develop from your participation in groups and organizations.

School

Some of the most complex and difficult relationships you will experience will be at school. You often attend school with many of your friends. But some of your friendships may not last because you have different schedules and classes, participate in various activities, meet new people, and change your interests. It may be difficult to see long-time friends become friendly with others you do not know. You may be hurt when your friends criticize you for not spending as much time with them as you used to or when they accuse you of "thinking you are too good for them."

As you meet other students in classes and through group activities, you face decisions about new relationships and friendships. You will certainly meet people whom you do not like very well. You will struggle to maintain positive relationships whenever you have to interact with them. Interactions and relationships will change as you attend classes and after-school activities and participate in the various meetings, activities, and informal gatherings that occur throughout the school year. Classes will have different requirements and rules.

Work with team members to identify three different types of relationships—one based on family or friendships, one related to your school activities, and one connected to work and careers. As a team, choose a creative way to illustrate the importance of each type of relationship and how it differs from the others. For example, you could write a short story, poem, song, or rap lyrics, or you could create a drawing, poster, or collage. Present your creation to the class.

THINK *CRITICALLY*

What are the differences and similarities among the three types of relationships? Is one of the relationships more important than the others? Did you express this in your presentation? What did you learn about relationships by working on this activity?

Teachers will have different expectations and personalities. Interactions with other students will also be affected by how well you know each other, the setting, and the purpose for getting together.

Work and Career

Moving into the work world presents a new set of relationships. Employer–employee, business person–customer, coworkers, and work teams are all examples of the relationships related to work and careers. Work relationships are defined by job descriptions, work rules, and the expectations of managers and customers.

As a beginning worker, you may feel nervous and insecure. You can be influenced in either positive or negative ways by the actions of your coworkers and managers. You can affect the satisfaction of customers and their loyalty to the business by how you treat them. The types of relationships you have with others at your job will have an important effect on your enjoyment of work, the amount of stress you feel, and much of the satisfaction and success you experience in your work life.

Intimate Relationships

As close friends spend time together and get to know each other, they may develop deeper feelings. When two people have special affection and commitment for each other based on understanding, caring, and trust, they have an **intimate relationship**. Television, movies, and music may lead you to believe that intimate relationships are based on physical attraction. A physical attraction by itself does not result in a relationship that will be long-lasting and positive. In intimate relationships, each person respects and cares for the other person, provides support for the other person's goals and activities, and works to maintain and strengthen the relationship.

It is not easy to recognize an intimate relationship. At first, an attraction to another person may seem like a close, intimate relationship. But generally those types of relationships occur suddenly with people you do not know well. They are often based on a first impression of the

A TEAM EFFORT
This activity provides students with a creative way to look at different types of relationships. In addition to the examples listed, students could create a skit or series of short vignettes to perform for the class.

Think Critically Answers
Answers will vary. Relationships are different and often complex.

TEACH
Ask students how they think relationships with others in the workplace can contribute to or detract from their job satisfaction and career advancement.

Ask students what they think might be the dangers of basing an intimate relationship on a first impression of the other person. What do they think intimate relationships should be based on? Have several students explain their answers.

ONGOING ASSESSMENT
Use the Checkpoint as an opportunity to conduct on-going assessment of student comprehension of the lesson material.

TEACH
Ask students to think of the "typical" student in their school. Does that student make positive contributions to the school, create problems and spread negativity, or just "coast" somewhere between the two? How do they think they can help get more students to engage in positive relationships with others?

TEACHING STRATEGIES
Limited English Proficiency Students
Students from other cultures often feel left out of activities or isolated from the majority culture. Ask students how they think they can build more effective relationships with others in their school. Do they see differences in the responsibilities of those students in the majority and the minority cultures? What would they like to see done to make all students feel more accepted?

other person as being interesting, attractive, or fun. With an attraction, people are more concerned about immediate happiness and personal satisfaction and less about long-term commitment, trust, and the individual goals and plans of each person. People in an intimate relationship are committed to the long-term success of the relationship more than short-term pleasure.

CHECKPOINT

Why is school a place where you will experience some of the most complex and difficult relationships?

Friendships may not last due to different classes and schedules, participation in

different activities, friendships with new people, and changing interests.

CHARACTERISTICS OF EFFECTIVE RELATIONSHIPS

Think of two different types of students in your school. The first type is not the most popular student, the top athlete, the student with the best grades, or the student council president. However, this person is well known to other students, is a friend to many, and is recognized for a positive attitude and sense of humor. This type of student is willing to become involved, is active in the events of the school, and helps out when needed. He or she seldom makes judgments about others, does not tease students who do not seem to fit in, and is one of the first to make positive comments, offer thanks, and provide encouragement to others. This student is well liked and well respected and helps to make the school a better place.

Now think of another type of student in your school. This student is not as well known, but those who know the student are more likely to be aware of problems rather than contributions. This student has a small group of friends, but most of those friendships do not last long. It is difficult to identify ways that this student has contributed positively to the school. This type of student is more often negative than positive, tears other students down rather than building them up, and is not actively involved in school activities. You avoid activities and events where you know you will have to deal with this student. If this type of student is involved, you expect the experience to be negative or to result in problems rather than being enjoyable.

Do you see yourself, your friends, and even the "typical" student in your school as more like the first example or the second one? There are few students in any school who fit either of these two examples. Most students are somewhere in the middle. Remember that relationships are the way you deal and interact with others. What are the actions of people who make positive contributions to the success of families, clubs, school, work, or personal relationships?

Your actions affect others in positive and negative ways. Answer the questions in Figure 10.1 to determine whether or not your attitudes and actions contribute to effective relationships.

FIGURE 10.1 **Actions Affect Your Relationships**

For each of the following choices, when it comes to your actions, are you more likely to:

___ 1a. Accept and respect differences in backgrounds, cultures, and beliefs, or

___ 1b. Base your comments about others and your actions toward them on biases and stereotypes?

___ 2a. Expect the best from others and offer them encouragement, or

___ 2b. Make negative comments about people when they do not perform well?

___ 3a. Give everyone a chance and treat each person fairly, or

___ 3b. Play favorites and bend the rules for your friends when you can?

___ 4a. Be open-minded and think carefully before making judgments, or

___ 4b. Condemn or ridicule ideas and beliefs you disagree with?

___ 5a. Show respect for authority and help leaders and people in authority do their jobs, or

___ 5b. Set your own agenda, be uncooperative, and disrupt activities you do not enjoy or where you are not in charge?

___ 6a. Show respect for and take good care of the things you own and the property of others, or

___ 6b. Take things that do not belong to you, misuse and abuse your own things or those of others, and fail to pick up or clean up after yourself?

___ 7a. Remember policies, rules, and procedures and try to follow them, even if they may create problems for you from time to time, or

___ 7b. Feel that rules and procedures do not apply to you, especially if they are inconvenient or you get attention by not doing what is asked or expected?

___ 8a. Show interest in and concern for others and offer them help when needed even if they are not your close friends, or

___ 8b. Act self-centered, have a small group of close friends, and let others know you have little concern about them or things that are important to them?

___ 9a. Look out for the interests of family, friends, team members, and people in your organization, or

___ 9b. If it comes down to your interests or those of others, always choose your own and let others take care of themselves?

___ 10a. Keep the commitments you make and avoid getting in situations where a decision you make or actions you take will cause problems for others, or

___ 10b. Be unreliable, do what is convenient or benefits you even if you know it will likely inconvenience or harm others?

___ 11a. Help others to improve and succeed and give them credit for accomplishments, or

___ 11b. Be extra-competitive, try to prevent others from doing well, and grab the limelight whenever possible?

___ 12a. Find opportunities to volunteer, help out, do more than your fair share, and make things easier for others, or

___ 12b. Do only what is necessary to get by and only what benefits you and avoid situations where you might have to do extra work?

___ 13a. Avoid "gossiping" about others and protect information shared with you in confidence, or

___ 13b. Spread rumors if it hurts those you do not like and try to gather information that can be used against others to your advantage?

___ 14a. Be an effective member of the groups and organizations you participate in and set a good example for others, or

___ 14b. Use the organization to your benefit, give up when you do not get your way, and look for ways to cause problems for those you do not like?

___ 15a. Value the history and future of the groups and organizations in which you participate and work to make them better and stronger, or

___ 15b. Selfishly take everything you can from a group and work it to your benefit with no regard for its values or for the needs of future group members?

TEACH

Have students complete the questionnaire in Figure 10.1 to understand how their actions affect their relationships with others.

After students have completed the questionnaire in Figure 10.1 and have scored their answers, ask them if they are surprised by the results. For every *b* answer, have students write at least one positive action they can take to improve their behavior in that area.

TEACHING STRATEGIES
Kinesthetic Learners

Have students give a copy of the questionnaire in Figure 10.1 to a member of their family or to a close friend and ask that person to answer each question as it relates to the students. Have them compare their responses to the responses of their family member or friend. How do they compare? Do they view themselves differently from the way others view them?

TEACHING STRATEGIES
Kinesthetic Learners

Have students create a poster, computer-generated presentation, or flyer entitled "Your Actions Affect Your Relationships." Students should present examples of positive behaviors and encourage positive relationships among all students.

ONGOING ASSESSMENT

Use the Checkpoint as an opportunity to conduct ongoing assessment of student comprehension of the lesson material.

If you have more *a*'s than *b*'s that describe your typical actions, you value interpersonal relationships and try to contribute to the success of the groups and organizations to which you belong. If the *b*'s outnumber the *a*'s, you may want to consider why your own needs and interests outweigh those of others to the point that you are willing to cause harm to the groups and organizations to which you belong if it benefits you.

Relationships are effective when each person's needs are met. That occurs when people who are working together realize that their individual needs are no more or less important than the needs of others. They understand that if there are conflicts among the members of a group, the group will suffer if the conflicts cannot be resolved. They understand that the success of each member leads to the success of the group and that a strong team contributes to the success of each member.

© Adam Crowley/Photodisc/Getty Images

CHECKPOINT

What can you do as a group member to ensure that both your needs and the group's needs are met?

As a group member, you can realize that your needs are no more or less important than the needs of others in the group. The group will suffer if conflicts cannot be resolved.

Follow UP

UNDERSTAND LEADERSHIP CONCEPTS

Circle the best answer for each of the following questions.

1. **When people are brought together to complete an activity or achieve a goal, they are involved in a(n) _____ relationship.**
   a. virtual
   b. formal
   c. informal
   d. intimate

2. **Effective relationships occur when each person's _____ are met.**
   a. responsibilities
   b. commitments
   c. needs
   d. all of the above

THINK *CRITICALLY*

Answer the following questions as completely as possible. If necessary, use a separate sheet of paper.

3. **Do you believe that people who are effective in one type of relationship, such as a family or club, are more likely to be effective in other relationships? Why or why not?**
   Answers will vary. People who are effective in one type of relationship are more likely to be effective in other relationships because they realize the importance of meeting the other person's needs as well as their own, and they understand that the success of each person in the relationship contributes to the success of everyone else involved.

4. **What are the differences between an instant attraction and an intimate relationship? What actions and behaviors might suggest an attraction rather than a strong, lasting relationship?**
   Instant attractions occur suddenly and are based on first impressions. They are more concerned with immediate satisfaction and are less about long-term commitment, trust, and each person's goals and plans. Intimate relationships are based on understanding, caring, respect, trust, and mutual support for the other person's goals and plans.

5. **When a new group is formed with people who do not know each other well, what can be done to develop effective relationships among the group members?**
   Answers will vary but may include sharing each other's stories and backgrounds, working together on assignments, projects, or committees, and developing friendships with those who may have similar interests.

ASSESS
Reteach
Have students list the six most common types of relationships. For each type, have students write one or two sentences describing the key points discussed in the text.

Enrich
Have students create a poster that represents the various relationships in which they are involved. They might include a picture of themselves in the center and then surround themselves with photos of their family and friends, groups in which they participate, and items that represent their workplace (if employed).

Close
Ask students whether they think virtual communications help to improve relationships among individuals or if they tend to isolate people from others.

Respect and Fairness

SHOWING RESPECT FOR OTHERS AND PROPERTY

Boyd, Mike, and Mario walked into their third-period class and headed for the back row of desks. They knew their teacher, Mr. Hildahl, did not like them sitting together since they usually disrupted the class, but they always liked to test him. A guest speaker was scheduled for today's class, so they thought he might be too busy to notice. But just before class started, he walked back to the three friends. "Since you do not have time to change seats, I will let the three of you sit together if you promise to show respect for our guest." Each of them smiled and nodded, but they had no intention of sitting and listening.

They waited about fifteen minutes and then started making comments to each other under their breath that gradually got louder. Mr. Hildahl's disapproving looks did not deter them. Soon their comments were loud enough that the guest speaker was clearly uncomfortable and other students were glaring at them. They knew that Mr. Hildahl would stop the class and that they would probably have to serve detention. But it was worth it. Once again, they were in control.

Having **respect** means showing consideration and regard for people and property. You are respectful when you are courteous and pleasant in your dealings with others. You show respect when you do

Jack Star/PhotoLink/Photodisc/Getty Images

not intentionally insult, degrade, or ridicule people, their appearance, actions, or beliefs. You are also respectful in the way you treat things of value—your property, the property of others, and all of the things that surround you and that are part of your daily life. Being respectful does not mean that you always agree with people or that you allow them to mistreat or disrespect you. But your positive actions show your willingness to accept others and cooperate with them rather than create conflict and problems. Respect for property does not mean that you do not use those resources. It does mean that you do not damage or misuse them for a selfish purpose.

Respecting Others

Boyd, Mike, and Mario did not demonstrate respect in their third-period class. They showed no respect for Mr. Hildahl as their teacher. Each day, he has the responsibility to plan for and guide several classes. He took extra effort to obtain a guest speaker for the day. He hoped all of the students would treat the guest with respect for volunteering his time to meet with the class and provide his professional knowledge. Their actions disrespected the guest and probably made him question why he took the time to prepare for and deliver his presentation to the class.

The three boys also did not respect the other students who were interested in the class and the speaker and who want guests to have a good impression of the school. They even failed to respect themselves. They were willing to act childishly and face the penalty of detention just for the personal enjoyment of disrupting the class and gaining negative attention. While they may have thought the few giggles from other students was a sign of approval, they would soon see that most other students view them in a negative way, try to avoid them, and do not want them involved in any important activities where their inappropriate actions could disrupt and cause problems.

COMMUNICATE
Ask students why maintaining an open line of communication with parents is a sign of respect. Ask them how they can improve communication with parents.

Think Critically Answers
Answers will vary but may include regular, positive conversations, talking about school activities and letting parents know where you are going when you leave home.

▌Respecting Property

Respect also applies to the way you treat property, including your own property and the property of others. How do you feel when you find that a brother, sister, or friend has taken or used something of yours? Even if the person returns it to you, typically you are upset that he or she did not ask to borrow the item. If it becomes damaged or lost, you are clearly upset. You expect people to respect what belongs to you.

Do you also show respect for your things, or do you believe that since they belong to you, you can treat them any way you choose? Some people fail to take care of their property. They do not use it carefully, they misplace it, or they just get tired of it and want to replace it even if it is still useful. The lack of respect for personal property may result because a person has enough money or has family members with enough resources to replace it. Perhaps the person has not yet developed personal responsibility.

© Jack Star/PhotoLink/Photodisc/Getty Images

Respect for property includes a belief in the value, worth, and usefulness of something. As long as property has a purpose and can still be used, it should not be discarded or destroyed. It is usually possible to find other uses or other people who can use almost all property. Considering the value or usefulness of property is an important part of demonstrating respect for property.

You probably are aware of others who intentionally damaged public property, school equipment, or the belongings of others. It may have been minor damage, or it may have taken the form of major vandalism. Are you bothered by the major vandalism but not the minor damage? Does it matter to you if someone else's neighborhood or school is damaged as long as it is not yours? Do you feel that it is okay to draw graffiti on public buildings or business vehicles since taxpayer money or company profits can easily pay the cost of restoring the property? Respect must apply equally in all situations. You should not justify property damage based on the way it is damaged, who owns the property, and whether they have the resources to repair the damage.

▌Demonstrating Respect

Respect is an important part of effective interpersonal relations. Respect must be a characteristic of every family member and each person that is part of a club, an athletic team, a work group, or school. When there is a lack of respect or when there is disrespect toward others who are part of a group, the group will not be able to work well together. The lack of respect will affect trust, communication, and commitment to each other. It will result in leaders questioning whether they can count on group members to follow them, work well together, and accomplish goals without personal conflicts.

Consider your personal beliefs and actions that relate to respect in your family, school, and the groups, clubs, and activities in which you are involved. Also consider the ways you show respect for your close friends and others you interact with on a regular basis. Especially consider your feelings and actions toward those you do not know well or those with different beliefs and values. Finally, think about the way you respect property—your own property, the property of family members and friends, the materials and equipment in your school, and all of the resources that are part of your life. How do you show that you respect and value the people and things that are a part of your life? Have you done or said things that could be interpreted as a lack of respect? What are your feelings when you think that others have disrespected you or something of value to you? How have you responded when you see others, especially friends or members of groups to which you belong, clearly disrespecting other people or property? Showing respect is an important first step in demonstrating your character and showing people that you want to contribute to the success of the groups and organizations to which you belong.

CHECKPOINT

What does it mean to have respect for property?

Respect for property means showing consideration and regard for your own property and the property of others. It includes a belief in the value, worth, and usefulness of items.

TREATING OTHERS FAIRLY

"Play fair," you said to your playmates when you felt they were taking advantage of you in a game. "That is not fair," you said to your parents when you felt a brother or sister was getting special treatment. "It was a fair test," you said to yourself when the questions on an exam reflected what you had learned and what you had prepared for. **Fairness** is the act of being free from favoritism, self-interest, or bias. A **bias** is a preference that influences your judgment. In general, you want to be treated fairly, and you try to treat others fairly. People who are viewed as being fair are respected and trusted. When you believe people are willing to cheat, bend the rules, or play favorites, you will be cautious about working with them, believing what they say, or trusting what they do.

Fairness is a character trait that is important to long-term relationships. People will not want

© Digital Vision/Getty Images

LEADERSHIP TIP
Ask students why they think it is important for a leader to be open to the views of everyone in the group. How do they think that a willingness to listen and understand opposing viewpoints shows respect for others?

ONGOING ASSESSMENT
Use the Checkpoint as an opportunity to conduct ongoing assessment of student comprehension of the lesson material.

TEACH
Ask students to think about the character trait of fairness. How do they decide what is or is not fair? How do they feel when people treat them unfairly?

to be part of a group if they believe that they do not have an equal opportunity or that the rules will not be applied in the same way to everyone. It is difficult to be a member of a team, work group, or class with people whom you do not trust and who you believe will take advantage of you or others if it is in their self-interest.

Fairness by Individuals

Each of us has control over the way we treat others. Fair treatment of others involves three types of behaviors. First, you must be as objective as possible when interacting with other people. Being **objective** means that you can look at the facts without letting your personal feelings influence your views. You may feel strongly about your beliefs and the positions you take in disagreements. But to be fair, you need to be both open-minded and objective. Your beliefs are not always shared by others. The person who disagrees with you may have a good point. You will never know unless you are willing to listen, discuss all sides of an argument or disagreement, and consider the facts and information carefully. When you can interact with others without any biases, you will be viewed as fair.

© Jules Frazier/Photodisc/Getty Images

The second way to act fairly is to avoid favoritism. **Favoritism** means giving some people special treatment due to bias or a close relationship. When people are willing to "bend the rules" for people they know or try to make it more difficult for those they dislike, those actions will be viewed as unfair. Each qualified person should be given the same opportunity or consideration when people are being selected for a position, activity, or recognition. Some people may look for reasons to disqualify those they do not like. People may also try to find reasons why those they favor are more qualified. If the people making those decisions are trying to justify their decision rather than make an unbiased decision, they are not acting fairly.

Finally, acting fairly means not taking advantage of others. You certainly would not think it was fair if the top player on the varsity basketball team competed against a beginning junior high player. Would you believe it was fair if one team in an academic competition knew about the topics for the questions while the other teams had to prepare without that information? While winning is a good feeling, winning because you have an unfair advantage over the other person will always make you wonder if you would have won if everything was equal. If others learn about your unfair advantage, how do you think they will feel about your victory and about you?

Fairness by Organizations

Organizations and their leaders also have a responsibility to be fair. The policies, rules, and procedures of an organization can give some people an advantage while unfairly harming others. Any organization should look carefully at how its group members are treated. You should ask the following questions to determine if an organization is operating fairly or unfairly:

- How are people chosen to be part of the organization?
- How are leaders selected or promotions given?
- Are there special assignments or preferred activities? If so, how are people assigned to those activities?
- How are people chosen to receive awards and recognitions?
- Are there informal or formal activities or communications that involve some people more often than others?
- Are rules clear and understandable? Are they applied the same way each time and to everyone?
- Does everyone have a chance to have their ideas and concerns heard?
- Are penalties and punishments appropriate for the offense? Are they applied in an unbiased way?

Fairness does not mean that everyone in an organization or group has to be treated the same way. It means that everyone has a fair opportunity and that no one has an intentional or unintentional advantage or disadvantage that they do not deserve.

CHECKPOINT

What are three types of behaviors that show a person is being fair in his or her relationships with others?

Three types of behaviors that show a person is being fair in relationships with others include being objective, avoiding favoritism, and not taking advantage of others.

© Ryan McVay/Photodisc/Getty Images

Follow **UP**

UNDERSTAND LEADERSHIP CONCEPTS

Circle the best answer for each of the following questions.

1. **Giving some people consideration or special treatment due to bias or a close relationship is**
   a. fairness
   b. respect
   c. favoritism
   d. objectivity

2. **Which of the following statements about fairness in organizations and groups is not true?**
   a. Everyone has to be treated the same way.
   b. Everyone deserves to have a fair opportunity.
   c. No one should have an intentional or unintentional advantage or disadvantage that they do not deserve.
   d. All are true.

THINK *CRITICALLY*

Answer the following questions as completely as possible. If necessary, use a separate sheet of paper.

3. **How do activities like recycling and protecting the environment relate to the characteristic of respect?**
   Answers will vary. Recycling and protecting the environment show respect for the earth and its limited resources. They also show respect for others—especially future generations.

4. **What would you do if you are part of an organization that has rules and procedures that are not fair to some people but that do not affect you?**
   Answers will vary. Because everything the organization does reflects on the values and character of its members, its unfair rules and procedures do affect you. You should work hard to change them by working with others who agree with you. You may need to withdraw from the organization if it is in conflict with your values.

5. **What are some specific examples of how respect and fairness can be demonstrated among members of a family?**
   Answers will vary but may include asking permission before using the property of other family members, letting your parents know where you are and who you are with when you are not at home, and offering to help with your fair share of the responsibilities at home.

ASSESS
Reteach
Have students review each of the goals for the lesson and then write several sentences describing the key points for each goal.

Enrich
Have students conduct research in their community to learn about groups or organizations that are in need of donations of good used items. Also have them research the recycling programs in their community. Have them design a plan for ways to communicate the information in the school and community.

Close
Ask students to think about their personal beliefs as well as their actions relating to respecting others at home, at school, and in groups or organizations to which they belong. Do their actions consistently represent their beliefs?

Trust, Loyalty, and Caring

- Describe how trust strengthens relationships.
- Explain the importance of loyalty.
- Recognize how caring for others affects your actions.

- trust
- loyalty
- disloyal
- caring

WHO DO YOU TRUST?

Gloria really liked Thomas. Ever since they had been in the same freshman English class, their friendship had grown. Gloria liked his smile when they ran into each other at school and his funny sense of humor when they had a chance to talk. He always had encouraging words for her when things were not going well. But as they got closer, one thing about Thomas was beginning to bother Gloria. He seemed to be concerned about whom Gloria was friends with and what she was doing. She knew that he had asked her girlfriends if she was talking to other boys. He called her home most nights saying that he liked to talk to her. But he seemed to be checking up on her to see what she was doing and if anyone was visiting her. He seemed to be jealous of any time she was spending with her other friends. Gloria was concerned that Thomas did not trust her, and it was affecting her feelings. While Thomas was special to her, she had many friends. She did not feel she had to justify her other friendships to him.

Whether the relationship is a special friendship like Gloria and Thomas, teammates on an athletic team, employees working together on a project, or members of a family, trust is essential for a positive relationship. **Trust** means having complete confidence in another person. You believe the other person is honest and reliable

© PhotoLink/Photodisc/Getty Images

SCHEDULE
Block 45 minutes
Regular 1 class period

FOCUS
Ask students to think about trust and loyalty among their family members and friends. Do they think it is possible to have a close, caring relationship with another person if trust and loyalty are missing?

TEACH
Ask students if they have ever trusted someone who then did something to betray their trust. What, if anything, did the person do to try to rebuild their trust? How did that loss of trust affect their relationship with them? Were they more cautious about trusting others?

and will do what he or she has committed to do. Members of a team can work together to improve their performance knowing that they can count on each other. But just because there is trust between group members does not mean that the group will always achieve its goals. Each member of an athletic team can do his or her part and the team can perform at its best, but it still may not be enough to win. However, the fact that the team worked together and no one let the team down will result in a stronger team.

What happens when you have earned the trust of parents, teachers, coaches, or group leaders? They have confidence in you and give you greater freedom, knowing that you will do your best to show that you deserve the trust they have placed in you. It will give you a greater feeling of personal responsibility and confidence knowing that you are trusted to do your job and make the right decisions.

On the other hand, if you lose their trust, things are quite different. They will monitor you much more closely and ask questions about what you are doing and why. It will be difficult to get permission to do something if they are unable to check on you since they cannot trust you to make the right decision or to act responsibly. While you may believe you can be trusted, it will take a long time to rebuild that trust once it is lost.

To understand the importance of trust, you need to consider situations where you trusted someone and that person did not follow through on his or her commitment. How did you feel when you told a friend something very personal in confidence and he betrayed you by spreading the information to others? What was your reaction when you worked hard on a team project only to learn that one of the team members had not completed her part? The way you are affected when people break your trust in them is the same way people will feel about you when you fail to meet your obligations to them. Trust may be one of the most important factors in strong, lasting relationships. Once trust is broken, it will be very difficult to repair the relationship.

 CHECKPOINT

How does being trusted affect a person's feelings about himself or herself?

Being trusted to do their job and make the right decisions gives people a greater

feeling of personal responsibility and confidence.

THE USE AND MISUSE OF LOYALTY

Loyalty may be one of the most difficult character traits to understand as well as to demonstrate. Students are expected to be loyal to their school, but what does that mean? Can you sing the school song? Do you attend school events when you are not participating? Do you try to do things that uphold and improve the image of your school?

Loyalty is a personal commitment to support the values and goals of a person, group, or organization. Loyalty can be demonstrated in many ways, some that are appropriate and some that are inappropriate. *Blind allegiance,* meaning unthinking support, suggests that people do not think for themselves and will do whatever is asked of them. Loyalty should not extend beyond your personal beliefs and values.

Loyalty develops over time. When you first join a group, start a job, or even make a new friendship, you will not immediately feel a strong loyalty. As you get to know the group, business, or new friend better, learn more about their goals and values, and see that they match with yours, you will develop a stronger loyalty. Even if you do not feel a strong sense of loyalty, you should not be disloyal. To be **disloyal** means to take actions that intentionally harm a relationship. If you feel you cannot be loyal to a person or group, you should be honest about the reasons and end the relationship in a positive way. You should not be disloyal and attempt to damage the relationship.

Occasionally, you may be caught in conflicting loyalties. You may want to support a friend who is running for an office in an organization to which you both belong. However, because you know your friend very well, you may realize that he is not nearly as well qualified as the other candidate. In this case, your loyalty to your friend conflicts with your loyalty to do what is best for the organization.

Loyalty goes beyond simply being a good member of a group. It means you are committed to devote time and energy to the group, to promote the group to others, and to help the group be the best it can be. It does very little good to be a part of a relationship or a member of a group and do nothing to support it. A club will not be successful if members join but do not attend meetings, participate on committees, and volunteer for other activities. A business cannot succeed if its employees do not give their best efforts and do their jobs as well as they possibly can. In return, the business must demonstrate its loyalty to employees by providing a good work environment and rewarding their performance. A person cannot expect loyalty from a friend, a group, or an employer if there is a lack of respect in return.

© Ryan McVay/Photodisc/Getty Images

 CHECKPOINT

What problems can occur if someone has blind allegiance rather than loyalty?

Having blind allegiance to another person or group means that you might do things or

behave in ways that conflict with your personal beliefs and values.

TEACH

Ask students to think about someone that they view as a caring person. What personal characteristics of this person lead students to believe that he or she is a caring individual? List their answers on the board.

Ask students to list the people and things that they care most about. Next to the name of each person or thing, have students write a brief description of the ways they show or express their care and concern. Are there people or things that they have listed for which they currently are not showing their care? If so, ask them to think of ways they can begin to express their concern for those people or things.

CARING FOR OTHERS

Caring is the most basic component of relationships. It is the way you feel about others. **Caring** means feeling and acting with concern and empathy for others. If you are uncaring, you are selfish, self-centered, and will easily take advantage of others. If you are caring, you have concern for the welfare of others, feel bad when they experience pain or disappointment, and are happy for their success.

Caring for Those Close to You

Caring is a human instinct. You care about the people you love—your family and close friends. You care about things that are important to you—your home, neighborhood, and school. When you care about people and things, you will go to great lengths to support, protect, and improve them. If your family is struggling financially, you will try to find ways to earn money to help. If a brother or sister has a serious illness, you will offer comfort and try to get the medicines or treatments that will restore them back to health. If your neighborhood is filled with litter, you will participate in a clean-up day. If you care about education, you will study, improve your skills, take challenging classes, and treat your school and teachers with respect.

Caring When It Does Not Directly Affect You

It is more difficult to care for people you do not know, have never met, or that you view as different from you, your family, and friends. It is not easy to care about things that do not affect you or that are not important to you. If people in a distant part of the world suffer from

© Jack Star/PhotoLink/Photodisc/Getty Images

hunger, poor health care, or a lack of education, it is easy to ignore those problems and to be more concerned about the things that directly affect you. There may be endangered species that need protection, a growing pollution problem, or low-quality schools in another part of your city or state. But since you do not believe there is any way you can really solve these problems, it seems easier not to care about those issues. In fact, you may question the reasoning of people you know or see on television who are very concerned about one of those issues and are attempting to persuade others to share their concern and to work for a solution.

It is understandable that people care for their loved ones and for things that are important to them. But why should you care for those you do not know or about things that do not have an immediate effect on you? Why would you invest energy, effort, and money to respond to the needs of others and problems that seem to have no solutions or to support changes that may not occur in your lifetime?

But you see examples of that type of caring every day. When the tsunami struck South Asia in 2004, people throughout the world raised funds, sent aid, and traveled to the affected countries to provide rescue efforts, health care, and rebuilding. When you watched on television as Hurricane Katrina destroyed the Gulf Coast and New Orleans, religious organizations, non-profit groups, and individuals from far-away cities and towns traveled to the affected areas with clothing, food, building materials, and other types of aid. Children raised funds on their neighborhood streets as celebrities held concerts on national television seeking donations. The same types of efforts occur regularly in every town and city to help families in need, repair homes for the elderly, and offer help to victims of natural disasters.

Assume you are the leader of a committee in your school that is trying to get other students to volunteer their time for a number of community charities and projects. What would you say to students to convince them of the importance of the volunteer efforts and the benefits to them? Of course, there is the fun and socializing that will occur when a group of students works together. Students should get personal satisfaction from seeing the result of their volunteer efforts and the effect it has on others. But caring means more than obtaining personal satisfaction. People care when they are willing to do things to benefit others and participate in solving problems with no personal rewards. Caring is demonstrated by the anonymous donor and the volunteers who use their own time and money without expecting recognition or compensation. Caring is also demonstrated by the student organization that completes a community-service project for reasons other than "because it is a requirement to win an award." In those situations, you care because you are concerned about others, you want the best for everyone, and you want to help others who are in need. Differences between caring and not caring are identified in Figure 10.2.

TEACH
Ask students to think of an experience they may have had that started out as a required service project but ended up being personally meaningful to them. How did their changing views make them feel?

TEACHING STRATEGIES
Auditory Learners
Ask students to brainstorm a list of ways they can demonstrate caring for people, situations, or causes that do not directly affect them. Possible suggestions might include becoming more informed about other people and events and volunteering with an organization such as Habitat for Humanity or the American Red Cross.

ONGOING ASSESSMENT
Use the Checkpoint as an opportunity to conduct ongoing assessment of student comprehension of the lesson material.

FIGURE 10.2   *Caring Do's and Don'ts*

People who are caring:

- show appreciation
- try to understand others
- are considerate
- are helpful
- respect the rights of others
- volunteer
- overcome differences
- are concerned about the treatment of others
- work cooperatively

People who are not caring:

- are self-centered
- put their own interests ahead of others
- have negative opinions of others
- do not care about the feelings of others
- do not believe in sharing their time and resources
- use negative peer pressure, insults, and abuse

 CHECKPOINT

What is meant by "caring is a human instinct"?

Just as animals are born with certain instincts, humans are born with the instinct to care

for the people and things closest to them, such as their families, friends, and homes.

Follow UP

UNDERSTAND LEADERSHIP CONCEPTS

Circle the best answer for each of the following questions.

1. **Feeling and acting with concern and empathy for others is called**
   a. loyalty
   b. trust
   c. caring
   d. character

2. **It is more difficult to care for**
   a. people in another country who have been affected by a disaster
   b. your family
   c. close friends
   d. issues that affect you directly

THINK *CRITICALLY*

Answer the following questions as completely as possible. If necessary, use a separate sheet of paper.

3. **Provide examples of things that people do that suggest they do or do not care about their job and the people with whom they work.**

   Answers will vary but may include showing up on time and doing a fair share of the

   work, respecting their employer's property, treating coworkers with respect, and

   working cooperatively with others.

4. **Describe a time when you have lost the trust of someone you know. How did you (or how will you) regain that person's trust?**

   Answers will vary.

5. **Why do you think loyalty is an important quality for a member of a group or an organization?**

   Loyalty is an important quality for a member of a group or an organization because

   groups must have the support of their members to be effective. A group or an

   organization cannot succeed if members do not attend meetings, participate on

   committees, and volunteer for other activities.

ASSESS

Reteach
Have students provide examples of how trust and loyalty are important attributes in effective relationships.

Enrich
Have students research a recent international, national, or local disaster that had a negative affect on the lives of many people. Have them prepare a brief report about the response of people from all over the world to help those affected.

Close
Have students review the list of Caring Do's and Don'ts in Figure 10.2. Ask them to check the bullet points that apply to them in each list. For each check in the "People who are not caring" column, ask students to think of a positive step they could take to become more caring.

Organizational and Community Citizenship

THE MEANING OF CITIZENSHIP

Do you ever think about what it means to be part of a group or organization? Some people would suggest that they participate in organizations because of what they can gain or how they can personally benefit. The concept of citizenship suggests a different view of the role of group members. **Citizenship** is responsible involvement in a group or organization. **Responsible** means acting with mature judgment. **Involvement** means being fully committed to the work required. A good citizen does not just expect personal benefits but is actively and positively involved in the work of a group or organization. When describing the citizenship responsibilities of Americans, President John F. Kennedy said, "Ask not what your country can do for you; ask what you can do for your country."

Not Getting Your Way

Kwan really wanted to be vice-president of the Connections Club, a school group that worked to get every student in the school involved in extra-curricular activities. He knew that if he won that election, the next step would be president. He felt that he was ready for a leadership role and knew it would look very good on his college applications. Kwan campaigned hard before the election and was very disappointed when he lost by eight votes. The loss meant that he not only would not be an officer this year but also would have a difficult time becoming president next year.

After the loss, Kwan's attitude toward the club changed. He no longer volunteered for committees. When he was assigned to an activity, he often would not show up or would give a half-hearted effort. He attended meetings but often would argue against the recommendations presented by the officers. He frequently made comments to others

© Jack Star/PhotoLink/Photodisc/Getty Images

TEACH
Ask students to describe their experiences with someone who tried to "sabotage" the success of a group or organization because they did not get their way. How did they view that person's behavior? Would they consider that person a potential leader after seeing those actions?

Have students think about the different groups to which they belong. Do they think most members are committed to the success of each group, or are most of them members because their friends belong or because they think it will make them more popular?

TEACHING STRATEGIES
Print Learners
Have students obtain and review the written purpose, history, rules, and procedures of an organization to which they belong in order to learn more about the background and mission of the organization.

about how the organization was not effective. In fact, he discouraged some students from joining the club.

Kwan's attitude and actions were not demonstrating good citizenship as a member of the Connections Club. Clearly he was disappointed about losing the election. His leadership goals were disrupted, and he felt that the members who did not vote for him had let him down. The club had been important to him in the past, but now his personal feelings were more important than the success of the club. Instead of exploring other leadership opportunities and showing the members that he still wanted the club to be successful, Kwan chose to get back at the club through his immature and inappropriate behavior. Not only did the club suffer from Kwan's actions but his friends, teachers, and other students began to have a different view of him.

Effective Organizational Citizenship

The goal of good citizenship in a group or organization is to contribute energy and talents to its success. You are a member because you support the goals and purpose of the group. You also are a member because you respect and care about the other people who are part of the group. You enjoy participating in the organization and the relationships you have developed with the other members.

Your most important citizenship responsibilities are related to the important groups and organizations in which you participate—your family, clubs, teams, school, and work. Think about all of the groups in which you currently participate. What is the primary purpose of each one? Why are you a member—what makes the group important to you? Do you feel you have been a good citizen in the group? Most people agree on the following expectations of good citizenship for members of groups and organizations.

- Understand the purpose, history, and goals
- Maintain positive relationships with other members
- Respect and follow all rules and procedures
- Commit the necessary time and energy to activities
- Help the organization obtain needed finances
- Participate actively in discussions and decisions
- Contribute your ideas and opinions but welcome those of others
- Be willing to discuss and debate without being negative
- Celebrate achievements and share credit with others
- Commit to the success of the group and each of its members

Think back to the groups in which you are a member. Review these expectations of good citizenship for each of the groups. What are your

© Ryan McVay/Photodisc/Getty Images

citizenship strengths and where do you need to improve? Are you a better citizen in some groups than in others? What do you need to do in each group to become a better citizen?

 ## CHECKPOINT

How do responsibility and involvement relate to good citizenship?

Citizenship means responsible involvement—acting with mature judgment and being fully committed to the work required.

COMMUNITY CITIZENSHIP

Citizens are an important part of every community. Citizens not only become elected leaders but also are responsible for making their communities what they are. Citizens vote, pay taxes, and follow the laws. They also speak out about their beliefs, look out for their friends and neighbors, and work to make their communities better places to live. Citizens want the best government, the best schools and libraries, and the best roads, parks, and playgrounds. They may not agree on politics, religious beliefs, or even the best sports teams, but they do agree that their community is the best place to live, and they are committed to making it better. Citizens are concerned about a good life for themselves but are even more committed to a better life for future generations.

That description of citizenship may seem a bit idealistic and may not always reflect what you see around you. However, it is important to

ONGOING ASSESSMENT
Use the Checkpoint as an opportunity to conduct on-going assessment of student comprehension of the lesson material.

BUILDING COMMUNITIES
Ask students if there are areas in their neighborhood, school, or community that need to be "spruced up." What are some simple things they could do to help? Possible answers may include cleaning up litter, planting grass seed, flowers, or trees, or painting. How might they take the lead to get others to help with the clean-up?

Think Critically Answers
1. Answers will vary. The adults could attend city council meetings and request funding. In the absence of city funds, they could also organize committees and hold fundraisers in the neighborhood to improve the park themselves.
2. Answers will vary. The young people in the neighborhood could organize clean-up crews to pick up litter and clear weeds.

Building COMMUNITIES

A park in your neighborhood has become very rundown and is no longer a safe place for children and families. It used to have basketball courts and a large field used for baseball, soccer, and touch football. It also had shady areas with playground equipment where families and other groups could gather, relax, and have picnics. Now the basketball goals are broken, the fields are littered and overgrown, and the playground equipment is rusted and damaged. People in the neighborhood talk about the need for a play area and recall how their families used the park in the past. You and your friends want a place to hang out, socialize, and even get together for an informal game of basketball or skateboarding. However, the city council does not seem interested in improving the park. It says there is not enough money in the city budget right now.

THINK *CRITICALLY*

1. What are some things the adults in the neighborhood can do to try to influence the decisions of the city council about the park?
2. What are some of the ways you could work with other young people in the neighborhood to develop solutions to this problem?

TEACH
Have students brainstorm a list of things they can do to be helpful to current neighbors as well as newcomers in their neighborhood. How will those activities help them become good community citizens? How might it change the feelings and relationships among neighbors?

TEACHING STRATEGIES
Auditory Learners
On the board, write the sentence, "Bloom where you are planted." Ask student how they think this expression relates to community citizenship.

ONGOING ASSESSMENT
Use the Checkpoint as an opportunity to conduct ongoing assessment of student comprehension of the lesson material.

recognize the ideals of good citizenship. Just because your relationships with family and friends are not always what you would like them to be does not mean that you give up on them and accept less than you can have. You are also aware that there are problems with your country, your community, or your neighborhood. As citizens, you must take responsibility for working to correct those problems. Cooperating with others who have the same concerns and working to make changes increases the chances that you can solve the problems. If you give up on those responsibilities, the problems will get worse rather than better. If citizens do not get involved, there is no way in a democracy for change to occur and problems to be solved.

Good citizenship starts in your neighborhood and community. You are also a citizen of your state and country and should be aware of the issues at those levels that affect you today and that are important to your future. As you get older, you may become more active in state and national events and activities. Today, however, you are most affected by events in your community and can be most helpful as a citizen in your local neighborhood and community. Schools, recreational facilities, youth services, and jobs are mostly local community issues. You have a right to voice your opinions and ideas and a responsibility to help make each part of your community as good as it can be. Figure 10.3 describes things you, your family, and your friends can do to be effective community citizens.

FIGURE 10.3   *Characteristics of a Good Community Citizen*

A good community citizen:

- is a good neighbor
- stays informed about local news, events, and issues
- shows respect for everyone despite differences in age, culture, or economic status
- welcomes new people into the neighborhood and helps them fit in
- provides help to those in need
- takes responsibility for the care of the neighborhood by participating in clean-up days and improvement projects that benefit the community
- works to support and improve community institutions and services such as schools, libraries, hospitals, and community centers

- informs the appropriate officials and agencies about damage, needed repairs, or safety issues
- becomes involved in community groups and organizations
- is active in the political process, encourages and supports effective leaders, votes, attends meetings, and expresses ideas and views
- is courageous in standing up for the community and working to keep it safe, clean, prosperous, and a great place to live

---

CHECKPOINT

List several responsibilities of a good community citizen.

Responsibilities of a good community citizen include all of the characteristics listed in Figure 10.3.

Follow UP

UNDERSTAND LEADERSHIP CONCEPTS

Circle the best answer for each of the following questions.

1. **Organizational citizenship applies to which of the following?**
   a. families
   b. clubs
   c. school
   (d.) all of the above

2. **Good citizenship starts in your**
   a. country
   b. state
   (c.) neighborhood and community
   d. school

THINK *CRITICALLY*

Answer the following questions as completely as possible. If necessary, use a separate sheet of paper.

3. **List several examples of your citizenship responsibilities as a member of your family, your school, and a team or club.**

Answers will vary.

4. **Explain what President John F. Kennedy meant when he said, "Ask not what your country can do for you; ask what you can do for your country." What are some ways you can respond to his challenge?**

Answers will vary. President Kennedy meant that good citizens are more concerned about making a positive contribution to their country than they are about getting personal benefits.

5. **Look around your community. What are some local issues in which you can get involved to demonstrate community citizenship?**

Answers will vary.

ASSESS
Reteach
Have students review the Characteristics of a Good Community Citizen in Figure 10.3. For each characteristic listed, have students list one or more things they can do to fulfill that "requirement" for good community citizenship.

Enrich
Have students conduct research in the library or on the Internet about the Peace Corps, which was established in 1961 by President John F. Kennedy to provide a way for ordinary citizens to make a difference in the lives of people throughout the world.

Close
Ask students to explain why it is important for them to become responsible citizens in their local communities.

Chapter Assessment

TEACHING RESOURCES
ExamView® CD, Ch. 10

REVIEW LEADERSHIP CONCEPTS

Write the letter of the term that matches each definition. Some terms will not be used.

a. bias
b. caring
c. citizenship
d. disloyal
e. fairness
f. favoritism
g. formal relationships
h. informal relationships
i. intimate relationship
j. involvement
k. loyalty
l. objective
m. respect
n. responsible
o. trust
p. virtual relationships

___e___ 1. The act of being free from favoritism, self-interest, or bias

___h___ 2. Relationships that occur voluntarily based on the interests people have in each other

___j___ 3. Being fully committed to the work required

___p___ 4. Purposeful, continuing interactions and communications between two or more people that are carried on primarily via computer networks

___o___ 5. Having complete confidence in another person

___f___ 6. Giving some people special treatment due to bias or a close relationship

___d___ 7. To take actions that intentionally harm a relationship

___m___ 8. Showing consideration and regard for people and property

___c___ 9. Responsible involvement in a group or organization

___k___ 10. Personal commitment to support the values and goals of a person, group, or organization

___i___ 11. When two people have special affection and commitment for each other based on understanding, caring, and trust

___b___ 12. Feeling and acting with concern and empathy for others

Circle the best answer.

13. Which of the following statements about relationships is *not true*?
    a. The first important relationship in your life is with your family.
    b. Relationships can be either personal or professional.
    c. Relationships cannot be established through technology.
    d. Informal relationships occur voluntarily.

14. Which of the following is *not* a behavior that demonstrates fair treatment of others?
    a. being as objective as possible when dealing with other people
    b. avoiding favoritism
    c. avoiding rules that give some people an advantage
    d. finding reasons to justify why you did not allow a highly qualified individual to join your team

15. When people do not think for themselves and will do whatever is asked of them, they are demonstrating
    a. loyalty
    b. blind allegiance
    c. respect for others
    d. a caring attitude

ASSESS
Reteach
Have students prepare an outline of the chapter by listing the lesson titles and heads within each lesson. Ask students to list one or two key points below each outline item.

Enrich
Invite a local government official, such as a member of your city council, to speak to the class about community citizenship. Have students prepare questions in advance to ask the guest speaker.

CLOSE
Have students discuss how their relationships with others affect their character either positively or negatively.

16. What are some of the characteristics of an effective relationship? What are some characteristics of an ineffective relationship?

In effective relationships, people have a positive attitude and are willing to become involved and help out when needed. They are encouraging to others and are seldom judgmental. In ineffective relationships, people are more negative than positive and are not actively involved in activities. They tear others down instead of building them up.

17. Do you agree or disagree that schools offer some of the most complex and difficult relationships you will experience? Provide examples to justify your answer.

Answers will vary. It often is difficult to maintain long-term friendships in school because of different classes and schedules. Also, school provides opportunities to meet new people, participate in new activities, and develop new interests.

18. Review the items in Figure 10.1. Which of the actions listed are the ones that most often contribute to poor interpersonal relationships? Justify your choices.

Answers will vary.

19. How can you disagree strongly with other people's ideas, beliefs, and values and still treat them with respect?

You can disagree strongly with other people's ideas, beliefs, and values and still show consideration and regard for them. By showing respect, you are demonstrating your willingness to accept other people and cooperate with them rather than to create conflict and problems.

20. Make a list of the things you believe students should do to demonstrate good citizenship in your school? Do you believe good citizenship makes a difference in the school climate? Why or why not?

Answers will vary but may include maintaining a positive relationship with other students and faculty, respecting and following school rules, and being committed to making your school a success.

21. **Research**   *Review newspapers to find stories of people demonstrating good citizenship in their communities. Select three stories that you believe are the best examples. Write a two-paragraph summary of each story that describes the actions of the person or persons and why you believe the individual(s) became involved in the activity. Also describe how this person's actions will benefit others.*

Answers will vary.

22. **Technology**   *Use a graphics program on a computer to create an illustration of how several types of technology can be used for virtual relationships. Identify those that are most often used for informal relationships and those that are best used for formal relationships. Write a short description of each one and the types of problems that might prevent you from developing and maintaining effective relationships.*

Answers will vary.

23. **Communication**   *Partner with another class member of the opposite sex. Review the scenario at the beginning of Lesson 10.3 involving Gloria and Thomas. Discuss how the two friends might resolve the problem that is facing them and restore their relationship. Then role play a conversation they would have to accomplish that goal. After the role play, discuss how you would feel about the other person based on the conversation.*

Answers will vary but may include having an open and honest conversation to clearly

define the boundaries of their relationship.

24. **Problem Solving**   *Lack of respect for others and their property has been identified as one of the major problems facing many schools today. Televised messages are often developed by public relations businesses to raise awareness of important issues. Team with several other students. Plan and produce a one-minute video for your school that emphasizes the importance of respect.*

Answers will vary.

LEARNING TO LEAD

FOCUS

Participate in team competitive events.

DESCRIPTION

Among the key skills required for success in the twenty-first century are teamwork, collaboration, and interpersonal skills. Many student organizations offer opportunities and activities to develop and demonstrate those skills. One of the most challenging and rewarding opportunities is team competition.

Each student organization offers a number of choices of competitive events that require the cooperative efforts of several team members to solve a business problem and present a solution to judges. The solution typically involves both a written report and an oral presentation. Learn about team competitive events and work with other students to select and prepare for an event.

LEARNING TO LEAD
This project is written for use with student organizations such as BPA, DECA, and FBLA. Student organizations can help students prepare for key leadership roles. After students complete the activities, discuss what they learned about their student organization.

ACTIVITIES

1. *Go to the competitive events section on the national web site of your student organization. Review each team event carefully to determine the types of team activities required and the skills needed by team members for successful participation.*

2. *Study information on effective teams and interpersonal relationships. List the interpersonal,* *leadership, followership, and communication skills necessary for a team to participate effectively in the competition.*

3. *Meet with other students in your student organization who would make good team members based on shared interests and the diversity of skills needed for an effective team. Discuss the strengths and commitment each person could bring to a successful team.*

SHARE YOUR RESULTS

1. *Form a team with other chapter members interested in preparing for a team competitive event. Agree as a team on the event or activity and study the requirements. Clarify expectations with your chapter adviser.*

2. *Plan activities to: (1) improve interpersonal relationship skills, focusing on decision making, communication, problem solving, and time management, and (2) prepare for competition by completing the research, developing the materials, and practicing the team presentation. Make sure to meet the deadlines set by your state and national organization.*

3. *Once every two weeks, conduct a team feedback meeting in which each member discusses the strengths of the team and areas needing improvement. Use the feedback to develop team improvement goals for the next two weeks.*

4. *Ask a teacher, a local business person, and an experienced student from your local chapter to serve as mentors for your team. Have the mentors evaluate your team's performance and offer suggestions for improvement using the evaluation criteria for team competition provided by your national student organization.*

Activities
1. Answers will vary.
2. Answers will vary. To better organize a list of needed skills, students may find it helpful to create a table with column headings of *interpersonal*, *leadership*, *followership*, and *communication*.
3. Answers will vary. When discussing team competitions with prospective team members, students should try to match the strengths of each member with the skills listed on their table.

Share Your Results
1. Requirements will vary based on the event selected.
2. Students should establish a time line or calendar.
3. Students should agree on goals that will improve the overall team effort.
4. Mentors should understand the time commitment required.

By asking for help from the
foreign language depart-
ment in her school and by
bringing in speakers from
the community, Ashley is
organizing a collaborative
effort that will involve not
only the school but also
the larger community.

Ask students to think of
ways they could help pro-
mote cultural awareness
and sensitivity and resolve
conflicts among groups in
their own school.

ACCEPTING THE CHALLENGE

CASE STUDY 10—EDUCATION IS THE KEY

In the opening scenario, What Would You Do?, *you learned that Ashley wants to make a difference in her school and community. Though Ashley and her friends are only sophomores and represent a small number of students in their large school, their sensitivity to the change in attitudes and relationships in their community and school implies that they have a desire for unity in their community and school. Ashley decides she would like to start an after-school program to educate students about other cultures. She discusses her idea with the principal and explains the purpose of the program. Her plan is to have a weekly meeting after school to discuss different cultures. The meeting would be jam packed with reading materials, visual presentations, and speakers from the community who represent the various cultures. Ashley is hoping that the foreign language department in her school will help sponsor the program. She thinks it may generate interest among students to learn another language. The goal of the program would be to build cultural awareness and sensitivity in her school, which she hopes will then expand to the community.*

THINK *CRITICALLY*

1. *What character traits do you recognize in Ashley that indicate she knows how to show or demonstrate respect for others?*

Answers will vary. Ashley's actions demonstrate regard, consideration, and caring for

others, particularly students of different cultures. She wants everyone in her school to

be treated fairly and with respect.

2. *Having observed the unfair treatment of students from different ethnic backgrounds and different cultures, Ashley takes action to bring this negative behavior to an end. Do you think her plan is a good one? Why or why not?*

Answers will vary.

3. *What lessons can you learn from Ashley about caring for others who are not being respected or treated fairly even when the negative behavior is not directly affecting you. Why is this an important lesson in today's society?*

Answers will vary. An important lesson is to look beyond yourself and your immediate

family and friends and to care for others who may need help because they are not

being treated with respect or fairness. Those negative attitudes and actions will have a

negative effect on the community or organization if not resolved. To be a leader, you

must be able to care about issues that may not necessarily affect you personally.

APPLY *WHAT YOU HAVE LEARNED–Evaluate Your Relationship Skills*

DIRECTIONS: *In an attempt to learn how you treat and respect your friends and family, complete the* Relationship Rating Survey *below or on your Student Activity CD. Enter the word "True" or "False" to indicate whether the statement accurately represents your "relationship style."*

RELATIONSHIP RATING SURVEY

MY FRIENDS WOULD SAY THAT:

_____ 1. I respect others, no matter their ethnicity or culture.

_____ 2. I respect only those individuals who are most like me.

_____ 3. Relationships with my friends are important to me because of what they bring to my life.

_____ 4. Relationships with my friends are important to me because of who they represent (e.g., status and popularity).

_____ 5. I am better at engaging in virtual relationships (e.g., e-mail, chat rooms, instant messaging).

_____ 6. I am better at engaging in personal and intimate relationships.

_____ 7. I am more effective in formal relationships.

_____ 8. I am more effective in informal relationships.

_____ 9. I treat those who are different from me fairly.

_____ 10. I treat those who are different from me unfairly.

_____ 11. I am a loyal friend.

_____ 12. I am only loyal if it benefits me.

MY FAMILY WOULD SAY THAT:

_____ 13. I am respectful of other family members' feelings.

_____ 14. I disregard the feelings of other family members.

_____ 15. I respect other family members' property.

_____ 16. I do not bother to take care of other family members' property.

_____ 17. I am more loyal to family than to friends.

_____ 18. I am more loyal to my friends than to family members.

_____ 19. I am a caring person toward others.

_____ 20. I am usually more caring when it benefits me the most.

   Do your responses in the survey suggest that you are well respected by your friends and family? Focus on the areas viewed negatively by either your friends or family. On the lines below or on your Student Activity CD, create a SMART goal (including a completion date) for improving your relationship skills. Enter your goal in a monthly calendar (on the CD or your own). Then enter your thoughts, ideas, and discussions related to your goal in a journal (on the CD or your own) to help plan and track your progress. Choose a goal-setting partner to help you reach your goal and evaluate your progress.

_____

_____

_____

ACCEPTING THE CHALLENGE
Apply What You Have Learned—Evaluate Your Relationship Skills Note that students can complete this part of the *Accepting the Challenge* activity in the book or on the Student Activity CD. Instructions are provided on the CD.

After students have answered the questions in this activity, instruct them to write a SMART goal (including a completion date) that will help them improve their relationship skills. Have them enter their goal on a monthly calendar. Students can use the monthly calendar on the Student Activity CD or their own calendar. Explain to students that they may also use weekly calendar pages (on the Student Activity CD or their own calendar) to plan activities and tasks that will help them achieve their goals. Finally, direct students to use a journal (on the Student Activity CD or their own) to track and evaluate their progress in achieving their goal.

A goal-setting partner can add an element of accountability and can offer positive feedback to help students stay on track to achieve their goals.

Students should be given the opportunity to reflect on the progress they have made toward achieving their goal. To do this, students can complete the *Evaluate Your Progress* activity on the Student Activity CD. Stress to students that it is important to complete this activity on the original target completion date even if they have not met their goal at that time.

Chapter 11

Modeling and Mentoring: Helping Others to Lead

© Buccina Studios/Photodisc/Getty Images

11.1 *Role Models*

11.2 *Finding Role Models*

11.3 *Mentors and Mentoring*

What would **YOU** do?

YVETTE SEEKS ADVICE

Yvette was the youngest child in her family. As her four brothers and one sister all matured and married, she was the only child left at home with her parents. Her parents were very strict and did not allow Yvette to participate in many high school activities. However, she still felt her life was quite full because of the time she spent with her sister, Shirley, and her four sisters-in-law—Joyce, Anna, Priscilla, and Jean. Yvette had always looked up to them for the positive ways they lived their lives. She also admired each of them for their personal and professional accomplishments. They included Yvette in most of their family and community activities. She considered them her biggest cheerleaders. She always went to them for advice about dating, clothes, school activities, class work, and life in general.

When Yvette was ready to choose a college, she knew she wanted to go to a college nearby so she could continue to live at home. She did not want to leave her comfort zone. She discussed this with her sister, Shirley, fully expecting her to support her decision. However, Yvette was surprised to learn that Shirley disagreed with her decision. Shirley thought it would be a good idea for Yvette to attend a college away from home to gain the experience of living on her own. Shirley thought Yvette had lived a fairly sheltered life and had not developed the skills needed to live independently.

Yvette decided to ask her sisters-in-law for their opinions on selecting a local college or an out-of-state college. Surprisingly, they agreed with Shirley. They explained to Yvette that by living on her own she would become more mature and responsible as she began to make her own decisions. They encouraged her to take a step toward independence.

Yvette was not sure what to do. She had always turned to her sister and sisters-in-law for advice and had placed trust in their good judgment and guidance. Should she trust their judgment once again?

THINK *CRITICALLY*

1. If you were Yvette's friend, what would you advise her to do? Explain why.

2. Why do you think Yvette places so much emphasis on her family's opinions?

3. Why is it important for everyone to have someone to look up to who can offer support and advice?

TEACHING RESOURCES
Instructor's Resource CD
Lesson Plans, Ch. 11
PowerPoint Slides, Ch. 11

Student Activity CD, Ch. 11

thomsonedu.com/school/
leading
Crossword Puzzle, Ch. 11
Flash Cards, Ch. 11

Exam*View*® **CD**, Ch. 11

CHAPTER OVERVIEW
Chapter 11 discusses role modeling and mentoring as a way to help individuals become leaders.

Lesson 11.1
Explains the purpose of a role model and describes different types of role models.

Lesson 11.2
Describes where to find role models and explains why others may view you as a role model.

Lesson 11.3
Describes the mentoring relationship and explains how to find the right mentor.

WHAT WOULD YOU DO?
Ask students to think about the people whom they have always turned to for advice and guidance. Would they hesitate to take the advice offered if it was out of their comfort zone?

Think Critically Answers
1. Answers will vary.
2. Answers will vary. Yvette has always looked up to them, and she trusted their guidance.
3. Answers will vary. All individuals need people in their life who wish the best for them and want to see them succeed.

Role Models

- Explain the purpose of a role model.
- Describe the different types of role models.

- role model
- public role models
- personal role models
- formal role models
- informal role models

SCHEDULE
Block 45 minutes
Regular 1 class period

FOCUS
Ask students to list the people whom they look up to and admire. What personal characteristics do they admire about each person listed?

WHAT IS A ROLE MODEL?

A **role model** is someone whose character, behavior, attitude, personality, or skills serve as a good example to follow. A role model could be anyone, including a parent, teacher, or sibling. People tend to look for role models to fill some need in their lives. The lack of total self-acceptance, whether physical or emotional, may drive them to try to find someone or something else to imitate. Even little children select role models, such as Dora the Explorer and the Muppets. The desire to strengthen a personal characteristic, develop leadership skills, or fulfill a role to which you aspire, such as an athlete or a musician, can lead you to seek role models. Your goal should be to select positive people to imitate. It is important to take the time to observe, study, and research potential role models. It is even a good idea to ask others about your choice of role models.

On television today, you often hear the debate about athletes, musicians, political figures, and actors being role models. Some people in these roles say that young people should not look up to them and try to model their behavior. On the other hand, many adults believe that because famous people are public figures who benefit financially from their fans, they should behave in appropriate ways and be a positive influence on others. While many of these role models are good people and get publicity for their positive contributions, a few generate negative publicity through their actions. You sometimes read about them using drugs, engaging in violent behavior, or using vulgar language in public. Many of them believe that the public has no say in what they do in their personal life when they are not performing.

© SW Productions/Photodisc/Getty Images

You and your friends are big fans of Fantasy Football and have chosen Larry Johnson of the Kansas City Chiefs and Peyton Manning of the Indianapolis Colts as your star players. Because of the skills and other character traits and behaviors they exhibit on the field and in their communities, you view these players as role models. This type of role model falls into the category of someone you probably will not meet in real life and will not get to know personally. But you still identify them as role models.

THINK *CRITICALLY*

1. Name a celebrity or athlete that you consider to be a role model. Describe the characteristics he or she possesses that impressed you to choose them as a role model.

2. If you had a chance to "walk in the shoes" of your role model, would you feel pressured to act as a role model to people you do not even know. Explain why or why not.

Keeping It Real

As people play out their roles, you sometimes become impressed with their talent, skill, behavior, or personality, and you want to be like them. How many times have you thought that it would be good to take up golf because Tiger Woods has been such a positive role model for young people, especially minority youths? How many times have you seen young girls trying to imitate the latest female pop star? As you look at these personalities, they are "star studded" and out of reach for most people who are just beginning to recognize their interests and talents. They are people with whom you have no personal relationship, but as you purchase their CDs or buy the products they endorse, you somehow begin to attach yourself to them in a deeply emotional and almost personal way. You may begin to imitate the behaviors that they exhibit.

Some of these athletes and entertainers are *false role models*. Many of them have public identities that are different from their personal identities. They are not interested in being a role model and are not concerned about the effect they have on their fans and others who look up to them. *True role models* are people who try to consistently behave in a positive manner because they are aware of their influence on others and they want to set a good example.

Sometimes role models are taken from history. In school as you study persons from the past—from George Washington and George Washington Carver to Ghandi and Dr. Martin Luther King, Jr.—you learn something about their courage in times of great challenge. As you learn about their life experiences and contributions to society, you obtain information about their character, values, attitudes, and leadership styles. Although they no longer live today, their contributions have helped to shape the world in which you now live. The character traits they demonstrated may appeal to your sense of what you want to be or do in your own life. Historical role models have laid the groundwork and have motivated others to continue their life's work.

TEACH
Have students review the role models on their list. Ask them to indicate why they chose each person. What need does each person fill in their lives?

Ask students to think about any entertainers or athletes they may look up to and try to emulate. Why do they think those individuals are true role models?

Discuss historical role models. Ask students to provide additional examples of historical role models and their contributions to society.

WHAT ABOUT ME?
Ask students why they think people choose role models whom they do not personally know and probably will not ever meet in real life. Do they see any harm in these "fantasy" role models?

Think Critically Answers
1. Answers will vary.
2. Answers will vary.

© Amanda Clement/Photodisc/Getty Images

All That Glitters Is Not Gold

Each day, a variety of entertainment, sports, and art comes into your living room and presents you with a variety of people, groups, or teams that challenge your concept of reality.

The reality shows and other entertainment that invite you into the personal lives of people on television can be misleading. When the camera is on, people sometimes exaggerate their lifestyles, personalities, attitudes, and conversations to create a specific type of impression for the viewers. The way they appear to live in their lavish homes with swimming pools, video and game rooms, and unlimited access to all kinds of luxuries is a setup provided by the producers of the show. They actually are "unreality" shows.

You often invest your time, dedication, loyalty, energy, and money in these personalities. You may buy their CDs, posters, or the clothing and sports equipment they endorse. Because you listen to their music or watch every game they play, you feel connected to them. Your emotional investment in these famous personalities sometimes leads you to see them as role models. But the reality is that many of these famous people have no desire to be considered role models. Because they are public figures, they must always try to act in acceptable ways in every part of their lives. If they behave in real ways, you would see that they have flaws just as everyone else does. Try to remember that they are really just "regular" people when they are not entertaining. Do not try to live up to a role model whose image is not real. You could be setting yourself up for disappointment.

CHECKPOINT

What can you gain from learning about historical role models?
Historical role models have made contributions that have helped shape the world. They have laid the groundwork and have motivated others to continue their life's work.

TYPES OF ROLE MODELS

When individuals are looking for a role model, they do so according to the need in their own personal lives. Sometimes the need is simply for "dreaming" about the possibility of becoming a professional athlete or famous entertainer. At other times, the need for a role model arises from a person's lifestyle or home environment. For example, some people who come from a single-parent home or are an only child may feel they need the help of a role model to fill a void in their life. Then there are times when a role model is needed to help a person find the courage to make important personal changes and improvements. Whatever the reason, there are different types of role models to fit particular needs. Examine the following types of role models to see if any of them fit a possible need or desire in your life. Keep in mind that one person may serve more than one role.

Public and Personal Role Models

Public role models are people whom you admire because of their impact on the community or on society. You may be impressed by their leadership skills in getting things done or by their interpersonal skills in knowing how to treat people. The mayor, city council members, school board members, and well-known members of the business community fit into this category. Athletes and celebrities can also be public role models.

People in your household or neighborhood that you have known for a long time and whose behavior you admire are **personal role models**. You may find traits in your family members that you want to imitate. Maybe you have an older sibling that you admire because of his or her academic ability or popularity with others. Sometimes a personal role model can be another relative or family friend who has accomplished something that you admire or who has shown commitment in achieving a goal. Personal role models can be family members or personal friends who play an important role in enhancing the quality of your life. Children frequently see parents as role models and plan to follow in their footsteps in their career choices. You may see the strength and character in a family member—particularly during difficult times—and desire to model those character traits.

Formal and Informal Role Models

Formal role models are those persons who have earned your admiration in a formal or professional way. When you start going to the dentist or orthodontist, for example, you have a formal relationship with that person. After you have been the doctor's patient for a while, your relationship may become friendlier. Because of this person's skill, practice, and care for you, you may become interested in this type of career and look to this person for advice.

Those persons whom you know casually and whose skills and talents you admire are **informal role models**. Perhaps you admire someone at school because she has the talent to play basketball or the courage to run for Student Council president. Perhaps you know someone who is popular among the student body because he treats everyone fairly and respectfully. Informal role models can also be members of a team or group to which you belong. There is something about the way they carry themselves—either their personality, attitude, social intelligence, or emotional stability. You may be friendly with them, but you do not consider yourselves friends. Many times you come to admire some traits about these people and decide to pattern your life after them in some way.

 CHECKPOINT

What are the four different types of role models?

The four types of role models include public, personal, formal, and informal role models.

TEACH
Ask students to think of the people who have leadership roles in their community. What characteristics of these individuals make them good role models for others in the community?

Ask students if there are others in their school whom they admire and consider to be informal role models. What traits about these individuals do they admire and want to emulate?

TEACHING STRATEGIES
Limited English Proficiency Students
Have students make four columns on a piece of paper—labeling one for each of the four types of role models. In each column, have students write brief descriptors to identify the type of person who might be included in that particular category of role models.

ONGOING ASSESSMENT
Use the Checkpoint as an opportunity to conduct ongoing assessment of student comprehension of the lesson material.

ASSESS
Reteach
Have students list the various types of role models—public, personal, formal, and informal as well as true, false, and historical. Ask students to write one or two sentences describing each type of role model.

Enrich
Divide students into small groups and have each group create a computer-generated presentation showing well-known individuals from the areas of business, government, entertainment, and athletics. Have each group share its presentation with the class. As each person's image is shown, have the class discuss whether that person is a true role model or a false role model.

Close
Ask students to explain why individuals look for role models to imitate.

UNDERSTAND LEADERSHIP CONCEPTS

Circle the best answer for each of the following questions.

1. Formal role models are
   a. persons you interact with casually
   b. persons you interact with in a professional way
   c. persons from history who are studied in your curriculum
   d. persons you consider to be your friends

2. Which of the following is not a type of role model?
   a. informal role models
   b. personal role models
   c. reality role models
   d. public role models

THINK *CRITICALLY*

Answer the following questions as completely as possible. If necessary, use a separate sheet of paper.

3. Why do you think people often choose entertainers or professional athletes as role models?

People often choose entertainers or professional athletes as role models because they admire their talent, skills, and abilities and dream of being just like them. Even though they have no personal relationship with these individuals, because they buy their CDs or sports jerseys, they become emotionally attached to them.

4. What do you think a person can learn from a role model who lived many years ago?

The actions of role models who lived many years ago reveal their character, values, attitudes, and leadership styles. You can use these examples as a guide for what you may want to do in your own life.

5. What is the difference between false role models and true role models?

False role models have public identities that are different from their personal identities. They are not concerned about the effect they have on people who look up to them. True role models try to consistently behave in a positive manner. They are aware of their influence on others, and they want to set a good example.

Finding Role Models

- Describe where to find role models.
- Explain why others may view you as a role model.

- peer role models
- underrepresented groups

WHERE DO YOU FIND ROLE MODELS?

Why do you think that you and many others often view famous people as role models? Is it because of their contributions to their community, or is it because of their glamorous lifestyles? Perhaps it is because you live in a situation where there seem to be few close or personal role models and so you look to these well-known people to provide you with someone to admire and imitate. However, there are many other places closer to you where you can look for role models.

Home

Your home is likely the most realistic place to find a role model. Think back to some of the televised award shows for entertainers. When giving their acceptance speech for receiving the award, they often thank one or both of their parents for being there for them and helping them along the way. They do not necessarily use the words *role model*, but remember that home is the first place you begin to learn about appropriate actions and behaviors. Many children admire their parents and want to imitate their behavior, position, and values.

SCHEDULE
Block 45 minutes
Regular 1 class period

FOCUS
Have students brainstorm a list of places where they might find appropriate role models. Write their answers on the board.

TEACH
Ask students if they think that glamour, fame, possessions, or money are good enough reasons to admire a person and try to model their behavior and attitudes. Have them explain their answers.

Ask students why they think home is the most realistic place to find role models. Among their family members, who do they consider to be a good role model? Have them explain their answer.

© Don Tremain/Photodisc/Getty Images

With your classmates, create a list of role models from among the students in your school. After compiling the list, have the person who selected each role model explain why he or she chose that person. Meet with your school administrators and let them know that you believe these people represent your school well and that they deserve this honor. Also let the students who were selected know that you honored them in this way.

THINK *CRITICALLY*

What are the character traits that you should look for in individuals when selecting them to be honored as role models? What are some things you could do to show that you appreciate their positive influence in your school?

A TEAM EFFORT
Before they begin compiling their list of role models from among the students in their school, students should discuss the criteria they will use for the selection process.

Think Critically Answers
Answers will vary. Possible ways to show appreciation might be to recognize them in a school assembly, to present them with a certificate of appreciation, or to publish an article about their positive influence on others in the school newspaper.

TEACH
Have students name several people they admire in their community who care for the needs of others. Ask students what they think they can learn from each of these role models.

Ask students to think about the teachers in their school. What character traits do they exhibit that would make them positive role models?

Community

Consider the people in your community. You admire many of them because of their attitude in caring for the needs of others. It could be a supervisor at your local Boys and Girls Club because she accepts others regardless of their differences. It could be one of your coaches who demonstrates self-control even when the team does not perform as well as it can. It could be a religious leader who is patient and demonstrates a caring attitude toward people with needs in the community as well as those in his or her congregation. It could be your friend's mother who always nurtures you and boosts your self-esteem. You might consider any one of these people a role model.

School

Look at the teachers in your school who support your academic efforts while encouraging you to take advantage of leadership opportunities. They make you feel like you have what it takes to be successful and help build your self-confidence. You may want to model some of the character traits of these teachers in your own life.

In your school, there are also many **peer role models**, or other students who exhibit character traits that you respect and appreciate. How many times have you been impressed by a friend who already has set a career goal for her future and takes classes and participates in the right clubs to ensure her road to success? How many times have you admired the courage of someone whose disability requires the use of a wheelchair for mobility? How many times have you admired the integrity of a fellow classmate who stands up for the rights of all students, not just for certain groups of students.

When you recognize your admiration for the character traits you see in others, you will begin to realize that you view them as role models, even if it is only in a small way. You see something in them that either affirms a trait in you or is a trait that you desire.

Job

You may have a part-time job, and in that setting, you may have discovered that you admire someone with whom you work. Having a role model on the job can be valuable as you are thinking about your future career. There are many people in the workplace who demonstrate good character and leadership traits and who are eager to serve as role models for young people or new employees.

Role Models for Minority Groups

For **underrepresented groups**—groups of individuals from minority cultures—finding role models in school or in the workplace who are like them, based on race, culture, gender, or ethnicity, is sometimes difficult to do. In some local communities, minority groups may have access to personal role models because they live in "cultural cities" or neighborhoods that are made up of a majority of their ethnic or racial group. However, in other communities, people from minority racial or ethnic backgrounds are more isolated.

Increasingly, underrepresented groups can find role models in public figures. On the national level, minorities serve in important roles in government, such as Dr. Condoleezza Rice as Secretary of State and Justices Clarence Thomas and Ruth Ginzberg on the U.S. Supreme Court. In the areas of entertainment and athletics, there are many more minorities who can serve as role models. When choosing a role model that is a public figure, remember to choose a true role model—not a false role model. True role models try to maintain a positive image in all aspects of their life.

Underrepresented individuals can also turn to role models who are different from them. Personality, attitude, and social and emotional intelligence are character traits that must sometimes guide you in choosing a role model. Even though the experiences and viewpoints of the minority culture may differ from another culture, it is possible to find someone who can understand, respect, and relate to the difficulties and struggles in another person's life.

CHECKPOINT

Name four places where you can find role models.

Four places where you can find role models are your home, community, school, and job.

© Andrew Wakeford/Photodisc/Getty Images

TEACH
Ask students to read the quote in the margin. Have students research information about Tiger Woods. Based on the information they have learned about him, do they think Tiger Woods would be a positive role model for young people? Why or why not?

Ask students to brainstorm a list of public figures (other than the examples provided in the text) whom they consider to be true role models for underrepresented groups of individuals. Write their answers on the board.

TEACHING STRATEGIES
Tactile Learners
Have students design and create a "Role Model of the Year" award to be presented to the teacher in their school who supports and encourages others to become successful student leaders. After the award has been created, students should vote to decide on the teacher who will receive the award.

As an alternate idea, students could create a "Peer Role Model of the Year" award to present to the student they most admire.

ONGOING ASSESSMENT
Use the Checkpoint as an opportunity to conduct ongoing assessment of student comprehension of the lesson material.

© Doug Menuez/Photodisc/Getty Images

SOMEBODY IS WATCHING YOU!

You may be surprised to realize that while you are watching others, someone may also be watching you. Just because no one has approached you to tell you that they admire you does not mean that you are not a role model to others. On the other hand, you may have had someone compliment you on your caring attitude, your friendly personality, or your positive approach when working with other people. How many times has one of your teachers or coaches picked you to be in charge of a group of your peers? They most likely believe in your leadership abilities and know you have the discipline to get things done while treating people fairly. They consider you to be a good role model.

Even if you, by chance, engage in negative or disruptive behavior, somebody is watching you. People who admire you may model your behavior even though they know that it is negative role modeling. That is why gangs and people who engage in bullying behavior seem to have a following. People who participate in these types of groups believe in and support the leader and the group for the wrong reasons. When people engage in this type of behavior, they are seeking ways to meet their own needs and to gain a sense of belonging. Their lives and daily experiences do not provide a positive climate in which they can safely and successfully exist.

Be aware that people are watching you and try to avoid negative behaviors. When you work to serve as a positive role model, others may follow your lead and avoid hanging out with the groups that will lead them into increasingly negative behaviors.

 CHECKPOINT

Why do people engage in negative or disruptive behavior?

People who engage in negative or disruptive behavior are seeking ways to gain a sense of belonging. Their daily lives do not provide a positive climate in which they can safely exist.

Follow UP

UNDERSTAND LEADERSHIP CONCEPTS

Circle the best answer for each of the following questions.

1. The most realistic place to find a role model is
   a. at school
   b. on television
   c. in the community
   d. at home *(circled)*

2. Underrepresented groups include individuals identified by
   a. ethnicity
   b. gender
   c. race
   d. all of the above *(circled)*

THINK *CRITICALLY*

Answer the following questions as completely as possible. If necessary, use a separate sheet of paper.

3. Describe a role model whom you might choose from among professional athletes.
Answers will vary.
_____
_____
_____
_____

4. Explain why you believe it is sometimes necessary to select a role model in your same racial or ethnic group.
Answers will vary. People sometimes need to select a role model in their same racial or ethnic group to have someone "like them" with whom to identify. It may be easier to establish a relationship with someone from the same racial or ethnic group because he or she is more likely to have the same viewpoints and to have had the same experiences.

5. Describe one positive characteristic that you possess that would cause one of your peers or siblings to consider you a role model.
Answers will vary.
_____
_____
_____
_____

ASSESS
Reteach
Have students list each of the places where they can find role models—home, community, school, and job. For each location, have them write one or two sentences explaining how they would benefit from a role model in that area.

Enrich
Have students create a "Fishbowl" poster or bulletin board. They should visually represent the characteristics of a positive role model who is "living in a fishbowl"—having his or her actions constantly being observed by others.

Close
Have students explain the value of having positive peer role models. Then have them explain the value of being a positive peer role model.

Mentors and Mentoring

THE MENTORING RELATIONSHIP

A **mentor** is a person who engages in a supporting and guiding relationship with another person, usually over an extended period of time. A mentor provides caring, motivation, mutual trust, respect, guidance, support, encouragement, constructive comments and suggestions, and expertise in some area of need in another person's life. The **mentee** is the individual who is the recipient of the support. The mentee benefits from the kindness, patience, and generosity of the person who is acting as the mentor. Many times, a mentor is seen as a role model and as someone with whom the mentee wants to develop a relationship in order to imitate or achieve some of the mentor's positive traits or characteristics. However, the relationship between the mentor and mentee is more personal than that of most role models. The mentor works with the mentee to provide support and encouragement. This relationship usually exists between a more mature or experienced person and a less experienced person.

Mentoring is a planned set of interactions and opportunities that occur during the relationship between the mentor and mentee. Persons

© Emma Lee/Life File/Photodisc/Getty Images

serving in the role of mentor are sometimes called adviser, counselor, tutor, teacher, coach, or sponsor. Many times people are involved in a mentoring relationship, but they do not call the other person their mentor. Examine some of the relationships in your life to discover if you have anyone serving as a mentor that you may be calling by another title or name.

The Relationship Makes the Difference

The presence of a relationship and friendship at a somewhat personal level is the major difference between a role model and a mentor. Many of the role models you select—especially those who are famous—will never be in a personal relationship with you because your lives have no intersecting point or opportunity.

Although negative mentoring can take place, most mentoring is about a positive personal relationship between individuals in which interactions occur on a regular basis as determined by those involved. The mentor is usually a more mature and older, experienced, skilled or creative person than the mentee. There are times, however, when the age difference is not important, and a mentor can be someone of your own age. People who are your age may have had very different life experiences caused by family type or size, culture, geographic location, financial status, mental/emotional stability, self-awareness/self-esteem, or physical health. These different life experiences may result in one person being more experienced or more skilled in a particular area than another person. People's history can make a difference in how they come to be who they are. A person's needs or leadership abilities are often a direct result of his or her history.

Young people searching for personal direction can become involved in gangs or in groups that engage in a variety of negative activities. Even in these types of relationships, a type of mentoring can and does occur. A new gang member may want to imitate the actions and behaviors of the gang leader and may view that person as a role model who can become a mentor. For some students, this type of belonging is important to them because it gives them a group relationship and personal support. As is often said, negative attention is better than no attention at all. Although you may see this behavior as inappropriate and wrong, there are many individuals who believe that they benefit from these negative behaviors. Sometimes they even take part in these types of groups to survive in the neighborhoods where they live or to provide protection for others whom they believe have been victimized in some way.

On the other hand, there are the healthy, positive mentoring relationships that create constructive and supportive opportunities between individuals. They can lead to measurable growth, performance, achievement, and maturity for the person being mentored. Do

TEACH
Have students think about the relationships in which they are involved. Are there any relationships in which they feel they are the mentor rather than the mentee? In what way do they feel they are providing support and guidance to another person?

Discuss how a person's background or history can result in a mentoring relationship. If a person's background is lacking of certain experiences, a mentor can help fill in the gaps.

TEACHING STRATEGIES
Auditory Learners
Ask students to brainstorm a list of ways that they think they could benefit from having a mentor. When they are finished, have them discuss the items on their list.

you know individuals who work as leaders in community youth organizations? Persons volunteering in these roles serve as mentors. Do you or any of your friends serve as tutors for other students? In those tutoring sessions, do you find yourself offering advice to the young person you are tutoring on topics other than academics? If so, you are mentoring the person in that area. If you are an athlete, do you find yourself being approached by other less-capable team members to help them with their skills? Start paying closer attention to your relationships. You may discover that you are offering some level of mentoring to others and can have a positive impact on their lives.

Although the mentoring relationship can be positive or negative, it is in the best interest of the mentee to seek a positive and healthy person who can help improve the quality of the mentee's life in some measurable way.

A Mentor Is a Role Model

Keep in mind that a mentor is a role model, but a role model is not always a mentor. The entertainers, athletes, historical figures, and others who are often viewed as role models cannot be mentors to most people because their lives are far removed from those who look up to them. Tiger Woods, Michael Jordan, Sammy Sosa, Bruce Lee, Mia Hamm, Nelson Mandela, Venus Williams, Bill Gates, or Peyton Manning can be role models for many people but are only able to mentor people close to them.

CHECKPOINT

What is the major difference between a role model and a mentor?

Mentors have a close supportive relationship with their mentees. Many role models cannot be mentors because their lives are far removed from those who admire them.

FINDING THE RIGHT MENTOR

There are many different times in your life when you may need someone to help, guide, or assist you in some way. The reasons can range from needing someone to fill an adult role when a parent is not available to someone who will help you build the confidence and self-esteem you need to maintain your attendance, grades, and commitment to graduating from high school or college. There are times when you need a push to help you stay the course toward some particular goal or mission. Having a mentor serve as a "cheerleader" can be important to your present and future success.

When trying to find a mentor, it may be difficult to find a person who has all of the desired traits you would like to develop. Finding a mentor who meets the most urgent needs that you have in your life may be the best solution. You will have the opportunity to be mentored by many people in your lifetime and each can offer guidance and support in specific areas.

FIGURE 11.1   *The Role of a Mentor*

Mentor responsibilities include:

- Being available to the mentee—both physically and emotionally
- Providing direction and guidance on personal and school matters
- Providing support to enhance self-esteem
- Helping to identify strengths, skills, talents, and areas of weakness
- Helping to establish goals—both short-term and long-term—and providing motivation to achieve the goals

- Focusing on improving attitude, personality, social intelligence, and emotional stability
- Sharing knowledge and expertise in the areas of responsibility, accountability, communication, and teamwork
- Introducing you to and getting you involved in organizations that will enhance your learning experiences
- Providing encouragement and direction for leadership

Before choosing a mentor, consider his or her role. Figure 11.1 lists some of the most important responsibilities of a mentor. To get the most out of a mentor–mentee relationship, be sure the mentor you choose is able to meet these responsibilities.

Identifying Potential Mentors

Sometimes mentors come into your life because they see a need, void, or talent in your life that they believe they can help meet, fill, or support. You may already know them in another role, such as a teacher, coach, spiritual adviser, student organization leader, tutor, counselor, sister, brother, or friend. At other times, a mentor may enter your life because you have a specific need and have identified someone you admire who possesses character traits that you believe can help you.

When trying to identify people to serve as mentors, you might be guided by the characteristics of your personal identity as well as by issues you are facing in your personal, school, social, and family life. A few of the variables you may use to select a mentor include gender, nationality, race, religion, mutual interests, personality, attitude, academic expertise, or skills and talents.

Gender

Gender is sometimes important when choosing a mentor. In some types of athletics, people may prefer a mentor of the same gender, while in others the gender of the mentor may not be important. When a young child is matched with a Big Brother or Big Sister, those pairings are usually made by gender.

Nationality and Race

Finding a mentor from the same nationality can sometimes present a problem. Individuals living as a minority in a majority culture often prefer to have someone from their own nationality, culture, or ethnicity as a mentor. They may believe that someone from their own culture will have a better understanding of the unique issues that they are

TEACH
Have students review the variables that they might use to select a mentor. What variable do students feel is the most important one for them when selecting a mentor?

Ask students to name some situations in which the gender of the mentor might be important to the mentoring relationship.

Have students discuss the reasons that an individual might want to have a mentor of the same nationality or race. Ask students what, if any, benefits can result from having a mentor from a different nationality or race. Have them explain their answers.

© Duncan Smith/Photodisc/Getty Images

facing. Unfortunately, individuals fitting their profile may not be available in certain geographic regions. If they live in a college town or an urban area, there is a greater possibility of finding a mentor based on nationality. A good way to find a mentor based on nationality may be to ask others close to you for recommendations.

Individuals often seek a mentor who is of the same race. Finding role models is not as difficult because they can be found in the entertainment industry, athletics, politics, or business. However, finding a local mentor may be more difficult, particularly if the person desiring the mentor is one of only a few minorities in his or her school, town, or job site. All too often, students in minority groups realize that their experiences, viewpoints, and ways of doing things do not fit into the mainstream or majority population. Therefore, if you are a member of one of these groups and you find yourself being the "only one" or "one of a few" in your school, class, organization, or team, you may feel the need to make uncomfortable changes in order to fit into the majority group. A mentor of the same race can show you how to embrace the uniqueness of your ethnicity while being the best you can be.

Religion

People who are affiliated with a religious organization often turn to their religion to find a mentor. Mentors from the area of religion reach out as spiritual advisers to people who share their faith as well as to others in the community. They try to create a safe and open environment in which the relationship can exist. Mentors may also be found in private church schools in which the curriculum, the student body, and the administration embrace the religious beliefs that are important to them. There are also religious clubs that meet and worship on some public school campuses with the school district's approval and support. Individuals for whom this is important should research the available options for practicing their faith. Mentors can help answer spiritual questions and offer guidance in making moral and ethical decisions.

Mutual Interest

The basis for many mentoring relationships is a mutual interest such as a hobby, technical skill, or career area. The mutual interest may be obvious at the beginning of the mentoring relationship, or it may be discovered as the relationship grows. An older, more experienced mentor who has built his or her interest over time can offer valuable advice to younger mentees who are in the early stages of developing their interest.

Personality, Attitude, Academic Expertise, and Skill or Talent

Character traits such as personality, attitude, academic expertise, and skill or talent can make or break a mentoring relationship. Individuals with the right character traits have the potential of making excellent role models and mentors. If having a mentor is of great importance to you, you should be open-minded to a diverse group of people. Who the person is may not be as important as the characteristics that person possesses. A good mentor is a person who

- Is a positive role model
- Is emotionally stable and can tolerate frustrating situations
- Has positive self-esteem and self-awareness
- Devotes time and attention to the mentee
- Engages in positive interactions with the mentee
- Communicates well on the mentee's level and is a good listener
- Provides effective leadership
- Has the knowledge and expertise needed to guide the mentee

Mentoring Considerations

Mentoring relationships have existed for centuries. There has always been a need for people to learn and grow from the experience, knowledge, skills, and know-how of one another. During the mentoring process, there are many things to consider. Four common considerations in a mentoring relationship include the level of formality, the mentoring location, the number of individuals being mentored, and the time frame for the commitment.

Level of Formality

Both formal and informal levels of mentoring exist. Formal activities may include tutoring, educational guidance, and career development. Informal activities involve casual time spent together that may or may not be directly related to the area of mentoring. Informal activities usually encourage personal growth in the areas of self-esteem, culture, or social and interpersonal skills.

Mentoring Location

Mentors and mentees may meet and interact in their home, community, school, or workplace or by Internet or e-mail. The mentoring location may depend upon the goals of the mentoring relationship. If leadership development is the goal, mentoring may take place in the community. Academic support may be provided at school. Job advice may come from a mentor at work. Providing general advice and information may take place using the Internet or e-mail.

Number of Individuals Being Mentored

The number of individuals being mentored can vary. Mentoring can take place one-on-one, in a team or group, or even as part of a family. Mentoring activities may involve individual tutoring sessions. Individual or group sessions may be used for personal and professional

TEACH
Based on the characteristics listed in the text, have students compile a short list of individuals whom they would like to have as potential mentors.

TEACH
Write the words *formal* and *informal* on the board. Ask students to name mentoring activities that they consider to be formal activities and mentoring activities that they consider to be informal activities. List their answers on the board under each heading and discuss.

Ask students if they think a mentor and mentee can develop a satisfactory mentoring relationship using only the Internet or e-mail instead of meeting in person. What, if any, limitations do they see to an online mentoring relationship?

Ask students if they think an individual can effectively mentor more than one person, such as a group or a team, or if a successful mentoring relationship needs to be one-on-one only. Have them explain their answers.

TEACHING STRATEGIES
Kinesthetic Learners
Have students create a poster or computer-generated presentation of the things that need to be considered during the mentoring process.

development. Families may meet with counselors for support and guidance of the family unit. Whole families may work with a counselor to serve as mentors for one family member who needs specific assistance.

Time Frame for Commitment

The mentor and mentee should jointly decide the time frame for the mentoring relationship. How long will the relationship continue? The time frame is affected by the goal the individual has set and the time constraints of the mentor and the mentee. Ideally, the mentoring relationship would continue until the mentee achieves his or her goal. The time frame that the mentor and mentee are willing to commit to the relationship will affect the types of activities and experiences involved. In the mentoring relationship, activities and experiences may include tutoring, spending casual time together, and exploring personal, educational, and career options. The more time a mentor and mentee can devote to the mentoring relationship, the more benefits the mentee will gain.

Start with a Self-Appraisal

A self-appraisal is a good place to start the process of selecting the right mentor. To conduct the self-appraisal, ask yourself the following questions:

- What are my needs?
- What are my strengths and weaknesses?
- What are my immediate goals?
- What skills and talents do I want to improve?
- Am I willing to work with someone of a different gender, nationality, race, or religion?
- Am I willing to work with someone who has a very different personality than mine?
- What are my career interests?
- What type of training or support do I need or desire?
- How much effort am I willing to put into the mentoring relationship?

 CHECKPOINT

What variables might you use to select a mentor?

Variables for selecting a mentor may include gender, nationality, race, religion, mutual interests, personality, attitude, academic expertise, and skills or talents.

Follow UP

UNDERSTAND LEADERSHIP CONCEPTS

Circle the best answer for each of the following questions.

1. Mentors are
   a. people you admire from a distance
   b. individuals who engage in caring relationships with another person over time to provide caring and guidance
   c. people who always work with only one person at a time
   d. people who are always older than the person being mentored

2. An example of a mentoring relationship is
   a. a student who is interested in science and a biology teacher
   b. a professional athlete and an adoring fan at home
   c. a student and a historical character
   d. all of the above

THINK *CRITICALLY*

Answer the following questions as completely as possible. If necessary, use a separate sheet of paper.

3. Describe a relationship in your personal life that compares to the relationship between a mentor and a mentee.
Answers will vary.
_____
_____
_____
_____

4. Describe a situation in which you believe a person can mentor more than one individual at a time.
Answers will vary but may include mentoring a team or an academic group or even
providing support and counseling for an entire family.
_____
_____

5. Describe a need or situation in your life in which you believe having a mentor could support you in a nurturing and helpful way.
Answers will vary.
_____
_____
_____
_____

ASSESS
Reteach
Have students list the variables they can use to identify a mentor. For each variable, have them write one or two sentences explaining the value of using that variable to select a mentor.

Enrich
Have students develop a plan for the creation of a mentoring program in their school to help new students feel more comfortable and become acclimated to their new school environment. Have them present their plan to the school administration.

Close
Ask students to explain why conducting a self-appraisal is a good way to start the process of selecting the right mentor.

Chapter Assessment

TEACHING RESOURCES
ExamView® CD, Ch. 11

a. formal role models
b. informal role models
c. mentee
d. mentor
e. mentoring
f. peer role models
g. personal role models
h. public role models
i. role model
j. underrepresented groups

REVIEW *LEADERSHIP CONCEPTS*

Write the letter of the term that matches each definition. Some terms will not be used.

___h___ 1. People whom you admire because of their impact on the large-scale growth of your community

___b___ 2. Persons whom you know casually and whose skills and talents you admire

___c___ 3. The recipient of the kindness, patience, and generosity of the person acting as the mentor

___i___ 4. Someone whose character, behavior, attitude, personality, or skills serve as a good example to follow

___d___ 5. A person who engages in a relationship with another person and provides expertise in some area of need

___f___ 6. Other students who exhibit character traits that you respect and appreciate

___g___ 7. People in your household or neighborhood that you have known for a long time and whose behavior you admire

___e___ 8. Actions, behaviors, experiences, and opportunities that occur during the relationship between the mentor and mentee

___a___ 9. Persons who have earned your admiration in a professional way

Circle the best answer.

10. *Role models are always*
    a. found in your local community
    b. mentors
    c. older than you
    d. none of the above

11. *A mentoring relationship*
    a. is one-on-one all of the time
    b. can include more than one mentee
    c. is always short-term
    d. none of the above

12. *Four common considerations in mentoring relationship are*
    a. location, time frame, income, athletic ability
    b. time frame, number of individuals in the relationship, location, age of mentor
    c. time frame of the commitment, location, number of individuals being mentored, level of formality
    d. none of the above

ASSESS

Reteach

Have students write ten true-or-false questions from material in the chapter. Then have students exchange papers with a classmate and answer their partner's questions. Have students and their partners check their answers for accuracy.

Enrich

Organize a panel discussion with several guest speakers who can talk to the class about the benefits of mentoring. The panel should include both mentors and mentees who can discuss various aspects of the mentoring relationship. Have students prepare questions in advance to ask panel members after their presentation.

CLOSE

Ask students to explain the differences between role models and mentors. Have them discuss the benefits of each.

THINK *CRITICALLY*

13. Find a historical role model that you admire and describe your reasons for this admiration.

Answers will vary depending on the historical role model.

_____

_____

_____

_____

14. Which of the four common considerations in mentoring relationships do you think has the greatest influence on the relationship? Explain why.

Answers will vary depending on which of the four common considerations in the

mentoring relationship is chosen—level of formality, mentoring location, number of

individuals being mentored, or time frame for the commitment.

_____

_____

15. Unfortunately, not all role models are positive ones. Identify an athlete or entertainer who has exhibited negative or inappropriate behavior. Describe the behavior and its impact on how you now view that person.

Answers will vary depending on the athlete or entertainer students identify.

_____

_____

_____

_____

16. Why is it important for you to realize that others may be watching you and viewing you as a role model or potential mentor?

It is important to realize that others who admire you may model your behavior. In

order to be a positive role model, you must try to avoid negative or disruptive behavior

that could be a harmful influence on others.

_____

_____

17. What is meant by the saying, "A mentor is a role model, but a role model is not necessarily a mentor"?

A mentor engages in a supporting and guiding relationship with others. That person

can also be a role model if his or her character and behavior set a positive example for

others. A role model, on the other hand, may not necessarily be a mentor because

some role models, such as entertainers and athletes, do not have a personal

relationship in which they provide support and guidance to those who admire them.

MAKE CONNECTIONS

18. **Research**   It is important to have some role models that are of the same race or gender as you. Use the Internet, magazines, and other documentation to create a pictorial representation of role models of your own race, culture, ethnicity, or gender. Describe your feelings of connectedness to these role models.

Answers will vary.

_____

_____

_____

_____

_____

19. **Media**   Watch a television program or movie that has an ethnically diverse cast. Select one of the characters and describe why you think that person could be viewed as a role model by others. Then select another character from the program or movie that you believe should not be viewed as a role model and explain why.

Answers will vary.

_____

_____

_____

_____

_____

20. **Research**   Use the Internet or other sources to learn about a local community outreach program for youth. Research the services they offer and determine if they have a mentoring program. Describe the mentoring program and the requirements for serving as a mentor. Would you like to be a mentor in this program? Explain why or why not.

Answers will vary.

_____

_____

_____

_____

21. **Communication**   Select someone who has been a personal role model or mentor to you. Write a note, thanking that person for his or her presence and influence in your life.

Answers will vary.

_____

_____

_____

_____

LEARNING TO LEAD

FOCUS

Learn about member and chapter recognition in student organizations.

DESCRIPTION

Recognitions and rewards are powerful motivators. While recognitions and rewards should not be the primary reason for the work of student organization members, seeing their efforts valued by others increases self-esteem and personal satisfaction. When they are recognized, members have increased loyalty and respect for each other and their leaders. They take greater pride in the organization and its work. In this activity, you will learn about the opportunities and types of individual member, team, and chapter recognitions that are available through your student organization and the requirements for members and chapters to earn recognition for their work.

LEARNING TO LEAD
This project is written for use with student organizations such as BPA, DECA, and FBLA. Student organizations can help students prepare for key leadership roles. After students complete the activities, discuss what they learned about their student organization.

ACTIVITIES

1. *Visit the web sites of your national and state student organizations. Identify the types of recognitions and rewards that are available to individual members, teams, and the entire chapter. Take notes on each type of recognition, what type of activity or achievement is being recognized, and the procedures to follow to earn the recognition.*

2. *Review student organization publications and find news stories about members and chapters that recently received recognition for their activities and achievements. Learn more about what was done that resulted in the recognition and how the recipients felt about the honor.*

3. *Survey several students to determine how the possibility of earning recognitions and rewards influences their decision to participate in a group, complete an activity, or put extra effort into their school work, job, or community service activity.*

Activities
1. Answers will vary.
2. Answers will vary.
3. Answers will vary. Students should create a short questionnaire that others can complete.

Share Your Results
1. The recognition program, individual assignments, and plan for completion should be agreed upon by all group members.
2. The team should schedule regular meetings to make sure everyone is on track with individual assignments.
3. Whether or not the team wins recognition or a reward from the student organization, it is important to recognize the team's successful completion of the project.

SHARE YOUR RESULTS

1. *In a small group, identify a team or chapter recognition program you would like to complete. Obtain approval to work on the activity from your chapter adviser. As a team, develop a plan of activities to complete. Assign one or more activities to each team member.*
2. *Implement the plan your team has developed. Provide support and feedback to each other to make sure each activity is completed according to the standards required for the recognition. Make sure you prepare the necessary reports and materials to document your work and to apply for the recognition.*
3. *Continue to evaluate your efforts to determine whether they will meet the requirements for the recognition. At the completion of the project, prepare a celebration for your team to recognize the contributions of each member and the accomplishments of the team.*

ACCEPTING THE
CHALLENGE
Case Study 11
Ask students to think of
the members of their own
family. Are there family
members whom they ad-
mire and instinctively turn
to for support and advice?
Do they recognize those
individuals as mentors?

ACCEPTING THE CHALLENGE

CASE STUDY 11—HONORING YOUR ROLE MODELS AND MENTORS

As you learned in the opening scenario, What Would You Do?, Yvette greatly admired her sister and sisters-in-law. Because they were older and had more life experiences, she trusted their opinions. She took their advice and went to a college out of state. She lived on campus and easily made many new friends. She approached all of her activities with confidence and enthusiasm, which, in turn, motivated those around her to do the same. Both her friends and professors often complimented her on her can-do, positive attitude. She always gave credit to those wonderful women in her life. Yvette explained how they had loved, supported, and counseled her in many ways, helping her become the person she had become. They were always there to help point her in the right direction. They approached everything with a positive attitude and a pleasant personality. As she described the influences of her family, Yvette realized that her sister and sisters-in-law were not only her family but also her role models and mentors in life. Yvette encouraged her friends to develop mentoring relationships of their own to help them be the best they could be.

THINK CRITICALLY

1. *In what ways were Yvette's sister and sisters-in-law her mentors? In what areas of her life did they mentor her?*

Yvette's sister and sisters-in-law offered her support and advice in her personal life as well as her academic life. By advising her to attend college away from home, they helped her develop independence, self-confidence, and maturity.

2. *Why do you think Yvette recommended that her friends seek out mentors? Do you think mentoring relationships are valuable? Why or why not?*

Answers will vary. Because Yvette had such a positive experience in the mentoring relationship with her sister and sisters-in-law, she wanted to see her friends enjoy the benefits of a similar positive experience with a mentor.

3. *Describe ways to recognize and show appreciation to the family members who serve as role models or mentors in your life.*

Answers will vary but may include writing a thank-you note or letter of appreciation to let them know that your successes are due in part to their help and support.

APPLY WHAT YOU HAVE LEARNED–Honor Roll

DIRECTIONS: *In order for you to reflect on the role models and mentors who have helped guide and direct you in some way, complete the following* Honor Roll of Role Models and Mentors *using the form below or on your Student Activity CD. In the last column of the Honor Roll, describe the impact your role model or mentor has had on your life.*

HONOR ROLL OF ROLE MODELS AND MENTORS

Name	Type of Role Model (public, personal, formal, informal)	Role Model or Mentor?	Impact on My Life

After reflecting on the importance of role models or mentors in your life, consider taking on these roles yourself. On the lines below or using your Student Activity CD, create a SMART goal (including a completion date) that will help you to become a role model or mentor to someone else. Record your goal in a monthly calendar (on the CD or your own). Then enter your thoughts, ideas, and discussions related to your goal in a journal (on the CD or your own) to help you plan and track your progress. Recruit a goal-setting partner to help you put your plan into action.

_____

_____

_____

_____

_____

ACCEPTING THE CHALLENGE

Apply What You Have Learned—Honor Roll Note that students can complete this part of the *Accepting the Challenge* activity in the book or on the Student Activity CD. Instructions are provided on the CD.

After students have answered the questions in this activity, instruct them to write a SMART goal (including a completion date) that will help them to become a role model or mentor to others. Have them enter their goal on a monthly calendar. Students can use the monthly calendar on the Student Activity CD or their own calendar. Explain to students that they may also use weekly calendar pages (on the Student Activity CD or their own calendar) to plan activities and tasks that will help them achieve their goals. Finally, direct students to use a journal (on the Student Activity CD or their own) to track and evaluate their progress in achieving their goal.

A goal-setting partner can add an element of accountability and can offer positive feedback to help students stay on track to achieve their goals.

Students should be given the opportunity to reflect on the progress they have made toward achieving their goal. To do this, students can complete the *Evaluate Your Progress* activity on the Student Activity CD. Stress to students that it is important to complete this activity on the original target completion date even if they have not met their goal at that time.

Leading into the Future

© Digital Vision/Getty Images

12.1 *Future Leadership Roles*

12.2 *What Employers Expect*

12.3 *Visionary Leadership*

What would **YOU** do?

RODERICK'S DESTINY

Roderick's interest in medicine began in high school with his participation in the Medical Explorers, a Boy Scouts program in New York. During his high school years, Roderick was also a Red Cross volunteer. Roderick was mentored by doctors at the famous Blueberry Hill Hospital of New York. They taught him how to take patients' blood pressure and vital signs. The doctors were good mentors for Roderick. He enjoyed hanging out with them, even in the emergency room. On several occasions, he was taught how to suture a wound for a patient. This experience was quite exciting for a teenager who believed that becoming a doctor was his destiny.

Roderick continued pursuing his dream of becoming a doctor by enrolling in medical school in Tennessee. Roderick's experience at Blueberry Hill Hospital gave him an advantage over the other medical students and interns. During his residency, he was selected over other doctors to perform a heart and liver transplant on an important state official. After the successful operation and the patient's recovery, Roderick received much praise.

Although Roderick was happy about his decision to become a doctor, doubts started creeping into his mind. During high school, he had also participated in another Boy Scouts program called the Police Explorers. Roderick enjoyed the adventurous experiences he had while a member of that group. He began having visions of becoming a state trooper with the New York State Police. Was being a doctor really his destiny? Roderick thought long and hard about what he should do. He knew that he wanted to do something that would make a difference in other people's lives. He decided that practicing medicine was the best way for him to do that. Today, Roderick is a distinguished surgeon in a rural community hospital where he works to improve the quality of life for others.

THINK *CRITICALLY*

1. How did Roderick prepare himself for a future leadership role in medicine?

2. Describe the important role Roderick's mentoring relationships with other doctors played in helping him fulfill his destiny.

3. If you had doubts or concerns about some of your career choices, what would you do to resolve them?

TEACHING RESOURCES
Instructor's Resource CD
Lesson Plans, Ch. 12
PowerPoint Slides, Ch. 12

Student Activity CD, Ch. 12

thomsonedu.com/school/ leading
Crossword Puzzle, Ch. 12
Flash Cards, Ch. 12

Exam*View*® **CD**, Ch. 12

CHAPTER OVERVIEW
Chapter 12 discusses future leadership roles and employers' expectations and defines visionary leadership.

Lesson 12.1
Describes leadership roles in a changing society and explains coaching techniques.

Lesson 12.2
Explains future trends in the workforce and identifies future career opportunities.

Lesson 12.3
Discusses the importance of visionary leadership and explains the value of cultural competence in the workplace.

WHAT WOULD YOU DO?
Ask students to think about their own career interests. What steps can they take to help them prepare for their future career?

Think Critically Answers
1. Roderick joined the Medical Explorers program, became a Red Cross volunteer, and was mentored by other doctors.
2. The doctors at Blueberry Hill Hospital were good role models. Roderick's experiences gave him an advantage over other medical students and interns.
3. Answers will vary but may include seeking advice from a trusted adviser or mentor.

Future Leadership Roles

- Describe some future leadership roles in our changing society.
- Explain how coaching techniques are used to mentor others.

- legacy
- self-directed leader
- facilitator
- change agent

SCHEDULE
Block 45 minutes
Regular 1 class period

FOCUS
Ask students to think about the concept of change. How does change affect a leader's role?

YOUR LEGACY AS A LEADER

Preparing for future leadership roles begins with your first position as a leader and continues with many life experiences. It starts within you as a self-directed person who is willing to lead your classmates and friends, whether as captain of your high school baseball team or as president of a student organization.

Due to changes in our society, leadership roles are also changing. Future leadership roles will focus more on relationships with others rather than on the traditional authoritarian approach of directing and controlling others. Future leaders will often be mentors as well as coaches. Your positive relationships with others will increase your effectiveness in future leadership roles. Positive relationships involve working together with others in harmony to accomplish a goal or resolve a particular problem.

Building relationships with others is the beginning of your legacy as a leader. Regardless of the leadership roles you undertake, your **legacy** involves how your classmates, friends, teachers, and others will remember you. Have you ever thought about the legacy you want to leave behind as a leader in your school?

A successful legacy begins with a commitment to make a difference as a leader in the lives of your classmates, friends, and family, and it continues into adulthood. As you develop as a leader beyond high school, you can find ways to make a difference and contribute to society. Are you ready to make a difference in your school and community? What legacy will you leave behind?

© Ryan McVay/Photodisc/Getty Images

Cecilia was a rising senior in high school, but she was struggling with her assignments and tests in her science class. She always studied hard, but she still could not seem to grasp the concepts taught by her teacher or covered in her textbook. Cecilia decided to get a science tutor to help her improve her grades. After a few weeks of tutoring sessions, Cecilia was much more confident about her knowledge and understanding of the subject. A big test was coming up, and Cecilia felt ready for it.

During the test, Cecilia noticed that one of her classmates was using a cell phone to take pictures of the science test to share with others. She was shocked and disappointed to see this type of unethical behavior in one or her classmates. Cecilia had worked so hard to prepare for the test, and she did not think it was fair for others to have an unfair advantage.

THINK *CRITICALLY*

What would you do in this situation? Do you think there should be rules about using personal technology products in school?

▌Self-Directed Leadership Role

What drives your passion to become an effective leader? Do you think that you have a "higher calling" to be a leader in the future? Do you try to do the right thing even though you may not always do everything right? If so, you may be a self-directed leader. A **self-directed leader** is a person with the character, values, purpose, and courage to do the right thing even when no one is watching.

Your willingness to do the right thing is a matter of choice and not circumstances. There are no exceptions, reasons, or excuses for doing something that you know is not right. Your character and values influence you to do the right things. Even if others are making a different choice, you can rely on courage. Courage will help guide you when you are tempted or encouraged by those around you to make a decision that challenges or goes against what you believe is the right thing to do. It also gives you the strength to take positive risks that can lead to your growth as a leader.

As a self-directed leader, you have focused on an important purpose in your life and are moving toward it. Sometimes, you may stumble, make a mistake, or lose focus. When that happens, you will have the courage to recover and go forward. Everyone makes mistakes sometimes, but leaders with character have the courage to recognize them and learn from them. This is part of the recovery process. In most cases, you can recover from unintentional mistakes, but difficulties may occur if you cannot move on in positive ways. Are you willing to forgive yourself if you make a mistake? More important, how long will it take you to get over the incident and move on toward your goals? Although it is understandable to feel bad after making a mistake, you should not let it reduce your effectiveness as a leader. Taking the first step in the recovery process can be difficult but also personally rewarding. Learn from the mistakes, then put them behind you and focus on what you can do now to accomplish your mission.

TEACH
Ask students why they think a collaborative approach to leadership is more effective than a traditional authoritarian approach. What skills or qualities do they think a future leader must have in order to work collaboratively with others?

Have students think about a time when they made a mistake or lost their focus. How were they able to recover and continue moving toward their goal?

TECH ETHICS
Ask students if they have ever been aware of a classmate behaving unethically, such as cheating on a test. How did it make them feel? What, if anything, did they do? Discuss some of the ethical issues in the classroom relating to technology.

Think Critically Answers
Answers will vary.

CHARACTER *Builder*

When it comes to change, check your attitude. How well you manage change says a lot about your character. Try to view change as an exciting new beginning rather than something to fear.

As a leader, you should strive for excellence, but not perfection. Always remember that all leaders make mistakes from time to time. If you try to be perfect, you will be setting yourself up for failure. It also may cause you to be too careful and reluctant to make hard decisions. Be the best person and leader that you can possibly be. It is your choice.

Your Future Roles as a Leader

During your leadership journey, you will be faced with many challenging roles. These roles will demonstrate your ability to lead others by showing that you have what it takes to be an effective leader. One such role is that of a facilitator. A **facilitator** is someone who assists, guides, and supervises others in order to reach a desired outcome. The facilitator is willing to delegate responsibilities and empower others to become leaders. Are you willing to empower others in your group or organization to help them grow and develop as successful leaders? More important, are you committed to spending quality time with the members of your group to enhance their leadership development? If you take the time to empower members of your group and offer advice and guidance when they need it, you will more likely get positive results while helping to improve their leadership skills.

Another role you may take on as a leader is that of a change agent. A **change agent** is someone who makes meaningful changes that add value to a group or an organization. Making a difference should be the ultimate goal of a leader. But making a difference often means making changes. Changes may involve how things are done, who does them, and when things are done.

Because people often resist change, being a change agent might not be easy. People fear what they do not understand. You have to be sure the members of your group understand the reasons for the change. You also have to be willing to listen to others' concerns and address them. Why do we have to redesign the school newspaper when the old design already looks good? Why does our group have to meet twice a week instead of once a week? As a change agent and leader, you have to have valid answers to these questions. Support your reasons for making change by explaining or showing how it will benefit the members of the group as well as those people the group serves.

CHECKPOINT

Explain why it is important for a facilitator to spend quality time with members of the group.

It is important for a facilitator to spend quality time with members of the group in order to enhance their leadership development.

COACHING TECHNIQUES

You have learned that a mentor is someone who engages in a supporting and guiding relationship with another person. A leader can be a mentor by providing advice, constructive suggestions, and encouragement in order to improve the mentee's chances of achieving his or her important personal goals. If you accept the role of mentor, you are making a commitment to share your expertise and advice with others. You are agreeing to nurture their development as future leaders.

Future leadership roles may require you to use coaching techniques as part of the mentoring process. *Coaching* involves teaching, motivating, directing, and encouraging others to reach their potential. This particular leadership technique is not about athletics even though that is where you often hear about coaching. Coaching can be used in all parts of life as a way to motivate others to be productive and successful.

Coaching techniques take mentoring to a much higher level. This leadership role requires you to be responsible and committed to the learning process. Being someone's coach is similar to a teacher and student relationship. Coaching is based on a positive relationship that has a strong professional foundation. Developing positive relationships with others as a part of helping them to improve should not be confused with being a "buddy" to them. You can be friendly, but as a coach, you must maintain your professionalism and remain focused on the task at hand.

There may be opportunities to be a short-term coach without being a mentor. These opportunities may include tutoring a younger student to help him or her become more proficient in a subject area, helping a member of your local student organization prepare for a competitive event, or teaching a new coworker the correct way to complete a job task. The goal of using coaching techniques as a teaching tool is to improve the performance of others through personal attention and support.

CHECKPOINT

What are the leadership responsibilities of a coach?

The leadership responsibilities of a coach include teaching, motivating, directing, and encouraging others to reach their potential.

ONGOING ASSESSMENT
Use the Checkpoint as an opportunity to conduct ongoing assessment of student comprehension of the lesson material.

TEACH
Have students list the current opportunities they may have to be a short-term coach to another person. Are there any coaching opportunities on their list that they could pursue right now to enhance their leadership development?

TEACHING STRATEGIES
Gifted Students
Limited English Proficiency Students
Assign students to work with a partner in a coaching role. Students may help their partners improve performance in an academic subject or in the completion of a project or task. (LEP students also may benefit from having a "conversation partner" to help them understand colloquial expressions.)

Follow UP

UNDERSTAND LEADERSHIP CONCEPTS

Circle the best answer for each of the following questions.

1. Preparing for future leadership roles may begin by
   a. serving as a facilitator
   b. serving as a change agent
   c. serving as a coach
   d. all of the above *(circled)*

2. A self-directed leader should have all of the following traits except
   a. good character
   b. a purpose in life
   c. a perfectionist attitude *(circled)*
   d. courage

THINK *CRITICALLY*

Answer the following questions as completely as possible. If necessary, use a separate sheet of paper.

3. Describe the legacy that you plan to leave behind after graduating from high school, college, or in your first job.

Answers will vary.
_____
_____
_____

4. As a self-directed leader, can you think of an exception or excuse that would allow you to do something that you know is not right? Explain your answer.

There are no exceptions, reasons, or excuses for doing things that you know are not

right.
_____
_____
_____

5. What is a change agent? Describe how you could be a change agent as the leader of a student organization.

A change agent is someone who makes meaningful changes that add value to a group

or an organization. As the leader of a student organization, you must be able to show

the members of the group why the change is necessary and how it will benefit

everyone involved.
_____

ASSESS
Reteach
Have students list the various future leadership roles—facilitator, change agent, and coach—and write a brief description of the characteristics of each role.

Enrich
Invite a coach to speak to the class about the types of techniques coaches use. (The speaker may be a business coach, personal coach, or athletic coach.)

Close
Ask students to describe how coaching takes mentoring to a much higher level.

What Employers Expect

- Explain the future trends that are occurring in the workplace.
- Identify the career areas and future career opportunities in the workplace.

- trend
- career clusters

FUTURE TRENDS IN THE WORKFORCE

After graduating from high school, you will be faced with many life decisions. You will have to decide whether to continue on to college, enter the military services, or take the first steps toward your dream job or career. What decisions have you made concerning your future? What type of employment or work do you see yourself doing in the near future? Your answers to these questions could determine your future career path.

When thinking about your future career, you might want to consider the trends. A **trend** is the general direction in which things are moving. Future trends that can affect your career will include major changes or innovations in the workplace and society. Technology will continue to improve and change the way you do things at home and work. Other trends that will affect your life include an increase in international business, which will require employees to be well prepared to work in a global work environment. Additionally, trends include flexible employment schedules. Telecommuting will allow millions of people to work from their home computers. A greater emphasis on character qualities, such as ethics, honesty, integrity, caring, self-discipline, and forward-thinking, is also becoming a trend. Future trends in the workplace should be exciting to future leaders who are willing and eager to accept the challenges of a rapidly changing, high-tech, and service-oriented workplace.

© Patagonik Works/Photodisc/Getty Images

SCHEDULE
Block 45 minutes
Regular 1 class period

FOCUS
Ask students what qualities or characteristics they think employers expect new employees to have. Write their answers on the board.

During the job fair at your school for summer employment, you were surprised to see that several of your friends and classmates shared your interest in the same employer—a local television station. In talking with the others, you learned that, although your career goals were different, all of you shared interests in the television industry. It was exciting to know that different career goals could possibly be met through the same company.

You decided it would be a good idea to organize a support group to learn more about the career opportunities in the field of television and video production. The group meetings would also help members prepare for the interviews for summer employment. Everyone was excited about the idea of learning and studying as a team.

THINK CRITICALLY

Explain what approach your team could take to examine job opportunities in a particular area of interest. Do you think a support group is a good way to learn about and prepare for careers? Why or why not?

Meeting the Employment Needs of the Future

What are the best jobs of the future? Can you find a job that meets your personal goals and interests, utilizes your skills and educational preparation, and offers good prospects for future employment? Most career areas offer a variety of opportunities with entry level jobs right out of high school and advanced, high-skilled jobs requiring additional education and experience.

There are many career areas to consider. Engineering jobs are a growth area for the future. The need for engineers represents a serious shortage in the United States because other countries are producing more engineering graduates. China produces more than 600,000 new engineers each year, and India produces 350,000. In comparison, the United States produces only 70,000 new engineers each year. U.S. employers will be challenged to maintain a competitive edge over these other countries.

Another career area projected to have high growth is that of education and training. If you are interested in becoming a teacher, now is the time to begin to prepare yourself. In the next ten years, the United States will need millions of new teachers to replace the aging population of retiring teachers.

Although there is a demand for new teachers in most academic areas, there is a greater demand for mathematics and science teachers. Foreign language is another projected high growth area in education. Consider taking all the math and science courses that you can as well as learning one or more foreign languages. They will improve your chances of success in the workplace even if you decide not to pursue a teaching career.

If you are excited about being a teacher but do not choose a career in education, there is a wide range of jobs in corporate training. Businesses have a rapidly growing need to train and retrain their workforce due to new technology and increasing demands for higher productivity.

Traditional training roles will require instructors to lead training classes for new employees. People with advanced technology skills will be needed to develop computerized simulations and training videos for corporations. Distance learning is a major trend in delivering training around the world. People with web-design and other computer skills will be needed to plan and carry out distance learning programs.

In addition to the career areas already discussed, there are many other career areas that offer attractive future opportunities. Whether your interests lie in technical careers, the sciences, service careers, or arts and theater, you can find jobs that meet your interests and needs if you are well informed and well prepared.

© Keith Brofsky/Photodisc/Getty Images

Employers' Expectations

Are you knowledgeable about future high-tech jobs and careers needed in the workplace? Are you aware of what employers might expect from you in terms of job readiness skills and leadership qualities? Your future success with employers will be based more on preparation than on luck. Remember the saying that "luck is preparation meeting opportunity."

Employers want hard-working employees who have good leadership qualities, strong character, strong interpersonal skills, enthusiasm, and motivation. The more skills you take to a job, the more valuable you are to your employer. These skills will result in more job responsibilities, faster promotions, and career advancements.

The expectations that employers have of you as a high school graduate are within your reach to meet. As you reflect on your leadership development, you should realize that the qualities of a leader and the expectations of employers are basically the same. For example, employers expect you to possess

- foundational skills, or basic skills in reading, writing, and mathematics
- communication skills
- a positive attitude that demonstrates responsibility and accountability
- a good work ethic
- interpersonal or social skills, such as being friendly, respectful, and courteous to others
- honesty and trustworthiness
- decision-making skills
- a willingness to adapt to frequent changes in the high-tech workplace
- a spirit of collaboration and teamwork
- cultural diversity awareness that is accepting and respectful of people from other ethnicities, races, and religious backgrounds

TEACH
Have students review the list of employers' expectations in the text and make a note of any quality or skill in which they may need improvement. For each item they have listed, have them write a statement indicating how they might improve that particular skill. How are employer expectations and leadership qualities similar?

TEACHING STRATEGIES
Gifted Students
Have students interview local employers about what they expect from their employees. What qualities do they value most in new employees? Have students report their findings to the class.

TEACHING STRATEGIES
Kinesthetic Students
Have students create a questionnaire to be distributed to local employers listing the ten expectations that employers have of employees. Have them ask employers to rank the items in order of importance, with 1 being the most important and 10 being the least important. Have students tally the results and report their findings to the class.

Consider how well you meet employer expectations. Determine your strengths and areas of weakness and work to improve them.

 CHECKPOINT

List three expectations that employers have of high school graduates entering the workplace.

Employers expect basic skills, a positive attitude, a good work ethic, social skills, honesty, decision-making skills, a willingness to adapt, teamwork, and cultural diversity awareness.

MAKING YOUR CAREER DECISION

As you consider your future employment choices, you will find that there are many career areas or pathways and future career opportunities for you to explore. Whether you are interested in pursuing a technical, liberal arts, engineering, science, or teaching career, the 16 career clusters developed by the U.S. Department of Education may be a valuable source in helping you make decisions. **Career clusters** are categories of related occupations and careers and include the following:

- Agriculture, Food, and Natural Resources
- Architecture and Construction
- Arts, Audio/Visual Technology, and Communications
- Business, Management, and Administration
- Education and Training
- Finance
- Government and Public Administration
- Health Science
- Hospitality and Tourism
- Human Services
- Information Technology
- Law, Public Safety, Corrections, and Security
- Manufacturing
- Marketing, Sales, and Service
- Science, Technology, Engineering, and Mathematics
- Transportation, Distribution, and Logistics

The clusters are designed to provide assistance for more effective coordinated career planning. They are used by state educational agencies, local schools and students, colleges and universities, employers, and other interested groups. A primary goal of the clusters is to help students investigate a range of occupations in an industry and match their course choices while in school to career decisions. This helps students learn what they need to do now and in the future to prepare for their chosen career. As you study the clusters, you will see that there are good careers in many different areas. Choosing the best one for you should be based on your personal interests and strengths as well as your future educational plans.

Review the clusters with your career counselor, teachers, and parents and family members. They can assist you in making your career decision by asking you thought-provoking questions. Keep in mind, however, that your career choice and your career plans are your own responsibility. Use the information to make the best choices related to your courses, student organizations and activities, and future education goals.

Job/Career Outlook

The Bureau of Labor Statistics is a good source for learning more about careers. It provides career information in its *Occupational Outlook Handbook (OOH)*, which describes job responsibilities, working conditions, training and education requirements, earnings, and job prospects for a wide range of jobs and careers. The Bureau of Labor Statistics also provides employment projections and job market trends. Its current employment projections through the year 2014 include the following:

- Total employment in the United States will increase by 18.9 million jobs, or 13 percent.
- Professional and service jobs are projected to account for 6 out of every 10 new jobs created.
- Nine of the 10 fastest-growing jobs are health and computer related.
- The number of women in the work force will grow by 10.9 percent, and women will make up 46.8 percent of the total work force.
- An associate or bachelor's degree is the most common source of postsecondary education or training for 6 of the 10 fastest-growing occupations.
- By 2014, the Hispanic U.S. work force is expected to reach 25.8 million.
- The 10 fastest-growing occupations ranked from highest to lowest are as follows: home health aides, network systems analysts, medical assistants, physician assistants, computer software engineers–applications, physical therapist assistants, dental hygienists, computer software engineers–systems software, dental assistants, and personal and home care aides.

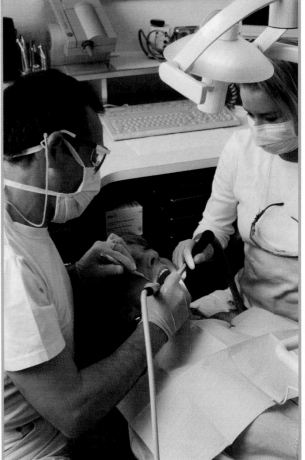

© Andrew Wakeford/Photodisc/Getty Images

TEACH
Have students review the employment projections discussed in the text. (They also may want to visit the Bureau of Labor Statistics' web site for additional employment trends and projections.) How will these projections affect their career decisions?

TEACHING STRATEGIES
Visual Learners
Have students create a poster representing the ten fastest-growing occupations in the country.

ONGOING ASSESSMENT
Use the Checkpoint as an opportunity to conduct ongoing assessment of student comprehension of the lesson material.

✓ CHECKPOINT

List at least three jobs/careers where there is a growing need.

Jobs/careers with a growing need include computer-related jobs, such as network systems analysts, and jobs in the health field, such as home health aides.

Follow UP

UNDERSTAND LEADERSHIP CONCEPTS

Circle the best answer for each of the following questions.

1. **There is a demand for new teachers in most academic areas, but there is a greater demand for**
   a. music teachers, especially band directors
   (b.) mathematics and science teachers
   c. physical education teachers and coaches
   d. art teachers

2. **Employers are looking for employees with**
   a. leadership qualities
   b. interpersonal skills
   c. foundational skills
   (d.) all of the above

THINK *CRITICALLY*

Answer the following questions as completely as possible. If necessary, use a separate sheet of paper.

3. **Identify your first and second career choices and explain why you chose them.**
   Answers will vary.
   _____
   _____
   _____

4. **Why is the United States facing a challenge to maintain a competitive edge in the engineering field over other countries? How do you think this problem can be solved?**
   Engineering jobs represent a growth area for the future, but there is a shortage of
   engineering graduates. Other countries are producing many more engineering
   graduates than the United States. Recommended solutions to the problem will vary.
   _____

5. **Explain why employers spend billions of dollars to train and retrain their employees. What benefits do they expect to get from spending that much money?**
   Employers spend billions of dollars each year to train and retrain their employees due
   to new technology and increasing demands for higher productivity. Employers hope to
   gain a competitive edge by having employees who are more knowledgeable and
   better skilled.
   _____

ASSESS

Reteach
Have students review the goals for the lesson and write one or two paragraphs identifying the key points for each goal.

Enrich
Have students interview an individual who is working in their chosen career field. Have them ask about the education and experience required for both entry-level and advanced positions in the field.

Close
It is projected that by 2014 the Hispanic U.S. work force will exceed 25 million workers. Ask students what they think this projection might mean for future leaders. (Possible answers may include an understanding of diversity and Hispanic culture and the ability to communicate effectively in Spanish.)

Visionary Leadership

GOALS

GOALS

- Define *visionary leadership* and discuss its importance.
- Explain the importance of cultural competence in the workplace.

TERMS

- destiny
- visionary leadership
- optimism
- pessimism
- imagination
- creativity
- cultural competence

FULFILLING YOUR DESTINY AS A LEADER

How often do you think about your future as a leader? What type of leader do you envision yourself to be? Do you see a person who has effective personal leadership qualities? More important, do you see a person who is preparing to fulfill his or her destiny? Your **destiny** is what you determine your life should be. Destiny is different from *fate,* which is an event that is uncontrollable. Unlike fate, you can control your destiny. Staying focused on fulfilling your destiny may be difficult at times. You must have a strong work ethic and be willing to commit your time and energy in order to do it.

How would you rate yourself on the following leadership qualities: optimism, imagination, creativity, forward and visionary thinking, cultural competence, and relationship building? **Visionary leadership** looks beyond the typical roles of a leader and embraces a forward-thinking attitude that looks to the future. It creates a welcoming climate in which diverse individuals can work together, share their ideas, and express their opinions without fear of rejection.

© Andrew Wakeford/Photodisc/Getty Images

SCHEDULE
Block 45 minutes
Regular 1 class period

FOCUS
Ask students to think about their future as a leader. What qualities do they think they will need to become a forward-thinking leader?

TEACH
Ask students whether they believe they have a destiny to fulfill. Discuss how destiny can be controlled.

Ask students to think of someone they know (or know of) whom they would call a truly visionary leader. What sets this individual apart from others?

COMMUNICATE

Visionary leadership skills give you the ability to communicate ideas that you think will enhance people's lives. As a visionary leader, you are a forward thinker who looks for creative ways to deal with challenging issues facing your school and community.

You are now the newly elected leader of the Junior/Senior Prom planning committee for your school's annual event. You are excited about your leadership role. You want to provide a new direction for this year's prom that will include the diverse cultural dress and customs that are represented in your school and community instead of the traditional formal dress. Your school's student body is very diverse, and you think this will help develop a sense of unity within the school. However, several members of the planning committee are not buying into your ideas to change the format of the prom. Everything has been placed on hold until an agreement can be reached. Finding support for your vision will be challenging.

THINK *CRITICALLY*

How will you communicate your vision and its benefits to the planning committee and the student body in order to gain support for your idea? What will you do if you cannot get support for your vision in time to complete the necessary planning?

Visionary leadership can provide the creative edge needed to reenergize the performance of others. Ultimately, it can enhance the success of your group or organization.

Optimism versus Pessimism

Optimism is the belief that things will work out for the best. Optimistic people look on the bright side of things and expect positive outcomes. The power of optimism is usually contagious. Others will want to follow or mirror your optimistic attitude as a leader. It takes creative thought, energy, and effort to maintain an optimistic attitude on a daily basis. You can do it by continuing to say to yourself, "I am who I say I am—a visionary leader with a positive outlook on life." Even during moments of disappointment, remind yourself of the potential, desire, and drive in you. Optimism can overcome the disappointment.

Try not to let pessimism creep into your life. **Pessimism** is the feeling that things are likely to turn out badly. Pessimistic people have a negative outlook on life and expect the worst outcome in all situations. Pessimism can have a negative effect on your life. It can cause you to lose faith in your abilities and lose hope in the future.

On the other hand, optimism can lead you to believe in yourself and your abilities. Optimistic people look to the future with anticipation and excitement. Optimism leads to positive health benefits, such as reduced stress and enhanced emotional well being. Your optimistic attitude will contribute to greater success as you continue your visionary leadership journey.

Imagination and Creativity

Albert Einstein, one of the world's most famous scientists, believed that imagination and creativity were greater than intelligence. He said that intelligence stops at a given point, but your imagination and creativity continue without any limits. **Imagination** is the power of your mind to form a mental image of something that is not present. On the other hand, **creativity** is your ability to generate new ideas or concepts. Some people are said to have a creative imagination. Imagination and creativity are often associated with originality. People with these traits often have ideas for new ways of doing things. Both qualities can be developed over time. You can improve both your imagination and creativity by

- reading a variety of books, magazines, trade journals, and newspapers
- visiting museums, art galleries, and design studios
- being a regular consumer of music, photography, movies, and plays
- studying different types of designs used in buildings, bridges, and other structures and objects
- learning about different countries, cultures, religions, and philosophies

These suggestions are just some of the ways to stir your imagination and see things in a new light. Creativity and imagination allow you to take something that exists in one form and envision how it might be used in another form or in another way.

As a leader, if your imagination is too far ahead of your group or organization, it can lead to frustration, miscommunication, and disruptive behavior from group members. You can avoid this problem by keeping your visionary ideas within a reasonable range. But you also want to communicate with others and encourage them to be open, accepting, and optimistic. The idea is to get others to see a new vision, accept it, and to keep stretching to reach it. Remember the words of Henry David Thoreau: "A person's reach should exceed his grasp."

Ensuring Your Success

Character education is a broad term used to describe many aspects of teaching and learning for moral, personal, social, and emotional development. You are constantly developing, demonstrating, and testing your character. Your good character comes down to good citizenship and a good reputation in your school and community, where you treat everyone as you would like to be treated, consider the consequences of your actions, and admit to your mistakes and learn from them.

As part of your personal development as a leader with character, you should seek out opportunities to learn and practice leadership and positive character traits. Practice good citizenship in your family, school, and community. Do not be afraid to accept leadership challenges in class projects, student organizations, athletics, and at work. Seek out the help and support of mentors and coaches. Ask for feedback from your family members, friends, teachers, and bosses and use that feedback to make personal improvements. Develop a plan, set goals, and monitor your progress. Taking these steps will help build your confidence, enhance your reputation, and ensure your success as an individual who has the character, values, and personal skills needed by a visionary leader.

 CHECKPOINT

Describe one of the visionary leadership qualities that can enhance your performance as a leader.

Visionary leadership qualities that can enhance your performance as a leader include

optimism, imagination, and creativity.

TEACH
Ask students what they think Thoreau meant when he said that "a person's reach should exceed his grasp." How do they think that saying relates to the idea of visionary leadership?

TEACH
Ask students to list some of the opportunities in their school that would allow them to learn and practice leadership and positive character traits. From their list, have students select one or two opportunities that they would most like to pursue.

Have students discuss the definition of *hope* as it relates to the marginal quote. Ask them why they think it is important for leaders to keep hope alive among members of a group or organization. What do they think would happen to a group with no hope?

ONGOING ASSESSMENT
Use the Checkpoint as an opportunity to conduct ongoing assessment of student comprehension of the lesson material.

TEACH
Ask students what it means to be culturally competent. Discuss why it is important. You may want to provide some statistics on the growing immigrant population in the United States to reinforce the importance of cultural competence.

Ask students to name some ways that they can increase their cultural competence. (If their school does not have a diverse student population, ask students to think of ways they might gain cultural competence through community interaction or perhaps joint projects with another school.)

ONGOING ASSESSMENT
Use the Checkpoint as an opportunity to conduct ongoing assessment of student comprehension of the lesson material.

CULTURAL COMPETENCE

The workplaces in our nation have always been diverse. That has been one of the unique strengths of America. That diversity will increase at an even faster rate in the near future with the employment of larger numbers of people from even more countries and cultures. You will hear different languages and experience different values and beliefs. This continuing change will result in a bigger emphasis on cultural competence and its effect on interactions among individuals and work groups in the workforce of the future. Future leaders will be expected to be skilled in cultural competence.

Cultural competence is your ability to function effectively in a multicultural workplace and global community with people from other countries and cultures. What do you know about people who are culturally different from you in terms of ethnicity, socioeconomic status, gender, and religious beliefs and values? More important, what is your knowledge and understanding of the different cultures that exist in your school and community?

As a visionary leader, you will be expected to demonstrate cultural competence because many of your coworkers will be from Africa, China, India, Korea, South America, and Eastern and Western Europe. Even people whose families have lived in the United States for many generations represent different cultures, religions, and beliefs. Your understanding of individual differences and skills in cross-cultural communication will be a major consideration for employers who are trying to determine how well you will fit into their organizations.

Cultural competence is needed in many settings other than work. Many of you already live in diverse communities and attend schools with students whose backgrounds, attitudes, and beliefs are quite different than yours. Those differences may show up in their language, dress, habits, and views. If this does not describe your current situation, you can expect that, in the future, you will find yourself in a more diverse neighborhood, social group, college, or organization.

Interacting with others from different cultures and backgrounds is the best way to improve cultural competence. Limited experience with other cultures often leads to misunderstandings, inaccurate information, or stereotyping. Become involved rather than being culturally isolated. Find opportunities to interact with others and learn from them. Be willing to share your experiences, beliefs, and values and allow others to do the same.

 CHECKPOINT

Why is it important for future leaders to have cultural competence in the workplace?

Future leaders need to have cultural competence in the workplace because many of their coworkers will be from different cultures, religions, and beliefs.

Follow UP

UNDERSTAND LEADERSHIP CONCEPTS

Circle the best answer for each of the following questions.

1. Your destiny
 a. cannot be controlled
 b. is what you determine your life should be
 c. is your fate
 d. all of the above

2. Which of the following is not a visionary leadership quality?

 a. optimistic attitude
 b. creativity
 c. cultural isolation
 d. cultural competence

THINK *CRITICALLY*

Answer the following questions as completely as possible. If necessary, use a separate sheet of paper.

3. Explain how visionary leadership can provide a competitive edge for a group or organization.

Visionary leadership can provide a competitive edge for a group or organization by

reenergizing the performance of group members to enhance the success of the group.

_____

_____

_____

4. Describe the power of an optimistic attitude and why it is important for you as a leader.

The power of optimism is contagious. Having an optimistic attitude makes people

want to follow you and mirror your optimism as a leader.

_____

_____

_____

5. Describe some ways that you can improve your imagination and creativity other than those ways already discussed in the lesson.

Answers will vary.

_____

_____

_____

_____

ASSESS
Reteach
Write the phrase *Visionary Leadership* on the board. Discuss all of the qualities that relate to visionary leadership—forward thinking, optimism, imagination, creativity, relationship building, character, and cultural competence.

Enrich
To enhance imagination and creativity, give students a variety of art materials (colored paper, markers, stickers, paints, modeling clay, glue, glitter, etc.). Ask them to create something that represents one or more of the key points in the lesson.

Close
Ask students to explain why a visionary leader must be able to show cultural competence.

Chapter Assessment

TEACHING RESOURCES
ExamView® CD, Ch. 12

REVIEW *LEADERSHIP CONCEPTS*

Write the letter of the term that matches each definition. Some terms will not be used.

a. career clusters
b. change agent
c. creativity
d. cultural competence
e. destiny
f. facilitator
g. imagination
h. legacy
i. optimism
j. pessimism
k. self-directed leader
l. trend
m. visionary leadership

__a__ 1. Categories of related occupations

__i__ 2. The belief that things will work out for the best

__m__ 3. Looks beyond the typical roles of a leader and embraces a forward-thinking attitude

__l__ 4. The general direction in which things are moving

__h__ 5. How others will remember you

__d__ 6. Ability to function effectively in a multicultural workplace

__j__ 7. The feeling that things are likely to turn out badly

__c__ 8. Ability to generate new ideas or concepts

__f__ 9. Someone who assists, guides, and supervises others to reach a desired outcome

__k__ 10. Person with the character, values, purpose, and courage to do the right thing even when no one is watching

Circle the best answer.

11. Someone who expects things to have a negative outcome is
    a. optimistic
    b. pessimistic
    c. imaginative
    d. none of the above

12. A facilitator does not
    a. empower others to become leaders
    b. delegate responsibilities to others
    c. spend quality time with group members
    d. expect group members to work without assistance and guidance

13. All of the following are future trends in the workplace except
    a. telecommuting
    b. increased emphasis on character qualities
    c. decrease in international business
    d. improvements in technology

14. Visionary leadership qualities involve
    a. optimism
    b. imagination and creativity
    c. cultural competence
    d. all of the above

ASSESS

Reteach
Have students list each of the terms from the lesson and write a brief definition for each term. Then have students exchange papers with a classmate and review their definitions.

Enrich
Divide students into three groups and assign each group one of the lessons from the chapter. Have students present the material from their assigned lesson to the class in a creative way, such as a skit, a game format, or a computer-generated presentation.

CLOSE
Have students discuss why visionary leaders need to be open to change.

THINK CRITICALLY

15. *What are some things you can do now to help you meet and exceed the expectations that future employers will have of you?*

Answers will vary but may include developing solid foundational, communication, interpersonal, and decision-making skills as well as finding opportunities to interact with individuals from diverse backgrounds in order to develop cultural competence.

16. *Do you think you have what it takes to be a self-directed leader? Explain your answer.*

Answers will vary.

17. *As you continue your leadership journey, explain how you will help others to grow and develop as leaders.*

Answers will vary but may include mentoring or coaching activities, such as tutoring another student in an academic subject or helping a member of your local student organization prepare for a competition.

18. *Describe the difference between coaching someone and being their "buddy."*

As a coach, you must maintain a professional relationship. You can be friendly, but it will be more difficult for you to stay focused on the task at hand if you are viewed as a "buddy."

19. *Describe your career plans after graduating from high school. What are your future plans and what are you currently doing to prepare for them?*

Answers will vary.

20. **Problem Solving**   *Although over 60 percent of the jobs in the future will require more education than a high school diploma, many high school graduates will not continue their education. How might you help your classmates and friends to understand that education is a lifelong process for maintaining a better quality of life?*

Answers will vary but may include presenting research on the education and ongoing

training that is required for the jobs in which they are interested.

_____

_____

_____

_____

21. **Research**   *The future workplace of the United States may look very different than it does today. Use the Internet to learn about some of the workplace trends of the future. Describe three of them and explain how each one will affect workers. Discuss whether you view the changes as positive or negative and explain why.*

Answers will vary based on the three workplace trends selected.

_____

_____

_____

_____

_____

22. **Creative Thinking**   *The local United Way has asked you to develop a public service campaign to promote its community youth mentoring program. Develop a creative ad for the local newspaper to try to gain support and volunteers from the citizens in your community.*

Answers will vary.

_____

_____

_____

_____

_____

23. **Communication**   *You have been selected as the "leader of the month" at your high school. Write a short article for your school newspaper describing your future visions for the school.*

Answers will vary.

_____

_____

_____

_____

_____

LEARNING TO LEAD

FOCUS

Prepare to be a student organization officer.

DESCRIPTION

There are many leadership opportunities available to members of student organizations. Members should identify and prepare for the leadership roles that match their interests and abilities. Accepting leadership roles strengthens abilities and contributes to the organization's success.

Many students never consider the possibility of leading as an officer of the local chapter, much less running for a state or national office. However, each member has the potential to develop into one of the top leaders of the organization. Accept the challenge of becoming a local, state, or national officer by completing this activity.

ACTIVITIES

1. Select a current state or national officer of your student organization who has a background and interests similar to your own. E-mail that person and ask why he or she decided to run for election, what concerns arose when making the decision, and what advice he or she would give to someone considering running for a local, state, or national office.

2. List your academic preparation, interests, hobbies, and previous leadership experiences. Study the descriptions of the local, state, and national officer positions for your student organization. Divide them into two categories—those that seem to match your interests and academic preparation and those that do not appear to match them.

3. Identify specific leadership goals for the rest of your high school career—for example, a local officer position this year or next, followed by a state leadership position and a national leadership position. Prepare a statement for each position describing why you want to work in that position and what you can contribute to your student organization in each role.

SHARE YOUR RESULTS

1. Select one local officer position (or a state position if you already are a local officer) that you would be interested in applying for this year or next year. Use a computer to design a brochure or one-page flyer that describes your qualifications and your platform as a candidate.
2. Ask three of your friends to role play an officer candidate interview with you. They should ask you questions about why you want to run, your qualifications for the position, and your goals if you are elected. After the interview, ask them how you can improve your interview skills.
3. Prepare a three-minute campaign speech you could give to the members of your organization to encourage them to vote for you as a candidate. Make sure you emphasize your leadership preparation and philosophy. After practicing the speech, deliver it to friends and family and ask them for feedback on the content and delivery of the speech.

ACCEPTING THE
CHALLENGE
Case Study 12
Have students think
about the individuals with
whom they are ac-
quainted. Does someone
need help or encourage-
ment in pursuing his or her
own career dream? Ask
students what they can do
to support and encourage
that individual.

ACCEPTING THE CHALLENGE

CASE STUDY 12—A VISION FOR THE FUTURE

As you learned in the opening scenario, What Would You Do?, Roderick had experienced great success and satisfaction from his career as a doctor. He wanted his legacy to be that of a strong, influential leader who gave back to his community. Although Roderick's contributions as a doctor were great, he felt there was more he could do, especially for the youth in his community. He thought back to a time when he had struggled with his career choice. He was fortunate to have had many positive role models and mentors in his life to guide him in making career decisions. Had his role models and mentors not been there to encourage him to take advantage of every learning opportunity, he may not have succeeded in life.

Roderick decided that the best way to help the youth in his community was to take on the role of a mentor himself. One of his young patients, Catie, had often spoken to Roderick about her interest in a health career. However, she was very pessimistic about her chances of ever fulfilling her dream. She felt overwhelmed by the career options in this field. She didn't know where or how to focus her attention. Roderick wanted to help turn Catie's pessimistic attitude into an optimistic one. He told Catie that he believed in her abilities and that she needed to start believing in herself too. He offered to provide the assistance, advice, and encouragement she needed in her journey to find a fulfilling and satisfying career. In return Catie had to promise not to let go of her vision for the future.

THINK CRITICALLY

1. *What qualities does Roderick seem to have that make him a visionary leader? How is he using visionary leadership when working with Catie?*

Roderick possesses several qualities of a visionary leader. He is optimistic, forward and

visionary thinking, and is focused on relationship building. He is using all of these

qualities when working with Catie in order to encourage her to develop an optimistic

attitude and believe that she can fulfill her career goal.

2. *Why is it important that Catie start believing in herself and being optimistic about her future?*

It is important for Catie to believe in herself and become more optimistic about her

future because optimistic people look on the bright side of things and expect positive

outcomes. Pessimism, on the other hand, could cause her to lose faith in her abilities

and to lose hope for the future.

3. *Describe your major areas of interest and passion. What do they reveal about your possible future career? Describe at least one person in your area of interest who could serve as a potential mentor to help guide and support your career plans.*

Answers will vary.

APPLY *WHAT YOU HAVE LEARNED–Career Exploration*

DIRECTIONS: *Career planning is one of the most important things you will do in life. Take the lead by planning ahead and exploring career options. By doing so, you will more likely find a career that matches your interests. Use the Internet, library, or your school's career center to do a job analysis for one job or career that interests you. The Bureau of Labor Statistics and the* Occupational Outlook Handbook *are good resources for this activity. Complete the job analysis form below or on your Student Activity CD.*

Job/Career Analysis

Job/Career Title _____

Job Responsibilities or Tasks _____

_____

_____

Work Environment (working conditions and hours) _____

_____

_____

_____

Training and Education Requirements _____

_____

_____

_____

Job Outlook (growth rate/job opportunities) _____

_____

Average Hourly/Yearly Income _____

Related Jobs/Careers _____

_____

_____

_____

After exploring your chosen career, does it still interest you? Discuss why or why not. On the lines below or using your Student Activity CD, create a SMART goal (including a completion date) to help you fulfill your career aspirations. Record your goal in a monthly calendar (on the CD or your own). Then enter your thoughts, ideas, and discussions related to your goal in a journal (on the CD or your own) to help you plan and track your progress. Choose a goal-setting partner to help you stay focused on your goal.

_____

_____

_____

_____

_____

_____

_____

_____

Note that students can complete this part of the *Accepting the Challenge* activity in the book or on the Student Activity CD. Instructions are provided on the CD.

After students have answered the questions in this activity, instruct them to write a SMART goal (including a completion date) that will help them fulfill their career aspirations. Have them enter their goal on a monthly calendar. Students can use the monthly calendar on the Student Activity CD or their own calendar. Explain to students that they may also use weekly calendar pages (on the Student Activity CD or their own calendar) to plan activities and tasks that will help them achieve their goals. Finally, direct students to use a journal (on the Student Activity CD or their own) to track and evaluate their progress in achieving their goal.

A goal-setting partner can add an element of accountability and can offer positive feedback to help students stay on track to achieve their goals.

Students should be given the opportunity to reflect on the progress they have made toward achieving their goal. To do this, students can complete the *Evaluate Your Progress* activity on the Student Activity CD. Stress to students that it is important to complete this activity on the original target completion date even if they have not met their goal at that time.

Glossary

accountable to accept responsibility for your actions (p. 42)

affirmation the act of agreeing with, validating, or confirming the actions or behaviors of another person (p. 8)

analyzers team members who listen and then offer a solid response based on what they believe is the right direction, goal, or task for the team (p. 152)

attitude the way you deal with and treat yourself and other people (p. 12)

authoritarian leadership a leadership style that uses a top-down approach in working with members of the group, team, or organization (p. 35)

behavior an action caused by or a reaction to the surrounding environment (p. 16)

belief something you accept as true (p. 116)

bias a preference that influences your judgment (p. 253)

body language the combination of gestures, movements, and physical mannerisms that you use to communicate to others (p. 45)

career clusters categories of related occupations (p. 310)

career track a series of related jobs ranging from entry-level to advanced positions that help fulfill career goals (p. 66)

caring feeling and acting with concern and empathy for others (p. 260)

challengers/confronters team members who question or oppose the leader in order to keep the leader honest and committed to the team's goal (p. 152)

change agent a person who makes meaningful changes that add value to a group or an organization (p. 304)

character the combination of qualities and attributes (traits) that makes one person different from others (p. 59)

citizenship participating effectively in an organization, supporting its goals, and contributing to its success (p. 66); responsible involvement in a group or organization (p. 263)

climate physical and relational feeling within your school environment (p. 91)

code of ethics a written statement of the beliefs and values that should guide the actions of a specific group or organization (p. 72)

collaborating cooperating and working together in a joint effort (p. 142)

compensation what you will receive in return for completing the task (p. 179)

conflict resolution the ability to find acceptable solutions to problems and experiences to benefit both you and the others involved (p. 8)

consistent the same time after time (p. 121)

constructive criticism feedback that encourages improvement and is given in a positive way (p. 21)

creativity ability to generate new ideas or concepts (p. 314)

cultural competence ability to function effectively in a multicultural workplace (p. 316)

culture the beliefs, values, language, and dress that are characteristic of a certain group of people (p. 170)

decoding interpretation or translation of a message by the receiver (p. 48)

demographics the characteristics of a population, such as gender, age, race, ethnicity, and level of education and income (p. 196)

destiny what you determine your life should be (p. 313)

discrimination the unfair way you favor or treat other people according to some standard that you or your group has chosen (p. 191)

disenfranchised groups those whose rights and privileges have been denied on a regular and unfair basis (p. 191)

disloyal to take actions that intentionally harm a relationship (p. 259)

diversity inclusion of people who are different from one another (p. 147)

empathy the ability to understand the feelings and experiences of others (p. 192)

encoding putting the message into a form that is understood by the receiver (p. 47)

ethics the decisions and actions of individuals and groups based on an understanding of right and wrong (p. 70)

extrovert a person who directs attention and interests toward the outer world of people and things (p. 14)

facilitator a person who assists, guides, and supervises others to reach a desired outcome (p. 304)

fading out losing your sense of self in order to fit in with a particular crowd or group (p. 204)

fairness act of being free from favoritism, self-interest, or bias (p. 253)

favoritism giving some people special treatment due to bias or a close relationship (p. 254)

feedback the receiver's response to the sender's message (p. 48)

field experience gaining practical experience by working with various organizations (p. 101)

fitting in changing who you are to meet the expectations of others (p. 201)

focus group a listening session conducted by a small group of students (p. 95)

followership the act of following a leader's guidance and direction (p. 172)

formal relationships interactions of people brought together to complete an activity or achieve a goal (p. 243)

formal role models those persons who have earned your admiration in a formal or professional way (p. 279)

gatekeeper a member who oversees the daily operations and activities of the group (p. 173)

habitual acting in a certain way with little thought due to repeated behavior (p. 215)

heterogeneous consisting of dissimilar or diverse ingredients or constituents (p. 196)

homogeneity the quality or state of being the same (p. 196)

honest without deception; not misleading (p. 216)

imagination power of your mind to form a mental image of something that is not present (p. 314)

independent operating individually (p. 141)

informal relationships voluntary relationships based on the interests people have in each other (p. 243)

informal role models those persons whom you know casually and whose skills and talents you admire (p. 279)

integrity a commitment to following a set of values and is often associated with ethics (p. 72)

interdependent depending on the help of others (p. 141)

interpersonal relations connections, interactions, or affiliations between two or more people (p. 123)

intimate relationships special affection and commitment two people share based on understanding, caring, and trust (p. 245)

introvert a person who tends to focus on inner thoughts and ideas (p. 14)

involvement being fully committed to the work required (p. 263)

joint leadership a leadership style where leaders agree to take joint control of the group (p. 36)

leader a person with the ability to guide others toward accomplishing a goal (p. 4)

leadership the ability to influence others to achieve a common goal (p. 32)

learning contract a written agreement to reinforce the learning process (p. 92)

legacy how others will remember you (p. 302)

loyalty a personal commitment to support the values and goals of a person, group, or organization (p. 258)

macro diversity the larger or more global events related to diversity that are reported in the media every day (p. 191)

media channels of communication including radio, television, music, movies, the Internet, books, newspapers, and magazines (p. 115)

mediators team members who work to find a solution or an acceptable compromise (p. 152)

mental practice imagining yourself completing each of the steps of an activity correctly (p. 130)

mentee the individual who is the recipient of the support (p. 286)

mentor a person who engages in a supporting and guiding relationship with another person, usually over an extended period of time (p. 286)

mentoring a planned set of interactions and opportunities that occur during the relationship between the mentor and mentee (p. 286)

micro diversity diversity that takes place in your home, school, community, church, and local businesses and organizations (p. 192)

motivation the driving force that persuades individuals to take action (p. 39)

myths fictional or unproven beliefs (p. 21)

networking interacting with others and developing beneficial relationships (p. 86)

nurturers/caregivers team members who are concerned about the feelings and emotions of other team members (p. 151)

objective looking at the facts without letting your personal feelings influence your views (p. 254)

one-by-five plan strategy that encourages a leader to spend more time with his or her classmates by giving them individualized attention—one minute per day for five consecutive days (p. 96)

optimism belief that things will always work out for the best (p. 314)

peer evaluation constructive feedback from classmates (p. 102)

peer-mentor a person who serves as a role model and provides motivation and encouragement to others (p. 39)

peer role models other students who exhibit character traits that you respect and appreciate (p. 282)

personal characteristics the individual attributes that make up your personality and guide your actions (p. 60)

personal history diverse life experiences of each team member (p. 154)

personality the total set of emotions, traits, and behaviors that makes each person unique (p. 113)

personality type an indication of how you deal with the different situations and experiences in your life (p. 13)

personal plan foundation and guide to enhance your leadership development (p. 84)

personal role models people in your household or neighborhood that you have known for a long time and whose behavior you admire (p. 279)

pessimism feeling that things are likely to turn out badly (p. 314)

practical experience application of knowledge to improve learning (p. 84)

prejudice a hostile and negative attitude toward people's characteristics (p. 191)

priority an activity that receives more attention than alternative activities (p. 129)

procedures a series of steps and actions that must be followed to complete an activity (p. 71)

process how the team gets things done (p. 153)

protective factors situations that could potentially decrease your chances of being involved in inappropriate or dangerous behaviors (p. 16)

public role models people whom you admire because of their impact on the community or on society (p. 279)

relationship development discussion session designed by teachers and students to explore ways to positively relate to each other (p. 92)

relationships the ways you interact and deal with others (p. 60)

reliability consistency in performance or behavior (p. 221)

reputation how a person is viewed by most other people (p. 58)

resources the materials, finances, and people needed to run an organization or team (p. 147)

respect consideration and regard for people and property (p. 250)

responsibility a duty or obligation (p. 225)

responsible acting with mature judgment (p. 263)

risk factors situations that could potentially increase your chances of being involved in inappropriate or dangerous behaviors (p. 16)

role identification the process of identifying the strengths, talents, and creativity of each member to help define each member's role on the team (p. 151)

role model a person whose character, behavior, attitude, personality, or skills serve as a good example to follow (p. 276)

rule a written statement of appropriate action that people are expected to follow (p. 71)

self-concept your full set of beliefs and feelings about yourself at a particular time (p. 121)

self-control the responsibility for managing your immediate actions (p. 228)

self-directed leader person with the character, values, purpose, and courage to do the right thing even when no one is watching (p. 303)

self-discipline the ability to forgo something that will provide immediate satisfaction in order to achieve an important, longer-term goal (p. 228)

self-esteem the general feeling of value you have about yourself (p. 121)

self-image the mental picture you have of yourself (p. 121)

servant leadership a commitment to serve the needs of others (p. 98)

skill a learned ability or strength that allows an individual to do something well (p. 7)

skill level a measure of a person's ability, talent, or expertise in performing a task (p. 7)

social dynamics interpersonal relationships among group members (p. 166)

social group a group of people that depend on each other for their wellbeing (p. 64)

social intelligence the ability to communicate and interact with members of your family, school, and community (p. 44)

social responsibility a duty and obligation to be responsive (p. 99)

stereotype to pass judgment on a group based only on your experiences with one member (p. 170)

success environment people, conditions, and resources that support rather than detract from your personal improvement efforts (p. 232)

supportive climate an environment that encourages creativity among group members in a noncompetitive way (p. 166)

tolerance a level of acceptance or understanding of differences (p. 192)

transactional leadership a leadership style based on an exchange of rewards for the accomplishment of tasks or goals (p. 36)

transformational leadership a leadership style based on persuading others to commit to a vision in order to enhance performance or reach group goals (p. 36)

trend the general direction in which things are moving (p. 307)

trust having complete confidence in another person (p. 257)

truthful providing accurate and complete information while respecting the circumstances and the persons receiving the information (p. 218)

underrepresented groups groups of individuals from minority cultures (p. 283)

value a strongly held belief that guides individual action (p. 61)

vignette a short theatrical scene performed by student-actors about an issue (p. 92)

virtual relationships purposeful continuing interactions and communications between two or more people that are carried on primarily via computer networks (p. 242)

vision an idea or a project that you imagine turning into reality by undergoing some type of change (p. 18)

visionary leadership ability to look beyond the typical roles of a leader and embrace a forward-thinking attitude (p. 313)

work ethic a person's character, values, beliefs, and behavior as related to work (p. 177)

worker bees team members who do whatever it takes to get the job done (p. 152)

zero tolerance rules to protect schools from acts of violence and disruptive behaviors (p. 95)

Index

Note: Page numbers in bold type indicate definitions.

A

Academic ability, 8-9
Academic groups, 167
Accountability, **42**
Achievement altitude, 87
Actions, words versus, 88, 120
Active followers, 173
Affirmation, **8**
African-Americans, 190, 204
Agenda, 41
Analyzers, **152**
Appearance, physical, 7, 15-16
Athletic teams/groups, 168
Attitude
    actions and, 88
    defined, **12**
    negative, 87
    positive, 86-87
    self-evaluation of, 12-13
Attractiveness, physical, 7
Authoritarian leadership, **35**
Avoidance, 41

B

Babies, development of, 113
Behavior
    beliefs and, 120-122
    defined, **16**
    self-evaluation of, 16
    values and, 117-118
Beliefs
    behavior and, 120-122
    defined, **116**
Bias, **253**
Blind allegiance, 259
Body language, **45**-46
Bottom-up approach, 36
Bureau of Labor Statistics, 311
Business Professionals of America (BPA), 169

C

Career clusters, **310**
Career-oriented groups, 168-169

Career planning, 310-311, 323
Career track, **66**, 308-309
Caregivers/nurturers, **151**-152
Caring
    as character component, 60, 123
    defined, **260**
    degree of closeness and, 260-261
    as leadership skill, 41
    not caring versus, 261
    school climate and, 91-96
Challengers/confronters, **152**
Change agents, **304**-305
Character
    babies and, 113
    checklist, 74
    components of, 59-60
    consistency of, 121, 214-215, 239
    defining, 58-**59**
    development of, 60-62, 112-116, 125-130
    effects of poor, 67-68
    ethics and, 74
    evidence of, 62, 122, 123
    importance of, 68
    interpersonal relations and, 123
    of leaders, 41
    media influence on, 115
    personal characteristics and, 122
    plan for developing, 128-130
    self-concept and, 121
    self-examination of, 126-127
    shortcomings in, 126-127
    social influences on, 64-67, 113-116
    survey, 81
Character education, 315
Child development, 113-114, 228-229
Citizenship
    as character component, 60, 123
    community, 265-266
    defined, **66**, **263**
    effective, 264-265, 266
    organizational, 264-265

in school setting, 66
Climate
    creating caring, 92-96
    defined, **91**
    effects of positive, 91-92
    home climate
        survey, 137
    supportive, 166-167
Clothing, 15-16
Coaching, 305
Code of conduct, 72
Codes of ethics, 72-73
    athletes', 73
    defined, **72**
    healthcare business, 73
    types, 73
Collaboration, **142**, 163
Commitment, 128, 153
Communication
    channels of, 48
    cultural differences in, 198
    parent-adolescent, 251
    persuasive speaking, 232
    process of, 47-48
    teams and, 154-155, 156
    verbal language, 45
    See also Communication
        skills
Communication skills, 7-8, 40-41, 42
Community
    citizenship in, 265-266
    knowledge of, 88
    leadership in, 88-89
    relationship building and, 88-89
    resource organization, 89
    role models in, 282
    school as, 91-96
    social woes, 99
Compensation, **179**
Conflict resolution, **8**, 40
Congeniality, 34
Consensus, 39
Consistency of character, **121**, 214-215, 239
Constructive criticism, **21**
Cosby, Bill, 83
Courage, 34
Courageous followers, 174
Covey, Stephen R., 173
Creativity, **314**-315
Criticism, constructive, **21**
Cultural competence, **316**

Culture
    body language and, 45-46
    communication and, 198
    defined, **170**
    diversity and, 190

D

DECA, 169
Decision-making skills, 8, 39
Decoding messages, **48**
Dedication, 34
Demographics, **196**
Destiny, **313**
Differences
    acceptance of, 203-204
    visible, 201-202
    See also Diversity
Disagreements, handling, 121
Discipline, 95
Discrimination, **191**, 204
Disenfranchised groups, **191**
Disloyal behavior, **259**
Diversity
    acceptance of, 203-204
    in contemporary
        society, 196
    defined, **147**, 190
    embracing, 198-199
    fitting in and, 201-203
    groups and, 197, 199
    macro, 191-192
    micro, 192
    recognition of, 190-191
    respecting, 193-194
    self-evaluation about, 211
    teams and, 147, 149, 154
    valuing, 194, 197-198
    visible differences, 201-202
Dubois, W. E. B., 204

E

Eastwood, Clint, 85
Education, as career, 308-309
Emotional stability, 9, 40
Empathy, **192**
Employers
    expectations held by, 309-310
    school involvement of, 94

Encoding messages, 47-48
Engineering, as career, 308
Ethical behavior, 38
Ethics
    character and, 74
    codes of, 72-73
    defined, **70**
    rules and procedures, 71
    values and, 70, 71
Expectations
    employers', 309-310
    reliability and, 222, 223
Extrovert, **14**

Facilitators, **304**
Fading out, **204**
Fairness
    as character component, 60, 123
    defined, **253**
    honesty and, 216-217
    by individuals, 254
    by organizations, 255
Family
    character influenced by, 64-65, 113-115
    relationships in, 243
    role models in, 281
    teamwork in, 140
Family, Career and Community Leaders of America (FCCLA), 169
Favoritism, 42, **254**
Feedback, **48**, 102
Field experience, **101**-102
Fitting in, **201**-203
Focus groups, **95**-96
Followers
    leaders and, 172-173
    leaders developing from, 175
    reasons for becoming, 172
    types, 173-175
    wrong reasons of, 173
Followership, **172**
Formal relationships, **243**
Formal role models, **279**
Forward thinking, 34
Friends
    character influenced by, 64-65
    relationships with, 243-244
Future Business Leaders of America-Phi Beta Lambda (FBLA-PBL), 169

Garner, John, 315
Gatekeepers, **173**
Ginzberg, Ruth, 283

Goal setting
    as leadership skill, 40
    personal, 19, 28
    for self-improvement, 230-231
Golden Rule, 117
Groups
    culture of, 170
    diversity and, 197, 199
    effective, 166-167
    joining, 170, 187
    relationships in, 244
    size of, 167
    types, 166-169
    See also Organizations; Teams

Habits, **215**
Head, qualities of, 100
Health, 35
Health Occupations Students of America (HOSA), 169
Heart, qualities of, 100
Heterogeneity, **196**
History, personal, 139, **154**
Home climate survey, 137
Homogeneity, **196**
Honesty
    as character component, 60, 122
    defined, **216**
    leadership and, 9
    with others, 217
    with self, 216, 232
Honor code, invisible, 179-180

Imagination, **314**-315
Independence, **141**
Informal relationships, **243**
Informal role models, **279**
Information Age, 177
Integrity
    ethics and, 72
    personal, 33-34, 179
Interdependence, **141**
Interpersonal relations
    as character component, 60, 123
    defined, **123**
    group social dynamics, 166
    networking, 86
    skills in, 40, 42
    See also Relationships; Social intelligence
Intimate relationships, **245**-246
Introvert, **14**
Involvement, **263**

Japanese proverb, 62
Joint leadership, **36**
Jordan, Michael, 31, 32

Kennedy, John F., 263
King, Martin Luther, Jr., 149

Language
    barriers to, 46
    non-verbal, 45-46
    verbal, 45
    written, 46
Lao-Tzu, 230
Leaders
    beliefs about, 4
    as change agents, 304-305
    character of, 41
    as coaches, 305
    defined, 4
    as facilitators, 304
    followers and, 172-173
    followers developing into, 175
    legacy of, 302
    mistakes of, 41-42
    myths about, 21
    qualities of, 4, 6, 29
    self-directed, 303-304
    team, 151, 153, 155
    See also Mentors; Role models
Leadership
    academic ability and, 8-9
    changing roles in, 302
    characteristics of, 33-35, 55
    childhood examples of, 5, 32
    community, 88-89
    defined, **32**
    development of, 32-33
    emotional stability and, 9
    honesty/truthfulness and, 9
    opportunities for, 6-9
    physical attractiveness and, 7
    physical size and, 6
    pledge, 38
    servant, 98-102
    skills for, 7-8, 38-41
    treatment of others and, 9
    types, 35-36
    visionary, 313-316
Learning contracts, **92**-93
Leave It to Beaver (television show), 214
Legacy, **302**
Listening, 32-33, 34
Loyalty, 60, 123, **258**-259

Macro diversity, **191**-192
Mann, Thomas, 33
Marsalis, Wynton, 213, 238
Mechanical skills, 8
Media
    character influenced by, 115
    defined, **115**
Mediators, **152**-153
Mental practice, **130**
Mentees
    defined, **286**
    self-appraisal by, 292
Mentoring
    considerations in, 291-292
    defined, **286**
    negative, 287
    positive, 287-288
    relationship as key to, 287
    time frame for, 292
Mentors
    defined, **286**
    effective, 291
    finding, 288-292
    gender of, 289
    "Honor Roll" of, 299
    and mutual interests, 290
    nationality of, 289-290
    race of, 290
    religion of, 290
    responsibilities of, 289
    as role models, 288
    selection of, 289-291
Merrill, A. Roger, 173
Merrill, Rebecca R., 173
Messages
    decoding, 48
    encoding, 47-48
    sending/receiving, 47
Micro diversity, **192**
Minority groups, role models for, 283
Motivation, **39**
Myths, **21**

National FFA Organization, 168-169
Negative attitude, 87
Negative followers, 174-175
Negatives, overcoming, 20
Networking, **86**
No Child Left Behind Act, 192
Non-verbal language, 45-46
Nurturers/caregivers, **151**-152

Objectivity, **254**
Occupational Outlook Handbook, 311
One-by-five plan, **96**
Optimism, 34, **314**

Organizational skills, 20
    resource organization, 89
Organizations
    citizenship in, 264-265
    fairness in, 255
    resources of, 147, 149,
        154, 156
    service, 167-168
    See also Groups
Others, treatment of.
    See Interpersonal relations;
        Relationships

Passive followers, 173-174
Past, overcoming one's, 20
Peer evaluation, **102**
Peer-mentor, **39**
Peer role models, **282**
Personal characteristics, **60**,
    122, 213-233
    honesty, 9, 60, 122,
        216-217
    reliability, 60, 122,
        221-224
    responsibility, 60, 122,
        224-226
    self-discipline, 60, 122,
        228-230
    self-improvement of,
        230-232
    truthfulness, 9, 60, 122,
        218-219
Personal history, 139, **154**
Personal integrity, 33-34, 179
Personality, 13-15, **113**
Personality type, **13-14**
Personal needs
    assessment, 109
Personal plan, **84**
Personal role models, **279**
Persuasive speaking, 232
Pessimism, **314**
Physical appearance, 15-16
Physical attractiveness, 7
Physical size, 6
Pippen, Scottie, 174
Planning
    for character
        development, 129-130
    for personal goals, 19-20
Pollard, C. William, 223
Positive attitude, 86-87
Practical experience, **84**
Prejudice, **191**
Priorities, **129**
Procedures, **71**
Process, **153**
Protective factors, for
    behavior, **16**
Public role models, **279**, 283

Readiness for skills, 20-21
Receiving messages, 47
Record keeping skills, 34

Relationship building, 32,
    88-89
Relationship development, **92**
Relationships
    defined, **60**, 242
    effective, 246-248
    family, 243
    formal versus informal,
        123, 243
    with friends, 243-244
    group, 244
    intimate, 245-246
    in mentoring, 287
    school, 244-245
    survey, 273
    variety of, 242-243
    virtual, 242
    work, 245
    See also Interpersonal
        relations
Reliability
    benefits of, 224
    as character component,
        60, 122
    consistent quality/effort
        and, 222
    defined, **221**
    effects on others,
        221-222
    effects on self, 223
    meeting expectations
        and, 222
    rule following and, 222
    time commitments and,
        221-222
Religion, and values, 117
Reputation, **58**
Resources
    community, 89
    team/organization, **147**,
        149, 154, 156
Respect
    as character component,
        60, 123
    defined, **250-251**
    importance of, 252
    leadership and, 9
    for others, 251
    for property, 252
    showing, 253
    truthfulness and, 218-219
Responsibility
    acceptance of, 225-226
    as character component,
        60, 122
    defined, **225**, **263**
    parts of, 225
    taking, 224, 226
Rice, Condoleezza, 283
Right/wrong
    ethics and, 70-71
    learning, 113-114
Risk factors, for behavior, **16**
Risk taking, positive, 34
Rogers, Fred, 113
Role identification, **151**
Role models
    defined, **276**
    false, 277
    famous figures as, 276-278
    finding, 281-283

formal, 279
    historical, 277
    "Honor Roll" of, 299
    informal, 279
    mentors as, 288
    minority group, 283
    need for, 278
    peer, 282
    personal, 279
    public, 279, 283
    selection of, 276
    serving as, 284
    true, 277
    types, 278-279
Rules, **71**, 72, 114-115

School
    character influenced by,
        65-66
    citizenship in, 66
    community/climate, 91-96
    relationships in, 244-245
    role models in, 282
    social woes, 98-99
    work issues
        common to, 94
Self-awareness, 11-12
Self-concept, **121**
Self-control
    defined, **228**
    development of, 228-229
    skills in, 8
Self-directed leaders, **303-304**
Self-discipline
    as character component,
        60, 122
    characteristics of, 229-230
    defined, **228**
    self-improvement through,
        230-232
Self-esteem, **121**
Self-evaluation, 11-16
    accepting yourself, 12
    attitude, 12-13
    behavior, 16
    comparison of self to
        others, 11-12
    personality, 13-15
    personal needs
        assessment, 109
    physical appearance,
        15-16
    self-awareness, 12
    self-image, 12
    strong points, 84
Self-image, 12, **121**
Self-improvement
    goal identification,
        230-231
    honesty with self, 232
    networking, 86
    practical experience,
        84-85
    priority setting, 231
    success environment,
        231-232
Sending messages, 47

Servant leadership
    defined, **98**
    field experience,
        101-102
    peer evaluation, 102
    qualities of heart/
        head, 100
    social responsibility,
        99-100
    social woes, 98-99
Service clubs/organizations,
    167-168
Silence, appropriateness
    of, 45
Situational followers, 174
Skill level, **7**
Skills
    communication, 7-8,
        40-41, 42
    conflict resolution, 40
    decision-making, 8, 39
    defined, **7**
    development of, 38-41
    emotional stability, 40
    ethical behavior, 38
    goal setting, 40
    interpersonal relations,
        40, 42
    motivation, 39
    organizational, 20
    peer-mentoring, 39
    practical experience and,
        84-85
    readiness for, 20-21
    self-control, 8
    social, 7
    teams and, 154, 156
    teamwork, 39
    technical/mechanical, 8
    time management, 41
    vision, 40
SkillsUSA, 169
SMART goals, 28
Social dynamics, **166**
Social groups
    defined, **64**
    family/friends, 64-65
    school, 65-66
    work, 66-67
Social intelligence, 44-46
    defined, **44**
    importance of, 44-45
    language barriers, 46
    verbal language, 45
    written language, 46
Social responsibility, 99-100
Social skills, 7
Social woes/problems, 98-99
Stereotyping, **170**
Strengths, evaluation of
    personal, 84
Success environment, **232**
Supportive climate,
    166-167

Teaching, as career, 308-309
Team leadership, 36

Teams
  athletic, 168
  character of, 146-147
  diversity on, 147, 149, 154
  effective, 153-155
  formation of, 141-142
  functioning of, 142-144
  goal/task level, 144
  group level, 143
  individual level, 143
  ineffective, 155-156
  member characteristics,
    147-149
  roles, 151-153, 154
  school/community impact
    level, 144
  See also Groups;
    Teamwork
Teamwork
  collaboration survey, 163
  in families, 140
  as leadership skill, 32, 39
  necessity of, 141
  See also Teams
Technical skills, 8
Thomas, Clarence, 283
360-degree feedback
    appraisal, 102
Time management, 41
Tolerance, **192**
Tolstoy, Leo, 101
Top-down approach, 35
Transactional leadership, **36**

Transformational
    leadership, **36**
Trends, in workplace, **307**
Trust
  as character component,
    60, 123
  defined, **257**
  importance of,
    257-258
  reliability and, 223
  teams and, 155, 156
Truthfulness
  as character component,
    60, 122
  defined, **218**
  leadership and, 9
  respect and, 218-219

Underrepresented
    groups, **283**

Validation of others, 21
Values
  behavior and, 117-118
  defined, **61**

development of, 61-62,
    117
  ethics and, 70, 71
  examining one's,
    116-117
  religion and, 117
Verbal language, 45
Vignettes, **92**
Virtual relationships, **242**
Visible differences, 201-202
Vision
  creation of, 18
  defined, **18**
  lack of, 42
  as leadership skill, 40
  steps for fulfilling,
    19-21
Visionary leadership
  cultural competence, 316
  defined, **313**
  ensuring success at, 315
  imagination/creativity,
    314-315
  optimism, 314
Volunteering, 85, 99-100

Winfrey, Oprah, 243
Woods, Tiger, 277, 283

Work
  character influenced by,
    66-67
  cultural competence
    and, 316
  future of, 307-309,
    311
  nature of, 177-178
  relationships at, 245
  role models
    from, 283
  school issues common
    to, 94
Worker bees, **152**
Work ethic
  components of, 180
  contemporary, 179
  defined, **177**
  as honor code,
    179-180
  meaning/value of,
    177-178
  teams and, 155
Written communication,
    41, 46

Zero tolerance discipline
    policies, **95**